T0189933

Lecture Notes in Artificial Intelligence 13552

Subseries of Lecture Notes in Computer Science

More information about this subseries at https://link.springer.com/bookseries/1244

Wei Lu · Shujian Huang ·
Yu Hong · Xiabing Zhou (Eds.)

Natural Language Processing and Chinese Computing

11th CCF International Conference, NLPCC 2022
Guilin, China, September 24–25, 2022
Proceedings, Part II

Springer

Editors
Wei Lu ⓘ
Singapore University of Technology
and Design
Singapore, Singapore

Yu Hong
Soochow University
Suzhou, China

Shujian Huang
Nanjing University
Nanjing, China

Xiabing Zhou
Soochow University
Suzhou, China

ISSN 0302-9743   ISSN 1611-3349 (electronic)
Lecture Notes in Artificial Intelligence
ISBN 978-3-031-17188-8   ISBN 978-3-031-17189-5 (eBook)
https://doi.org/10.1007/978-3-031-17189-5

LNCS Sublibrary: SL7 – Artificial Intelligence

This Springer imprint is published by the registered company Springer Nature Switzerland AG
The registered company address is: Gewerbestrasse 11, 6330 Cham, Switzerland

Preface

Welcome to NLPCC 2022, the eleventh CCF International Conference on Natural Language Processing and Chinese Computing. Following the success of previous conferences held in Beijing (2012), Chongqing (2013), Shenzhen (2014), Nanchang (2015), Kunming (2016), Dalian (2017), Hohhot (2018), Dunhuang (2019), Zhengzhou (2020), and Qingdao (2021), this year's NLPCC was held in Guilin. As a premier international conference on natural language processing and Chinese computing, organized by CCF-NLP (the Technical Committee of Natural Language Processing, China Computer Federation, formerly known as the Technical Committee of Chinese Information, China Computer Federation), NLPCC serves as an important forum for researchers and practitioners from academia, industry, and government to share their ideas, research results, and experiences, and to promote their research and technical innovations.

The fields of natural language processing (NLP) and Chinese computing (CC) have boomed in recent years. Following NLPCC's tradition, we welcomed submissions in 10 areas for the main conference: Fundamentals of NLP; Machine Translation and Multilinguality; Machine Learning for NLP; Information Extraction and Knowledge Graphs; Summarization and Generation; Question Answering; Dialogue Systems; Social Media and Sentiment Analysis; NLP Applications and Text Mining; and Multimodality and Explainability. This year, despite the non-negligible influence of COVID-19, we still received 327 valid submissions to the main conference by the submission deadline.

After a thorough reviewing process, including meta reviewing, out of the 327 submissions (some of which were desk-rejected due to policy violations), 83 papers were finally accepted as regular papers to appear in the main conference, resulting in an acceptance rate of 25.4%. Each paper was reviewed in a double-blind manner by at least 3 members of the Program Committee, with the help of additional reviewers. In total, 73 of the accepted papers were written in English and 10 in Chinese. Among them, 62 submissions were presented as oral papers and 21 as poster papers at the conference. Six papers were nominated by our area chairs for the best paper award. An independent best paper award committee was formed to select the best papers from the shortlist. This proceedings includes only the accepted English papers; the Chinese papers will appear in the ACTA Scientiarum Naturalium Universitatis Pekinensis. In addition to the main proceedings, three papers were accepted to the Student workshop and 21 papers were accepted to the Evaluation workshop.

We were honored to have four internationally renowned keynote speakers, Jason Eisner (Johns Hopkins University), Ray Mooney (University of Texas at Austin), Alexander Rush (Cornell University), and Luke Zettlemoyer (University of Washington), sharing their findings on recent research progress and achievements in natural language processing.

We would like to thank all the people who contributed to NLPCC 2022. First of all, we would like to thank our 20 area chairs for their hard work recruiting reviewers, monitoring the review and discussion processes, and carefully rating and recommending submissions. We would like to thank all 330 reviewers for their time and efforts to review the submissions. We are also grateful for the help and support from the general chairs, Bonnie Webber and Ya Zhou, and from the organization committee chairs, Guimin Huang and Xiaojun Wan. Special thanks go to Yu Hong and Xiabing Zhou, the publication chairs. We greatly appreciate all your help!

Finally, we would like to thank all the authors who submitted their work to NLPCC 2022, and thank our sponsors for their contributions to the conference. Without your support, we could not have such a strong conference program.

We were happy to see you at NLPCC 2022 in Guilin and hope you enjoyed the conference!

August 2022

Wei Lu
Shujian Huang

Organization

NLPCC 2022 was organized by the China Computer Federation (CCF) and hosted by Guilin University of Electronic Technology. Publishers comprise Lecture Notes on Artificial Intelligence (LNAI), Springer, and ACTA Scientiarum Naturalium Universitatis Pekinensis.

Organization Committee

General Chairs

Bonnie Webber	University of Edinburgh, UK
Ya Zhou	Guilin University of Electronic Technology, China

Program Committee Chairs

Wei Lu	Singapore University of Technology and Design, Singapore
Shujian Huang	Nanjing University, China

Student Workshop Chairs

Zhongqing Wang	Soochow University, China
Piji Li	Nanjing University of Aeronautics and Astronautics, China

Evaluation Chairs

Yunbo Cao	Tencent, China
Youzheng Wu	JD AI Research, China

Tutorial Chairs

Hai Zhao	Shanghai Jiao Tong University, China
Yang Feng	Institute of Computing Technology, Chinese Academy of Sciences, China

Publication Chairs

Yu Hong	Soochow University, China
Xiabing Zhou	Soochow University, China

Journal Coordinator

Yunfang Wu   Peking University, China

Conference Handbook Chair

Jun Li   Guilin University of Electronic Technology, China

Sponsorship Chairs

Haofen Wang   Tongji University, China
Ruifeng Xu   Harbin Institute of Technology, Shenzhen, China
Guoyong Cai   Guilin University of Electronic Technology, China

Publicity Chairs

Jianxing Yu   Sun Yat-sen University, China
Siyou Liu   Macao Polytechnic University, China

Organization Committee Chairs

Guimin Huang   Guilin University of Electronic Technology, China
Xiaojun Wan   Peking University, China

Area Chairs

Fundamentals of NLP

Nanyun Peng   University of California, Los Angeles, USA
Zhenghua Li   Soochow University, China

Machine Translation and Multilinguality

Lei Li   University of California, Santa Barbara, USA
Jiajun Zhang   Chinese Academy of Sciences, China

Machine Learning for NLP

Zhiting Hu   University of California, San Diego, USA
Piji Li   Nanjing University of Aeronautics and Astronautics,
                                  China

Dialogue Systems

Lili Mou   University of Alberta, Canada
Weinan Zhang   Harbin Institute of Technology, China

Question Answering

Rui Zhang   Pennsylvania State University, USA
Nan Yang   Microsoft Research Asia, China

Summarization and Generation

Chenghua Lin   University of Sheffield, UK
Deyi Xiong   Tianjin University, China

Information Extraction and Knowledge Graph

Ruihong Huang   Texas A&M University, USA
Kang Liu   Chinese Academy of Sciences, China

Social Media and Sentiment Analysis

Anh Tuan Luu   Nanyang Technological University, Singapore
Rui Xia   Nanjing University of Science and Technology, China

NLP Applications and Text Mining

Jey Han Lau   University of Melbourne, China
Lemao Liu   Tencent, China

Multimodality and Explainability

Lizi Liao   Singapore Management University, Singapore
Mingxuan Wang   ByteDance

Treasurers

Yajing Zhang   Soochow University, China
Xueying Zhang   Peking University, China

Webmaster

Hui Liu   Peking University, China

Program Committee

Bo An   Institute of Ethnology and Anthropology, Chinese
     Academy of Social Sciences, China
Xiang Ao   Institute of Computing Technology, Chinese Academy
     of Sciences, China
Guirong Bai   Institute of Automation, Chinese Academy of Sciences,
     China
Yu Bao   ByteDance AI Lab, China
Qiming Bao   University of Auckland, New Zealand
Junwei Bao   JD AI Research, China
Xiangrui Cai   Nankai University, China

Yi Cai   South China University of Technology, China
Yuan Cao   Google Brain, USA
Yixin Cao   Singapore Management University, Singapore
Pengfei Cao   Institute of Automation, Chinese Academy of Sciences,
                            China
Jun Cao   ByteDance AI Lab, China
Zhangming Chan   Alibaba Group, China
Shuaichen Chang   Ohio State University, USA
Xiuying Chen   Peking University, China
Yufeng Chen   Beijing Jiaotong University, China
Xinchi Chen   Amazon AWS, USA
Kehai Chen   Harbin Institute of Technology, China
Bo Chen   Institute of Software, Chinese Academy of Sciences,
                            China
Yubo Chen   Institute of Automation, Chinese Academy of Sciences,
                            China
Yi Chen   Harbin Institute of Technology, Shenzhen, China
Shuang Chen   Harbin Institute of Technology, China
Wei Chen   Fudan University, China
Hanjie Chen   University of Virginia, USA
Pei Chen   Texas A&M University, USA
Yulong Chen   Zhejiang University and Westlake University, China
Jiangjie Chen   Fudan University, China
Chen Chen   Nankai University, China
Liang Chen   Peking University, China
Guanyi Chen   Utrecht University, The Netherlands
Shanbo Cheng   ByteDance AI Lab, Singapore
Chenhui Chu   Kyoto University, Japan
Yiming Cui   Joint Laboratory of HIT and iFLYTEK Research,
                            China
Cunli Mao   Kunming University of Science and Technology, China
Xiang Deng   Ohio State University, USA
Chenchen Ding   NICT, Japan
Qianqian Dong   ByteDance AI Lab, China
Ziyi Dou   University of California, Los Angeles, USA
Longxu Dou   Harbin Institute of Technology, China
Rotem Dror   University of Pennsylvania, USA
Xinya Du   University of Illinois Urbana-Champaign, USA
Jinhua Du   Huawei, UK
Chaoqun Duan   Harbin Institute of Technology, China
Junwen Duan   Central South University, China
Xiangyu Duan   Soochow University, China
Alex Fabbri   Salesforce AI Research, USA
Zhihao Fan   Fudan University, China
Biaoyan Fang   University of Melbourne, Australia
Zhiyuan Fang   Amazon, USA

Xiachong Feng	Harbin Institute of Technology, China
Jiazhan Feng	Peking University, China
Yansong Feng	Peking University, China
Shi Feng	Northeastern University, China
Yang Feng	Institute of Computing Technology, Chinese Academy of Sciences, China
Mauajama Firdaus	University of Alberta, Canada
Lea Frermann	Melbourne University, Australia
Qiankun Fu	Zhejiang University, China
Xingyu Fu	University of Pennsylvania, USA
Guohong Fu	Soochow University, China
Jun Gao	Harbin Institute of Technology, Shenzhen, China
Shen Gao	Peking University, China
Ruiying Geng	Alibaba Group, China
Yu Gu	Ohio State University, USA
Jiachen Gu	University of Science and Technology of China, China
Yi Guan	Harbin Institute of Technology, China
Tao Gui	Fudan University, China
Shaoru Guo	Institute of Automation, Chinese Academy of Sciences, China
Jiale Han	Beijing University of Posts and Telecommunications, China
Lifeng Han	University of Manchester, UK
Xudong Han	University of Melbourne, Australia
Tianyong Hao	South China Normal University, China
Yongchang Hao	University of Alberta, Canada
Hongkun Hao	Shanghai Jiao Tong University, China
Ziwei He	Shanghai Jiao Tong University, China
Ruifang He	Tianjin University, China
Yanqing He	Institute of Scientific and Technical Information of China, China
Ihung Hsu	University of Southern California, USA
Jingwen Hu	Harbin Institute of Technology, China
Minghao Hu	Information Research Center of Military Science, China
Chenyang Huang	University of Alberta, Canada
Ruihong Huang	Texas A&M University, USA
Jiangping Huang	Chongqing University of Posts and Telecommunications, China
Qingbao Huang	Guangxi University and South China University of Technology, China
Fei Huang	Tsinghua University, China
Changzhen Ji	Harbin Institute of Technology, China
Tong Jia	Northeastern University, China
Hao Jia	Soochow University, China

Zhongtao Jiang	Institute of Automation, Chinese Academy of Sciences, China
Xuhui Jiang	Institute of Computing Technology, Chinese Academy of Sciences, China
Jingchi Jiang	Harbin Institute of Technology, China
Yong Jiang	Alibaba DAMO Academy, China
Wenbin Jiang	Baidu Inc., China
Yiping Jin	FreeDa Language Space, Spain
Peng Jin	Leshan Normal University, China
Zhu Junguo	Kunming University of Science and Technology, China
Fajri Koto	University of Melbourne, Australia
Tuan Lai	University of Illinois Urbana-Champaign, USA
Yuxuan Lai	Peking University, China
Yuanyuan Lei	Texas A&M University, USA
Miao Li	University of Melbourne, Australia
Irene Li	Yale University, USA
Mingzhe Li	Peking University, China
Fei Li	Wuhan University, China
Fenghuan Li	Guangdong University of Technology, China
Mingda Li	Harbin Institute of Technology, China
Jiajun Li	University of Chinese Academy of Sciences and Institute of Computing Technology, Chinese Academy of Sciences, China
Zhenghua Li	Soochow University, China
Maoxi Li	Jiangxi Normal University, China
Jing Li	Hong Kong Polytechnic University, China
Mingda Li	University of California, Los Angeles, USA
Jiaqi Li	Harbin Institute of Technology, China
Yanran Li	Hong Kong Polytechnic University, China
Shasha Li	National University of Defense Technology, China
Lishuang Li	Dalian University of Technology, China
Yanyang Li	Chinese University of Hong Kong, China
Qintong Li	University of Hong Kong, China
Bin Li	Nanjing Normal University, China
Xinyi Li	National University of Defense Technology, China
Zuchao Li	Shanghai Jiao Tong University, China
Hongzheng Li	Beijing Institute of Technology, China
Zheng Li	Stockton University, USA
Xin Li	Alibaba Group, China
Haonan Li	University of Melbourne, Australia
Zhixu Li	Fudan University, China
Yucheng Li	University of Surrey, UK
Chenliang Li	Wuhan University, China
Dongfang Li	Harbin Institute of Technology, Shenzhen, China
Zujie Liang	Sun Yat-sen University, China
Lizi Liao	Singapore Management University, Singapore

Ying Lin	Apple, USA
Yuchen Liu	National Laboratory of Pattern Recognition, CASIA, China
Kang Liu	Institute of Automation, Chinese Academy of Sciences, China
Xiao Liu	Microsoft Research Asia, China
Pengyuan Liu	Beijing Language and Culture University, China
Xuebo Liu	Harbin Institute of Technology, Shenzhen, China
Qian Liu	Beihang University, China
Yongbin Liu	University of South China, China
Qingbin Liu	Tencent, China
Chunhua Liu	University of Melbourne, Australia
Chuang Liu	Tianjin University, China
Yan Liu	Tianjin University, China
Xianggen Liu	Sichuan University, China
Yuanxing Liu	Harbin Institute of Technology, China
Jian Liu	Beijing Jiaotong University, China
Zhicheng Liu	ByteDance, China
Lemao Liu	Tencent AI Lab, China
Qun Liu	Chongqing University of Posts and Telecommunications, China
Shujie Liu	Microsoft Research Asia, China
Puyuan Liu	University of Alberta, Canada
Yaojie Lu	Institute of Software, Chinese Academy of Sciences, China
Xin Lu	Harbin Institute of Technology, China
Hengtong Lu	Beijing University of Posts and Telecommunications, China
Yinglong Ma	North China Electric Power University, China
Longxuan Ma	Harbin Institute of Technology, China
Mingyu Derek Ma	University of California, Los Angeles, USA
Xuezhe Ma	University of Southern California, USA
Yunshan Ma	National University of Singapore, Singapore
Zhao Meng	ETH Zurich, Switzerland
Tao Mingxu	Peking University, China
Xiangyang Mou	Meta, USA
Yulia Otmakhova	University of Melbourne, Australia
Jiaxin Pei	University of Michigan, USA
Xutan Peng	University of Sheffield, UK
Jianzhong Qi	University of Melbourne, Australia
Jun Qi	Georgia Institute of Technology, USA
Xian Qian	ByteDance AI Lab, USA
Lihua Qian	ByteDance, China
Tao Qian	Hubei University of Science and Technology, China
Yanxia Qin	National University of Singapore, Singapore
Libo Qin	Harbin Institute of Technology, China

Liang Qiu	Amazon Alexa AI, USA
Yuqi Ren	Tianjin University, China
Shuo Ren	Microsoft Research Asia, China
Yubin Ruan	Harbin Institute of Technology, China
Lei Sha	University of Oxford, UK
Wei Shao	City University of Hong Kong, China
Lingfeng Shen	Johns Hopkins University, USA
Haoran Shi	Amazon Inc., USA
Xing Shi	ByteDance Inc., China
Lei Shu	Google Research, USA
Jyotika Singh	Placemakr, USA
Linfeng Song	Tencent AI Lab, USA
Kaiqiang Song	Tencent AI Lab, USA
Zhenqiao Song	ByteDance AI Lab, China
Haoyu Song	Harbin Institute of Technology, China
Jinsong Su	Xiamen University, China
Dianbo Sui	Institute of Automation, Chinese Academy of Sciences, China
Kai Sun	Cornell University, USA
Zewei Sun	ByteDance, China
Chengjie Sun	Harbin Institute of Technology, China
Simon Suster	University of Melbourne, Australia
Zhixing Tan	Tsinghua University, China
Minghuan Tan	Singapore Management University, Singapore
Ping Tan	Universiti Malaysia Sarawak, Malaysia
Yun Tang	Facebook, USA
Buzhou Tang	Harbin Institute of Technology, Shenzhen, China
Duyu Tang	Tencent, China
Jialong Tang	Institute of Software, Chinese Academy of Sciences, China
Xunzhu Tang	University of Luxembourg, Luxembourg
Zhiyang Teng	Westlake University, China
Lin Tian	RMIT University, Australia
Thinh Hung Truong	University of Melbourne, Australia
Zhaopeng Tu	Tencent AI Lab, China
Gisela Vallejo	University of Melbourne, Australia
Lijie Wang	Baidu, China
Le Wang	Chinese Academy of Military Science, China
Tao Wang	King's College London, UK
Xing Wang	Tencent, China
Shaolei Wang	Harbin Institute of Technology, China
Yunli Wang	Beihang University, China
Wei Wang	Shenzhen International Graduate School, Tsinghua University, China
Ruize Wang	Fudan University, China
Hongling Wang	Soochow University, China

Danqing Wang	Bytedance AI Lab, China
Liang Wang	Microsoft Research Asia, China
Yuxuan Wang	Zhejiang Lab, China
Lingzhi Wang	Chinese University of Hong Kong, China
Siyuan Wang	Fudan University, China
Zijian Wang	AWS AI Labs, USA
Jun Wang	University of Melbourne, Australia
Sijia Wang	Virginia Tech, USA
Bo Wang	Tianjin University, China
Yaqiang Wang	Chengdu University of Information Technology, China
Yufei Wang	Macquaire University, Australia
Hongwei Wang	Tencent AI Lab, USA
Qingyun Wang	University of Illinois Urbana-Champaign, USA
Tao Wang	ByteDance AI Lab, China
Zhen Wang	Ohio State University, USA
Jiaqiang Wang	ByteDance, China
Xuesong Wang	Harbin Institute of Technology, China
Xuepeng Wang	Tencent AI Lab, China
Xiao Wang	Fudan University, China
Wei Wei	Huazhong University of Science and Technology, China
Yang Wei	Bytedance AI Lab, China
Haoyang Wen	Carnegie Mellon University, USA
Yuqiao Wen	University of Alberta, Canada
Sixing Wu	Peking University, China
Yuxia Wu	Xi'an Jiaotong University, China
Shun Wu	Institute of Automation, Chinese Academy of Sciences, China
Liwei Wu	Bytedance AI Lab, China
Lijun Wu	Microsoft Research, China
Changxing Wu	East China Jiaotong University, China
Qingrong Xia	Soochow University, China
Congying Xia	Salesforce Research, USA
Yang Xiang	Peng Cheng Laboratory, China
Tong Xiao	Northeastern University, China
Ruiyu Xiao	Harbin Institute of Technology, China
Jun Xie	Alibaba DAMO Academy, China
Yuqiang Xie	Institute of Information Engineering, Chinese Academy of Sciences, China
Xin Xin	Beijing Institute of Technology, China
Kang Xu	Nanjing University of Posts and Telecommunications, China
Yan Xu	Hong Kong University of Science and Technology, China
Wenda Xu	University of California, Santa Barbara, USA
Xiao Xu	Harbin Institute of Technology, China

Zhixing Xu	Nanjing Normal University, China
Jinan Xu	Beijing Jiaotong University, China
Peng Xu	Google, Canada
Ying Xu	Oracle Australia, Australia
Jiahao Xu	Nanyang Technological University, Singapore
Yiheng Xu	Microsoft Research Asia, China
Wang Xu	Harbin Institute of Technology, China
Lingyong Yan	Baidu Inc., China
Yuanmeng Yan	Beijing University of Posts and Telecommunications, China
Hang Yang	Institute of Automation, Chinese Academy of Sciences, China
Ziqing Yang	iFLYTEK Research, China
Liner Yang	Beijing Language and Culture University, China
Shiquan Yang	University of Melbourne, Australia
Ziqing Yang	Peking University, China
Muyun Yang	Harbin Institute of Technology, China
Jun Yang	MarcPoint, China
Qiang Yang	KAUST, Saudi Arabia
Baosong Yang	Alibaba DAMO Academy, China
Songlin Yang	ShanghaiTech University, China
Zhiwei Yang	Jilin University, China
Liang Yang	Dalian University of Technology, China
Haoran Yang	Chinese University of Hong Kong, China
Wenlin Yao	Tencent AI Lab, USA
Jianmin Yao	Soochow University, China
Rong Ye	ByteDance AI Lab, China
Tiezheng Yu	Hong Kong University of Science and Technology, China
Dong Yu	Beijing Language and Culture University, China
Junjie Yu	Soochow University, China
Zhe Yu	Sun Yat-sen University, China
Heng Yu	Alibaba, China
Pengfei Yu	University of Illinois Urbana-Champaign, USA
Guoxin Yu	Institute of Computing Technology, Chinese Academy of Sciences, China
Chunyuan Yuan	Institute of Information Engineering, Chinese Academy of Sciences, China
Xiang Yue	Ohio State University, USA
Xiangrong Zeng	Kuaishou, China
Qi Zeng	University of Illinois Urbana-Champaign, USA
Daojian Zeng	Hunan Normal University, China
Shuang (Sophie) Zhai	University of Oklahoma, USA
Weidong Zhan	Peking University, China
Wenxuan Zhang	Alibaba DAMO Academy, Singapore
Zhirui Zhang	Tencent AI Lab, China

Zhihao Zhang	Beihang University, China
Shuaicheng Zhang	Virginia Polytechnic Institute and State University, USA
Peng Zhang	Tianjin University, China
Xiuzhen Zhang	RMIT University, Australia
Xingxing Zhang	Microsoft Research Asia, China
Dakun Zhang	SYSTRAN, France
Yuanzhe Zhang	Institute of Automation, Chinese Academy of Sciences, China
Zhuosheng Zhang	Shanghai Jiao Tong University, China
Biao Zhang	University of Edinburgh, UK
Yazhou Zhang	Zhengzhou University of Light Industry, China
Tongtao Zhang	Siemens Corporate Technology, USA
Kaiyan Zhang	Harbin Institute of Technology, China
Mengjie Zhao	LMU Munich, Germany
Zhenjie Zhao	Nanjing University of Information Science and Technology, China
Xiang Zhao	National University of Defense Technology, China
Jun Zhao	Fudan University, China
Yufan Zhao	Microsoft, China
Zhedong Zheng	National University of Singapore, Singapore
Wanjun Zhong	Sun Yat-sen University, China
Bo Zhou	Institute of Automation, Chinese Academy of Sciences, China
Guangyou Zhou	Central China Normal University, China
Wenxuan Zhou	University of Southern California, USA
Chunting Zhou	Meta AI, USA
Wangchunshu Zhou	Beihang Univeristy, China
Xin Zhou	Fudan University, China
Peng Zhou	Kuaishou, China
Junnan Zhu	Institute of Automation, Chinese Academy of Sciences, China
Qingfu Zhu	Harbin Institute of Technology, China
Tong Zhu	Soochow University, China
Rongxin Zhu	University of Melbourne, Australia
Yaoming Zhu	ByteDance AI lab, China
Jie Zhu	Soochow University, China
Conghui Zhu	Harbin Institute of Technology, China
Muhua Zhu	Meituan Group, China
Zhou Qian	ByteDance AI Lab, China

Organizers

Organized by the China Computer Federation, China

Hosted by the Guilin University of Electronic Technology

In Cooperation with Lecture Notes in Computer Science, Springer

ACTA Scientiarum Naturalium Universitatis Pekinensis

Sponsoring Organizations

Diamond Sponsor

Alibaba

Platinum Sponsors

Huawei

Tencent AI Lab

Baidu

GTCOM

ByteDance

Gold Sponsors

LeYan

WoFeng

Xiaomi

Vivo

Contents – Part II

Student Workshop (Poster)

Evaluation Workshop (Poster)

Contents – Part I

Information Extraction and Knowledge Graph (Oral)

Dialogue Systems (Oral)

Social Media and Sentiment Analysis (Oral)

NLP Applications and Text Mining (Oral)

Multimodality and Explainability (Oral)

Fundamentals of NLP (Poster)

Information Extraction and Knowledge Graph (Poster)

Summarization and Generation (Poster)

Question Answering (Poster)

Question Answering (Poster)

Faster and Better Grammar-Based Text-to-SQL Parsing via Clause-Level Parallel Decoding and Alignment Loss

Kun Wu[1(✉)], Lijie Wang[1], Zhenghua Li[2], and Xinyan Xiao[1]

[1] Baidu Inc., Beijing, China
{wukun04,wanglijie,xiaoxinyan}@baidu.com
[2] Institute of Artificial Intelligence, School of Computer Science and Technology,
Soochow University, Suzhou, China
zhli13@suda.edu.cn

Abstract. As a mainstream approach, grammar-based models have achieved high performance in text-to-SQL parsing task, but suffer from low decoding efficiency since the number of actions for building SQL trees are much larger than the number of tokens in SQL queries. Meanwhile, intuitively it is beneficial from the parsing performance perspective to incorporate alignment information between SQL clauses and question segments. This paper proposes clause-level parallel decoding and alignment loss to enhance two high-performance grammar-based parsers, i.e., RATSQL and LGESQL. Experiments on the Spider dataset show our approach improves the decoding speed of RATSQL and LGESQL by 18.9% and 35.5% respectively, and also achieves consistent improvement in parsing accuracy, especially on complex questions.

Keywords: Text-to-SQL parsing · Grammar-based parser · Clause-level alignment · Parallel decoding

1 Introduction

The text-to-SQL parsing task aims to automatically transform natural language (NL) questions into SQL queries based on the given databases (DBs) [9], as depicted in Fig. 1. As a key technology in an NL interface for relational DBs, it has attracted increasing attention from both academic and industrial community. Researchers have done many solid and interesting fundamental works on both dataset construction [7,20] and parsing model innovation [10,13].

Recently, several high-quality cross-domain text-to-SQL datasets have been released, strongly boosting the research interest and progress in this task [11,18,20]. Most early works generate SQL queries in a token-level seq2seq manner [4,20], or by filling DB elements into SQL slots [13,16], both of which are known as token-based parsers.

In contrast, grammar-based parsers incorporates some pre-designed SQL grammar into the decoder to guarantee the grammaticality of output SQL queries [15]. Concretely, a grammar-based parser builds a tree from top to down via a sequence of

W. Lu et al. (Eds.) NLPCC 2022, LNCS 13552, pp. 3–15, 2022.
https://doi.org/10.1007/978-3-031-17189-5_1

actions. Each action selects a production rule to expand a selected node. As representative grammar-based parsers, RATSQL [10] and LGESQL [1] achieve competitive performance on various text-to-SQL datasets.

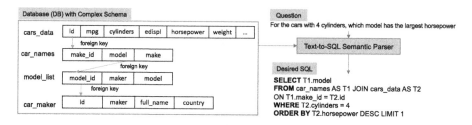

Fig. 1. An example of the text-to-SQL parsing task from the spider dataset.

In spite of their high performance, the number of actions for building a tree is usually much larger than the number of tokens in the SQL query, due to the generation of non-leaf nodes. Take the SELECT clause in Fig. 1 as an example. The SQL query clause "SELECT T1.model" consists of two tokens, but its corresponding sub-tree is built by seven actions in RATSQL (see Fig. 2). This makes the decoding process extremely inefficient. To improve efficiency, DuoRAT [8] uses a transformer-based decoder to replace the parent-feeding LSTM decoder in RATSQL [10], which can improve the training efficiency given gold-standard SQL queries. Unfortunately, their method does not influence the testing speed, which is very important in real applications.

As discussed by many previous works, one characteristic of the text-to-SQL task is that an SQL clause usually depends on a local segment of the input question [12,14,19]. Recent works try to exploit alignments between SQL clauses and question segments for better handling some specific SQL structures. Zeng et al. (2020) [19] propose a recursive parsing framework that can elegantly generate complicated nested SQL queries. The basic idea is explicitly encouraging the decoder to focus on different question segments when generating different nested layers. Based on a token-based parser, Yin et al. (2021) [14] incorporate an extra attention loss to capture such alignments, which is proved to be helpful for dealing with compositional SQL queries. However, how to effectively apply alignments on handling all SQL queries is still open.

To address the above two issues, we propose to enhance grammar-based parsers via clause-level parallel decoding and alignment loss. First, we propose to generate SQL clauses in parallel, that is, clauses are generated independently of each other and simultaneously. Compared with the sequential generation of SQL clauses, there is no dependency between clauses in parallel decoding. Second, we propose a clause-level alignment training loss to encourage the model to focus on only related question segment when generating a clause. We implement these two strategies based on two representative grammar-based parsers, i.e., RATSQL and LGESQL. Experiments on the Spider dataset show our approach improves the decoding speed of RATSQL and LGESQL by 18.9% and 35.5% respectively, and also achieves consistent improvement in parsing accuracy, especially on complex questions.

2   Related Works

In this section, we mainly discuss recent works on grammar-based parsers, token-level alignments between question words and DB schema items (i.e., schema linking), and segment-level alignments between questions and SQL queries.

Grammar-Based Parser. In order to ensure the grammaticality of generated SQL query, Yin et al. (2018) [15] propose TRANX, a transition-based abstract syntax parser for semantic parsing. TRANX employs the abstract syntax tree (AST) as an intermediate meaning representation, and uses the SQL grammar as external knowledge to guide the generation of AST. As shown on the left of Fig. 2, the AST of the SELECT clause is generated by the action sequence on its left side. Most recent state-of-the-art (SOTA) models are implemented on TRANX, such as IRNet [5], RATSQL [10] and LGESQL [1]. However, compared with parsers with a token-based decoder, the grammar-based parser is more inefficient in training and inference, as the sequence generated by the grammar-based decoder is much longer than that of the token-based decoder. Taking the SELECT clause "SELECT T1.model" in Fig. 2 as an example, the length of the action sequence in RATSQL is 7, whereas the length of output sequence in a seq2seq model [20] is 2. In order to reduce the training time, Scholak et al. [8] build DuoRAT, a re-implementation of the RATSQL model, by replacing RATSQL's LSTM-with-parent-feeding decoder with a transformer one. DuoRAT trains three times faster than RAT-SQL given gold-standard SQL queries. But it does not reduce the inference time, which is more important in real applications.

Schema Linking. In order to improve model performance on new DBs, recent studies encode the linking information between question words and DB schemas to enhance representations of question words [5,10,16]. TypeSQL [16] utilizes types extracted from DB content to help model better understand entities and numbers in the question. IRNet [5] recognizes DB schema items (i.e., columns and tables) mentioned in the question, and further assigns different matching types (e.g., exact matching, partial matching) to these items based on how they are mentioned in the question. Then IRNet encodes this matching information to enhance representations of question words. RAT-SQL [10] uses a relation-aware self-attention mechanism to handle various matching relations between question words and DB schema items. Lei et al. (2020) [6] systematically study the role of schema linking based on human-annotated schema linking information, and find that schema linking is the crux for cross-domain text-to-SQL task.

Segment-Level Alignment. Although schema linking has effectively enhanced input representations, how to make this token-level alignment work in decoding is still open [6,10]. Consequently, some studies aim to design better alignment mechanisms, i.e., segment-level alignment, to improve SQL generation in decoding [14,19]. Zeng et al. (2020) [19] propose a novel recursive semantic parsing framework to handle the generation of complicated nested SQL query. The basic idea is explicitly encouraging the decoder to focus on different segments of questions when generating SQL queries in different nested layers. To improve the generation of compositional SQL queries, Yin et al. (2021) [14] incorporate a supervised attention loss to capture segment-level align-

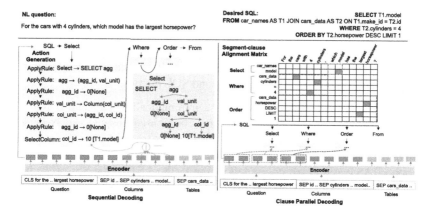

Fig. 2. An overview of our approach. The left side shows the generation process of sequential decoding in RATSQL, and the right side gives our proposed parallel decoding, where all clauses are generated independently. Meanwhile, according to alignments between SQL clauses and question segments, as shown by the segment-clause alignment matrix, a clause-level alignment loss is incorporated during training.

ments. But these methods are designed to handle special SQL structures and can not be directly applied to grammar-based parsers.

In order to improve both the inference efficiency and performance of grammar-based parsers, we propose clause-level parallel decoding and alignment loss.

3 Our Proposed Model

3.1 Grammar-Based Text-to-SQL Parsing

We adopt high-performance grammar-based parsers as our baseline models. Since all grammar-based parsers are implemented on TRANX, we take RATSQL as an example to introduce the mechanism of grammar-based decoder. As shown on the left side of Fig. 2, the decoder generates SQL queries via generating actions to select grammar rules in the depth-first search order. And it uses an LSTM to remember the current decoding status and select next actions.

Specifically, there are three types of actions, i.e., ApplyRule, SelectColumn and SelectTable. ApplyRule(r) applies a grammar rule r to expand the focus node, and is used to gradually create a skeleton tree without concrete DB elements. SelectColumn(c) and SelectTable(t) are used to fill a skeleton tree with concrete values by selecting a column name c or a table name t, respectively. Formally, based on the given input x and DB schema s, the generation process of a SQL query y can be formalized as follows.

$$P(y|x, s) = \prod_{t=1}^{T} p(a_t|x, s, a_{<t}) \tag{1}$$

where a_t is the action taken at time step t, $a_{<t}$ is the sequence of actions before t, and T is the number of total time steps of the whole action sequence.

For the action of ApplyRule[r], we compute its probability as follows:

$$\alpha_j = softmax_j(att(\mathbf{h}_t, \mathbf{m}_j)) \quad \mathbf{h}_t^{att} = \sum_{j=1}^{|m|} \alpha_j \mathbf{m}_j$$

$$P(a_t = ApplyRule[r]|a_{<t}) = softmax_R(g(\mathbf{h}_t^{att}))$$

where $\mathbf{m_j}$ is the output vector for x_j in encoder outputs; $\mathbf{h_t}$ is the LSTM hidden state at time t; $att(.)$ is a multi-head attention layer; $g(.)$ is a two layer MLP with a tanh activation unit; and r is the selected rule from the rule set R.

For the action of SelectColumn[c], we directly copy the i-th column from the column set. The probability of column i is computed as:

$$\widetilde{\lambda}_i = \frac{\mathbf{h}_t^{att} W_Q (\mathbf{m}_i^{col} W_K)^T}{\sqrt{d_x}}$$

$$P(a_t = SelectColumn[i]|a_{<t}) = softmax_i\{\widetilde{\lambda}_i\}$$

where W_Q and W_K are learned parameters, and $\mathbf{m}_i^{col}$ is the output vector for column i in encoder outputs. The calculation of SelectTable is similar with that of SelectColumn.

Figure 2 to illustrate the process of grammar-based decoder. Suppose that the decoder is at the "agg" node under the "Select" node. We call "agg" the current node and "Select" the father node, and denote them as n_i and f_i. We further suppose the next action is "ApplyRule(agg → agg_id val_unit)". Then the LSTM state of the decoder is updated as follows. Then we take an example in Fig. 2 to illustrate the update of LSTM state. Suppose that the decoder is at the "agg" node under the "Select" node. We call "agg" the current node and "Select" the father node, and denote them as n_i and f_i. We further suppose the next action is "ApplyRule(agg → agg_id val_unit)". Then the LSTM state of the decoder is updated as follows.

$$\mathbf{c}_{t+1}, \mathbf{h}_{t+1} = \text{LSTM}(\mathbf{c}_t, \mathbf{h}_t, \mathbf{i}_t)$$
$$\mathbf{i}_t = [\mathbf{e}_{a_t}; \mathbf{e}_{n_i}; \mathbf{e}_{\text{type}(n_i)}; \mathbf{z}_t; \mathbf{h}_{\text{tm}(f_i)}] \tag{2}$$

where $\mathbf{c}_t$ and $\mathbf{h}_t$ are the cell state and the output vector at step t; $\mathbf{e}_n$ represents the embedding vector of the input n; a_t denotes the previous action; $\text{type}(.)$ returns the type of a node[1]; $\mathbf{z}_t$ is the contextual representation vector after attending to the encoder outputs; $\text{tm}(f_i)$ denotes the timestamp when f_i has been just generated.

3.2 Clause-Level Parallel Decoding

During decoding, the grammar-based parser actually generates a SQL query by sequentially creating clauses (seeing Table 1) in a pre-defined order, as shown on the left side of Fig. 2. For instance, after completing the SELECT clause, the parser tries to expand the WHERE clause. If "WHERE → None" is selected by the decoder, it means that the

---

[1] The parser assigns a type for each node according to its role in SQL, such as "agg" for aggregations.

Table 1. Six types of clauses defined in RATSQL and used for parallel decoding in our work.

Clauses	Grammar rules for clause generation
SELECT	SELECT agg | SELECT agg, agg | ...
WHERE	WHERE | None
GROUP	GROUP_BY | GROUP_BY & HAVING | None
ORDER	ORDER_BY | ORDER_BY & LIMIT | None
IEU	INTERSECT | EXCEPT | UNION | None
FROM	FROM Table 1 | FROM Table 1, Table 2 | ...

final SQL query does not include a WHERE clause and the decoder will move on to generate the GROUP clause, and so on. In fact, the generation of different clauses is quite loosely connected. This motivates us that we may generate all SQL clauses independently and in parallel via batch processing, which obviously can improve decoding efficiency.

Specifically, major differences between parallel and sequential decoding lie in the initial LSTM state of each clause, reflected in c_0, h_0, and the previous action a_0 in Eq. 2. In sequential decoding, the initial status for a subsequent clause is inherited from and thus depends on the previous clause. In contrast, in parallel decoding, each clause has the same initial status, which we believe is more reasonable considering the loose dependency between adjacent clauses.

3.3   Clause-Level Alignment Loss

Figure 2 shows the alignment between question segments and SQL clauses. We use this alignment to improve clause generation by introducing a clause-level alignment training loss to encourage the model to focus on the aligned question segment in the clause generation.

Clause-Level Alignment Acquisition. Given a question/SQL pair, for each DB element and condition value in the SQL query, we search for some tokens from NL question to align them, so as to get a token-level alignment matrix. In this process, we use the string-matching method which is commonly used for token-level schema linking in recent works [5, 12]. As shown in the alignment matrix in Fig. 2, token-level alignments are marked in orange box.

Then we use a simple heuristic algorithm to extract a question segment for each SQL clause from existing token-level alignment results. For each clause, we take the shortest question segment that contains all DB elements and values in the clause as its aligned segment. As shown in the alignment matrix of Fig. 2, the question segment for a clause is marked by a dashed bounding box. Please note that the question segments for different clauses may have overlaps. Finally, there are about 23% question/SQL pairs missing segment-clause alignments. For these pairs, we align each clause to the whole question. We believe that higher-quality alignment may lead to higher gains, which we leave as future work.

Clause-Level Alignment Loss. After aligning SQL clauses with NL question segments, we design an extra training loss to inject such clause-level alignment into the parsing model. Intuitively, the model can be benefited by paying more attention to related aligned segments during clause generation.

In our grammar-based parser, a clause is generated by a sequence of actions. For instance, the SELECT clause in Fig. 2, i.e., "select T1.model", which is aligned to "which model", is generated by six ApplyRule actions and one SelectColumn action. For each ApplyRule(r) action, we define a prior token-wise alignment probability towards its corresponding segment.[2] Concretely, each token in the segment obtains an averaged probability, whereas tokens outside the segment receive zero.

$$P_{\texttt{align}}(x_i|r_j) = \begin{cases} 0 & x_i \notin S \\ 1/\texttt{len}(S) & x_i \in S \end{cases}$$

where r_j is the rule in the ApplyRule action; x_i is the i-th token in the sentence; and $\texttt{len}(S)$ is the number of tokens in the aligned segment S.

Then, we define an attention probability from the current decoder state to each question token as

$$P_{\texttt{att}}(x_i|r_j) = \texttt{softmax}(..., \mathbf{h_t}W_m\mathbf{m_i}, ...)$$

where t is the timestamp when executing ApplyRule(r_j); $\mathbf{h_t}$ is the time t's hidden state of LSTM decoder; $\mathbf{m_i}$ is the output vector for x_i in encoder outputs; W_m is a learned matrix.

Finally, we define the alignment loss as the squared distance between the aligned (prior) and attention (modeling) probabilities.

$$L_{align} = \sum_j \sum_i (P_{\texttt{align}}(x_i|r_j) - P_{\texttt{att}}(x_i|r_j))^2$$

In this way, we hope the model learn to attend to certain related question tokens for the sake of better rule selection.

4 Experiments

4.1 Experimental Setup

Dataset. We conduct experiments on Spider,[3] a complex and cross-domain text-to-SQL dataset. Spider contains 8,659/1,034/2,147 question/SQL pairs for training/dev/test sets over 146/20/40 DBs. We follow the original data splitting and use the exact matching (EM) accuracy as the evaluation metric. In our experiments, we use the corrected development set released on June 7, 2020.

---

[2] We don't use alignment loss for other two actions, since they tend to be closely related with one or two tokens in NL question. Forcing such action to align with too many tokens in a segment degrades the performance, which has been proved by our early-stage preliminary experiments.

[3] Leaderboard of the challenge: https://yale-lily.github.io/spider.

Table 2. EM accuracy and testing speed on Spider dev set. Results marked by * are obtained on an earlier-version dev set. For our models, we report mean and variance over three runs.

Models	EM accuracy	Parsing speed (query/s)
DuoRAT + BERT [8]	69.9	–
RATSQL [10]		
+ BERT	69.7*	–
+ GRAPPA [17]	73.4	–
LGESQL [1]		
+ BERT	73.5	–
+ GRAPPA	74.1	–
+ ELECTRA	75.1	–
RATSQL		
Orig. + BERT (rerun)	$71.1_{\pm0.4}$	7.48
Ours + BERT	$72.5_{\pm0.1}$ (+1.4)	9.14 (+18.4%)
w/o Align	$71.7_{\pm0.2}$ (+0.6)	9.21 (+18.9%)
w/o Parallel	$72.4_{\pm0.1}$ (+1.3)	–
Ours + GRAPPA	$74.2_{\pm0.4}$ (+0.8)	–
LGESQL		
Orig. + ELECTRA (rerun)	$75.1_{\pm0.7}$	11.69
Ours + ELECTRA	$75.7_{\pm0.6}$ (+0.6)	15.81 (+35.2%)
w/o Align	$75.3_{\pm0.6}$ (+0.2)	15.84 (+35.5%)
w/o Parallel	$75.6_{\pm0.4}$ (+0.5)	–

Baseline Parsers. We select two SOTA grammar-based parsers, namely RATSQL [10] and LGESQL [1], to verify our approaches. RATSQL utilizes schema linking and DB structures to build a complete graph, where a node in the graph is a DB schema item or a question word, and an edge in the graph represents the connection relation between nodes. Then RATSQL uses a relation-aware transformer encoder to model the connection relations between nodes. As RATSQL treats all relations, either 1-hop or multi-hop, in the same manner which may lead to the notorious over-smoothing problem, LGESQL proposes a novel line graph encoder to distinguish local and non-local connection relations for each node. By means of line graph: 1) messages propagate more efficiently through connections between nodes and the topology of directed edges; 2) local and non-local relations are integrated distinctively during the graph iteration.

Implementation. We implement our proposed strategies on RATSQL and LGESQL. For clause-level parallel decoding, the definitions of six clauses are shown in Table 1. For clause-level alignment, we take the summation of our proposed alignment loss and the original loss ($-log(P(y|x,s))$) as the final loss, i.e., $L = -log(P(y|x,s))+L_{align}$.

For each parser, we use the default parameter settings in their released code. We train all models on one A100 GPU and evaluate parsing speed on one V100 GPU. For fair comparison, we ignore time cost in the pre-processing step and set beam size as 1 during evaluating the parsing speed.

Table 3. EM accuracy over five types of SQL clauses.

Models	SELECT	WHERE	GROUP_BY	ORDER_BY	IEU
RATSQL					
Orig.+BERT	89.7	78.9	80.8	84.8	57.9
Orig.+BERT (w/Parallel)	90.6	**81.2**	82.1	85.1	46.8
Orig.+BERT (w/Align)	90.9	78.9	82.3	**85.6**	**60.1**
Ours+BERT	**91.4**	78.9	**82.6**	82.9	53.0
LGESQL					
Orig.+ELECTRA	91.8	82.6	82.1	**88.3**	62.1
Orig.+ELECTRA (w/Parallel)	**93.1**	81.6	**85.4**	87.3	53.9
Orig.+ELECTRA (w/Align)	**93.1**	**83.0**	81.1	86.5	**63.6**
Ours+ELECTRA	**93.1**	81.9	86.0	87.1	57.3

Table 4. EM accuracy on different hardness levels.

Hardness	Easy	Medium	Hard	Extra Hard	all
RATSQL					
Orig. + BERT	87.9	72.9	63.2	49.4	71.1
Ours + BERT	88.7 (+0.8)	74.9 (+2.0)	64.9 (+1.7)	50.0 (+0.6)	72.5 (+1.4)
LGESQL					
Orig. + ELECTRA	93.1	76.5	69.0	50.6	75.1
Ours + ELECTRA	93.1 (+0.0)	78.5 (+2.0)	69.0 (+0.0)	52.4 (+1.8)	75.8 (+0.7)

4.2   Results

Table 2 shows the main results on Spider dev set.[4] In the first major row, we select several high-performance grammar-based parsers from the Spider leaderboard. We report our results in the second and third major rows. For RATSQL, besides using BERT [3], we also give the results with GRAPPA [17], a task-specified pre-trained model. For LGESQL, we give results with another pre-trained model ELECTRA [2], with which LEGSQL achieves SOTA performance. In order to avoid the effect of performance vibrations, we run each model for 3 times with different random initialization seeds, then report the averaged EM accuracy and the variance ($\sqrt{\frac{\sum_{i=1}^{n}(x_i-\bar{x})^2}{n-1}}$).

Parallel Decoding. Parallel decoding aims to improve parsing efficiency of grammar-based parsers. As shown in the last column of Table 2, the parallel decoding improves parsing speed by 18.9% and 35.5% for RATSQL and LGESQL, respectively. Based on LGESQL, the parallel decoding achieves a larger improvement in parsing speed. We think this is because the action sequence generated by LGESQL is shorter, and we give a detailed analysis in Sect. 4.3.

More interesting, the parallel decoding achieves an average accuracy improvement of 0.6% and 0.2% on RATSQL and LGESQL. According to results in Table 3, we find

---

[4] Because of submission times limitation, we did not submit our models successfully.

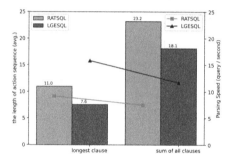

Fig. 3. Distribution of action numbers generated by different grammar-based parsers.

that performances on some clauses are improved in parallel decoding, especially on the SELECT and GROUP_BY clause, which proves that there is no strong generation dependency between these SQL clauses. But the performance on IEU clause is worse in parallel decoding, as the inter-clause dependency is important in this type. Taking SQL query "*SELECT Status FROM city WHERE Population > 1500 INTERSECT SELECT Status FROM city WHERE Population < 500*" for example, the clauses in the latter SQL query (i.e., the query after the INTERSECT operation) rely on the former SQL query, where this dependency is ignored in parallel decoding.

Clause-Level Alignment. The clause-level alignment loss aims to improve the generation of SQL clauses by encouraging the model pay more attention to related aligned question segments during clause generation. This loss improves RATSQL and LGESQL by 1.3% and 0.5%, although its incorporation slightly decreases the testing speed[5].

In order to deeply analyze the effect of alignment loss, we report EM results on different SQL hardness levels. Yu et al. (2018) [18] define the SQL hardness based on the number of clauses and the number of components in a clause. From Table 4, we can see that our clause-level alignment obtains larger gains on hard examples, e.g., improving performance by 2.0% on "Medium" and 1.5% on "Hard" with RATSQL, and obtaining gains by 2.0% on "Medium" and 1.8% on "Extra Hard" with LGESQL. Through data statistics, about 85% of SQL queries in "Medium" and "Hard" levels contain no less than three clauses. Thus, we conclude that the clause-level alignment can improve SQL generation, especially for multiple-clause queries.

4.3 Analysis

Analysis of Parallel Decoding. In order to analyze the factors that affects the speed improvements in parallel decoding, we count the number of actions generated by each base model both in sequential decoding and parallel decoding, as shown in Fig. 3. In sequential decoding, where the number of actions for an SQL query is the total number of actions for its clauses, the average action numbers for RATSQL and LGESQL are 23.2 and 18.1, respectively. In parallel decoding, the number of actions for an SQL

---

[5] We have not evaluation the model performance on different level of clause-segment alignment and leave it in our future work.

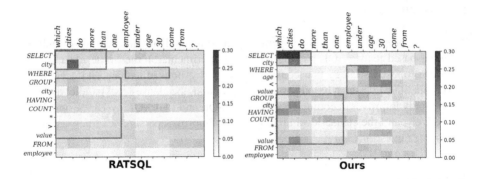

Fig. 4. Visualization of RATSQL attention scores. Red rectangles highlight alignment blocks that obtain high scores in our model but low scores in baseline. (Color figure online)

Table 5. Case study: comparisons with baseline (RATSQL) and our method show ours generate more accurate SQLs.

Q	What type of pet is **the youngest animal**, and how much does it weigh?
Base	SELECT Pets.PetType, Pets.weight FROM Pets ORDER BY Pets.weight Asc LIMIT 1
Ours	SELECT PetType, weight FROM Pets **ORDER BY pet_age LIMIT 1**
Gold	SELECT PetType, weight FROM Pets **ORDER BY pet_age LIMIT 1**
Q	Find the number of flights landing **in the city of Aberdeen or Abilene**
Base	SELECT Count(*) FROM airports JOIN flights WHERE airports.City ='Val' OR airports.AirportName ='Val'
Ours	SELECT count(*) FROM Flights AS T1 JOIN Airports AS T2 **WHERE T2.city = "Val" OR T2.city = "Val"**
Gold	SELECT count(*) FROM Flights AS T1 JOIN Airports AS T2 **WHERE T2.city = "Aberdeen" OR T2.city = "Abilene"**

query depends on that of the longest clause. And the average action numbers for RATSQL and LGESQL in parallel decoding are 11.0 and 7.6. In LGESQL, the average action number in parallel decoding is about 42% of that in sequential decoding. Then the parallel decoding improves parsing speed by 35.5% for LGESQL. However, in RATSQL, the average action number in parallel decoding is about 48% of that in sequential decoding, but the speed is improved by 18.9%. Through further data analysis, we find that the SELECT clause always takes the largest time cost, and its average action number accounts for 33.6% of that for the whole SQL query. Therefore, the parallel decoding obtains a lower speed improvement in RATSQL. Thus it can be seen that parallel decoding is more effective when there is little difference in the action numbers of all clauses.

Case Study. In order to verify the impact of clause-level alignments in the attention mechanism, we plot attention weights of original RATSQL and our RATSQL in Fig. 4. In our model, each clause has a higher attention weight with tokens in the corresponding aligned segment. Inversely, the base model doesn't have focus attention scores for some clauses, such as WHERE and GROUP, and it fails to generate the WHERE clause. Table 5 gives more cases, which shows our method focuses on relevant question segments in different clause generation.

5   Conclusions

This work proposes clause-level parallel decoding and alignment loss to enhance grammar-based text-to-SQL parsing models. Experiments on the Spider dataset show that our proposed strategy can consistently improve both efficiency and accuracy of two competitive grammar-based parsers. In particular, the clause-level parallel decoding substantially improves decoding speed of RATSQL and LGESQL by 18.9% and 35.5% respectively, and the clause-level alignment loss improves parsing accuracy, especially on complex questions.

References

1. Cao, R., Chen, L., Chen, Z., Zhao, Y., Zhu, S., Yu, K.: LGESQL: line graph enhanced text-to-SQL model with mixed local and non-local relations. arXiv preprint arXiv:2106.01093 (2021)
2. Clark, K., Luong, M.T., Le, Q.V., Manning, C.D.: ELECTRA: pre-training text encoders as discriminators rather than generators. arXiv preprint arXiv:2003.10555 (2020)
3. Devlin, J., Chang, M.W., Lee, K., Toutanova, K.: BERT: pre-training of deep bidirectional transformers for language understanding. In: Proceedings of the 2019 Conference of the North American Chapter of the Association for Computational Linguistics: Human Language Technologies, pp. 4171–4186 (2019)
4. Dong, L., Lapata, M.: Coarse-to-fine decoding for neural semantic parsing. In: Proceedings of the 56th Annual Meeting of the Association for Computational Linguistics (Volume 1: Long Papers), pp. 731–742 (2018)
5. Guo, J., et al.: Towards complex text-to-SQL in cross-domain database with intermediate representation. In: Proceedings of the 57th Annual Meeting of the Association for Computational Linguistics, pp. 4524–4535 (2019)
6. Lei, W., et al.: Re-examining the role of schema linking in text-to-SQL. In: Proceedings of the 2020 Conference on Empirical Methods in Natural Language Processing (EMNLP), pp. 6943–6954 (2020)
7. Li, F., Jagadish, H.V.: Constructing an interactive natural language interface for relational databases. PVLDB 8(1), 73–84 (2014)
8. Scholak, T., Li, R., Bahdanau, D., de Vries, H., Pal, C.: DuoRAT: towards simpler text-to-SQL models. In: Proceedings of the 2021 Conference of the North American Chapter of the Association for Computational Linguistics: Human Language Technologies, pp. 1313–1321 (2021)
9. Tang, L.R., Mooney, R.J.: Using multiple clause constructors in inductive logic programming for semantic parsing. In: De Raedt, L., Flach, P. (eds.) ECML 2001. LNCS (LNAI), vol. 2167, pp. 466–477. Springer, Heidelberg (2001). https://doi.org/10.1007/3-540-44795-4_40
10. Wang, B., Shin, R., Liu, X., Polozov, O., Richardson, M.: RAT-SQL: relation-aware schema encoding and linking for text-to-SQL parsers. In: Proceedings of the 58th Annual Meeting of the Association for Computational Linguistics, pp. 7567–7578 (2020)
11. Wang, L., et al.: DuSQL: a large-scale and pragmatic Chinese text-to-SQL dataset. In: Proceedings of the 2020 Conference on Empirical Methods in Natural Language Processing (EMNLP), pp. 6923–6935. Association for Computational Linguistics, November 2020. https://doi.org/10.18653/v1/2020.emnlp-main.562, https://aclanthology.org/2020.emnlp-main.562

12. Wu, K., et al.: Data augmentation with hierarchical SQL-to-question generation for cross-domain text-to-SQL parsing. In: Proceedings of the 2021 Conference on Empirical Methods in Natural Language Processing, Punta Cana, Dominican Republic, pp. 8974–8983. Association for Computational Linguistics, November 2021. https://aclanthology.org/2021.emnlp-main.707
13. Xu, X., Liu, C., Song, D.: SQLNet: generating structured queries from natural language without reinforcement learning. arXiv preprint arXiv:1711.04436 (2017)
14. Yin, P., et al.: Compositional generalization for neural semantic parsing via span-level supervised attention. In: Proceedings of the 2021 Conference of the North American Chapter of the Association for Computational Linguistics: Human Language Technologies, pp. 2810–2823 (2021)
15. Yin, P., Neubig, G.: TRANX: a transition-based neural abstract syntax parser for semantic parsing and code generation. In: Proceedings of the 2018 Conference on Empirical Methods in Natural Language Processing: System Demonstrations, pp. 7–12 (2018)
16. Yu, T., Li, Z., Zhang, Z., Zhang, R., Radev, D.: TypeSQL: knowledge-based type-aware neural text-to-SQL generation. In: Proceedings of the 2018 Conference of the North American Chapter of the Association for Computational Linguistics: Human Language Technologies, Volume 2 (Short Papers), pp. 588–594 (2018)
17. Yu, T., et al.: GraPPa: grammar-augmented pre-training for table semantic parsing. arXiv preprint arXiv:2009.13845 (2020)
18. Yu, T., et al.: Spider: a large-scale human-labeled dataset for complex and cross-domain semantic parsing and text-to-SQL task. In: Proceedings of the 2018 Conference on Empirical Methods in Natural Language Processing, pp. 3911–3921 (2018)
19. Zeng, Y., et al.: RECPARSER: a recursive semantic parsing framework for text-to-SQL task. In: Twenty-Ninth International Joint Conference on Artificial Intelligence, pp. 3644–3650 (2020)
20. Zhong, V., Xiong, C., Socher, R.: Seq2SQL: generating structured queries from natural language using reinforcement learning. arXiv preprint arXiv:1709.00103 (2017)

Two-Stage Query Graph Selection
for Knowledge Base Question Answering

Yonghui Jia[1], Chuanyuan Tan[1], Yuehe Chen[1], Muhua Zhu[2], Pingfu Chao[1],
and Wenliang Chen[1(✉)]

[1] Institute of Artificial Intelligence, School of Computer Science and Technology,
Soochow University, Suzhou, China
{cytan17726,yhchen2020}@stu.suda.edu.cn, {pfchao,wlchen}@suda.edu.cn
[2] Meituan Group, Beijing, China

Abstract. Finding the best answer to a question in Knowledge Base
Question Answering (KBQA) is always challenging due to its enormous
searching space and the interactive performance requirement. A typical
solution is to retrieve the answer by finding the optimal query graph,
which is a sub-graph of the knowledge graph. However, existing methods
usually generate a considerable number of sub-graph candidates, then fail
to find the optimal one effectively, resulting in a significant gap between
top-1 performance and the oracle score of all the graph candidates. To
address this issue, this paper presents a novel two-stage method based
on the idea of first reducing the candidates to form a shortlist, and then
selecting the optimal one from them. Before the selection, we generate
many, often hundreds of, candidates for each question. In the first selection stage, we sort the candidates and select a small set of query graphs
(top-k), while in the second stage we propose to rerank them to select the
final answer. We evaluate our system on both English and Chinese data,
and the results show that our proposed two-stage method achieves competitive performance on all datasets (Our code is publicly available at
https://github.com/EnernityTwinkle/KBQA-QueryGraphSelection.).

Keywords: Knowledge Base Question Answering · Query graph
generation · Query graph selection

1 Introduction

Knowledge Base Question Answering (KBQA) is defined to be a task that
answers natural language questions over knowledge bases, such as Freebase [3]
and Wikidata [22]. A representative stream of approaches to KBQA is based
on semantic parsing [10,19,21] which translates textual questions into some

Y. Jia and C. Tan—Contribute equally to this paper. This work was supported by the
National Natural Science Foundation of China (Grant No. 61936010 and 61876115)
and the Project Funded by the Priority Academic Program Development of Jiangsu
Higher Education Institutions.

W. Lu et al. (Eds.) NLPCC 2022, LNCS 13552, pp. 16–28, 2022.
https://doi.org/10.1007/978-3-031-17189-5_2

semantic representation. To this end, formal meaning representations such as $\lambda - DCS$ [15] are widely adopted to represent the semantics of questions. However, such meaning representations need to be mapped to logical constants or an ontology before they can be used to retrieve answers from the knowledge base. The mapping between the meaning representations and an ontology is restricted by the coverage of the ontology [12].

An alternative to formal meaning representations is to represent question semantics with a query graph [16, 26, 27], which can be regarded as a sub-graph of the knowledge base. In this way, the restriction incurred by the coverage of an ontology is overcome. With query graph as the semantic representation, the process of KBQA can be divided into two steps: query graph generation and query graph selection. During query graph generation, the question is parsed into a set of candidate query graphs [26]. In query graph selection, an optimal query graph is selected through ranking methods, and the answer node corresponding to the optimal query graph is returned as the answer to the question. In the process described above, query graph generation determines the upper bound of the performance that we can achieve, whereas query graph selection determines the final performance of a KBQA system. In this paper, we put focus on question graph selection which is thought to be more important and challenging.

Existing approaches to query graph selection generally build on single-stage ranking [1, 16, 26], which ranks query graphs according to the similarity between the question and each query graph. These approaches achieve a certain success. However, in our preliminary experiments, we find that there is a significant gap between top-1 performance and the oracle score of top-k candidates.[1] The reason behind might be that there are too many, often hundreds of candidates generated by the step of query graph generation. This makes it difficult for the selection model to choose the right answer. In addition, during error analysis we also find that in some bad cases the type of the retrieved answer is wrong.

To address the above problems, we propose a two-stage (ranking-reranking) method for query graph selection. Our idea is that we continuously reduce the number of candidates in each stage, and then the model can make the final decision based on a shortlist. In our method, we need a sorting model which can calculate the matching score between the input question and each graph candidate. However, computing such scores is non-trivial because of the mismatch problem between a word sequence and a graph. Thus, we propose a new sorting model to do this job by converting the graph into a sequence and computing the matching score between two sequences, for both two stages. In the first stage, we select top-k candidates according to the matching scores of all the candidates. In the second stage, we rerank the top-k candidates by considering two types of information: 1) the ranking information from the first stage; 2) a new feature of type information corresponding to the answer node of the query graph.

Our contributions in the paper are summarized as follows,

---

[1] By *oracle score of top-k candidates*, we mean the performance that we can achieve by always choosing the optimal query graph from the top-k set.

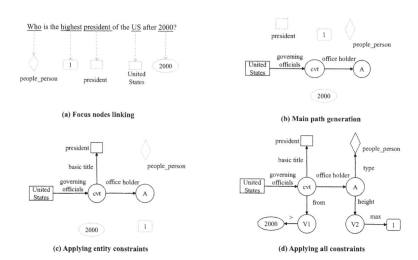

Fig. 1. Query graph generation procedure of "Who is the highest president of the US after 2000?".

- We propose the sorting model to effectually calculate the matching score between a question and a query graph, which can solve the mismatch problem.
- We propose the two-stage method for query graph selection to handle the problem of too many candidates. Our solution reduces the number of candidates from hundreds to tens and chooses the final answer from the shortlist. To our best knowledge, it is the first time that such a solution is proposed for KBQA.
- To prove our method is language-independent, we evaluate the proposed system on four datasets, two in English and the other two in Chinese. The experimental results show the effectiveness and generality of our method.

2   Our Approach

The system consists of two main components: query graph generation and query graph selection. In query graph generation, we utilize the staged query graph generation method to obtain a set of query graph candidates which often contains hundreds of items. In query graph selection, we propose a two-stage method to select the optimal query graph from candidates. Specifically, we rank the candidates to obtain top-k graphs in the first stage, then in the second stage, we rerank them to get the best one as the optimal query graph. Finally, the optimal query graph is used to retrieve the final answer from the Knowledge Base (KB).

2.1   Query Graph Generation

The goal of query graph generation is to parse the question into the form of query graph corresponding to the underlying KB. Due to the page limitation, here we briefly demonstrate the query graph generation method on English datasets, and the same applies to other languages. The details can be found in the paper of [16].

Given a question q, we first conduct focus nodes linking to recognize four node constraints, namely entities, type words, time words and ordinal words. For entity linking, we adopt the entity linking tool SMART [25] to obtain <mention, entity> pairs. For type word linking, we calculate word vector similarity scores between consecutive sub-sequences (up to three words) in the question and all types in KB, and select top-10 <mention, type> pairs as type candidates. For time word linking, we use regular expressions to extract time words from the question. For ordinal word linking, we use a predefined ordinal number dictionary and the "number + superlative" pattern to extract ordinal numbers. Figure 1(a) shows an example of the focus nodes linking.

After focus nodes linking, we perform one-hop and two-hop searches to obtain the main path based on the linked entities, as exemplified in Fig. 1(b). Then, the entity constraint is added to the main path as a constraint node, and we add type constraint, time constraint, and ordinal constraint subsequently to form a complete query graph, as shown in Fig. 1(c) and (d), respectively.

During the above procedure, the focus nodes are not fully disambiguated. Moreover, the one-hop and two-hop searches may have different paths. Thus query graph generation may generate more than one, usually hundreds of candidate query graphs, represented as a candidate query graph set $G = \{g_1, g_2, ..., g_m\}$ for each question.

2.2   Two-Stage Query Graph Selection

The goal of query graph selection is to select the optimal query graph g^* from the candidate query graph set G. In this section, we first describe the sorting model which can compute the matching score between the input question and each candidate query graph. And then we introduce our two-stage selection method which can obtain g^* from G.

Sorting Model. By this model, we calculate the matching score between the question and each candidate query graph. To encode the question and a query graph, we choose to convert the query graph into a query graph sequence, which makes the query graph and the question both in the unified sequence form. This choice simplifies the matching strategy of the question and the query graph, and the mature sequence matching methods can be used.

Specifically, we first transform the query graph into the sequence form according to its composition. In general, a query graph consists of up to five sub-paths: MainPath, TypePath, EntityPath, TimePath, and OrdinalPath, corresponding to the main path and four types of node constraints, respectively. Each sub-path can be converted into a word sequence. Taking the main path in Fig. 1 as an example, the corresponding main path sequence is "united states governing officials office holder A". We combine the five sub-path sequences into a query graph

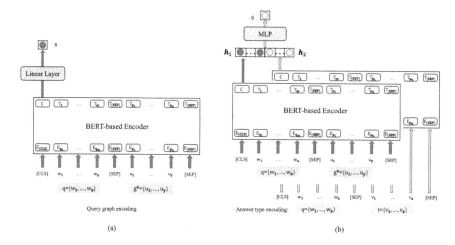

Fig. 2. (a) The matching framework for query graph ranking. During encoding, the question q and the query graph sequence g^s are considered. (b) The matching framework for query graph reranking. During encoding, the question q, the query graph sequence g^s and answer type t are considered.

sequence according to a fixed sub-path order, denoted as $g^s = \{u_1, u_2, ..., u_y\}$, where u_i is a token.

After the query graph sequence g^s is obtained, the task of query graph ranking is transformed into a matching task between two sequences: the question and the query graph sequence. We use BERT [8] to encode the question and the query graph sequence. Specifically, for query graph sequence $g^s = \{u_1, u_2, ..., u_y\}$, we combine it with the question $q = \{w_1, w_2, ..., w_x\}$ to form a sentence pair $qg^s = \{[CLS], w_1, ..., w_x, [SEP], u_1, ..., u_y, [SEP]\}$. Then the sentence pair qg^s is fed into BERT for encoding. The encoding framework is shown in Fig. 2(a). We use the output of the $[CLS]$ node in BERT as the semantic representation of the question and the query graph sequence, denoted as $\mathbf{h}$.

$$\mathbf{h} = BERT(qg^s), \tag{1}$$

The semantic representation vector $\mathbf{h}$ is mapped to a specific score through a linear layer.

$$s = Linear(\mathbf{h}), \tag{2}$$

where s is the similarity score between the question and the query graph.

Stage I: Top-K Selection. By using Eq. (2), we can calculate the scores of all the candidates in this stage. Then rank the candidates and obtain the top-k graphs. For training data construction, we randomly select n negative examples for each positive example. That is, a positive query graph and n negative query graphs form group examples $C = \{g_0^+, g_1^-, ..., g_n^-\}$, corresponding to label $Y = \{y_0, y_1, ..., y_n\}$. After query graph scoring, we can get the score set

$S = \{s_0, s_1, ..., s_n\}$ of each group examples C. In the optimization process, we use the cross-entropy loss function to optimize the score s_i of each query graph, and the optimization objective is:

$$s_i^* = \frac{exp(s_i)}{\sum_{i=0}^{n} exp(s_i)},$$ (3)

$$L = -\sum_{i=0}^{n} y_i log(s_i^*) + (1 - y_i)log(1 - s_i^*),$$ (4)

where y_i is the query graph label (1 represents a positive example and 0 represents a negative example). After this stage, we obtain top-k query graphs.

Stage II: Top-1 Selection. Obviously, we can rank all candidate query graphs according to the scores given in Stage I, and select the one with the highest score as the optimal query graph. However, in the preliminary experiments, we find that there is a significant gap between top-1 performance and the oracle score of top-k candidates. Thus, we propose to rerank the top-k candidates to obtain the final answer.

In addition, we use the type of the answer node in query graph as a feature in this stage, where the answer type information is from KB. As shown in Fig. 2(b), we adopt the same way used in Stage I to calculate the matching feature h_1 of the question and the query graph sequence.

$$h_1 = BERT_1(qg^s),$$ (5)

Besides, we utilize another BERT to encode the question and the answer type. Given a question $q = \{w_1, w_2, ..., w_x\}$ and answer type sequence $t = \{v_1, v_2, ..., v_z\}$ of the query graph, they are spliced into a sequence qt, and then fed into BERT for semantic encoding. We also use the output vector of its $[CLS]$ node as the semantic feature of the question and the answer type.

$$h_2 = BERT_2(qt),$$ (6)

Then, the feature is mapped to a score through a multilayer perceptron layer.

$$s = MLP([h_1; h_2]),$$ (7)

We use the ranking information of Stage I for choosing negative examples during the training phase in this stage. For training data construction, we no longer randomly select negative examples like Stage I. Instead, we select n negative examples from high to low according to the ranking scores from Stage I. As for the optimization objective, Stage II also uses Eq. (3) and (4).

3   Experiments

3.1   Experimental Setup

Table 1. The partitions of the Chinese and English datasets.

Dataset	Train	Validation	Test
WebQ	3,023	755	2,032
CompQ	1,000	300	800
CCKS2019-KBQA	2,298	766	766
CCKS2021-KBQA	5,184	1,297	1,191

Datasets. We conduct experiments on four datasets, namely WebQuestions (WebQ) [2], ComplexQuestions (CompQ) [1], CCKS2019-KBQA[2] and CCKS2021-KBQA.[3] The English datasets WebQ and CompQ are in the form of question-answer pairs, and use Freebase as the knowledge base, while the Chinese datasets CCKS2019-KBQA and CCKS2021-KBQA use pkubase[4] as the knowledge base. The Chinese datasets contain both the answer and the corresponding SPARQL query to the question. Similar to previous studies, four datasets are divided into training set, validation set and test set. The partitions of datasets are listed in Table 1.

Implementation Details. In Stage I and Stage II, we both use BERT-BASE for BERT model initialization, and use Adam as the optimizer for optimization. We choose the settings of hyper-parameters in the systems according to the performance on the validation sets. The learning rate is set to 5×10^{-5}, and the maximum training epoch is 5. For English and Chinese datasets, the maximum sequence length of BERT is 100 and 150, respectively. In Stage I, the number of negative examples n in Chinese and English are 30 and 120 respectively. In Stage II, the number of negative examples n in Stage II for Chinese and English are 30 and 40 respectively. During testing, the top-k in the Chinese and English datasets are set to 10 and 20, respectively. As for the evaluation metrics, we report the average F1-score (F1) that has been used in the previous studies [16], and also report the average precision (P) and average recall (R).

---

[2] https://www.biendata.xyz/competition/ccks_2019_6/data/.

[3] https://www.biendata.xyz/competition/ccks_2021_ckbqa/data/.

[4] http://pkubase.gstore.cn/.

3.2 Main Results

Table 2. Main results on the English datasets.

Method	WebQ(%)			CompQ(%)		
	P	R	F1	P	R	F1
Ranking	54.64	64.01	55.30	42.90	56.73	44.40
Reranking	**55.48**	**66.25**	**56.36**	**44.11**	**57.89**	**45.49**

Table 2 shows the performance of our systems on the WebQ and CompQ datasets, where "Ranking" refers to the system that we only use the Stage I to obtain the top-1 answer and "Reranking" refers to the two-stage system proposed in this paper. From the table, we find that compared to the Ranking system, the Reranking system achieves much better performance. Specifically, we obtain an absolute improvement of 1.06% F1 on the WebQ dataset and 1.09% F1 on the CompQ, respectively. These facts indicate that the proposed two-stage method is quite effective.

Table 3. Main results on the Chinese datasets.

Method	CCKS2019-KBQA (%)			CCKS2021-KBQA (%)		
	P	R	F1	P	R	F1
Ranking	73.09	74.63	72.64	76.19	77.77	75.38
Reranking	**74.93**	**75.71**	**74.14**	**78.07**	**79.22**	**77.28**

We further conduct experiments on two Chinese datasets and Table 3 shows the corresponding results. Compared with Ranking, Reranking also improves the system performance on Chinese datasets consistently. As shown in the table,

Table 4. The comparison results with the previous methods on English datasets.

Category	Method	WebQ (F1%)	CompQ (F1%)
Using Query Graph	Bao et al. (2016) [1]	52.4	40.9
	Hu et al. (2018) [10]	53.6	–
	Luo et al. (2018) [16]	52.7	42.8
	Chen et al. (2020) [5]	53.4	43.1
	Lan and Jiang (2020) [13]	–	43.3
	Qiu et al. (2020) [18]	54.8	45.0
	Ma et al. (2022) [17]	–	41.4
Others	Berant et al. (2013) [2]	36.4	–
	Jain(2016) [11]	55.6	–
	Chen et al. (2019) [6]	51.8	–
	Xu et al. (2019) [24]	54.6	–
Ours	Reranking	**56.4**	**45.5**

the Reranking method achieves 1.50% and 1.90% F1 score improvement on CCKS2019-KBQA and CCKS2021-KBQA, respectively, which further proves the effectiveness of our two-stage query graph selection method.

Table 4 shows the comparison results of our systems and the previous systems. According to whether to use query graph, the previous systems are divided into two categories: "Using Query Graph" and "Others". In the previous "Using Query Graph" systems, they utilize a single-stage ranking strategy and adopt the predefined query graph features to improve the performance of query graph selection. Compared with them, our method is based on a two-stage strategy and does not rely on any predefined query graph features. Among all the systems, our two-stage system achieves the best result on the WebQ and the CompQ, which indicates our two-stage query graph selection system is quite powerful.

Table 5. The comparison results with the previous methods on Chinese datasets.

Category	Methods	CCKS2019-KBQA (F1%)	CCKS2021-KBQA (F1%)
Teams	First	73.55	78.86
	Second	73.08	78.79
	Third	72.51	78.52
	Fourth	70.45	76.37
Ours	Reranking	74.14	77.28
	+Model fusion	**75.09**	**79.25**

We further compare the performance of the two-stage system with other methods on Chinese datasets. Table 5 shows the corresponding results, where "Teams" represents the top-4 system results in the CCKS competition. For Chinese datasets, the above competition systems adopt the corresponding model fusion strategy. Therefore, we also train five reranking models for model fusion with five different random seeds. The results show that our Reranking method has achieved competitive results. After model fusion, the two-stage system achieves the best performance on the CCKS2019-KBQA and CCKS2021-KBQA.

3.3 Discussion and Analysis

In this section, we perform further analysis on the results of our systems. We first discuss the necessity of the two-stage strategy. Then we check the effect of different components in Stage II.

Necessity of Two-Stage Query Graph Selection. Regarding the oracle score of top-k candidates in Stage I, as shown in Fig. 3, it is clear that the score shows a rapid initial growth, but tends to be stable eventually. This phenomenon means that most of the correct query graphs are the top candidates in the ranking list, but not necessarily to be the best one. Therefore, it is possible to improve the performance through the two-stage strategy based on the top-k candidates. Besides, when fewer candidates are obtained by ranking of Stage I, the reranking of Stage II also becomes less time-consuming. As a result, it is necessary and feasible to introduce the two-stage strategy to further improve the system performance.

Ablation Study for Stage II. Compared to the Ranking (Stage I) system, our Reranking (Stage II) system has two changes: 1) using a different negative examples sampling strategy to construct training data based on the ordering information from Stage I; 2) adding the answer type feature of query graph. In order to explore the influence of the above two changes on Stage II, we remove the answer type feature from the final system. The results are shown in Table 6, where "Reranking-Base" refers to the Stage II system without the information of answer type and "Reranking-Full" refers to our final two-stage system. From the table, we can find that after removing the answer type, the performance of the system is reduced. But compared to one-stage Ranking, the Reranking-Base still performs better. This shows that both two changes contribute to the system.

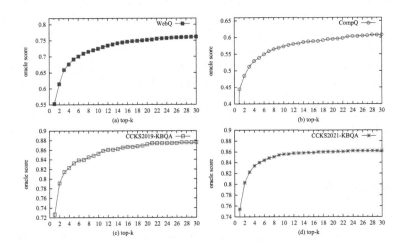

Fig. 3. The top-k oracle score in Stage I.

Table 6. The effect of using different components.

Method	WebQ	CompQ	CCKS2019-KBQA	CCKS2021-KBQA
Ranking	55.30	44.40	72.64	75.38
Reranking-base	55.68	44.62	73.57	76.37
Reranking-full	56.36	45.49	74.14	77.28

4   Related Work

Tracing back to the solutions for knowledge base question answering, there are two mainstream approaches: information retrieval(IR) based methods and semantic parsing (SP) based methods. Among them, IR-based methods [23] first recognize entities in the question, then search related candidate answers according to entities and returns the most relevant answers. The core of IR-based methods is the matching between questions and answers, which is usually realized by deep learning approaches [6,9]. For example, Bordes et al. (2014) [4] propose calculate the similarity between the question and the answer by learning the low-dimensional embedding of the question and the subgraph of the answer. There are also some works that focus on multi-hop reasoning by adopting Key-Value Memory Neural Networks [24] or performing a transition-based search strategy [7]. Besides, knowledge base embeddings are also used to improve multi-hop question answering and achieve success [20].

Different from IR-based methods, SP-based approaches pay more attention to the semantic information of questions, trying to parse the question into structured representation [1,5,14]. For example, the question can be parsed into $\lambda - DCS$, and then map to the knowledge base to obtain answers [2]. As for complex questions, Sun et al. (2020) [21] design a novel skeleton grammar to express complex questions and improve the ability to parse complex questions. Besides, query graph is also a widely-used formal meaning representation in SP-based systems which is also used in this paper. Yih et al. (2015) [26] are the pioneer in query graph research for KBQA. Following this line, the encoding method of complex query graph [16] and the construction method of multi-hop complex query graph [13] are also proposed. In this paper, we propose a two-stage method of query graph selection, which makes the query graph based method more effective.

5   Conclusions

In this paper, we propose a simple yet effective two-stage method for query graph selection in KBQA. In Stage I, we calculate the similarity between the question and the query graph sequence to obtain the top-k query graph candidates. In Stage II, we further rerank the top-k candidate query graphs. The experimental results show that the proposed method provides the competitive results on the Chinese and English datasets.

References

1. Bao, J., Duan, N., Yan, Z., Zhou, M., Zhao, T.: Constraint-based question answering with knowledge graph. In: Proceedings of COLING, pp. 2503–2514 (2016)
2. Berant, J., Chou, A., Frostig, R., Liang, P.: Semantic parsing on Freebase from question-answer pairs. In: Proceedings of EMNLP, pp. 1533–1544 (2013)

3. Bollacker, K., Evans, C., Paritosh, P., Sturge, T., Taylor, J.: Freebase: a collaboratively created graph database for structuring human knowledge. In: Proceedings of SIGMOD, pp. 1247–1250 (2008)
4. Bordes, A., Chopra, S., Weston, J.: Question answering with subgraph embeddings. In: Proceedings of EMNLP, pp. 615–620 (2014)
5. Chen, Y., Li, H., Hua, Y., Qi, G.: Formal query building with query structure prediction for complex question answering over knowledge base. In: Proceedings of IJCAI, pp. 3751–3758 (2020)
6. Chen, Y., Wu, L., Zaki, M.J.: Bidirectional attentive memory networks for question answering over knowledge bases. In: Proceedings of NAACL-HLT, pp. 2913–2923 (2019)
7. Chen, Z., Chang, C., Chen, Y., Nayak, J., Ku, L.: UHop: an unrestricted-hop relation extraction framework for knowledge-based question answering. In: Proceedings of NAACL-HLT, pp. 345–356 (2019)
8. Devlin, J., Chang, M., Lee, K., Toutanova, K.: BERT: pre-training of deep bidirectional transformers for language understanding. In: Proceedings of NAACL-HLT, pp. 4171–4186 (2019)
9. Dong, L., Wei, F., Zhou, M., Xu, K.: Question answering over Freebase with multi-column convolutional neural networks. In: Proceedings of ACL, pp. 260–269 (2015)
10. Hu, S., Zou, L., Zhang, X.: A state-transition framework to answer complex questions over knowledge base. In: Proceedings of EMNLP, pp. 2098–2108 (2018)
11. Jain, S.: Question answering over knowledge base using factual memory networks. In: Proceedings of NAACL-HLT, pp. 109–115 (2016)
12. Kwiatkowski, T., Choi, E., Artzi, Y., Zettlemoyer, L.: Scaling semantic parsers with on-the-fly ontology matching. In: Proceedings of EMNLP, pp. 1545–1556 (2013)
13. Lan, Y., Jiang, J.: Query graph generation for answering multi-hop complex questions from knowledge bases. In: Proceedings of ACL, pp. 969–974 (2020)
14. Liang, C., Berant, J., Le, Q.V., Forbus, K.D., Lao, N.: Neural symbolic machines: learning semantic parsers on freebase with weak supervision. In: Proceedings of ACL, pp. 23–33 (2017)
15. Liang, P.: Lambda dependency-based compositional semantics. arXiv preprint arXiv:1309.4408 (2013)
16. Luo, K., Lin, F., Luo, X., Zhu, K.: Knowledge base question answering via encoding of complex query graphs. In: Proceedings of EMNLP, pp. 2185–2194 (2018)
17. Ma, L., et al.: Syntax-based graph matching for knowledge base question answering. In: Proceedings of ICASSP, pp. 8227–8231 (2022)
18. Qiu, Y., et al.: Hierarchical query graph generation for complex question answering over knowledge graph. In: Proceedings of CIKM, pp. 1285–1294 (2020)
19. Reddy, S., Lapata, M., Steedman, M.: Large-scale semantic parsing without question-answer pairs. Trans. Assoc. Comput. Linguist. $\mathbf{2}$, 377–392 (2014)
20. Saxena, A., Tripathi, A., Talukdar, P.P.: Improving multi-hop question answering over knowledge graphs using knowledge base embeddings. In: Proceedings of ACL, pp. 4498–4507 (2020)
21. Sun, Y., Zhang, L., Cheng, G., Qu, Y.: SPARQA: skeleton-based semantic parsing for complex questions over knowledge bases. In: Proceedings of AAAI, pp. 8952–8959 (2020)
22. Vrandecic, D., Krötzsch, M.: Wikidata: a free collaborative knowledgebase. Commun. ACM $\mathbf{57}$(10), 78–85 (2014)
23. Wang, Z., Ng, P., Nallapati, R., Xiang, B.: Retrieval, re-ranking and multi-task learning for knowledge-base question answering. In: Proceedings of EACL, pp. 347–357 (2021)

24. Xu, K., Lai, Y., Feng, Y., Wang, Z.: Enhancing key-value memory neural networks for knowledge based question answering. In: Proceedings of NAACL-HLT, pp. 2937–2947 (2019)
25. Yang, Y., Chang, M.: S-MART: novel tree-based structured learning algorithms applied to tweet entity linking. In: Proceedings of ACL, pp. 504–513 (2015)
26. Yih, S.W.T., Chang, M.W., He, X., Gao, J.: Semantic parsing via staged query graph generation: question answering with knowledge base. In: Proceedings of ACL, pp. 1321–1331 (2015)
27. Yih, W., Richardson, M., Meek, C., Chang, M., Suh, J.: The value of semantic parse labeling for knowledge base question answering. In: Proceedings of ACL, pp. 201–206 (2016)

Plug-and-Play Module for Commonsense Reasoning in Machine Reading Comprehension

Damai Dai, Hua Zheng, Zhifang Sui$^{(\boxtimes)}$, and Baobao Chang

MOE Key Lab of Computational Linguistics, Peking University, Beijing, China
{daidamai,huaz,szf,chbb}@pku.edu.cn

Abstract. Conventional Machine Reading Comprehension (MRC) has been well-addressed by pattern matching, but the ability of commonsense reasoning remains a gap between humans and machines. Previous methods tackle this problem by enriching word representations via pretrained Knowledge Graph Embeddings (KGE). However, they make limited use of a large number of connections between nodes in Knowledge Graphs (KG), which can be pivotal cues for building the commonsense reasoning chains. In this paper, we propose a **P**lug-and-play module to **I**ncorporat**E** **C**onnection information for commons**E**nse **R**easoning (**PIECER**). Beyond enriching word representations with knowledge embeddings, PIECER constructs a joint query-passage graph to explicitly guide commonsense reasoning by the knowledge-oriented connections between words. Further, PIECER has high generalizability since it can be plugged into any MRC model. Experimental results on ReCoRD, a large-scale public MRC dataset requiring commonsense reasoning, show that PIECER introduces stable performance improvements for four representative base MRC models, especially in low-resource settings (The code is available at https://github.com/Hunter-DDM/piecer.).

Keywords: Machine Reading Comprehension · Commonsense reasoning · Connection information

1 Introduction

Machine Reading Comprehension (MRC) is a pivotal and challenging task in Natural Language Processing (NLP), which aims to automatically comprehend a context passage and answer related queries. In recent years, especially after the proposal of various large-scale Pre-Trained Models (PTM) [5,14], MRC has achieved great success on multiple datasets such as SQuAD [20] and NewsQA [25]. However, current state-of-the-art models perform worse on ReCoRD [37], a large-scale MRC dataset that requires commonsense reasoning. This may suggest that existing MRC models are adept at pattern matching [9,10,19], but they still lag behind in the ability of commonsense reasoning.

Figure 1 illustrates the difference between SQuAD and ReCoRD. In the SQuAD example, both keywords in the query ("a course of study" and "called")

© Springer Nature Switzerland AG 2022
W. Lu et al. (Eds.) NLPCC 2022, LNCS 13552, pp. 29–41, 2022.
https://doi.org/10.1007/978-3-031-17189-5_3

SQuAD	**Passage**	… Teachers may use a lesson plan to facilitate student learning, providing <u>a course of study</u> which is <u>called</u> **the curriculum** …
	Query	What is <u>a course of study</u> <u>called</u>?
	Answer	**the curriculum**
ReCoRD	**Passage**	… a Tennessee teacher who kidnapped and fled with his 15-year-old student was arrested … "I'm glad this is over," 50-year-old **Tad Cummins** said after his arrest … **Elizabeth Thomas** was found safe in a remote <u>cabin</u> …
	Query	Snipers surrounded the <u>cabin</u> as **X** exited the <u>cabin</u> and was taken into custody.
	Answer	**Tad Cummins**

Fig. 1. Two examples selected from SQuAD and ReCoRD. The SQuAD example requires only simple pattern matching, while the ReCoRD example requires commonsense reasoning. We mark the same keywords using the same underlines.

directly appear around the correct answer in the passage, so we can easily find the answer ***the curriculum*** by pattern matching. By contrast, the ReCoRD example requires commonsense reasoning, where we need to select a candidate entity (marked in bold) in the passage to be filled into the blank (denoted by a bold red **X**) in the query. Firstly, few keywords (only "cabin") in the query are covered by the passage. Secondly, there are confusing entities (***Elizabeth Thomas*** as the hostage vs. ***Tad Cummins*** as the kidnapper) that require external knowledge for differentiation. Therefore, it is almost impossible to find the correct answer by only pattern matching. Instead, with the commonsense knowledge that "be taken into custody" is similar to "be arrested", we can infer that ***Tad Cummins*** is the answer. These two examples suggest that pattern matching can not tackle difficult MRC that requires commonsense reasoning.

In order to make up for the deficiency in commonsense reasoning, previous methods attempt to leverage knowledge stored in Knowledge Graphs (KG) [3,17, 23]. KnReader [16] encodes knowledge as a key-value memory and enriches each word by memory querying. KB-LSTM [34] and KT-Net [33] enrich each word by applying the attention mechanism to its KG neighbors. SKG [18] updates the representation of each word by aggregating knowledge embeddings of its KG neighbors via graph attention [38]. These methods enrich each word separately by fusing pretrained knowledge embeddings. However, how to explicitly leverage knowledge-oriented connections between words, which can be pivotal cues for building the commonsense reasoning chains, is barely investigated.

In this paper, we propose a **P**lug-and-play module to **I**ncorporat**E C**onnection information for commons**E**nse **R**easoning (**PIECER**). Beyond leveraging knowledge embeddings, PIECER constructs a joint query-passage graph to explicitly guide commonsense reasoning by the knowledge-oriented connections. PIECER is composed of three submodules: (1) a **knowledge embedding injection** submodule that enriches words with background knowledge;

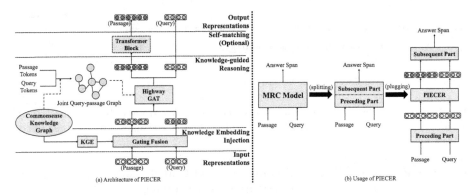

Fig. 2. Illustrations for PIECER. Subplot (a) illustrates how PIECER leverages external knowledge. Subplot (b) illustrates how to plug PIECER into an MRC model.

(2) a **knowledge-guided reasoning** submodule that leverages knowledge-oriented connections to facilitate commonsense reasoning; and (3) a **self-matching** submodule that further adapts the knowledge-enhanced information to a specific MRC task.

Our contributions are summarized as follows: (1) Beyond leveraging only knowledge embeddings, we propose to incorporate the connection information in KGs to guide commonsense reasoning in MRC. (2) We design a plug-and-play module called PIECER, which can be plugged into any MRC model to enhance its ability of commonsense reasoning. (3) We evaluate PIECER on ReCoRD that requires commonsense reasoning. Experimental results and elaborate analysis validate the effectiveness of PIECER, especially in low-resource settings.

2 Methodology

2.1 Task Formulation

Let $\mathcal{P}$ denote a context passage consisting of N words $\mathcal{P} = \left\{ w_i^{(p)} \right\}_{i=1}^{N}$ and $\mathcal{Q}$ denote a query consisting of M words $\mathcal{Q} = \left\{ w_i^{(q)} \right\}_{i=1}^{M}$. Given $\mathcal{P}$ and $\mathcal{Q}$, MRC requires reading and comprehending them and then predicting an answer to the query. Specifically, in this paper, we tackle the extractive MRC that requires extracting a continuous span in $\mathcal{P}$ as the answer, i.e., answer $= w_{s:t}^{(p)}$, where s and t are the answer boundaries.

2.2 Proposed Module: PIECER

As illustrated in Fig. 2 (a), PIECER is composed of three submodules: (1) a knowledge embedding injection submodule, (2) a knowledge-guided reasoning submodule, and (3) an optional self-matching submodule.

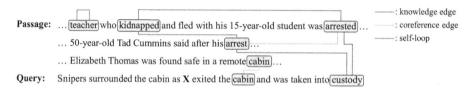

Fig. 3. An example of the joint query-passage graph. We draw only several edges in each category for readability. Red **X** in the query denotes the answer blank to be filled. (Color figure online)

Knowledge Embedding Injection. In an MRC model, word representations are learned based on the data distribution in the training set and are thus limited within the dataset. However, commonsense reasoning usually requires background knowledge beyond the dataset as shown in Fig. 1. In order to inject external background knowledge into words, this submodule adopts a gating mechanism to fuse word representations with pretrained knowledge embeddings.

First, we adopt Knowledge Graph Embedding (KGE) methods, such as TransE [1] or DistMult [35], to pretrain knowledge embeddings for each entity in a KG:

$$\{\mathbf{e}_i\} = \text{KGE}(\mathcal{G}),$$

where $\{\mathbf{e}_i\}$ is the entity embedding set and $\mathcal{G}$ is the selected KG.

Then, for each word w in $\mathcal{P}$ and $\mathcal{Q}$, we retrieve from $\mathcal{G}$ all unigram entities e_i that have the same lemma with w, and adopt a gating mechanism to fuse the word representation and the retrieved knowledge embeddings:

$$\mathbf{e} = \text{Mean}(\{\mathbf{e}_i|\text{lemma}(e_i) = \text{lemma}(w)\}),$$
$$gate = \sigma(\mathbf{W_g}[\mathbf{w}; \mathbf{e}] + \mathbf{b_g}), \quad \mathbf{w}' = \mathbf{w} \cdot gate + \mathbf{e} \cdot (1 - gate),$$

where lemma($\cdot$) denotes lemmatization, $\mathbf{w}$ is the input word representation, σ denotes sigmoid, $\mathbf{W_g}$ and $\mathbf{b_g}$ are trainable parameters, and $\mathbf{w}'$ is the output word representation with background knowledge.

Knowledge-Guided Reasoning. Although the knowledge embedding injection submodule injects background knowledge into each word, the connections between words are not explicitly leveraged. In order to incorporate the connection information, this submodule constructs a joint query-passage graph according to the structure of $\mathcal{G}$ and designs a Highway GAT for multi-hop reasoning.

In order to construct the joint graph, we treat words in $\mathcal{P}$ and $\mathcal{Q}$ as nodes and consider three categories of edges: knowledge edge, coreference edge, and self-loop. For **knowledge edge**, we first link each word in the passage or query to an entity in $\mathcal{G}$ by lemma matching. Then, for each pair of words, if they are connected in $\mathcal{G}$, we add an edge between them. For **coreference edge**, we assume that two words with the same lemma are coreferential and add an edge between them. For **self-loop**, we add an edge between each word and itself. In particular, we exclude all edges connecting stop words and punctuations. An example of the joint query-passage graph is shown in Fig. 3.

After constructing the joint query-passage graph, we design a **Highway GAT** that combines Highway Networks [24] and GAT [27] for multi-hop reasoning. Under the guidance of the joint graph, the Highway GAT expressly amplifies the interactions between knowledge-related nodes, which can help to build the commonsense reasoning chains. All nodes are updated for L times. At the l-th layer, we first calculate the updated representation $\mathbf{h}_i'^{(l)}$ for each node i by averaging K attention heads:

$$\mathbf{h}_i'^{(l)} = \frac{1}{K} \sum_{k=1}^{K} \sum_{j \in \mathcal{N}(i)} \alpha_{k,i,j}^{(l)} \mathbf{W}_k^{(l)} \mathbf{h}_j^{(l-1)},$$

$$\alpha_{k,i,j}^{(l)} = \text{Softmax}_j \left(e_{k,i,j}^{(l)} \right),$$

$$e_{k,i,j}^{(l)} = \sigma_r \left(\mathbf{a}_k^{(l)^T} \left[\mathbf{W}_k^{(l)} \mathbf{h}_i^{(l-1)}; \mathbf{W}_k^{(l)} \mathbf{h}_j^{(l-1)} \right] \right),$$

where $\mathbf{h}_i^{(l)}$ denotes the hidden state of node i at the l-th layer, and specially, we set $\mathbf{h}_i^{(0)}$ to $\mathbf{w}_i'$. $\mathcal{N}(i)$ denotes the neighbor set of node i in the joint graph, Softmax_j denotes softmax along dimension j, σ_r denotes LeakyReLU, and $\mathbf{W}_k^{(l)}$ and $\mathbf{a}_k^{(l)}$ are trainable parameters.

Then, inspired by Highway Networks, we use a highway connection to control the updating ratio to obtain the final output at the l-th layer $\mathbf{h}_i^{(l)}$:

$$\mathbf{w} = \sigma(\mathbf{W}_\mathbf{h}^{(l)} \mathbf{h}_i^{(l-1)} + \mathbf{b}_\mathbf{h}^{(l)}),$$

$$\mathbf{h}_i^{(l)} = \mathbf{w} \odot \mathbf{h}_i^{(l-1)} + (1 - \mathbf{w}) \odot \mathbf{h}_i'^{(l)},$$

where $\mathbf{w}$ is the weight vector, σ denotes sigmoid, $\odot$ denotes the Hadamard product, and $\mathbf{W}_\mathbf{h}^{(l)}$ and $\mathbf{b}_\mathbf{h}^{(l)}$ are trainable parameters. After L-layer Highway GAT updating, $\mathbf{h}_i^{(L)}$ is the final output of this submodule, which captures the interactions with its knowledge-related L-hop neighbors.

Self-matching. After the above knowledge enhancement, the self-matching submodule finally adapts the knowledge-enhanced information to the MRC task. We use a Transformer block [26] to implement this submodule:

$$\mathbf{o}_{1:N}' = \text{SelfAttention}(\mathbf{h}_{1:N}^{(L)}) + \mathbf{h}_{1:N}^{(L)},$$

$$\mathbf{o}_i = \text{FC}_2(\text{ReLU}(\text{FC}_1(\mathbf{o}_i'))) + \mathbf{o}_i',$$

where FC_x denotes fully connected layers, and $\mathbf{o}_i$ is the final output of PIECER. Specially, if an MRC model has its own matching submodule, we do not need another one in PIECER. Therefore, this submodule is optional.

2.3 Plugging PIECER into MRC Models

As a plug-and-play module, PIECER has high generalizability since it can be plugged into any MRC model. Figure 2 (b) demonstrates the usage of PIECER.

For an MRC model, we first split it into two sequential parts: (1) the preceding part that takes $\mathcal{P}$ and $\mathcal{Q}$ as inputs and outputs their representations, and (2) the subsequent part that takes these representations as inputs and predicts the final answer. Then, we can plug PIECER between them.

3   Experiments

3.1   Datasets

We conduct experiments on ReCoRD [37], a large-scale public MRC dataset requiring commonsense reasoning. ReCoRD contains a total of 120,730 examples, 75% of which require commonsense reasoning and is split into training, development, and test sets with 100,730, 10,000, and 10,000 examples, respectively. Each example contains a context passage and a query, where the passage has 169.3 tokens on average and the query has 21.4 tokens on average. Given an example, ReCoRD requires predicting an entity span in the context passage as the answer, which can be filled into the entity blank in the query, as shown in Fig. 1.

For the commonsense knowledge source, we select the English subset of ConceptNet [23]. This subset contains 1,165,190 nodes and 3,423,004 relational facts.

3.2   Base Models

In order to validate the effectiveness and generalizability of PIECER, we plug it into four representative MRC models. (1) **QANet** [36] is an outstanding MRC model without using PTMs. It contains five modules for embedding, encoding, passage-query attention, self-matching, and prediction. (2) BERT [5] is one of the most widely-used PTMs, which uses Transformers [26] as the encoder. We select both **BERT**$_{\text{base}}$ and **BERT**$_{\text{Large}}$ as our base models. (3) RoBERTa [14] is a modified PTM based on BERT, and is also widely-used. We select **RoBERTa**$_{\text{base}}$ as one of the base models. For MRC, both BERT and RoBERTa are followed by a linear layer to predict the answer span.

3.3   Experimental Settings

For pretrained knowledge embeddings, we select TransE [1] implemented by OpenKE [8] as the KGE method, use Adam [11] with a rate of 10^{-5} as the optimizer, set the embedding dimension to 100, and train for 10,000 epochs. For PIECER, we tune hyper-parameters on the development set. For a fair comparison, we first tune the base models to achieve the best performance, and then fix these hyper-parameters before plugging PIECER. Generally, we use AdamW [15] as the optimizer, apply exponential moving average with a decay rate of 0.9999, set all dropout rates to 0.1, set the number of Highway GAT layers to 3, and set the number of attention heads to 4. Other hyper-parameters, including learning rate, hidden dimension, and batch size, are different for each base

Table 1. Main evaluation results on ReCoRD. Δ EM and Δ F1 denote the improvements. Results on the test set are returned by the SuperGLUE online evaluation system.

Model	Dev				Test			
	EM	Δ EM	F1	Δ F1	EM	Δ EM	F1	Δ F1
QANet	36.79	–	37.32	–	38.4	–	38.9	–
QANet + PIECER	39.69	2.90↑	40.20	2.88↑	40.6	2.2↑	41.1	2.2↑
BERT$_{base}$	62.12	–	62.76	–	62.2	–	62.8	–
BERT$_{base}$ + PIECER	63.40	1.28↑	64.01	1.25↑	63.2	1.0↑	63.8	1.0↑
BERT$_{large}$	71.86	–	72.55	–	72.4	–	72.9	–
BERT$_{large}$ + PIECER	72.39	0.53↑	73.04	0.49↑	73.6	1.2↑	74.3	1.4↑
RoBERTa$_{base}$	78.89	–	79.52	–	79.7	–	80.3	–
RoBERTa$_{base}$ + PIECER	79.42	0.53↑	80.04	0.52↑	80.1	0.4↑	80.7	0.4↑

model. Due to the space limit, we put them into the technical Appendix in our GitHub repository.[1]

3.4 Main Results

Following previous work, we use Exact Match (EM) and F1 as the evaluation metrics. We show in Table 1 the main evaluation results. For each of the four base models, we compare the performance of the original model and the PIECER-plugged version (denoted as $X + PIECER$). From the table, we have the following observations: (1) PIECER introduces stable EM and F1 improvements for all base models. This validates the effectiveness of PIECER to enhance MRC that requires commonsense reasoning. (2) Comparing the performance improvements on four base models, QANet benefits the most from PIECER as an MRC model without using PTMs, while PTMs like BERT and RoBERTa gain moderate improvements. We explain this difference by the knowledge overlaps between PTMs and PIECER: PTMs have already encoded certain knowledge in their representations implicitly, which will overlap with commonsense knowledge introduced by PIECER. (3) We further investigate three PTMs that contain overlapping knowledge, and observe that PIECER still introduces stable performance improvements. This is due to the difference in how to leverage knowledge: PTMs encode knowledge in an uncontrollable and implicit way, while PIECER can actively select related commonsense knowledge stored in a KG for explicit use.

3.5 Analysis and Discussions

Ablation Study. In order to validate the effectiveness of each submodule in PIECER, we provide ablation experimental results of PIECER on the development set of ReCoRD in Table 2. We select RoBERTa$_{base}$ + PIECER as the baseline and attempt to remove the knowledge embedding injection submodule,

---

[1] https://github.com/Hunter-DDM/piecer/blob/main/Technical%20Appendix.pdf.

Table 2. Ablation study of PIECER based on RoBERTa_base + PIECER.

Model	EM	F1
RoBERTa_base + PIECER	79.42	80.04
w/o knowledge embedding injection	79.25 (−0.17)	79.92 (−0.12)
w/o knowledge-guided reasoning	78.98 (−0.44)	79.67 (−0.37)
RoBERTa_base	78.89 (−0.53)	79.52 (−0.52)

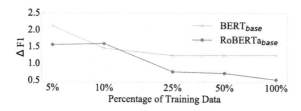

Fig. 4. F1 improvements of PIECER with different training and pretraining data.

the knowledge-guided reasoning submodule, and the whole PIECER, respectively. We observe that removing any submodule will result in a performance drop, especially for the knowledge-guided reasoning submodule. This suggests that each submodule is necessary for PIECER, and the connection information in a KG is more essential than knowledge embeddings for commonsense reasoning.

PIECER in Low-Resource Settings. Since PIECER has the ability to leverage external commonsense knowledge, we hypothesize that it can alleviate the problem of data insufficiency. In order to verify our hypothesis, we compare the performance of PIECER with different training data. Figure 4 shows the results, where we use the F1 improvement introduced by PIECER (denoted by ΔF1) as the metric. From the figure, we find that for both BERT_base and RoBERTa_base, PIECER can introduce more improvements when the amount of training data is smaller. Therefore, PIECER is a quite simple and cheap solution when facing the problem of insufficient training resources.

Robustness to Different Knowledge Embeddings. In order to get a deeper understanding of the impact of knowledge embeddings on PIECER, we compare different pretraining ways. Table 3 shows the experimental results based on QANet+PIECER. From the table, we observe that: (1) A proper KGE method is essential, since the performance with knowledge embeddings pretrained by DistMult [35] is even worse than that without using knowledge embeddings (*w/o knowledge embedding injection*). Even so, the impact of different KGE methods is not significant for PIECER. (2) PIECER is robust to the hyper-parameters, such as pretraining epochs, since for both DistMult and TransE, the number of epochs has little influence on the performance.

Table 3. Performance with different pretrained knowledge embedding configurations.

Method (pre-training epochs)	EM	F1
DistMult (1,000 epochs)	38.82	39.27
DistMult (5,000 epochs)	39.09	39.55
TransE (1,000 epochs)	39.64	40.15
TransE (10,000 epochs)	39.69	40.20
w/o knowledge embedding injection	39.18	39.66

Table 4. Performance of different GCN architectures.

Model	EM	F1
Highway GAT	63.40	64.01
Res GAT	62.54	63.16
w/o highway	58.39	59.46
Highway GCN	62.64	63.33
Highway GIN	62.66	63.29

These results prove that PIECER can keep a high performance even with a sub-optimal KGE configuration, since it mainly benefits from the connection information instead of knowledge embeddings. By contrast, methods that leverage only knowledge embeddings have to spend extensive efforts to search for the optimal KGE configuration. The robustness of PIECER to the pretraining KGE configuration eases the burden of hyper-parameter tuning.

Impact of GCN Architectures. In order to validate the design of the Highway GAT in PIECER, we compare other GCN architectures with it based on BERT$_{base}$ + PIECER. Firstly, as shown in Table 4, if we replace the highway connection with a simple residual connection (denoted by *Res GAT*), the performance will drop slightly. Secondly, if we remove the whole highway connection (denoted by *w/o Highway*), the performance will be severely degraded. These results suggest that the highway connection plays a key role in our Highway GAT. Thirdly, we replace GAT in our module with GCN [12] or GIN [32], and keep the highway connection for both of them for a fair comparison. We find that both Highway GCN and Highway GIN perform worse than Highway GAT. Fourthly, as shown in Fig. 5 (a), Highway GAT achieves the peak performance with 3 layers. The result is as expected, since too few layers build short reasoning chains, while too many layers may lead to the over-smoothing problem [13]. Finally, Fig. 5 (b) shows that Highway GAT achieves the best performance with 4 heads, which reveals that too many attention heads are redundant.

Impact of Graph Construction Methods. In order to study the impact of the joint query-passage graph, we compare different graph construction ways.

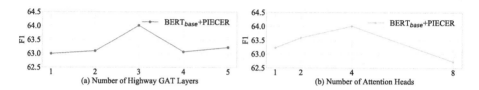

Fig. 5. Performance with different network architectures.

Table 5. Performance with joint query-passage graphs constructed in different ways.

Graph	EM	F1
Joint query-passage graph	63.40	64.01
w/o coreference edge	63.00	63.65
w/o knowledge edge	62.34	62.98
w/ complete graph	62.33	62.94

In Table 5, we present the results based on BERT$_{base}$ + PIECER. We have the following observations: (1) Removing either the coreference edge or the knowledge edge degrades the performance, which verifies the necessity of these edges. (2) A complete graph has the poorest performance, which indicates that too many redundant edges can not bring better performance, and also proves the construction method of our joint graph is reasonable.

4 Related Work

MRC is a longstanding task in NLP. In recent years, deep learning based methods such as Match-LSTM [28], BiDAF [21], DCN [31], R-Net [29], and QANet [36] have become the mainstream. As large-scale PTMs such as BERT [5] and RoBERTa [14] are proposed, MRC achieves further advance. However, their ability of commonsense reasoning still remains a question.

As MRC datasets requiring knowledge such as ReCoRD are proposed, various methods attempt to introduce external knowledge stored in KGs [3,17,23] into MRC. KnReader [16] encodes knowledge as a key-value memory and enriches each word by memory querying. KB-LSTM [34] and KT-Net [33] enrich each word by applying the attention mechanism to its KG neighbors and a sentinel vector. SKG [18] updates the representation of each word by aggregating knowledge embeddings of its KG neighbors. These methods enrich each word separately, but ignore the knowledge-oriented connections between words.

GCNs are effective to deal with graph-like data. Kipf et al. propose a fast approximate convolution method [12], which becomes one of the most popular spectral GCN models. Besides spectral GCNs, spatial GCNs such as GraphSAGE [7], GIN [32], and GAT [27] form another category of GCNs. In recent years, GCNs have been applied to various NLP tasks such as Relation Extraction [4,6],

Natural Language Inference [30], and Machine Reading Comprehension [2,18, 22]. However, existing GCN-based MRC methods do not thoroughly investigate the knowledge-oriented connections between words.

5 Conclusion

In this paper, we propose to enhance commonsense reasoning in MRC by explicitly incorporating the connection information in KGs. For high generalizability, we design a plug-and-play module called PIECER, which can be plugged into any MRC model. Experimental results on ReCoRD show that PIECER can improve the performance of existing MRC models. Also, we provide elaborate model analysis for PIECER to validate its design, including its submodules, the GCN architecture, and the graph construction method. Further, we reveal that PIECER is especially effective in low-resource settings.

Acknowledgement. This paper is supported by the National Key Research and Development Program of China 2020AAA0106701 and NSFC project U19A2065.

References

1. Bordes, A., Usunier, N., García-Durán, A., Weston, J., Yakhnenko, O.: Translating embeddings for modeling multi-relational data. In: NeurIPS 2013, pp. 2787–2795 (2013)
2. Cao, N.D., Aziz, W., Titov, I.: Question answering by reasoning across documents with graph convolutional networks. In: NAACL-HLT 2019, pp. 2306–2317 (2019)
3. Carlson, A., Betteridge, J., Kisiel, B., Settles, B., Hruschka, E.R., Mitchell, T.M.: Toward an architecture for never-ending language learning. In: AAAI 2010, pp. 1306–1313 (2010)
4. Dai, D., Ren, J., Zeng, S., Chang, B., Sui, Z.: Coarse-to-fine entity representations for document-level relation extraction. CoRR arXiv:2012.02507 (2020)
5. Devlin, J., Chang, M., Lee, K., Toutanova, K.: BERT: pre-training of deep bidirectional transformers for language understanding. In: NAACL-HLT 2019, pp. 4171–4186 (2019)
6. Guo, Z., Zhang, Y., Lu, W.: Attention guided graph convolutional networks for relation extraction. In: ACL 2019, pp. 241–251 (2019)
7. Hamilton, W.L., Ying, Z., Leskovec, J.: Inductive representation learning on large graphs. In: NeurIPS 2017, pp. 1024–1034 (2017)
8. Han, X., et al.: OpenKE: an open toolkit for knowledge embedding. In: EMNLP 2018: System Demonstrations, pp. 139–144 (2018)
9. Jia, R., Liang, P.: Adversarial examples for evaluating reading comprehension systems. In: EMNLP 2017, pp. 2021–2031 (2017)
10. Kaushik, D., Lipton, Z.C.: How much reading does reading comprehension require? A critical investigation of popular benchmarks. In: EMNLP 2018, pp. 5010–5015 (2018)
11. Kingma, D.P., Ba, J.: Adam: a method for stochastic optimization. In: ICLR 2015 (2015)

12. Kipf, T.N., Welling, M.: Semi-supervised classification with graph convolutional networks. In: ICLR 2017 (2017)
13. Li, Q., Han, Z., Wu, X.: Deeper insights into graph convolutional networks for semi-supervised learning. In: AAAI 2018, pp. 3538–3545 (2018)
14. Liu, Y., et al.: RoBERTa: a robustly optimized BERT pretraining approach. CoRR arXiv:1907.11692 (2019)
15. Loshchilov, I., Hutter, F.: Decoupled weight decay regularization. In: ICLR 2019 (2019)
16. Mihaylov, T., Frank, A.: Knowledgeable reader: enhancing cloze-style reading comprehension with external commonsense knowledge. In: ACL 2018, pp. 821–832 (2018)
17. Miller, G.A.: WordNet: a lexical database for English. Commun. ACM **38**(11), 39–41 (1995)
18. Qiu, D., et al.: Machine reading comprehension using structural knowledge graph-aware network. In: EMNLP-IJCNLP 2019, pp. 5895–5900 (2019)
19. Rajpurkar, P., Jia, R., Liang, P.: Know what you don't know: unanswerable questions for SQuAD. In: ACL 2018, pp. 784–789 (2018)
20. Rajpurkar, P., Zhang, J., Lopyrev, K., Liang, P.: SQuAD: 100,000+ questions for machine comprehension of text. In: EMNLP 2016, pp. 2383–2392 (2016)
21. Seo, M.J., Kembhavi, A., Farhadi, A., Hajishirzi, H.: Bidirectional attention flow for machine comprehension. In: ICLR 2017 (2017)
22. Song, L., Wang, Z., Yu, M., Zhang, Y., Florian, R., Gildea, D.: Exploring graph-structured passage representation for multi-hop reading comprehension with graph neural networks. CoRR arXiv:1809.02040 (2018)
23. Speer, R., Chin, J., Havasi, C.: ConceptNet 5.5: an open multilingual graph of general knowledge. In: AAAI 2017, pp. 4444–4451 (2017)
24. Srivastava, R.K., Greff, K., Schmidhuber, J.: Highway networks. CoRR arXiv:1505.00387 (2015)
25. Trischler, A., et al.: NewsQA: a machine comprehension dataset. In: Rep4NLP@ACL 2017, pp. 191–200 (2017)
26. Vaswani, A., et al.: Attention is all you need. In: NeurIPS 2017, pp. 5998–6008 (2017)
27. Velickovic, P., Cucurull, G., Casanova, A., Romero, A., Liò, P., Bengio, Y.: Graph attention networks. In: ICLR 2018 (2018)
28. Wang, S., Jiang, J.: Machine comprehension using match-LSTM and answer pointer. In: ICLR 2017 (2017)
29. Wang, W., Yang, N., Wei, F., Chang, B., Zhou, M.: Gated self-matching networks for reading comprehension and question answering. In: ACL 2017, pp. 189–198 (2017)
30. Wang, Z., Li, L., Zeng, D.: Knowledge-enhanced natural language inference based on knowledge graphs. In: COLING 2020, pp. 6498–6508 (2020)
31. Xiong, C., Zhong, V., Socher, R.: Dynamic coattention networks for question answering. In: ICLR 2017 (2017)
32. Xu, K., Hu, W., Leskovec, J., Jegelka, S.: How powerful are graph neural networks? In: ICLR 2019 (2019)
33. Yang, A., et al.: Enhancing pre-trained language representations with rich knowledge for machine reading comprehension. In: ACL 2019, pp. 2346–2357 (2019)
34. Yang, B., Mitchell, T.M.: Leveraging knowledge bases in LSTMs for improving machine reading. In: ACL 2017, pp. 1436–1446 (2017)
35. Yang, B., Yih, W., He, X., Gao, J., Deng, L.: Embedding entities and relations for learning and inference in knowledge bases. In: ICLR 2015 (2015)

36. Yu, A.W., et al.: QANet: combining local convolution with global self-attention for reading comprehension. In: ICLR 2018 (2018)
37. Zhang, S., Liu, X., Liu, J., Gao, J., Duh, K., Durme, B.V.: ReCoRD: bridging the gap between human and machine commonsense reading comprehension. CoRR arXiv:1810.12885 (2018)
38. Zhou, H., Young, T., Huang, M., Zhao, H., Xu, J., Zhu, X.: Commonsense knowledge aware conversation generation with graph attention. In: IJCAI 2018, pp. 4623–4629 (2018)

Social Media and Sentiment Analysis (Poster)

FuDFEND: Fuzzy-Domain for Multi-domain Fake News Detection

Chaoqi Liang, Yu Zhang[✉], Xinyuan Li, Jinyu Zhang, and Yongqi Yu

Harbin Institute of Technology, Harbin, China
{120L030706,7203610518,7203610523,7203610515}@stu.hit.edu.cn,
zhangyu@ir.hit.edu.cn

Abstract. On the Internet, fake news exists in various domain (e.g., education, health). Since news in different domains has different features, researchers have begun to use single domain label for fake news detection recently. Existing works show that using single domain label can improve the accuracy of fake news detection model. However, there are two problems in previous works. Firstly, they ignore that a piece of news may have features from different domains. The single domain label focuses only on the features of one domain. This may reduce the performance of the model. Secondly, their model cannot transfer the domain knowledge to the other dataset without domain label. In this paper, we propose a novel model, FuDFEND, which solves the limitations above by introducing the fuzzy inference mechanism. Specifically, FuDFEND utilizes a neural network to fit the fuzzy inference process which constructs a fuzzy domain label for each news item. Then, the feature extraction module uses the fuzzy domain label to extract the multi-domain features of the news and obtain the total feature representation. Finally, the discriminator module uses the total feature representation to discriminate whether the news item is fake news. The results on the Weibo21 show that our model works better than the model using only single domain label. In addition, our model transfers domain knowledge better to Thu dataset which has no domain label.

Keywords: Fake news detection · Social media · Multi-domain

1 Introduction

With the development of the Internet, social media platforms such as Sina Weibo and Twitter have become the main source of information. Fake news is also widely spread on social platforms. The fake news on social media is usually a short text, a picture and a short video that they can be understood in a few seconds. At the same time, the fake news incites people's emotions and stimulates users to forward, so they can be widely spread. Tavernise [1] showed that important social events were affected due to moderated fake news campaigns. The spread of fake news may result in people's panic and social dislocation. The quality of content on social media platforms has suffered greatly due to the spread of fake news, misinformation and unverifiable facts [2]. Therefore, it is meaningful to research into social media fake news detection today.

© Springer Nature Switzerland AG 2022
W. Lu et al. (Eds.) NLPCC 2022, LNCS 13552, pp. 45–57, 2022.
https://doi.org/10.1007/978-3-031-17189-5_4

At present, there are two methods of social media fake news detection. One is social background detection method, and the other is content-based detection method [3]. Social background method aims to study users' social network structure, users' personal information, microblog forwarding and reply relationship and rumor's propagation patterns. The content-based research method aims to detect the text, voice and video carried by microblog news. For example, Mouratidis et al. [4] analyzes linguistic features to distinguish between fake news and real news. Our work focuses on the content-based method.

On the Internet, fake news arises in many different domains. The task of detecting fake news in multiple domains is called Multi-domain Fake News Detection (MFND). There are two main challenges in MFND. First, the performance of techniques generally drops if news records are coming from different domains (e.g., politics, entertainment), and a possible explanation of this could be the rather unique content and style of each domain [5]. For example, during the 2020 US election, political fake news and Covid19 fake news were widespread simultaneously. It is difficult to detect both political fake news and Covid19 fake news at the same time, because of the different or even conflicting features between political fake news and Covid19 news. Thus, a variety of previous works [6–10] focused on rumor detection in a single domain. But herein lies another problem. In a single-domain, there may be too little data to train a good model. Therefore, Nan et al. [11] proposed a **M**ulti-**d**omain **F**ake **N**ews **D**etection Model (MDFEND) which use single domain label to solve the above two problems. Single domain label is to describe that a piece of news belongs to a certain domain, such as science and technology, education, health and so on. The model receives news content and single domain label as input. Utilizing these data, the model can extract the common features of fake news in all different domains, and can distinguish the specific features of certain domain by domain label.

Table 1. The difference between single domain label and fuzzy domain label.

News content	Single domain label	Fuzzy domain label
The new generation of iphone has added numbers of new technologies such as face recognition, which are popular with consumers. The next day, Apple shares rose sharply	Technology	Technology: 70% Business: 20% Finance: 10%

We build this paper on that work [11] by recognizing that there are two problems. (i) A piece of news may have features of several domains. There is an example showed in Table 1. This news has the features from three domains. Single domain label can't help the model extract this kind of news with multi domain features. (ii) Their model can't be transferred to datasets without domain label. Therefore, we propose a novel model, **Fu**zzy-**d**omain **F**ake **N**ews **D**etection Model (FuDFEND). FuDFEND is an improved model based on the MDFEND proposed in [11]. The improvement is made by introducing a fuzzy inference mechanism into the model. The fuzzy inference mechanism can solve the above two problems. The fuzzy inference mechanism constructs a fuzzy domain label for each news item. Compared with single domain label, fuzzy domain label can better describe the domain features of news, so that help the model better extract the multi-domain features of news. We demonstrated this by the experiment on the weibo21. In addition, FuDFEND has better transfer ability than MDFEND. We will illustrate this through experiment on Thu dataset.

Our summarized contributions with this paper are:

- We propose a novel model, Fuzzy-domain Fake News Detection Model (FuDFEND), which can extract the multi-domain features of news content by the fuzzy domain label that fuzzy inference mechanism generate. The results on the Weibo21 show that FuDFEND works better than the model, MDFEND, using only single domain label.
- In order to describe the multi-domain features of news, we introduced fuzzy inference mechanism to the multi-domain fake news detection task. The fuzzy domain label constructed by fuzzy inference mechanism can more accurately describe the multi-domain features that news has.
- We solve the problem that model can't transfer to the dataset without domain label. We evaluate FuDFEND on Thu dataset which has no domain label. Experimental results show that FuDFEND can transfer domain knowledge better by utilizing the fuzzy inference mechanism.

2   Related Work

2.1   Fake News Detection Methods

Researchers have come up with number of ways to detect fake news.

Content-Based Methods. In [12], the authors proposed an ensemble classification model for fake news detection. Their model obtains relevant features from a fake news dataset and then uses an ensemble model to classify the extracted features, but these works are based only on news texts. In [13], the authors study and analyze whether fake news can be distinguished from mainstream news by text writing style and whether fake news can be detected only by writing style by building a model. Rawat et al. [2] proposed a method to automatically collect fake news detection tasks online. For each piece of news data, they collect evidence and generate their summaries as another input to the model to help detect news text. In [14] author found images have different distribution patterns and statistically distinctive patterns for fake and real news. It reveals that images in the real news are more diverse and much denser than those in the fake news. Therefore, they extract image features from the visual features and overall statistics of images in news events. Alonso-Bartolome et al. [15] used the early fusion method to fuse text and image information for rumor detection. In [16], an innovative RNN with attention mechanism (att-RNN) is proposed for effective multimodal feature fusion. In [17], author propose a Multi-domain Visual Neural Network (MVNN) framework consisting of three main parts to mix all the features together.

Social Background Detection Method. These researches mainly focused on propagation patterns, publisher-news relations and user-news interactions. In [18], the authors examined numerous features related to user, linguistic, network and temporal characteristics of rumors. They studied the spread patterns of rumors over time and the ability to track the precise changes in the predictive power of rumor features. However, the events of this volume (111 rumor and non-romors) may not be sufficient for summarizing the prediction performance, and the algorithm takes every feature into account did not achieve good results in short observation periods. Shu et al. [19] examined the correlation of publisher bias, news stance, and relevant user engagement. They studied the novel problem of exploiting social context for fake news detection and proposed a tri-relationship embedding framework TriFN, which model relations and interactions between publishers, news, and users simultaneously for fake news classification. But it requires the social context information to be included in the data. Meanwhile, there may be significant differences in social relations in different domains, and targeted detection in different domains is a promising concept. Alrubaian et al. [20] proposed a credibility analysis system consisting of a model based on reputation, a feature ranking algorithm, a credibility evaluation classifier engine, and a user expertise model, to assess the accuracy of information on Twitter so it can stop the promotion of disinformation.

2.2 Multi-domain Rumor Task

In [5], the author introduced two new English fake news datasets (FakeNewsAMT, Celebrity) covering six news domains, and the author analyzes the different performance of his model in different news domains. Nan et al. [11] construct Weibo21, a multi-domain fake news dataset in Chinese. Weibo21 contains more than 9000 pieces of real and fake news from nine domains and was manually marked the domain label for each piece of news. And they designed a Multi-domain Fake News Detection Model (MDFEND) for Weibo21. The model can extract the common features of fake news in all different domains, and can distinguish the specific features of certain domain through single domain label. However, this model relies on manually annotated datasets, which not only contain news text and true and false information, but also need to input the domain category to which the news belongs, then select the corresponding vector in the domain matrix according to the type of domain to calculate the weight of each domain experts (TextCNN), so it requires a lot of effort to obtain the data set that match the model. In the following we will propose our improvement strategy on the base of this model.

3   FuDFEND: Fuzzy-Domain Fake News Detection Model

FuDFEND is an improved model based on the MDFEND proposed in [11]. The improvement is made by introducing a fuzzy inference mechanism into the model. The fuzzy inference mechanism includes two modules: Membership Function and Gate.

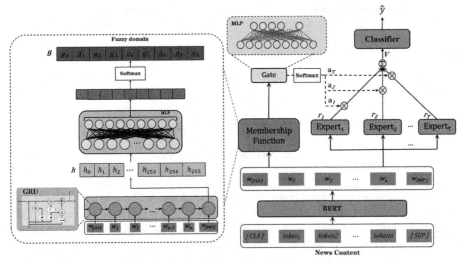

Fig. 1. Overall framework of FuDFEND.

Overall framework of FuDFEND is showed in Fig. 1. The working process of the model is as follows. Enter the news text into BERT [21, 22] to obtain a series of word embeddings $W = [w_{[CLS]}, w_1, w_2, ..., w_n, w_{[SEP]}]$. W is input into a mixture of experts to extract the features of different domains. Enter W into Membership Function to obtain fuzzy domain label. Then, Gate generates weight scores α by inputting fuzzy domain label. The output experts are weighted and summed by the weight scores α, so that obtain the total feature representation v. The classifier module uses the total feature representation v to discriminate whether the news item is fake news.

3.1 Membership Function

In traditional set theory, we define a set with a definite condition. For example, we define a tall set as those who are taller than or equal to 190 cm. The other belong to short set. If a person is 189 cm tall, very close to 190 cm but still belongs to short set. Obviously, the traditional way of describing sets is very crude. In order to describe the set more accurately, LA Zadeh proposed the concept of fuzzy sets in 1965. A fuzzy set is characterized by a Membership (characteristic) Function which assigns to each object a membership grade between zero and one [23]. As shown in Fig. 2, we can use a Membership Function to describe high set and short set. If a person is 189 cm tall, he belongs to a high set with a membership grade of 0.9 and belongs to a short set with a membership grade of 0.1.

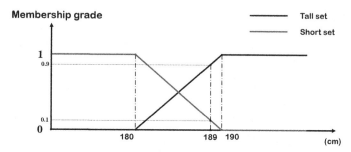

Fig. 2. An example of fuzzy set.

A piece of news may have features of different domains. Here is an example that "The new generation of iphone has added a number of new technologies such as face recognition, which are popular with consumers. The next day, Apple shares rose sharply." This news has the features of both science domain and financial domain. Therefore, we need to use fuzzy sets to more precisely measure the domains that news belongs to.

We will show how to use neural network to fit the Membership Function for the sets of news domains. The Membership Function consist of an *GRU*, a multi-layer perception (*MLP*) and a softmax function. Membership Function can generate a nine-dimensional membership grade vector g. We call this vector g as the fuzzy domain label. During training, we train it as training a classifier for news domains. When we use it, we regard it as a Membership Function. The specific process is as follows. For a piece of news, we put the news' word embeddings W into an *GRU*. The output h of *GRU* is fed into *MLP* which output is a nine-dimensional vector. Use softmax function to normalize the output of *MLP*. Then we obtain a vector g which has nine dimensions and sum of all dimensions is 1. The value of each dimension of the vector represents the membership grade of nine news domains (Science, Military, Education, Disasters, Politics, Health, Finance, Entertainment). We denote the Membership Function as $M(\cdot;\cdot)$, and θ, θ_1, θ_2 is the parameters in the Membership Function, *GRU*, *MLP*. g represents the fuzzy domain label:

$$g = M(W; \theta) = softmax(MLP(GRU(W; \theta_1); \theta_2)) \tag{1}$$

Membership Function's parameter is pre-trained. During the training of rumor detection task, the parameter of Membership Function is fixed. Membership Function is train as a as a classifier, its accuracy rate can only reach about 82% in the end. But as a Membership Function, We cannot think that its error rate is 18%, but should be understood as the correction of labels by large models. Because some domain labels labeled by the human are not necessarily suitable for machine. The machine reclassified things that it thought had the same features. Further, the outputs of Membership Function, g, is a probability distribution, which can provide enough noise for the model.

Figure 3 shows an execution of the Membership Function. Membership Function analysis shows that the content of the news has the features of entertainment domain and social domain.

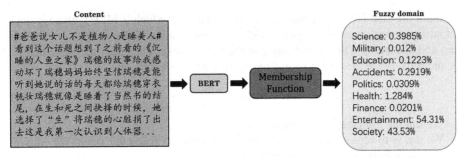

Fig. 3. An execution of the Membership Function. The single domain label of this news is "Society". The content of this news is that "# Dad said his daughter is not a vegetative person but a sleeping beauty # when I saw this topic, I was moved by the story of Mizuho in *The House Where the Mermaid Sleeps*. Mizuho's mother always believed that Mizuho could hear what she said. She dressed and dressed Mizuho every day. Mizuho was like falling asleep. Of course, at the end of the book, when choosing between life and death, she chose "living" to donate Mizuho's heart. This is the first time I realized the human body."

3.2 Feature Extraction

We use Mixture-of-Expert [24–26] to extract features of news' content. Each expert network is a TextCNN [27] in our model. Each expert has its own area of expertise and is good at extracting the features of certain domain. An expert network can be denoted by $E_i(\cdot;\cdot)$ $(1 \le i \le T)$. T is a hyperparameter, representing the number of the experts. r_i denote the output of the expert. φ_i are the trainable parameters of an expert:

$$r_i = E_i(W; \varphi_i) = TextCNN_i(W; \varphi_i) \tag{2}$$

3.3 Domain Gate

Because different experts can extract the features of different domains, we input the fuzzy domain label into the Domain Gate, to obtain the weight score. The weight score consists of T positive real numbers, corresponding to T experts. Then we use the weight score to aggregate the features extracted by experts. We denote the Domain Gate as $Gate(\cdot;\cdot)$. ψ is the trainable parameters of the Domain Gate. $\boldsymbol{\alpha}$ represent the weight score:

$$\boldsymbol{\alpha} = (\alpha_1, \alpha_2, \ldots, \alpha_T) = Gate(g; \psi) = softmax(MLP(g; \psi)) \tag{3}$$

3.4 Fake News Prediction and Loss Function

Through the weight score, we aggregate the features extracted by experts to obtain the total features vector v:

$$v = \sum_{i=1}^{T} \alpha_i r_i \tag{4}$$

Input the total features vector into a binary classifier which is MLP with a sigmoid output layer. And then we get our model's predicted value, $\hat{y}$. The value $\hat{y}$ is between zero and one and it is the probability that the news is fake. The larger the value of $\hat{y}$ is, the more likely the model is to conclude that the news is fake:

$$\hat{y} = sigmod(MLP(v, \xi)) \tag{5}$$

ξ represent the trainable parameters of the MLP.

We use y_i to represent value label and $\hat{y}_i$ to represent predicted value. We employ Binary Cross-Entropy Loss for training:

$$L = -\sum_{i=1}^{N}(y_i log\hat{y}_i + (1 - y_i)log(1 - \hat{y}_i)) \tag{6}$$

4   Experiment

FuDFEND is an improved model based on the MDFEND proposed in [11]. The improvement is made by introducing a fuzzy inference mechanism into the model. In order to show the effect of fuzzy inference mechanism, we compare our model FuDFEND with baseline method which mentioned in [11], especially MDFEND which hasn't fuzzy inference mechanism.

4.1   Dataset

In this section, we introduce the two datasets we use.

Weibo21 was released in this work [11] last year. It is a Chinese multi-domain fake news dataset. It consists of 4,488 pieces of fake news and 4,640 pieces of real news, covering nine different news domains: **Science, Military, Education, Accidents, Politics, Health, Finance, Entertainment**. The number of true and fake news contained in each domain is shown in Table 2.

Table 2. Data Statistics of Weibo21.

Domain	Science	Military	Education	Accidents	Politics
Real	143	121	243	185	306
Fake	93	222	248	591	546
All	236	343	491	776	852
Domain	Health	Finance	Entertainment	Society	All
Real	485	959	1000	1198	4640
Fake	515	362	440	1471	4488
All	1000	1321	1440	2669	9128

Table 3. Five Samples of Weibo21.

content	Single domain label	Fake label
【三星……年推出柔性折叠屏的产品，你会入手么？	Science	0
#四川……化工厂泄漏#紧急撤离！！大家注意安全	Accidents	1
#广州……料公布！居然是日本间谍！】@广东热搜	Politics	1
《哈利……面都是回忆[悲伤]http://t.cn/RURkC7V	Entertainment	0
#人民……。求@平安北京@通州警方在线给说法！！	Society	1

Each piece of news is labeled a specific domain. We show a few examples of the Weibo21 dataset in Table 3.

Another dataset we used is the Chinese Rumor Dataset released by thunlp [28, 29]. The news in this dataset has no domain label. The dataset consists of two parts. One is called rumors_V170613 [28], including 31669 rumors. Another named CEO_Dataset [29], including 1538 rumors and 1849 real news. We found that some rumors in CEO_Dataset coincide with the data in Weibo21, so we randomly selected 1560 pieces of fake news from rumors_V170613 and combined the fake news with the real news in the CEO_Dataset to form a new dataset that we called Thu dataset. We performed zero-shot learning on Thu dataset to test the model's capability of domain knowledge transfer.

4.2 Experiment Setting

BERT [21, 22] is fixed during training. The dimension of BERT's output embedding vectors is fixed to 768. The max length of the sentence is 170. We employ the Adam [30] optimizer for our training. The learning rate is $5e-4$. In order to enhance the credibility of our experiments, the process is performed for 5 times and the average f1-score is reported.

4.3 Train Membership Function and FuDFEND

As mentioned previously, we trained the Membership Function as a nine-classification classifier for domain label. We randomly selected 70% of the data from Weibo21 as the training set and the remain as the verification set. The mini-batch size is 32. After training 7 epochs using the crossentropy loss function, the f1-score on the validation set reaches 82.31%. We take the Membership Function from the 7th epoch training, because it has the highest f1-score. As training FuDFEND, the Membership Function is fixed. The mini-batch size is 64.

4.4 Experiment on Weibo21

Nan et al. [11] have showed the effectiveness of their multi-domain fake news detection model (MDFEND). Further, the results in Table 4 support that our idea is right. The fake news detection performance of FuDFEND compared with MDFEND demonstrates that the fuzzy domain label generated by fuzzy inference mechanism can better help the model extract the features for fake news detection task.

Table 4. Multi-domain Fake News Detection Performance on Weibo21 (F1-score).

Model	Science	Military	Education	Accidents	Politics
TextCNN_single	0.7470	0.7780	0.8882	0.8310	0.8694
BiGRU_single	0.4876	0.7169	0.7067	0.7625	0.8477
BERT_single	0.8192	0.7795	0.8136	0.7885	0.8188
TextCNN_all	0.7254	0.8839	0.8362	0.8222	0.8561
BiGRU_all	0.7269	0.8724	0.8138	0.7935	0.8356
BERT_all	0.7777	0.9072	0.8331	0.8512	0.8366
EANN	0.8225	0.9274	0.8624	0.8666	0.8705
MMOE	**0.8755**	0.9112	0.8706	0.8770	0.8620
MOSE	0.8502	0.8858	0.8815	0.8672	0.8808
EDDFN	0.8186	0.9137	0.8676	0.8786	0.8478
MDFEND	0.8301	0.9389	**0.8917**	0.9003	0.8865
FuDFEND (our)	0.8133	**0.9468**	**0.8917**	**0.9059**	**0.9013**
Model	Health	Finance	Entertainment	Society	All
TextCNN_single	0.9053	0.7909	0.8591	0.8727	0.8380
BiGRU_single	0.8378	0.8109	0.8308	0.6067	0.7342
BERT_single	0.8909	0.8464	0.8638	0.8242	0.8272
TextCNN_all	0.8768	0.8638	0.8456	0.8540	0.8686
BiGRU_all	0.8868	0.8291	0.8629	0.8485	0.8595
BERT_all	0.9090	0.8735	0.8769	0.8577	0.8795
EANN	0.9150	0.8710	0.8957	0.8877	0.8975
MMOE	0.9364	0.8567	0.8886	0.8750	0.8947
MOSE	0.9179	0.8672	0.8913	0.8729	0.8939
EDDFN	0.9379	0.8636	0.8832	0.8689	0.8919
MDFEND	0.9400	**0.8951**	0.9066	0.8980	0.9137
FuDFEND (our)	**0.9417**	0.8901	**0.9161**	**0.9174**	**0.9213**

4.5   Experiment on Thu Dataset

The news in Thu dataset hasn't domain label. FuDFEND has Membership Function module, so it only needs to enter news content and does not need to enter domain label. To demonstrate the transfer learning capabilities of our models, we use MDFEND as a baseline and used the hyperparameters provided in [11] to train MDFEND. MDFEND requires domain label, so we use Membership Function to label the single domain label for the dataset. The results are showed in Table 5. The results demonstrate that FuDFEND has good transfer ability with the help of fuzzy inference mechanism.

Table 5. Multi-domain Fake News Detection Performance on Thu dataset (F1-score).

Model	Science	Military	Education	Accidents	Politics
MDFEND	0.8157	**0.8407**	0.7995	0.6878	0.7938
FuDFEND (our)	**0.8760**	0.8301	**0.8568**	**0.7129**	**0.8148**
Model	Health	Finance	Entertainment	Society	All
MDFEND	0.8364	0.7535	0.8047	0.8642	0.8731
FuDFEND (our)	**0.8753**	**0.7930**	**0.8492**	**0.8653**	**0.8900**

5 Conclusion

Previous work has demonstrated that the use of single domain label can effectively improve the performance of fake news detection models. However, for news containing multi-domain features, models using single domain label do not synthesize multi-domain features well. In this work, we propose FuDFEND and provide a set of experiments to demonstrate that: (i) Fuzzy domain label more accurately portrays the multi-domain features of news content, so it can help the model to better extract the multi-domain features of news. (ii) Fuzzy inference mechanisms can be very helpful for model to transfer domain knowledge to dataset without domain label.

6 Future Work

We have received valuable comments from reviewers. For example, analyze good and bad cases and test more datasets and indicators. These suggestions give us great inspiration. However, due to time constraints and limited space, we cannot solve these problems one by one in this paper. We will study them in our future work.

References

1. Tavernise, S.: As fake news spreads lies, more readers shrug at the truth. The New York Times. Accessed 26 Jan 2017
2. Rawat, M., Kanojia, D.: Automated Evidence Collection for Fake News Detection. arXiv: 2112.06507 (2021)
3. Hangloo, S., Arora, B.: Fake news detection tools and methods — a review. Int. J. Adv. Innovat. Res. **8**(2) (IX), 100–108 (2021)

4. Mouratidis, D., Nikiforos, M.N., Kermanidis, K.L.: Deep learning for fake news detection in a pairwise textual input schema. Computation **9**(2), 20 (2021)

5. Pérez-Rosas, V., Kleinberg, B., Lefevre, A., et al.: Automatic detection of fake news. In: Association for Computational Linguistics, pp. 3391–3401 (2017)

6. Castillo, C., Mendoza, M., Poblete, B.: Information credibility on Twitter. In: WWW, pp. 675–684 (2011)

7. Jin, Z., Cao, J., Guo, H., Zhang, Y., Wang, Y., Luo, J.: Detection and analysis of 2016 US presidential election related rumors on Twitter. In: Lee, D., Lin, Y.-R., Osgood, N., Thomson, R. (eds.) SBP-BRiMS 2017. LNCS, vol. 10354, pp. 14–24. Springer, Cham (2017). https://doi.org/10.1007/978-3-319-60240-0_2

8. Kwon, S., et al.: Prominent Features of Rumor Propagation in Online Social Media, pp. 1103–1108. IEEE (2013)

9. Ma, B., Lin, D., Cao, D.: Content representation for microblog rumor detection. In: Angelov, P., Gegov, A., Jayne, C., Shen, Q. (eds.) Advances in Computational Intelligence Systems. AISC, vol. 513, pp. 245–251. Springer, Cham (2017). https://doi.org/10.1007/978-3-319-46562-3_16

10. Ma, J., et al.: Detecting rumors from microblogs with recurrent neural networks. IJCA. 3818–3824 (2016)

11. Nan, Q., et al.: MDFEND: Multi-domain Fake News Detection, pp. 3343–3347. ACM (2022)

12. Hakak, S., Alazab, M., Khan, S., Gadekallu, T.R., Maddikunta, P.K.R., Khan, W.Z.: An ensemble machine learning approach through effective feature extraction to classify fake news. Futur. Gen. Comput. Syst. **117**, 47–58 (2021)

13. Potthast, M., Kiesel, J., Reinartz, K., et al.: A stylometric inquiry into hyperpartisan and fake news. In: Association for Computational Linguistics, pp. 231–240 (2018)

14. Jin, Z., Cao, J., Zhang, Y., et al.: Novel visual and statistical image features for microblogs news verification. IEEE Trans. Multim. **19**(3), 598–608 (2016)

15. Alonso-Bartolome, S., Segura-Bedmar, I.: Multimodal Fake News Detection. arXiv:2112.04831 (2021)

16. Jin, Z.W., et al.: Multimodal Fusion with Recurrent Neural Networks for Rumor Detection on Microblogs, pp. 795–816. ACM (2017)

17. Qi, P., Cao, J., Yang, T., et al.: Exploiting Multi-domain Visual Information for Fake News Detection, pp. 518–527. IEEE (2019)

18. Kaist, K.S., Kaist, C.M., Snu, J.K.: Rumor detection over varying time windows. PLoS ONE **12**(1), e0168344 (2017)

19. Shu, K., Wang, S., Liu, H.: Beyond News Contents: The Role of Social Context for Fake News Detection, pp. 312–320. ACM (2019)

20. Alrubaian, M., et al.: A credibility analysis system for assessing information on Twitter. IEEE Trans. Dependab. Secure Comput. **15**(4), 661–674 (2016)

21. Jacob, D., et al.: BERT: pre-training of deep bidirectional transformers for language understanding. In: Association for Computational Linguistics, pp. 4171–4186 (2019)

22. Cui, Y., et al.: Revisiting Pre-trained Models for Chinese Natural Language Processing. In: Association for Computational Linguistics, pp. 657–668 (2020)

23. Zadeh, L.A.: Fuzzy sets. Inf. Control **8**(3), 338–353 (1965)

24. Jacobs, R.A., Jordan, M.I., Nowlan, S.J., Hinton, G.E.: Adaptive mixtures of local experts. Neural Comput. **3**(1), 79–87 (1991)

25. Ma, J., Zhao, Z., Yi, X., et al.: Modeling Task Relationships in Multi-task Learning With Multi-gate Mixture-of-Experts, pp. 1930–1939. ACM (2018)

26. Zhu, Y., Liu, Y., Xie, R., et al.: Learning to Expand Audience via Meta Hybrid Experts and Critics for Recommendation and Advertising, pp. 4005–4013. ACM (2021)

27. Kim, Y.: Convolutional neural networks for sentence classification. In: Empirical Methods in Natural Language Processing (EMNLP), pp. 1746–1751 (2014)

28. Liu, Z.Y., Zhang, L., Cunchao, T.U., et al.: Statistical and semantic analysis of rumors in Chinese social media. Sci. Sin. Inf. **45**(12), 1536–1546 (2015)
29. Song, C., Tu, C., Yang, C., et al.: CED: credible early detection of social media rumors. IEEE Trans. Knowl. Data Eng. **33**(8), 3035–3047 (2018)
30. Kingma, D., Ba, J.: Adam: a method for stochastic optimization. Comput. Sci. arXiv preprint arXiv:1412.6980 (2014)

NLP Applications and Text Mining
(Poster)

Continuous Prompt Enhanced Biomedical Entity Normalization

Zhaohong Lai[1,2], Biao Fu[1,2], Shangfei Wei[1,2], and Xiaodong Shi[1,2(✉)]

[1] Department of Artificial Intelligence, School of Informatics, Xiamen University,
Xiamen, China
{laizhaohong,biaofu,weishangfei}@stu.xmu.edu.cn,
mandel@xmu.edu.cn
[2] Key Laboratory of Digital Protection and Intelligent Processing of Intangible Cultural
Heritage of Fujian and Taiwan, Ministry of Culture and Tourism,
Xiamen, China

Abstract. Biomedical entity normalization (BEN) aims to link the entity mentions in a biomedical text to referent entities in a knowledge base. Recently, the paradigm of large-scale language model pre-training and fine-tuning have achieved superior performance in BEN task. However, pre-trained language models like SAPBERT [21] typically contain hundreds of millions of parameters, and fine-tuning all parameters is computationally expensive. The latest research such as prompt technology is proposed to reduce the amount of parameters during the model training. Therefore, we propose a framework **Prompt-BEN** using continuous **Prompt** to enhance **BEN**, which just needs to fine-tune few parameters of prompt. Our method employs embeddings with the continuous prefix prompt to capture the semantic similarity between mention and terms. We also design a contrastive loss with synonym marginalized strategy for the BEN task. Finally, experimental results on three benchmark datasets demonstrated that our method achieves competitive or even greater linking accuracy than the state-of-the-art fine-tuning-based models while having about 600 times fewer tuned parameters.

Keywords: Prompt-BEN · Prompt learning · Contrastive loss

1 Introduction

Biomedical entities are an important part in biomedical text mining. Yet, existing medical literature have severe irregularities in entity name conventions. Normalizing the extracted named entities is critical for enhancing the accuracy of applications like biomedical relation extraction [38] and literature search engines [35].

Entity normalization (also known as entity linking or entity disambiguation) is the process of mapping detected mentions in text to concepts in structured sources (such as Unified Medical Language System (UMLS) [2]), where scopes of mentions are typically a string of words that describes a concept and the knowledge base is a database of large numbers of concepts.

Due to the ambiguity, abbreviations and morphological variations of medical entity representations, language understanding confronts considerable problems in

© Springer Nature Switzerland AG 2022
W. Lu et al. (Eds.) NLPCC 2022, LNCS 13552, pp. 61–72, 2022.
https://doi.org/10.1007/978-3-031-17189-5_5

comparison to other areas. For example, The medical mentions "COVID-19 virus" and "SARS-CoV-2" are both assigned to the same Concept ID[1] (MeSH: C000656484), but they literally appear to be completely different. On the other hand, "SARS-CoV-2" (MeSH: C000656484) and "SARS-CoV" (MeSH: D045473), which seem to be highly similar literally, are two different concepts. "Diabetes Mellitus, Type 2" is also written as "DM2" and "lung cancer" is also known as "lung neoplasm malignant" and so on. These examples demonstrate the importance of developing latent representations of biomedical entities in order to capture semantic information about them.

Recently, the "pre-training + fine-tuning" paradigm achieves the state-of-the-art performance in the BEN task. These approach [1, 16, 21] are pre-trained on a large-scale unsupervised biomedical text corpus and then fine-tune on a BEN dataset. Previous works, however, required fine-tuning all parameters of the pre-trained model, which is computationally costly since the pre-trained model traditionally has hundreds of millions of parameters. Since the BEN task is to search for standard answers in a huge knowledge base space, the number of negative examples is often much larger than that of positive examples when constructing training data. However, the traditional method does not take into account the imbalance of positive and negative samples during training.

In order to reduce the number of parameters for model training and alleviate the problem of samples imbalance, we propose a **Prompt-BEN** framework for BEN task. The main contributions of this paper can be summarized as follows:

- In order to better mine the semantic information in the pre-trained model and reduce the number of parameters for model training, we propose a new framework **Prompt-BEN** which introduces the prompt learning approach to the BEN framework.
- We extended the synonym marginalization strategy [34] and designed a novel contrastive loss function for BEN task, which alleviated the imbalance of positive and negative samples to a certain extent.
- Experiments prove the effectiveness of our method, which can reach a new state-of-the-art in BEN task. It is worth mentioning that our model is only trained with 1.8M parameters.

2   Related Work

2.1   Biomedical Entity Normalization

In the biomedical domain, entity normalization is particularly challenging due to the evolving nomenclature. There are many types of medical entities, including diseases, signs, tests and devices etc. Early research focused on capturing the string similarity of mentions and terms based on hand-defined rules [5,6,27]. These approach are highly interpretable and simple, but only rely on mentions' morphological information, and rarely consider their semantics.

To avoid manual formulation of rules, many machine learning methods [2,12,15, 31] automatically learn the semantic similarity between mentions and terms from the

---

[1] Medical Subject Headings (MeSH) unique ID finds descriptor, qualifier, and supplemental concept records by their record unique identifier.

training set. DNorm [31] uses TF-IDF to model entity vectors. [12] normalizes clinical terms using learned edit distance patterns. And TaggerOne [15] uses semi-Markov models to train named-entity recognition (NER) and entity normalization. They all just model entities with simple sparse vectors and do not consider semantics correlations.

With the development of early pre-trained word embeddings word2vec [25] and Glove [28], deep learning has been applied to NLP tasks. [18,39] introduce CNN and RNN to rank candidate terms based on static word embeddings. Neither of them take long distant context semantics into account.

Bidirectional Encoder Representations from Transformers (BERT) [4] uses pre-training deep bidirectional representations from unlabeled text. Then, many BERT-based biological entity normalization systems have been proposed. [9] proposed an entity normalization framework based on pre-trained language models and conducted experiments on BERT [4]/BioBERT [16]/ClinicalBERT [1]. Experiments show that these models perform better than all previous methods. The best biomedical entity normalization performance at present is produced by SAPBERT [21] in conjunction with a framework called BioSyn [34]. Recently, a number of lightweight medical entity normalization frameworks [3,13] have been proposed in order to saving computing resources or alleviating the lack of access to large-scale computational power.

2.2 Prompt Learning and Contrastive Loss

Prompt Learning. While "pre-training + fine-tuning" paradigm obtains good performance, it is memory consuming during training because gradients and optimizer states for all parameters must be stored. Prompt learning is an idea of filling slot $[X]$ with the text x and tuning only the slot which is called prompts [22]. Specifically, the language model parameters are fixed and the prompt parameters are the only trainable parameters. This method achieves good performance on many tasks with low resource data [17,24]. The early prompt learning was to add prompt tokens [10,37]. Since the model is intrinsically continuous, from an optimization point of view, the optimality can never be achieved with discrete natural prompts [23]. Prefix-tuning [19] is a method that proposes to replace prompts tokens with a sequence of continuous task-specific vectors to the input, while keeping the LM parameters frozen. P-tuning V2 [23] can be thought of as an optimized version of prefix-tuning, a method designed for NLU tasks. Prompt learning is a good way to reduce the amount of parameters for model training. However, how to make full use of prompt learning in BEN tasks without reducing the performance of the model needs further research.

Contrastive Loss. In recent years, contrastive learning has gained popularity in the image domain. The goal of contrastive learning is to learn an embedding space such that close the distance between similar samples and distance between different samples [8]. [20] proposed Focal Loss to address class imbalance by reshaping the standard cross entropy loss such that it down-weights the loss assigned to well-classified examples. There is also a problem of class imbalance in the NLP field. The results of experiments in [36] suggests that when all the classes are equally, the Focal Loss does not improve the classification performance. However, if the objective is to detect the minority class, the Focal Loss achieves the best performance. And we know that in the BEN task, when it is regarded as a classification task, its classes are extremely unbalanced.

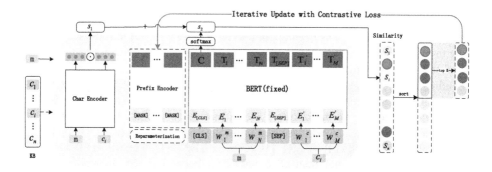

Fig. 1. Prompt-BEN: a framework based on continuous prefix prompt and contrastive loss for BEN.

In our work, dense representation of entity is inspired by P-tuningV2 [23] which is a prefix-tuning method for NLU tasks. To fully exploit the performance of the UMLS-based biomedical pretrained model and increase biomedical entity normalization accuracy, we introduce the continuous prefix prompt [19] to improve the biomedical entity normalization framework. Moreover, we reshape Focal Loss formula by a synonym marginalization strategy to alleviate the problem of unbalanced classes in the BEN task.

3   Our Method

Our framework **Prompt-BEN** which illustrated in Fig. 1 designed to reduce the amount of model training parameters and alleviate the problem of class imbalance for the BEN task. Given an entity mention m extracted from biomedical text and a knowledge base (KB) comprising of concepts, each with its own unique identifier (CUI).[2] Each CUI contains one or more synonyms form a set $\varepsilon = \{c_1, c_2, \ldots\}$. So the number of CUIs in KB is less than the number of concepts. The goal of BEN is to predict CUI_m that corresponds to each m. Our framework calculates character-based similarity through Char Encoder for m and c_i, and calculates semantic-based similarity through Prefix Encoder and BERT. We sum the two similarity results, and sort all the similarities in the knowledge base, and select the top-k concepts to train our model by contrastive loss.

3.1   Prompt Enhanced Scoring Mechanism

Sparse Representation Score. To handle out-of-vocabulary words, we adopt a Char Encoder based on the TF-IDF algorithm to capture character-level features for each

---

[2] In UMLS, CUI is the Concept Unique Identifier.

word. This has the additional benefit of teaching our model to recognize word morphological changes. We input the mention m and a term c_i into the Char Encoder, and the output of the model is a character-level representation of these two sequences. We obtain e_m^{sparse} and $e_{c_i}^{sparse}$ as the sparse vector representation. TF-IDF is calculated based on the character-level n-grams statistics computed over all concepts. Then we calculate a similarity score for a pair of TF-IDF vectors through their inner product, and obtain the similarity score S_{sparse} of the sparse representation of m and c_i

$$S_{sparse}(m, c_i) = e_m^{sparse} \odot e_{c_i}^{sparse} \tag{1}$$

Prompt Enhanced Dense Representation Score. We think of BEN task as a sentence pair classification task in order to obtain the semantic similarity of the input two strings m and c_i. For each pair (m, c_i), we construct a sequence "$[CLS]\, m\, [SEP]\, c_i$" as input for the BERT where $[CLS]$ is the special word used for classification result output, $[SEP]$ is used for s special word that separates m and c_i. Then we add trainable continuous prefix prompt by Prefix Encoder to the original sequence of input embeddings for first layer of pretrained model.

$$[prefix]\, e_{[CLS]m[SEP]c_i} \tag{2}$$

Verbalizer [32] has been a central component in previous prompt tuning approaches, however, [23] indicates that there is no significant difference between performances of verbalizer and $[CLS]$ in the supervised setting. If c_i is mapping concept for m, the classifier label is 1, otherwise the label is 0. Dense representation score uses the conventional $[CLS]$ label classified probability value that the label classification is 1:

$$S_{dense} = P(label = 1\,|m, c_i) = P(c_i\,|m; \theta) \tag{3}$$

The probability of label = 1 was computed with a softmax function.

Prefix Prompt Reparameterization. Many studies have shown that continuous prompts are effective for natural language processing tasks [19,23,30]. P-tuning V2 [23] shows how reparameterization can increase some NLU tasks training speed and robustness. However, different reparameterization (e.g. MLP for prefix-tuning [19] and LSTM for P-tuning [24]) procedures are required for various tasks and datasets. For medical entity normalization tasks, we adopt the MLP for reparameterization [19]. The language model parameters are fixed and the prefix parameters are the only trainable parameters.

Pairwise Similarity Score. Given that sequence similarity can include character-based expressions and semantic similarity. S_{dense} is obviously more important, but S_{sparse} can help recall two synonyms with completely distinct expressions. The similarity score of m and c_i are expressed using the following formula:

$$S(m, c_i) = S_{dense} + \lambda S_{sparse} \tag{4}$$

where λ is a trainable scalar weight. Using λ, model learns appropriate weight for the sparse similarity and the dense similarity.

3.2   Contrastive Loss Enhanced Training Mechanism

In general, m and the entity in the synonym set ε with the same CUI code are considered positive samples, whereas the rest of the entities in the knowledge base have the opportunity to be considered negative samples. It is conceivable that the number of positive and negative samples is unbalanced. Traditional entity normalization algorithms usually consist of two stages: recall and rank. This method depends greatly on the effect of the first step recall. Recalling failed mentions, no matter how precise the ranking model is, is impossible to link to the correct result. Models trained on pair-wise datasets often rely on the quality of the negative sampling [7].

Hard Negative Mining. The goal of hard negative mining is to discover the most informative negative instances for the model. These are the samples that are closest to the decision border, and the model will almost certainly classify them incorrectly. Given the large space of possible negative name pairs, we can only train our model on a subset of them. For each mention m, we recall k terms in total separately according to S_{sparse} and S_{dense}. Input m and KB to the model, model computes S_{sparse} and S_{dense} for all terms in KB. Among the recalled k candidate terms, the ratio of the number of candidate terms based on sparse score to the number of candidate terms based on dense score is $\alpha(0 \leq \alpha \leq 1)$. Since the sparse score is obtained from a static vector computed by TF-IDF, so the samples of each iteration mainly occur among the samples based on the S_{dense}. Through our training strategy, training samples are getting harder. The model is trained to a more accurate similarity measure for the input sequence pairs, which ultimately enables the model to better distinguish the correct terms.

Synonym Marginalized Contrastive Loss Function. We adopt Focal Loss function [20] to make the score of the positive candidates higher than the score of the negative candidates. From iterative top candidates, BIOSYN [34] maximize the marginal probability of positive terms, which in one synset have the same CUI. The following formula $P(c_i \mid m; \theta)$ represents the predicted probability of c_i:

$$P(c_i \mid m; \theta) = \frac{\exp(S(m, c_i))}{\sum_{c_j \in N_{1:k}} \exp(S(m, c_j))} \qquad (5)$$

And then maximize the marginal probability of positive terms:

$$P'(m, N_{1:k}) = \sum_{\substack{n \in N_{1:k} \\ EQUAL(m,c_i)=1}} P(c_i \mid m; \theta) \qquad (6)$$

where $EQUAL(m, c_i) = 1$ means m and c_i belong to the same concept and have the same CUI. We only accumulate among top k candidates.

At last, the contrastive loss we designed for the BEN task is as follows:

$$FL(P'(m, N_{1:k})) = -(P'(m, N_{1:k}))^\gamma \log(P'(m, N_{1:k})) \qquad (7)$$

where γ is a hyperparameter. Here we follow prior work [20] and set $\gamma = 2$.

Table 1. Data statistics of three biomedical entity normalization datasets.

Dataset	Documents			Mentions		
	Train	Dev	Test	Train	Dev	Test
NCBI-disease	592	100	100	5134	787	960
BC5CDR-disease	500	500	500	4182	4244	4424
BC5CDR-chemical	500	500	500	5203	5347	5385

4   Experiments and Analysis

4.1   Dataset and Evaluation

In our work, we employed two datasets: NCBI [14] and BC5CDR [11], and the specific
data details are shown in the Table 1:

NCBI Disease Corpus.[3] NCBI Disease Corpus [14] contains 792 PubMed abstracts,
divided into 692 training and development abstracts and 100 testing abstracts. In this
work, we used the July 6, 2012 version of MEDIC, which contains 11,915 $CUIs$ and
71,923 terms included in MeSH and/or OMIM ontologies, grouped into 9,664 disease
concepts.

Biocreative V CDR.[4] Biocreative V CDR (BC5CDR) [11] is a task to detect chemical-
s/drugs and diseases, and their relations in PubMed abstracts. BC5CDR corpus consists
of 1500 PubMed articles with 4409 annotated chemicals, 5818 diseases and 3116 chemicals. In this work, we use the November 4, 2019 version of the Comparative Toxicoge-
nomics Database (CTD) chemical dictionary containing 171,203 CUIs and 407,247
terms included in MeSH ontologies. We filter out mentions whose CUIs do not exist in
the dictionary, as [29] did previously.

Following prior work in biomedical entity normalization tasks, note that, since each
mention has only one correct CUI, we employ accuracy as an evaluation metric.

TP signifies that the CUI of the highest ranked candidate for inference is the actual
CUI of the mention m.

FP signifies that the CUI of the highest ranked candidate for inference is not the
actual CUI of the mention m.

$$Accuracy = \frac{TP}{TP + FP} \tag{8}$$

4.2   Data Preprocessing

Following from previous work, all terms in KB and the mention m are processed as
follows:

Spelling Correction: To resolve the typo issues in mentions from NCBI disease, we
used a spelling check list to replace all the misspelled words as in previous work [6, 18].
(e.g., smoll ← small, sytem ← system, etc.)

---

[3] https://www.ncbi.nlm.nih.gov/CBBresearch/Dogan/DISEASE.
[4] https://biocreative.bioinformatics.udel.edu/tasks/biocreative-v/track-3-cdr.

Abbreviation and Numeric Terms Resolution: Abbreviations are commonly employed in biological entities for efficient notation, making the work more difficult. We used the Ab3p [33] toolkit to detect abbreviations in each document and then substituted each short-form abbreviation with its long-form equivalent. As with earlier work [6, 18], we substituted all numerical words in mentions and terms with their matching Arabic numerals.

Other Preprocessing: We perform other preprocessings such as removing all the punctuations for both mentions and terms and converting all the tokens into lower case ASCII.

4.3   Experiment Setting

Char Encoder uses character-level uni-, bi-grams for tf-idf. Prefix Encoder used 2 layers MLP, which brings a consistent improvement over embedding. We use SAPBERT [21] as a pretrained model. The maximum sequence length of SAPBERT [21] is set to 50, while prefix prompt length is 10, which plays a central role in the hyper-parameter search of prompt tuning methods. And we use the conventional $[CLS]$ label classification paradigm with random-initialized linear heads to calculate dense score. The number of top candidate k in 20, and the ratio of the number of candidates based on sparse score to the number of candidates based on dense score is 0.5.

We set the learning rate to $1e - 5$, weight decay to $1e - 2$, and the mini-batch size to 8. To avoid overfitting, we adopt a dropout strategy with a dropout rate of 0.1. After hyperparameter tuning, several experiments have been performed, and the results on the best hyperparameter settings have been reported.

4.4   Overall Performance

We compare the performance of our best model with previous work on the test set. As demonstrated in Table 2. It can be seen that the performance of our model is better than that of the traditional framework, and it is slightly improved compared with the previous best-performing model, but the amount of parameters is almost negligible compared with the model framework of the traditional fine-tuning mode. Compared with the newly proposed lightweight framework ResCNN [13], not only the performance is better, but also the amount of parameters is only one tenth of it.

4.5   Ablation Study

To investigate the impact of different components employed in our model architecture on overall model performance, we compare **Prompt-BEN** to its many versions.

Effect of Different Pretrained Models. Table 3 shows the experimental results using different pre-trained models based on the **Prompt-BEN** framework. It can be seen that the performance of using SAPBERT [21] far exceeds other models. We estimate that

Table 2. Performance of different models.

Models	Top-1 accuracy (on test sets)			Nb. parameters
	NCBI-d	BC5CDR-d	BC5CDR-c	
BNE (2019) [29]	87.7	90.6	95.8	4.1M
CNN-based-Ranking (2017) [18]	89.6	–	–	4.6M
BERT-based-Ranking (2020) [9]	89.1	–	–	110M
TripleNet (2020) [26]	90.0	–	–	110M
BIOSYN (2020) [34]	91.1	93.2	96.6	110M
SAPBERT (Fine-tuned) (2021) [21]	92.3	93.2	96.5	110M
BIOSYN (SAPBERT) (2021) [21]	92.5	93.6	96.8	110M
Lightweight model (2020) [3]	89.6	–	–	4.8M
ResCNN (2021) [13]	92.4	93.3	**96.9**	1.8M
Prompt-BEN	**92.6**	**93.8**	96.7	**0.18M**

Table 3. Performance of using different pretrained models based on **Prompt-BEN**.

Models	Top-1 accuracy (on test sets)		
	NCBI-d	BC5CDR-d	BC5CDR-c
Prompt-BEN (BERT [4])	82.7	88.7	92.7
Prompt-BEN (BioBERT [16])	83.9	92.1	94.0
Prompt-BEN (ClinicalBERT [1])	84.7	91.4	93.6
Prompt-BEN (SAPBERT [21])	**92.6**	**93.8**	**96.7**

this is because SAPBERT is pre-trained with a large number of medical entities, and our training method is based on the prompt learning method. The feature of prompt learning is to mine the knowledge of the pre-trained model, which is closely related to task. Based on the above characteristics, it is expected that the model based on SAPBERT has the best performance. This also gives us a revelation that using this framework it is best to use the corpus trained by the pre-trained model to be closer to the task data.

Effect of Different Loss Function. Table 4 shows the impact of different loss functions on the performance of this framework. It can be seen that the above three loss function strategies have little difference in the performance of the framework. These three loss functions essentially contain the idea of contrastive learning, which alleviates the problem of unbalanced positive and negative sample data to a certain extent. The experimental results show that the Focal Loss function combined with the synonym marginalization strategy is better, so we use it in our framework.

Table 4. Performance of different loss, where "syn" means the synonym marginalization strategy in BioSyn [34].

Models	Top-1 accuracy (on test sets)		
	NCBI-d	BC5CDR-d	BC5CDR-c
Prompt-BEN (syn [34])	92.2	93.4	96.5
Prompt-BEN (focal loss [20])	92.5	93.8	96.6
Prompt-BEN (syn+focal loss)	**92.6**	**93.8**	**96.7**

5 Conclusion

In this paper, we design a framework called **Prompt-BEN** for biomedical entities normalization with the introduction of continuous prompt and contrastive loss function combined with the synonym marginalization strategy. **Prompt-BEN** achieves the best performance with an almost negligible amount of parameters. Moreover, this model mitigates the problem of data imbalance. We also experiment on three different datasets, demonstrating the effectiveness of this framework. Natural language processing tasks in other languages develop much more slowly than English, especially in the medical field. We will investigate Cross-lingual knowledge fusion entity representation in future work.

References

1. Alsentzer, E., et al.: Publicly available clinical BERT embeddings. In: Proceedings of the 2nd Clinical Natural Language Processing Workshop, Minneapolis, Minnesota, USA, pp. 72–78. Association for Computational Linguistics, June 2019. https://doi.org/10.18653/v1/W19-1909
2. Bodenreider, O.: The unified medical language system (UMLS): integrating biomedical terminology. Nucleic Acids Res. **32**(suppl_1), D267–D270 (2004)
3. Chen, L., Varoquaux, G., Suchanek, F.M.: A lightweight neural model for biomedical entity linking. arXiv e-prints (2020)
4. Devlin, J., Chang, M.W., Lee, K., Toutanova, K.: BERT: pre-training of deep bidirectional transformers for language understanding. In: Proceedings of the 2019 Conference of the North American Chapter of the Association for Computational Linguistics: Human Language Technologies, Volume 1 (Long and Short Papers), Minneapolis, Minnesota, pp. 4171–4186. Association for Computational Linguistics, June 2019. https://doi.org/10.18653/v1/N19-1423
5. Dogan, R., Lu, Z.: An inference method for disease name normalization. In: AAAI Fall Symposium (2012)
6. D'Souza, J., Ng, V.: Sieve-based entity linking for the biomedical domain. In: Proceedings of the 53rd Annual Meeting of the Association for Computational Linguistics and the 7th International Joint Conference on Natural Language Processing (Volume 2: Short Papers), Beijing, China, pp. 297–302. Association for Computational Linguistics, July 2015. https://doi.org/10.3115/v1/P15-2049

7. Fakhraei, S., Mathew, J., Ambite, J.L.: NSEEN: neural semantic embedding for entity normalization. In: Brefeld, U., Fromont, E., Hotho, A., Knobbe, A., Maathuis, M., Robardet, C. (eds.) ECML PKDD 2019. LNCS (LNAI), vol. 11907, pp. 665–680. Springer, Cham (2020). https://doi.org/10.1007/978-3-030-46147-8_40

8. Hadsell, R., Chopra, S., LeCun, Y.: Dimensionality reduction by learning an invariant mapping. In: 2006 IEEE Computer Society Conference on Computer Vision and Pattern Recognition (CVPR 2006), vol. 2, pp. 1735–1742 (2006). https://doi.org/10.1109/CVPR.2006.100

9. Ji, Z., Wei, Q., Xu, H.: BERT-based ranking for biomedical entity normalization. AMIA Jt. Summits Transl. Sci. **2020**, 269 (2020)

10. Jiang, Z., Xu, F.F., Araki, J., Neubig, G.: How can we know what language models know? Trans. Assoc. Comput. Linguist. **8**, 423–438 (2020)

11. Jiao, L., Sun, Y., Johnson, R.J., Sciaky, D., Lu, Z.: BioCreative V CDR task corpus: a resource for chemical disease relation extraction. Database J. Biol. Databases Curation **2016**, baw068 (2016)

12. Kate, R.J.: Normalizing clinical terms using learned edit distance patterns. J. Am. Med. Inform. Assoc. JAMIA **23**, 380–386 (2015)

13. Lai, T., Ji, H., Zhai, C.: BERT might be overkill: a tiny but effective biomedical entity linker based on residual convolutional neural networks. In: Findings of the Association for Computational Linguistics: EMNLP 2021, Punta Cana, Dominican Republic, pp. 1631–1639. Association for Computational Linguistics, November 2021. https://doi.org/10.18653/v1/2021.findings-emnlp.140

14. Leaman, R., Lu, Z.: NCBI disease corpus: a resource for disease name recognition and concept normalization. J. Biomed. Inform. **47**, 1 (2014)

15. Leaman, R., Lu, Z.: TaggerOne: joint named entity recognition and normalization with semi-Markov models. Bioinformatics **32**(18), 2839–2846 (2016)

16. Lee, J., et al.: BioBERT: a pre-trained biomedical language representation model for biomedical text mining. Bioinformatics **36**(4), 1234–1240 (2019). https://doi.org/10.1093/bioinformatics/btz682

17. Lester, B., Al-Rfou, R., Constant, N.: The power of scale for parameter-efficient prompt tuning. In: Proceedings of the 2021 Conference on Empirical Methods in Natural Language Processing, Punta Cana, Dominican Republic, pp. 3045–3059. Association for Computational Linguistics, November 2021. https://aclanthology.org/2021.emnlp-main.243

18. Li, H., et al.: CNN-based ranking for biomedical entity normalization. BMC Bioinform. **18**(11), 79–86 (2017)

19. Li, X.L., Liang, P.: Prefix-tuning: optimizing continuous prompts for generation. In: Proceedings of the 59th Annual Meeting of the Association for Computational Linguistics and the 11th International Joint Conference on Natural Language Processing (Volume 1: Long Papers), pp. 4582–4597. Association for Computational Linguistics, August 2021. https://doi.org/10.18653/v1/2021.acl-long.353

20. Lin, T.Y., Goyal, P., Girshick, R., He, K., Dollár, P.: Focal loss for dense object detection. In: Proceedings of the IEEE International Conference on Computer Vision, pp. 2980–2988 (2017)

21. Liu, F., Shareghi, E., Meng, Z., Basaldella, M., Collier, N.: Self-alignment pretraining for biomedical entity representations. In: Proceedings of the 2021 Conference of the North American Chapter of the Association for Computational Linguistics: Human Language Technologies, pp. 4228–4238. Association for Computational Linguistics, June 2021. https://doi.org/10.18653/v1/2021.naacl-main.334

22. Liu, P., Yuan, W., Fu, J., Jiang, Z., Hayashi, H., Neubig, G.: Pre-train, prompt, and predict: a systematic survey of prompting methods in natural language processing. arXiv:2107.13586 (2021)

23. Liu, X., Ji, K., Fu, Y., Du, Z., Yang, Z., Tang, J.: P-Tuning v2: prompt tuning can be comparable to fine-tuning universally across scales and tasks. arXiv preprint arXiv:2110.07602 (2021)
24. Liu, X., et al.: GPT understands, too. arXiv preprint arXiv:2103.10385 (2021)
25. Mikolov, T., Sutskever, I., Chen, K., Corrado, G.S., Dean, J.: Distributed representations of words and phrases and their compositionality. In: Advances in Neural Information Processing Systems, vol. 26 (2013)
26. Mondal, I., et al.: Medical entity linking using triplet network. In: Proceedings of the 2nd Clinical Natural Language Processing Workshop, Minneapolis, Minnesota, USA, pp. 95–100. Association for Computational Linguistics, June 2019. https://doi.org/10.18653/v1/W19-1912
27. Ning, K., Bharat, S., Zubair, A., Van, M., Kors, J.A.: Using rule-based natural language processing to improve disease normalization in biomedical text. J. Am. Med. Inform. Assoc. JAMIA **20**(5), 876–881 (2013)
28. Pennington, J., Socher, R., Manning, C.D.: GloVe: global vectors for word representation. In: Proceedings of the 2014 Conference on Empirical Methods in Natural Language Processing (EMNLP), pp. 1532–1543 (2014)
29. Phan, M.C., Sun, A., Yi, T.: Robust representation learning of biomedical names. In: The 57th Conference of the Association for Computational Linguistics (2019)
30. Qin, G., Eisner, J.: Learning how to ask: querying LMs with mixtures of soft prompts. In: Proceedings of the 2021 Conference of the North American Chapter of the Association for Computational Linguistics: Human Language Technologies, pp. 5203–5212. Association for Computational Linguistics, June 2021. https://doi.org/10.18653/v1/2021.naacl-main.410
31. Leaman, R., Islamaj Dogan, R., Lu, Z.: DNorm: disease name normalization with pairwise learning to rank. Bioinformatics **29**(22), 2909–2917 (2013)
32. Schick, T., Schütze, H.: It's not just size that matters: small language models are also few-shot learners. In: Proceedings of the 2021 Conference of the North American Chapter of the Association for Computational Linguistics: Human Language Technologies, pp. 2339–2352. Association for Computational Linguistics, June 2021. https://doi.org/10.18653/v1/2021.naacl-main.185
33. Sohn, S., Comeau, D.C., Kim, W., Wilbur, W.J.: Abbreviation definition identification based on automatic precision estimates. BMC Bioinform. **9**(1), 402 (2008)
34. Sung, M., Jeon, H., Lee, J., Kang, J.: Biomedical entity representations with synonym marginalization. In: Proceedings of the 58th Annual Meeting of the Association for Computational Linguistics, pp. 3641–3650. Association for Computational Linguistics, July 2020. https://doi.org/10.18653/v1/2020.acl-main.335
35. Sunwon, L., et al.: BEST: next-generation biomedical entity search tool for knowledge discovery from biomedical literature. In: Public Library of Science, p. e0164680 (2016)
36. Usuga-Cadavid, J.P., Grabot, B., Lamouri, S., Fortin, A.: Exploring the influence of focal loss on transformer models for imbalanced maintenance data in industry 4.0. IFAC-PapersOnLine **54**(1), 1023–1028 (2021). https://doi.org/10.1016/j.ifacol.2021.08.121, https://www.sciencedirect.com/science/article/pii/S2405896321008776. 17th IFAC Symposium on Information Control Problems in Manufacturing INCOM 2021
37. Wallace, E., Feng, S., Kandpal, N., Gardner, M., Singh, S.: Universal adversarial triggers for attacking and analyzing NLP. In: EMNLP (2019)
38. Wang, Y., et al.: A comparison of word embeddings for the biomedical natural language processing. J. Biomed. Inform. **87**, 12–20 (2018)
39. Wright, D.: NormCo: deep disease normalization for biomedical knowledge base construction. University of California, San Diego (2019)

Bidirectional Multi-channel Semantic Interaction Model of Labels and Texts for Text Classification

Yuan Wang[1,2], Yubo Zhou[1(✉)], Peng Hu[1], Maoling Xu[1], Tingting Zhao[1], and Yarui Chen[1]

[1] College of Artificial Intelligence, Tianjin University of Science and Technology, Tianjin 300457, China
`819635527@qq.com`
[2] Population and Precision Health Care, Ltd., Tianjin 300000, China

Abstract. Text classification, aiming for discovering corresponding relationships between labels and texts, is a pivotal task in Natural Language Processing (NLP). The existing joint text-label models help input texts to establish early global category semantic awareness via label embedding techniques, but they cannot simultaneously capture literal and semantic relationships between texts and labels. It may lead models to ignore obvious clues or semantic relations on different cognitive levels. In this paper, we propose a Bidirectional Multi-channel semantic Interaction model (BMI) to handle both explicit and implicit category semantics in texts for text classification. On the explicit semantic level, BMI designs a word representation similarity match channel for shallow interaction to get rid of semantic mismatch based on assumptions that words have different meanings under the same context. On the implicit semantic level, BMI provides a novel attended attention mechanism over texts and labels for deep interaction to model bidirectional text explanation for labels and label guidance for texts. Furthermore, a gated residual mechanism is employed to obtain core information of labels to improve efficiency. Experiments on benchmark datasets show that BMI achieves competitive results over 15 strong baseline methods, especially in the case of short texts.

Keywords: Text classification · Label embedding · Multi-channel semantic modeling

1 Introduction

Text classification is a fundamental NLP task with numerous real-world applications such as topic recognition [19], sentiment analysis [12], and question answering [2]. Text representation is a key step of converting human symbolic language into computable numeric numbers, and attracts broad attention in the task of text classification [1,6,9].

© Springer Nature Switzerland AG 2022
W. Lu et al. (Eds.) NLPCC 2022, LNCS 13552, pp. 73–84, 2022.
https://doi.org/10.1007/978-3-031-17189-5_6

To achieve good representations of texts, many techniques in neural network models have been employed to model implicit semantics of texts, including Recurrent Neural Networks (RNNs) [3,25], Convolutional Neural Networks (CNNs) [9,18,25] and attention mechanisms [7,11,16,17]. RNNs must back propagate through all previous words in a sequence. While, processing one word at a time makes RNNs difficult to parallelize, and thus RNNs suffer from expensive time cost especially when applied to long sequences. Unlike RNNs that learn knowledge across the entire text sequence, CNNs applie convolution computation on only a few words/characters at a time by a sliding window. Therefore, it is difficult to learn dependencies to long distances with CNNs. To tackle these two problems, attention mechanisms [1] have been introduced as an integral part of models employed for text classification [4]. The idea of attention mechanisms is motivated by the observation that different words in the same context are differentially informative, and the same word may be differentially important in a different context. It can thus provide complementary information to the distance-aware dependencies modeled by RNNs or CNNs.

Note that in classification tasks, neural networks lack global classification information when only modeling texts. It has been proved that label embedding can provide texts a priori knowledge about classification goals and achieve good results [5,21,22,24], label embedding refers to encoding label set into a mathematical form that the computer can understand, usually using one-hot coding, and then vectorizing the encoded results. Typically, HLAN [5] presents a new self-attention based text classification network. In order to effectively capture dependencies over long text sequences and overcome the large memory requirement of existing self-attention methods, HLAN divides the text into sentences and employ a hierarchical architecture to map the hierarchical structure of a text. Besides, to enhance the interpretability of model and prevent overfitting, HLAN proposes a new penalty term called class loss and combine it with the cross-entropy loss. LEAM [21] first investigates label embeddings for text representations and proposes the label-embedding attentive models. It embeds the words and labels in the same joint space and measures the compatibility of word-label pairs to attend the text representations. Label specific attention network (LSAN) [22] makes use of text content and label text to learn the label-specific text representation with the aid of self-attention and label-attention mechanisms, and an adaptive fusion is designed to effectively integrate these two attention mechanisms to improve the final prediction performance. Multi-Task Label Embedding (MTLE) [24] maps labels of text classification tasks into semantic vectors and implements unsupervised, supervised and semi-supervised models to facilitate multi-task learning, all utilizing semantic correlations among tasks and effectively solving the problems of scaling and transferring when new tasks are involved. Such early text-label interaction functions can help to fill the semantic gap between texts and labels.

Unfortunately, they only rely on one-way label-to-text modeling, that is, they only calculate the attention at the text level. This one-way modeling method makes the model unable to effectively model the attention information at the label level, it cannot distinguish which label should be given a higher weight for a specific word. At the same time, they ignore the different interactions between texts and labels at different semantic levels, that is, explicit and implicit interactions.

To give a comprehensive semantic understanding between texts and labels in the task, we propose a Bidirectional Multi-channel semantic Interaction model (BMI) to handle bidirectional semantics of both explicit and implicit category semantics in texts for text classification. On the explicit semantic level, BMI designs a word representation similarity match channel (shallow match channel) for obtaining shallow specific semantic interactive information of texts and labels, which can help to eliminate word semantic mismatch based on assumptions that different words own the same meanings under the same context. On the implicit semantic level, BMI provides a novel mutual look attended attention mechanism over texts and labels for deep interaction (a deep single interaction channel and a deep bidirectional interaction channel) to model bidirectional text explanation for labels and label guidance for texts. Furthermore, a gated residual mechanism is employed to obtain core information of labels in the training process to improve efficiency.

Our main contributions are the following:

- Our model efficiently handles shallow explicit specific semantic interactive information and deep implicit abstract semantic interactive information between texts and labels with a novel multi-channel structure.
- A bidirectional semantic learning mechanism is first introduced in text classification tasks to leverage both label-to-text and text-to-label alignment relationships.
- A gated residual mechanism is designed to obtain core information of labels to improve training effectiveness significantly.
- We consider different scenarios of text classification and experimental results on four large scale datasets demonstrate the effectiveness of BMI, especially in the case of short texts.

2   Model

In this section, we introduce the proposed Bidirectional Multi-channel semantic Interaction model, as shown in Fig. 1.

Motivated by the limitation of previous models for text classification, BMI consists of two parts. The first part aims to resolve category-related shallow specific semantics and deep abstract semantics in texts, including a shallow match channel, a deep single interaction channel and a deep bidirectional interaction channel. The second part helps the classification model to be trained on adaptive merged task-oriented dense text representations, including a fusion layer and a classification layer.

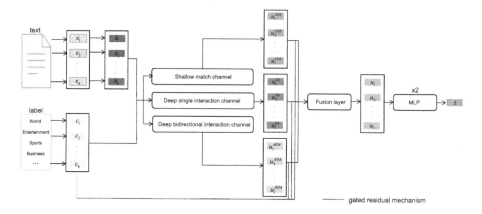

Fig. 1. The overall framework of BMI.

2.1 Preliminaries

Problem Definition. Let $D = \{(d_i, y_i)\}_{i=1}^N$ denote the set of texts, which consists of N texts with corresponding labels $Y = \{y_i \in \{0, 1, .., l\}\}$, here l is the total number of labels. Each text contains a sequence of words. Each word can be encoded to a low-dimensional space and represented as a d-dimension vector via GloVe technique [13]. Let $d_i = \{x_1, \cdots, x_p, \cdots, x_n\}$ denote the i-th text, $x_p \in \mathbb{R}^d$ is the p-th word vector in the text, n is the number of words in text d_i. For text classification, each label contains textual information. Given input texts and their associated labels D, BMI trains a classifier to assign a most relevant label to the new coming texts.

Input Text and Label Representation. To capture contextual information of text sequence, we adopt LSTM [6] to learn the word embeddings for each input text. At time-step t, the hidden state can be updated with the aid of input and t-1-th step output:

$$h_t = \text{LSTM}\,(h_{t-1}, x_t)\,, \tag{1}$$

where x_t is the embedding of the t-th word in the corresponding text, and $h_t \in R^d$ indicates the word context representations, respectively. Then, a text sequence can be represented by LSTM as $H = (h_1, h_2, \ldots, h_n)$, $H \in R^{n \times d}$. Similar to text words, input labels can be encoded as trainable embedding vectors $C = (c_1, \ldots, c_k, \ldots, c_l)$, where $c_k \in R^d$.

2.2 Bidirectional Multi-channel Semantic Interaction Model

In this subsection, we describe the model in detail, showing how it can be trained effectively. Based on input text and label representations, BMI captures bidirectional explicit and implicit complex semantic interaction signals of texts and labels by three parallel channels. For each channel, we employ a gated residual mechanism to obtain long-term semantic memory for texts. Next, a fusion layer is applied to aggregate the semantic interaction signals into a text-label joint space for input texts. Then a classification layer can make the final predictions. Next, we will show how to capture these characteristics within BMI.

Shallow Match Channel. The key idea of our shallow match channel is to infer clues whether and how a text and labels have explicit semantic relations on a shallow cognitive level. Thus we use attentive cosine similarity between a text and labels to measure obvious shallow interactions in original word embedding space. Specifically, we employ text representation H and label representations C to encode text-label shallow match representation $U^{COS} = \{u_1^{COS}, \ldots, u_l^{COS}\}$, $U^{COS} \in R^{l \times d}$. The implementation process for a text under the i-th label indication is as follows:

$$u_i^{COS} = \sum_{j=1}^{n} \bar{w}_{i,j} h_j, \tag{2}$$

where $\bar{w}_{i,j}$ is a label attentive weight to measure the compatibility of the pair $< h_j, c_i >$. To get compatibility weight, cosine similarities between label embedding c_i and each word embedding in $H = \{h_1, h_2, \ldots, h_n\}$ are computed, resulting in a similarity embedding weight $\{w_{i1}, w_{i2}, \ldots, w_{in}\}$, which should be normalized:

$$\{\bar{w}_{i1}, \bar{w}_{i2}, \ldots, \bar{w}_{in}\} = \text{Softmax}\, \{w_{i1}, w_{i1}, \ldots, w_{in}\}. \tag{3}$$

Deep Single Interaction Channel. The key idea of our deep single interaction channel is to learn implicit interactive of multi-faceted between texts and labels. Thus we employ an m-head self-attention mechanism [20] by treating label embeddings C as queries, and text context representation $H \in R^{n \times d}$ as keys and values to encode text-label deep single interaction representation $U^{SA} = \{u_1^{SA}, \ldots, u_l^{SA}\}$, $U^{SA} \in R^{l \times d}$. The implementation formula can be expressed as:

$$\text{head} = \text{softmax}\left(\frac{[CW_{q_i}] [HW_{k_i}]^{\mathrm{T}}}{\sqrt{d/m}} \right) [HW_{v_i}] \tag{4}$$

$$U^{SA} = [\text{ head }_1, \ldots, \text{ head }_m]\, W', \tag{5}$$

where $head_i$ refers to the i-th head of self-attention, $\{W_{q_i}, W_{k_i}, W_{v_i}\} \in R^{d \times d}/m$ and $W' \in R^{d \times d}$ are weight matrices for queries, keys, values, and multi-head attention, respectively.

Deep Bidirectional Interaction Channel. The key idea of our deep bidirectional interaction channel is to obtain implicit bidirectional semantic information interaction of labels and texts. Thus given label representations $C \in R^{l \times d}$ and a text context representation $H \in R^{n \times d}$, we first calculate a pair-wise interaction matrix: $M = CH^T$, where the value of each entry represents the correlation of a pair among labels and texts. With a row-wise softmax and column-wise softmax, we get text-to-label attention α, which represent label guidance for texts. And label-to-text attention β, which represent text explanation for labels:

$$\alpha_{ij} = \frac{\exp\left(M_{ij}\right)}{\sum_i \exp\left(M_{ij}\right)}, \tag{6}$$

$$\beta_{ij} = \frac{\exp(M_{ij})}{\sum_j \exp(M_{ij})}. \tag{7}$$

After column-wise averaging β, we get a text-level attention $\bar{\beta} \in R^n$:

$$\bar{\beta}_j = \frac{1}{l} \sum_i \beta_{ij}. \tag{8}$$

The final label-level attention $\gamma \in R^l$ is calculated by a weighted sum of each individual label-to-text attention α:

$$\gamma = \alpha\bar{\beta}^T. \tag{9}$$

By considering the contribution of each word explicitly, we learn the important weights for each word in the text. The final text representation of deep bidirectional interaction channel sum of label representations using the text attention to encode text-label deep bidirectional interaction representation $U^{AOA} = \{u_1^{AOA}, \ldots, u_l^{AOA}\}$, $U^{AOA} \in R^{l \times d}$. The implementation formula can be expressed as:

$$U^{AOA} = \gamma \cdot C. \tag{10}$$

Gated Residual Mechanism. The key idea of our gated residual mechanism is to obtain long-term memory of label information for three channels. The following takes gated residual mechanism for our shallow match channel as an example:

$$\partial_1 = \sigma\left(U^{COS}W_1 + CV_1 + b_1\right), \tag{11}$$

$$\bar{U}^{COS} = \partial_1 U^{COS} + (1 - \partial_1)C. \tag{12}$$

Among them $\{W_1, V_1\} \in R^{d \times d}$. Similarly, we can get $\{\bar{U}^{COS}, \bar{U}^{SA}, \bar{U}^{AOA}\} \in R^{l \times d}$.

Fusion Layer. We introduce a dynamic weighting strategy to generate task-orientated text representations after our shallow match channel, deep single interaction channel and deep bidirectional interaction channel. Specifically, we obtain the final text representation as follows:

$$U = \theta_0 \bar{U}^{COS} + \theta_1 \bar{U}^{SA} + \theta_2 \bar{U}^{AOA}, \tag{13}$$

where $\theta_0 + \theta_1 + \theta_2 = 1$. $\theta_0, \theta_1, \theta_2$ are automatically learned by the model during the training process to determine the importances among both explicit and implicit, unidirectional and bidirectional semantic relation information of texts and labels.

Classification Layer. In the classification layer, we use two full-connection layers named FC and FC' respectively. The first layer FC is used to compress a large text embedding dimension into a proper one, which reduces the dimension of the text representation to prevent overfitting. In this study, we empirically set $l \times 100$. The second layer FC' is used to encode the embedding dimension equal to l, which implements numerical mapping of text representation to label set:

$$z = FC'\left(FC(U)\right). \tag{14}$$

Thus, we can get the final probability distribution $z \in R^l$. Cross-entropy loss is widely used as the loss function for text classification tasks. It is computed as:

$$\mathcal{L} = \frac{1}{N} \sum_i \sum_{c=1}^{l} y_{ic} \log (z_{ic}) \tag{15}$$

where l is the number of categories, N is the number of texts, y_{ic} is the ground truth of labels and z_{ic} is the predicted probability distribution of labels.

3 Experiments

In this section, we design extensive experiments based on four benchmark datasets for text classification. We investigate the empirical performances of BMI and compare them with existing state-of-the-art baselines.

3.1 Experimental Settings

Datasets. There are many text classification datasets. However, only few of them have label text information to initialize label representation. Thus, in this paper, four benchmark text classification datasets, including two sentiment classification datasets (Yelp.F and Yelp.P) and two topic classification datasets (DBPedia and Yahoo), are used to construct the experiments. The detailed statistics of the data are shown in Table 1.

Yelp.F: The dataset is obtained from the 2015 Yelp Dataset Challenge, and the task is sentiment classification of polarity star labels for comments. The labels range from 1 to 5 are worst, bad, middle, good, and best.

Yelp.P: The same comments as the 2015 Yelp Dataset Challenge, considering only coarse-grained binary sentiment categories, where 1 and 2 are bad, 4 and 5 are good.

DBPedia: A categorized dataset containing Wikipedia text, with a total of 14 ontology classes.

Yahoo: Yahoo! Answers Comprehensive Questions and Answers dataset contains question titles, question contents and their corresponding best answers about 10 topics, including question title, question content and the best answer.

Table 1. Detailed statistics of datasets.

Dataset	Train	Dev	Test	Class	Classification task
Yelp.F	615 k	35k	38 k	5	Sentiment classification
Yelp.P	525 k	35k	38 k	2	Sentiment classification
DBPedia	490 k	70k	70 k	14	Ontology classification
Yahoo	1340 k	60k	60 k	10	Topic classification

Implementation Details. In experiments, we set $d = 300$ and use 300-dimensional GloVe 340B pre-trained word embedding [13] to initialize text embeddings and label embeddings. Among them, label embeddings use text content embeddings of description labels as input. The Adam Optimizer [10] with a learning rate of 1e-3 is used to train the model parameters, and the size of mini-batch is set to 100. The number of self-attention heads m is 4.

Baseline Methods. We evaluate and compare our BMI with a variety of strong baseline models, including (1) Deep learning models based on CNN/RNN: small/large word CNN [25], Gated CNNs [18] and LSTM [25]; (2) Simple linear models: Simple Word Embedding Models (SWEM) [15] and fastText [8]; (3)Self-attention models: Bi-directional Block Self-Attention Network (Bi-BloSAN) [17], Directional Self-Attention Network (DiSAN) [16], Self-Attentive Sentence Embedding Model (SASEM) [11], Cascaded Semantic and Positional Self-Attention Network (CSPAN) [7]; (4)Text-label models: LEAM [21], HLAN [5]; (5) Pretrained language models: Kernelinspired Encoder with Recursive Mechanism for Interpretable Trees (KERMIT) [23] and Pattern Exploiting Training (PET)[14].

Table 2. Test accuracy on text classification tasks, in percentage.(%)

Model	Yelp.P	Yelp.F	DBPedia	Yahoo
Small word CNN [25]	94.46	58.59	98.15	69.98
Large word CNN [25]	95.11	58.48	98.28	70.94
Gated CNNs [18]	93.75	61.42	98.51	–
LSTM [25]	94.74	58.17	98.55	70.84
SWEM [15]	93.76	61.11	98.42	73.53
fastText [8]	95.70	63.90	98.60	72.30
Bi-BloSAN [17]	94.56	62.13	98.77	76.28
DiSAN [16]	94.39	62.08	98.67	76.15
SASEM [11]	94.90	63.40	98.30	–
CSPAN [7]	96.18	65.95	–	77.75
LEAM [21]	95.31	64.09	99.02	73.53
HLAN [5]	95.83	63.78	**99.13**	77.55
KERMIT $_{ENC}$ + XLNet [23]	88.99	53.72	94.51	–
KERMIT $_{ENC}$ + BERT $_{base}$ [23]	87.58	52.02	97.73	–
PET $_{ENC}$ + RoBERTa $_{large}$ [14]	–	64.80	–	72.70
BMI	**96.70**	**67.07**	99.03	**78.01**

3.2   Results and Analysis

From Table 2, we can see that BMI achieves the highest test accuracy on Yelp.F, Yelp.P, and Yahoo datasets, and gets suboptimal results on DBPedia, which verifies the effectiveness of BMI on text classification tasks. Particularly, BMI consistently outperforms the deep learning networks based on CNN/RNN, such as small word CNN, large word CNN and LSTM by a substantial margin on all datasets. Meanwhile, BMI is mainly superior to the previous self-attention models and pre-trained language models. We notice that BMI performs better on sentiment classification tasks than on topic classification tasks. Because in the topic classification, the information of labels would probably appear in texts. The baseline models can extract the classification information of the text very well. But in the sentiment classification, the sentence structure is complex, which may include many aspects of sentiment semantics. BMI has greatly improved the effect by modeling both explicit and implicit information between labels and text simultaneously. Another possible reason why topic classification doesn't work well is that no existing words description for the label embedding initialization in topic classification datasets, such as DBPedia.

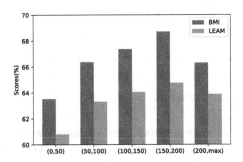

Fig. 2. Performance across different text length on Yelp.P dataset.

With text length varies among different texts, it is significant to explore how classification accuracy fluctuates among diverse text lengths. We employ experiments on Yelp.P dataset, which has the longest average length (145 words). As is illustrated in Fig. 2, we can see that the accuracy of our proposed model is higher than LEAM in the five-length intervals. Furthermore, we find that the effect of text classification on BMI is more pronounced in the case of short text length. It shows that BMI can handle both explicit and implicit semantic interaction well between texts and labels, make full use of the semantic information of external label, and make up for the lack of information in the short text itself.

To provide insight into the meaningfulness of the learned representations, we visualize the correlation between label embeddings and the text embeddings belonging to each label obtained by BMI based on the Yahoo dataset in Fig. 3. The rows are averaged per-class text embeddings, while columns are label embeddings. Therefore, the on-diagonal elements measure how representative the learned label embeddings are to describe their own classes, while off-diagonal elements reflect how distinctive the label embeddings are to be separated from other classes. The high on-diagonal elements and low off-diagonal elements in Fig. 3 indicate the superb ability of the text embeddings learned from BMI.

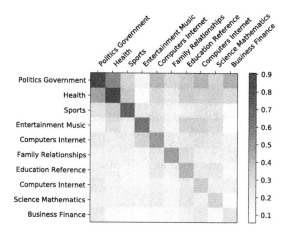

Fig. 3. Cosine similarity matrix on Yahoo dataset.

3.3 Ablation Test

We also carry out model ablations to further demonstrate the effectiveness of the proposed modules. The results are shown in Table 3. When we remove the shallow match channel (BMI-SM), the most significant decrease (0.29% in Yelp.P) appears, which indicates the shallow specific interactive is necessary especially for sentiment polarity detection in short texts. When we remove the deep single interaction channel (BMI-DS), the deep bidirectional interaction channel (BMI-DB) and the gated residual mechanism (BMI-GR), the most significant decrease all appears in Yelp.F with 0.76%, 0.39% and 0.40% respectively. These prove that the BMI model takes into account the bidirectional modeling dependencies between texts and labels, that is, not only the attention at the text level but also the attention at the label level is considered, can further refine the explicit and implicit interaction between texts and labels at different semantic levels through multi-channel design and effectively combine them and uses the gated residual mechanism to directly propagate the semantic information of the label embedding from the lower layer to the higher layer, which strengthens the propagation of label information to a certain extent and prevents network degradation during training.

Table 3. An ablation study of BMI.(%)

Model	Yelp.P	Yelp.F	DBPedia	Yahoo
BMI-SM	96.41	66.84	98.88	77.85
BMI-DB	96.60	66.24	98.99	77.83
BMI-DS	96.62	66.68	98.95	77.86
BMI-GR	96.56	66.67	98.99	77.72
BMI	**96.70**	**67.07**	**99.03**	**78.01**

4 Conclusions

In this paper, we proposed a novel bidirectional multi-channel semantic interaction model to capture both explicit specific and implicit abstract category semantics between labels and texts for text classification. We designed a shallow match channel, a deep single interaction channel and a deep bidirectional interaction channel to model semantic relationships of labels and texts in different levels, and effectively merged these three channels. Besides, a gated residual mechanism was employed to obtain core information of labels to improve efficiency. Extensive experiments on benchmarks showed the effectiveness of our model in text classification. Specifically, it inspired us two significant findings that 1) explicit symbolic information did help to text category information understanding in neural networks, and 2) labels and texts could be treated equally in the text classification.

References

1. Bahdanau, D., Cho, K., Bengio, Y.: Neural machine translation by jointly learning to align and translate. In: ICLR (2015)
2. Chen, J., et al.: End-to-end learning of lda by mirror-descent back propagation over a deep architecture. In: NIPS (2015)
3. Chung, J., Gülçehre Ç., Cho, K., Bengio, Y.: Empirical evaluation of gated recurrent neural networks on sequence modeling. CoRR (2014)
4. Gehring, J., et al.: Convolutional sequence to sequence learning. In: ICML (2017)
5. Gong, C., Shi, K., Niu, Z.: Hierarchical text-label integrated attention network for document classification. In: HPCCT (2019)
6. Hochreiter, S., Schmidhuber, J.: Long short-term memory. Neural Comput. **9**(8), 1735–1780 (1997)
7. Jiang, J., Zhang, J., Zhang, K.: Cascaded semantic and positional self-attention network for document classification. In: EMNLP (2020)
8. Joulin, J., Grave, E., Bojanowski, P., Mikolov, T.: Bag of tricks for efficient text classification. In: EACL (2017)
9. Kalchbrenner, N., Grefenstette, E., Blunsom, P.: A convolutional neural network for modelling sentences. In: ACL (2014)
10. Kingma, D.P., Ba, J.L.: Adam: A method for stochastic optimization. In: ICLR (2015)

11. Lin, Z., et al.: A structured self-attentive sentence embedding. In: ICLR (Poster) (2017)
12. Pang, B., Lee, L.: Seeing stars: exploiting class relationships for sentiment categorization with respect to rating scales. In: ACL (2005)
13. Pennington, J., Socher, R., Manning, C.D.: Glove: Global vectors for word representation. In: EMNLP (2014)
14. Schick, T., Schütze, H.: Exploiting cloze questions for few-shot text classification and natural language inference. In: EACL (2021)
15. Shen, D., et al.: Baseline needs more love: on simple word-embedding-based models and associated pooling mechanisms. In: ACL (2018)
16. Shen, T., Zhou, T., Long, G., Jiang, J., Pan, S., Zhang, C.: Disan: directional self-attention network for rnn/cnn-free language understanding. In: AAAI (2018)
17. Shen, T., Zhou, T., Long, G., Jiang, J., Zhang, C.: Bi-directional block self-attention for fast and memory-efficient sequence modeling. In: ICLR (2018)
18. Sun, J., Jin, R., Ma, X., Park, J.Y., Sohn, K.A., Chung, T.S.: Gated convolutional neural networks for text classification. Adv. Comput. Sci. Ubiquit. Comput. **32**(1), 309–316 (2021)
19. Tang, D., Qin, B., Liu, T.: Document modeling with gated recurrent neural network for sentiment classification. In: EMNLP (2015)
20. Vaswani, A., et al.: Attention is all you need. In: NIPS (2017)
21. Wang, G., et al.: Joint embedding of words and labels for text classification. In: ACL (2018)
22. Xiao, L., Huang, X., Chen, B., Jing, L.: Label-specific document representation for multi-label text classification. In: EMNLP (2019)
23. Zanzotto, F.M., Santilli, A., Ranaldi, L., Onorati, D., Tommasino, P., Fallucchi, F.: Kermit: complementing transformer architectures with encoders of explicit syntactic interpretations. In: EMNLP (2020)
24. Zhang, H., Xiao, L., Chen, W., Wang, Y., Jin, Y.: Multi-task label embedding for text classification. In: EMNLP (2018)
25. Zhang, X., Zhao, J., LeCun, Y.: Character-level convolutional networks for text classification. In: NIPS (2015)

Exploiting Dynamic and Fine-grained Semantic Scope for Extreme Multi-label Text Classification

Yuan Wang[1,2], Huiling Song[1], Peng Huo[1], Tao Xu[1(✉)], Jucheng Yang[1], Yarui Chen[1], and Tingting Zhao[1]

[1] Tianjin University of Science and Technology, Tianjin 300457, China
xutaowk0@mail.tust.edu.cn
[2] Population and Precision Health Care, Ltd., Tianjin 300000, China

Abstract. Extreme multi-label text classification (XMTC) refers to the problem of tagging a given text with the most relevant subset of labels from a large label set. A majority of labels only have a few training instances due to large label dimensionality in XMTC. To solve this data sparsity issue, most existing XMTC methods take advantage of fixed label clusters obtained in early stage to balance performance on tail labels and head labels. However, such label clusters provide static and coarse-grained semantic scope for every text, which ignores distinct characteristics of different texts and has difficulties modelling accurate semantics scope for texts with tail labels. In this paper, we propose a novel framework TReaderXML for XMTC, which adopts dynamic and fine-grained semantic scope from teacher knowledge for individual text to optimize text conditional prior category semantic ranges. TReaderXML dynamically obtains teacher knowledge for each text by similar texts and hierarchical label information in training sets to release the ability of distinctly fine-grained label-oriented semantic scope. Then, TReaderXML benefits from a novel dual cooperative network that firstly learns features of a text and its corresponding label-oriented semantic scope by parallel Encoding Module and Reading Module, secondly embeds two parts by Interaction Module to regularize the text's representation by dynamic and fine-grained label-oriented semantic scope, and finally find target labels by Prediction Module. Experimental results on three XMTC benchmark datasets show that our method achieves new state-of-the-art results and especially performs well for severely imbalanced and sparse datasets.

Keywords: Extreme multi-label text classification · Semantic scope · A dual cooperative network · Data sparsity

1 Introduction

Recent years have witnessed remarkable progress in XMTC, with a variety of approaches presented in the literatures and applied in real-world scenarios, such as dynamic search advertising [21] and query recommendation [8].

© Springer Nature Switzerland AG 2022
W. Lu et al. (Eds.) NLPCC 2022, LNCS 13552, pp. 85–97, 2022.
https://doi.org/10.1007/978-3-031-17189-5_7

Different from classical multi-label problems, only a few are head labels with sufficient positive training data, and most labels are tail labels with few positive training data due to large label dimensionality [18, 19, 23] in XMTC. This data sparsity issue leads to insufficient feature learning of tail labels, and hurts prediction performance on overwhelming tail label predictions.

To solve this problem, most existing XMTC methods [3,9,9,15,18,20,21,23] take advantage of label clusters obtained in early stage to balance performance on tail labels and head labels. The main motivation is that the semantics of head labels is easy to be recognized in the semantic space due to sufficient training data, while the semantics of tail labels is vague. The precise semantics of tail labels can be learned from head labels that may appear in the same cluster. However, existing label clusters are all pre-defined global category patterns due to fixed features of labels. The static and coarse-grained semantic scope provided by such label clusters is not always consistent with dynamic real-world semantic scenarios, where content of different text has different semantic granularity. The previous model establishes structures hierarchy for the labels of a single field, and if the user is likely to be interested in overlapping topics in that and other fields, then when he enters a query into the search engine, he only gets keywords for a single domain due to the prepared label clusters. Thus, we consider developing dynamic semantic scope in the form of fine-grained teacher knowledge to improve tail label predictions accuracy and alleviate the data sparsity issue. We introduce text relevance to increase exposure of tail labels and implement a dynamic label cluster structure to personalise relevant label subsets. In detail, for given instance, We can use the relevant labels of its neighbouring text to link more rare labels. We assume that if a text is related to a label, then the text is also related to its parent label. With the help of hierarchical label information, teacher knowledge is modeled to provide dynamic and fine-grained semantic scope to rich text semantics.

In summary, We propose a novel framework TReaderXML for XMTC containing a novel dual cooperative network based on multi-head self attention mechanism to embed both guidance knowledge and text into a shared semantic space for feature interaction, effectively improving the effect of teacher knowledge. The remainder of the paper is organized as follows. In Sect. 2, we review recent related work. Section 3 introduces TReaderXML. In Sect. 4, experimental results on three XMTC benchmark datasets are shown. Section 5 concludes this work.

2   Related Work

Many methods have been proposed for addressing the data sparsity issue of XMTC. They can be categorized into the following two types: 1) flat based label clusters [3,23]; 2) tree based label clusters [9,15,17,18,20,21]. Tree based label clusters include loss function-based and structure-based.

In flat based label clusters, SLEEC [3] uses text features for clustering. A new text is projected in corresponding clusters, and labels of a new text are obtained by K-Nearest Neighbor to alleviate the data sparsity issue. Based on SLEEC, AnnexML [23] uses label features for clustering based on graph embedding to improve the quality of clusters. In addition, in tree based label clusters, loss function-based method FastXML [21] learns an ensemble of trees which clusters the label space by optimizing a normalized Discounted Cumulative Gain (nDCG) loss function, and PfastreXML [9] replaces the nDCG loss in FastXML by its propensity scored variant which assigns higher rewards for tail label predictions. Furthermore, for structure-based methods in tree based label clusters, Parabel [15] generates a label tree by recursively clustering labels into two balanced groups to address the data sparsity issue. However, the clustering depth of Parabel is deep, which leads to error cascade problems and affects tail label predictions. Bonsai [18] uses shallow and diverse probabilistic label trees (PLTs) by removing the balance constraint in the tree construction of Parabel, which improves tail label predictions. This tree structure-based label cluster optimization is also applied to AttentionXML [17]. AttentionXML optimizes the structure of PLTs to obtain shallow and wide clusters, which improves tail label predictions.

These label cluster methods provide static and coarse-grained semantic scope for every text. It is not always consistent with dynamic real-world semantic scenarios, and reduces the precision of prior knowledge.

3   Methodology

3.1   Notation

Given a training set $\{(x_i, y_i)\}_{i=1}^{N}$ where x_i is text input sequence, and $y_i \in \{0,1\}^L$ is the label of x_i represented by L dimensional multi-hot vectors. Each dimension in y_i corresponds to a label where $y_{ij} = 1$ when the j-th label $L_{y_{ij}}$ is associated with x_i. In this paper, we introduce teacher knowledge in a training set $\{(x_i, y_i, y_i')\}_{i=1}^{N}$ where y_i' represents the text x_i's corresponding teacher knowledge.

3.2   TReaderXML

TReaderXML adopts dynamic and fine-grained semantic scope from teacher knowledge for an individual text to optimize text prior category semantic ranges. Before teacher knowledge helps read text semantics, we need a powerful feature extraction to obtain high dimensional features of semantic scope from teacher knowledge and a text respectively, and embed both of them into a shared semantic space. Then the high dimensional semantics of scope with prior knowledge helps read high dimensional semantics of a text. Based on the above motivations, we design four layers: 1) Encoding, 2) Reading, 3) Interaction and 4) Predicting. Furthermore, a dual cooperative network contains two layers of Reading and Interaction, and Fig. 1 shows the framework of TReaderXML.

Encoding. In this part, we design a structure of representation to obtain fine-grained semantic scope extended by teacher knowledge matrix $E_{y_i'}$ and E_{x_i}. Given a training text x_i, its vectorization is shown as follows:

$$V_{x_i} = \frac{\sum_{c=1}^{Len(x_i)} \text{Encode}(x_{ic})}{Len(x_i)}. \tag{1}$$

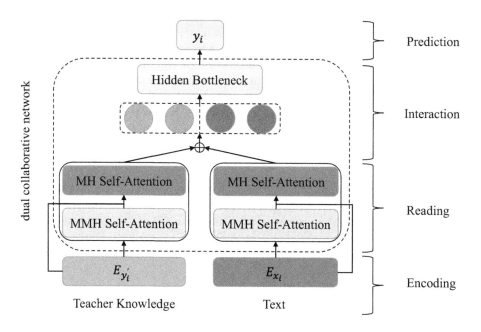

Fig. 1. An overview of TReaderXML.

Traverse x_z from training set and validation set to find the nearest neighbourhoods of x_i by using consine similarity:

$$score_{cos}(V_{x_i}, V_{x_z}) = \frac{(V_{x_i} \cdot V_{x_i})}{\| V_{x_i} \| \| V_{x_z} \|}. \tag{2}$$

and return top k nearest neighbourhoods $y_i^{nearest}$. To get the semantic scope, Gargiulo [7] uses all of ancestor labels of text labels y_i in a label tree to introduce hierarchical label information, effectively utilizing label semantic structural relation information. However, it leads to error cascade problems [18] due to the deep hierarchical structure. Furthermore, the semantics of deep hierarchical labels is often abstract, and it reduces the precision of prior knowledge. Inspired by these observations, we only use parent labels of child labels y_i in a hierarchical label tree to introduce hierarchical label information. With the advantage of low error and high precision of hierarchical label information, teacher knowledge is modeled to provide dynamic and fine-grained semantic scope to help read text semantics. As shown in Algorithm 1, we firstly find the most relevant labels of $x_i^{nearest}$ and its non-empty parent labels. And then we put them into the label subset $SET^{nearest}$. Each label description information can be generated with widely used tricks in Parabel [15]. To keep an input sequence consistent with the semantic scope of teacher knowledge, we also initialize an embedding for an input sequence x_i, and the processing formula is shown as: $E_{x_i} = \text{Encode}(x_i)$.

Reading. In this part, we design a structure of Reading to obtain high dimensional features of semantic scope from a teacher knowledge and a text respectively and embed both of them into a shared semantic space for the preparation of feature interaction. This component in a dual cooperative network plays a key role including a mask multi-head self attention (MMHSA) layer, a multi-head self attention (MHSA) layer and residual network.

To obtain high dimensional features of semantic scope from teacher knowledge and a text respectively, we design the structure of Reading based on the self-attention mechanism [2], which contains a MMHSA layer, a MHSA layer and a residual layer. MMHSA masks the future sequence information, and depends on existing sequence information to predict the next word in a sequence. We consider MMHSA as the first layer of Reading to capture more fine-grained semantic information due to the masking in MMHSA. Furthermore, MHSA makes each word contain other semantic information of words in a text input sequence, and we consider MHSA as the second layer of Reading to capture overall semantic information. The processing formula of masking in MMHSA is shown as follows:

$$d_k = d_{\text{model}}//h, \tag{3}$$

$$Q_{y_i'} = E_{y_i'}W_{y_i'}^q, \quad Q_{x_i} = E_{x_i}W_{x_i}^q, \tag{4}$$

$$K_{y_i'} = E_{y_i'}W_{y_i'}^k, \quad K_{x_i} = E_{x_i}W_{x_i}^k, \tag{5}$$

$$V_{y_i'} = E_{y_i'}W_{y_i'}^v, \quad V_{x_i} = E_{x_i}W_{x_i}^v, \tag{6}$$

$$Score_{y_i'} = \frac{Q_{y_i'} \cdot K_{y_i'}^T}{\sqrt{d_k}}, \quad Score_{x_i} = \frac{Q_{x_i} \cdot K_{x_i}^T}{\sqrt{d_k}}, \tag{7}$$

$$Score_{y_i'} = Mask(Score_{y_i'}, W_{y_i'}^{mask}), \tag{8}$$

$$Score_{x_i} = Mask(Score_{x_i}, W_{x_i}^{mask}), \tag{9}$$

$$H_i^{y_i'} = \text{Softmax}(Score_{y_i'}) \cdot V_{y_i'}, \tag{10}$$

$$H_i^{x_i} = \text{Softmax}(Score_{x_i}) \cdot V_{x_i}. \tag{11}$$

where d_{model} is dimension of embedding, and h is the number of attention heads. $W_{y_i'}^q$, $W_{y_i'}^k$, $W_{y_i'}^v$, $W_{x_i}^q$, $W_{x_i}^k$, and $W_{x_i}^v$ are weight matrices of random initialization. $W_{y_i'}^{mask}$ and $W_{x_i}^{mask}$ are upper triangular matrices. For $Mask(A, B)$, positions where the value of B is 0 are mapped into A, and the value of these positions are set to minus infinity in A. Then infinity values in A will become 0 after Softmax, and masking has been achieved. The attention output $H_i^{y_i'}$ and $H_i^{x_i}$

Algorithm 1. Encoding generation of teacher knowledge

Input: $y_i^{nearest}$

Output: $E_{y_i'}$

1: initialize $SET^{nearest} = \{\}$;
2: **for** $j = 0; j < L; j++$ **do**
3:    **if** $y_{ij}^{nearest} == 1$ and $Par(L_{y_{ij}}^{nearest})! = NULL$ **then**
4:       add $L_{y_{ij}}^{nearest}$ to $SET^{nearest}$
5:       add $Par(L_{y_{ij}}^{nearest})$ to $SET^{nearest}$
6:    **end if**
7: **end for**
8: **compute** $E_{y_i'} = \frac{\sum_{k=1}^{K} \text{Encode}(T_k^{nearest})}{K}$
9: **return** $E_{y_i'}$

---

learned by each head will be concatenated and transformed by multiplying a vector respectively. The output of MMHSA can be expressed by the formula given below:

$$MMHSA_{E_{y_i'}} = \tanh\left(\left\{H_1^{y_i'}, \ldots; H_h^{y_i'}\right\} \cdot W_{y_i'}^{MH}\right), \tag{12}$$

$$MMHSA_{E_{x_i}} = \tanh\left(\left\{H_1^{x_i}, \ldots; H_h^{x_i}\right\} \cdot W_{x_i}^{MH}\right). \tag{13}$$

Compared with MMHSA, the processing formula of MHSA omits formulas (6) and (7). To compensate for the loss of semantic information caused due to the masking techniques, we therefore introduce a residual network to enhance the robustness of the model and the expressiveness of the network:

$$E_{y_i'}^{residual} = E_{y_i'} + MMHSA(E_{y_i'}), \tag{14}$$

$$E_{x_i}^{residual} = E_{x_i} + MMHSA(E_{x_i}). \tag{15}$$

The design of Reading simulates the process of reading a text. Firstly a teacher and a student respectively read verbatim to understand details of texts with MMHSA, and then read comprehensively to understand themes of texts with MHSA. Furthermore, the first layer of a dual cooperative network simulates the preparation of a teacher teaching a student to read. A teacher will prepare the key points of a text and a student will preview a text to achieve the best performance of reading. The first preparation work for the process of cooperation in a dual cooperative network has been achieved, and both semantic scope and text have been embedded into a shared semantic space.

Iteraction. The high-dimensional semantic scope generated by the interaction process between the teacher knowledge and the text provides a deeper understanding of the semantics of the text.

We assume that $O_{y_i'}$ represents the output of Reading from teacher knowledge, and O_{x_i} represents the output of Reading from an input sequence. Firstly $O_{y_i'}$ and O_{x_i} are concatenated, then prior knowledge helps read text semantics with a MMHSA layer like the first layer in Reading. The processing formula is shown as follows:

$$O_{concat} = [O_{y_i'}; O_{x_i}], \tag{16}$$

$$O_{Interaction} = O_{concat} \cdot W^{HB}. \tag{17}$$

where W^{HB} represents the weight matrix of the hidden bottleneck layer. The bottleneck layer is properly constructed to significantly reduce the model size without degrading the network performance. The design of Interaction containing a MMHSA layer simulates the process of a teacher teaching a student to read word by word. The second cooperation work in a dual cooperative network has been achieved, and the semantics of semantic scope and text has been enhanced in this network for better label prediction.

Predicting. Finally, a softmax layer is applied to predict final labels. The processing formula is shown as follows:

$$Y = \text{Softmax}(O_{Interaction} \cdot W^{Output}). \tag{18}$$

where W^{Output} is the output weight matrix of fully connected layer.

Loss Function. We measure the performance with multi-label one-versus-all loss based on max entropy principle, which are widely used in classification taskes. Specifically, for a predicted score vector Y and a ground truth label vector y_i, the processing formula is shown as follows:

$$Loss_i(Y, y_i) = -\sum_{j=1}^{L} y_{ij} \times \log\left((1 + \exp(-Y_j))^{-1}\right)$$

$$+ (1 - y_{ij}) \times \log\left(\frac{\exp(-Y_j)}{1 + \exp(-Y_j)}\right). \tag{19}$$

4 Experiments

4.1 Datasets and Preprocessing

Datasets. Three XMTC benchmark datasets, which have rich hierarchical information and label descriptionare, used for experiments in this paper, including AmazonCat-13K [12], EURLex[1] and RCV1 [5]. Table 1 shows the statistics of three datasets.

---

[1] http://manikvarma.org/downloads/XC/XMLRepository.

Table 1. Data statistics of three XMTC datasets.

Dataset	Number of train points	Number of test points	Label dimensionality	Avg. labels per point
AmazonCat-13K	1,186,239	306,782	13,330	5.04
EURLex	15449	3865	3956	5.30
RCV1	23,149	781,265	103	3.18

Preprocessing Details. For AmazonCat-13K, we truncate each input sequence after 300 words, and label description after 4 words in the same way as Parabel [15]. Word embedding in AmazonCat-13K we use comes from AttentionXML [17]. For EURLex, we truncate each input sequence after 500 words, and each label description after 4 words. Word embedding in EURLex we use also comes from datasets. For RCV1, we truncate each input sequence after 250 words, and each label description after 16 words. Pre-trained Word2Vec [22] word embedding of 400 dimensions is used in RCV1.

The results of most these baseline methods are obtained from XMTC papers [11,14,17], and we have replicated unpublished results with original papers' codes. The word embedding training of RCV1 refers to methods [16,22]. The evaluation function implementation refers to the paper [10]. The framework of model training refers to the method [6]. The experimental code on tail labels refers to AttentionXML [17]. The implementation of MHSA refers to the paper [4], and the number of attention heads h in TReaderXML is set to 4. The initial learning rate for TReaderXML training is 0.0001. After the model converges, learning rate attenuation is used to further improve scores, and Adam [13] is used for all deep learning model training. Our experimental configuration has a GPU of RTX 2080 Ti, and 128GB memory. When duplicating AnnexML [23] on EURLex dataset, it cannot be duplicated due to memory problems.

4.2 Baselines

We compare our proposed TReaderXML to the most representative XMTC methods that address data sparsity issue including AnnexML [23], PfastreXML [9], Parabel [15], FastText [1], Bonsai [18], XML-CNN [11], and AttentionXML [17]. Table 2 compares TReaderXML with baseline methods, and the results with stars are from XMTC papers [11,14,17] directly.

The proposed TReaderXML outperforms all XMTC methods for most evaluation metrics, and for a few metrics it achieves results comparable to the current approaches. Our method TReaderXML outperforms all XMTC methods, except for being slightly worse than LightXML (P@1) on AmazonCat-13K. Compared to leading extreme classifiers, TReaderXML can up to 0.16% better in P@1 metric on RURLex. For the results of RCV1, TReaderXML has a substantial improvement at P@1. We consider that the precision of TReaderXML in the first predicting position is more accurate due to effective prior knowledge and TReaderXML remains close to existing XMTC methods in other evaluation metrics due to the small label dimensionality of RCV1.

4.3 Evaluation Metrics

Classification accuracy is evaluated according to Precision at k (P@k), normalized Discounted Cumulative Gain at k (nDCG@k) and Propensity Scored Precision at k (PSP@k) like AttentionXML [17]. refined

4.4 Ablation Study

We conduct an ablation study as shown in Table 3 to discuss proposed novel structures of a dual cooperative network in TReaderXML. In detail, we explore the effectiveness of the teacher knowledge branch and the Reading part.

Teacher Knowledge. Config. ID 0, 1 shows the effectiveness of teacher knowledge. With dynamic and fine-grained semantic scope from teacher knowledge, Config. ID 1 has improved 5.2% over Config. ID 0 without reading part.

Reading. Config. ID 2, 3, 4, 6 shows the plausibility of Reading structure. The structure of Config. ID 2 is similar to the effect of a person only reading word by word, and it cannot comprehensively understand themes of texts. The structure of Config. ID 3 is similar to the effect of a person only reading themes of texts, and it cannot carefully understand details of texts. The structure of Config. ID 4 is similar to the effect of a person reading themes of texts firstly then reading details of texts, and it is not always consistent with human reading habits. The structure of Config. ID 6 simulates the process of human reading, reading word by word to understand details of texts and reading comprehensively to understand themes of texts. It is feasible to simulate human reading with the Reading structure. Config. ID 5, 6 shows the effectiveness of residual layer. Config. ID 6 has improved 0.44% over Config. ID 5 with residual part.

4.5 Performance on Tail Labels

To evaluate performance of TReaderXML on tail labels, we discuss experiment results of tail labels on AmazonCat-13K dataset which has the most tail labels. From Table 4, we see that TReaderXML achieves SOTA effects at PSP@5, except for being slightly worse than PfastreXML [9] at PSP@1 and PSP@3. PfastreXML replaces the nDCG loss in FastXML [21] by its propensity scored variant which is unbiased and assigns higher rewards for the tail label predictions. However, it leads to a loss in prediction accuracy.

Table 2. Performance of TReaderXML and baseline methods over three datasets (The best results are highlighted in bold).

Datasets	Methods	P@1	P@3	P@5	nDCG@3	nDCG@5
AmazonCat-13K	AnnexML*	93.54%	78.37%	63.30%	87.29%	85.10%
	Parabel*	93.03%	79.16%	64.51%	87.72%	86.00%
	Bonsai*	92.98%	79.13%	64.46%	87.68%	85.92%
	PfastreXML*	91.75%	77.97%	63.68%	86.48%	84.96%
	XML-CNN*	93.26%	77.06%	61.40%	86.20%	83.43%
	AttentionXML*	95.92%	82.41%	67.31%	91.17%	89.48%
	X-Transformer*	96.70%	83.85%	68.58%	–	–
	APLC-XLNet	94.56%	79.82%	64.61%	88.74%	86.66%
	LigntXML	**96.77%**	84.02%	68.70%	–	–
	TReaderXML	96.64%	**85.57%**	**68.98%**	**93.99%**	**91.67%**
EURLex	AnnexML*	79.66%	64.94%	53.52%	68.70%	62.71%
	Parabel*	82.12%	68.91%	57.89%	72.33%	66.95%
	Bonsai*	82.30%	69.55%	58.35%	72.97%	67.48%
	PfastreXML*	73.13%	60.16%	50.54%	63.51%	58.71%
	XML-CNN*	68.01%	54.03%	43.93%	57.44%	51.83%
	AttentionXML*	87.12%	73.99%	61.92%	77.44%	71.53%
	X-Transformer*	87.22%	75.12%	62.90%	-	–
	APLC-XLNet	87.72%	74.56%	62.28%	77.90%	71.75%
	LigntXML	87.63%	75.89%	63.36%	-	–
	TReaderXML	**87.88%**	**78.07%**	**64.05%**	**80.70%**	**73.56%**
RCV1	AnnexML*	90.89%	76.48%	52.77%	–	–
	Parabel*	87.79%	64.84%	45.60%	77.01%	77.92%
	Bonsai*	85.23%	65.12%	45.89%	76.55%	77.59%
	PfastreXML*	68.82%	60.76%	43.28%	69.40%	71.24%
	XML-CNN*	93.63%	73.90%	52.16%	85.24	86.69%
	AttentionXML*	96.41%	**80.91%**	**56.38%**	**91.88%**	**92.70%**
	X-Transformer*	–	–	–	–	–
	APLC-XLNet	59.46%	43.79%	33.44%	–	–
	LigntXML	95.31%	78.40%	54.93%	–	–
	TReaderXML	**97.50%**	78.74%	54.67%	90.29%	90.94%

Table 3. Ablation study of TReaderXML on AmazonCat-13K (The best results are highlighted in bold).

Config. ID	Teacher knowledge	Reading	P@1	P@3	P@5	nDCG@3	nDCG@5
0	–	–	88.73%	69.12%	53.94%	78.78%	75.42%
1	True	–	93.93%	77.70%	58.53%	87.15%	81.79%
2	True	MMHSA+R	95.49%	83.45%	66.08%	92.00%	88.81%
3	True	MHSA+R	95.52%	83.46%	66.04%	92.03%	88.81%
4	True	MHSA+R+MMHSA	96.49%	85.44%	68.84%	93.86%	91.52%
5	True	MMHSA+MHSA	96.20%	84.89%	68.04%	93.33%	90.72%
6	True	MMHSA+R+MHSA	**96.64%**	**85.57%**	**68.98%**	**93.99%**	**91.67%**

Table 4. Performance on tail labels in AmazonCat-13K (The best results are highlighted in bold).

Methods	PSP@1	PSP@3	PSP@5
AnnexML*	49.04%	61.13%	69.64%
Parabel*	50.93%	64.00%	72.08%
Bonsai*	51.30%	64.60%	72.48%
PfastreXML*	**69.52%**	**73.22%**	75.48%
XML-CNN*	52.42%	62.83%	67.10%
AttentionXML*	53.76%	68.72%	76.38%
X-Transformer*	–	–	–
APLC-XLNet	52.22%	65.08%	71.40%
LigntXML	-	–	–
TReaderXML	57.15%	71.64%	**77.27%**

5   Conclusions

In this work, our method TReaderXML define semantic scope from teacher knowledge, which inherits the strength of hierarchical label information and meanwhile improves dynamic high level category information as semantic supplements and constraints. The proposed dual cooperative network learned semantic information in the way of people reading. Moreover, teacher knowledge can flexibly incorporate prior label information like semantic structures or descriptions.

Acknowledgements. This work was supported by the National Natural Science Foundation of China (No. 61976156 and No. 61702367), Tianjin Science and Technology Commissioner project (No. 20YDTPJC00560), the Natural Science Foundation of Tianjin (No. 19JCYBJC15300).

References

1. Armand, J., Edouard, G., Piotr, B., Matthijs, D., Herve, J., Tomas, M.: Fasttext. zip: compressing text classification models. arXiv preprint arXiv:1612.03651 (2016)
2. Ashish, V.: Attention is all you need. Adv. Neural. Inf. Process. Syst. **30**, 5998–6008 (2017)
3. Bhatia, K., Jain, H., Kar, P., Varma, M., Jain, P.: Sparse local embeddings for extreme multi-label classification. In: Advances in Neural Information Processing Systems, pp. 730–738 (2015)
4. Biqing, Z., Heng, Y., Ruyang, X., Wu, Z., Xuli, H.: Lcf: a local context focus mechanism for aspect-based sentiment classification. Appli. Sci. **9**, 3389 (2019)
5. Lewis, D.D., Yiming, Y., Rose, T.G., Fan, L.: Rcv1: a new benchmark collection for text categorization research. J. Mach. Learn. Res. **5**, 361–397 (2004)

6. Devlin, J., Chang, M.W., Lee, K., Toutanova, K.: Bert: pre-training of deep bidirectional transformers for language understanding. arXiv preprint arXiv:1810.04805 (2018)

7. Francesco, G., Stefano, S., Mario, C., Giuseppe, D.P.: Deep neural network for hierarchical extreme multi-label text classification. Appli. Soft Comput. **79**, 125–138 (2019)

8. Himanshu, J., Venkatesh, B., Bhanu, C., Manik, V.: Slice: scalable linear extreme classifiers trained on 100 million labels for related searches. In: Proceedings of the Twelfth ACM International Conference on Web Search and Data Mining, pp. 528–536 (2019)

9. Himanshu, J., Yashoteja, P., Manik, V.: Extreme multi-label loss functions for recommendation, tagging, ranking & other missing label applications. In: Acm Sigkdd International Conference on Knowledge Discovery & Data Mining, pp. 935–944 (2016)

10. Huang, X., Chen, B., Xiao, L., Jing, L.: Label-aware document representation via hybrid attention for extreme multi-label text classification. arXiv preprint arXiv:1905.10070 (2019)

11. Jingzhou, L., Wei-Cheng, C., Yuexin, W., Yiming, Y.: Deep learning for extreme multi-label text classification. In: Proceedings of the 40th International ACM SIGIR Conference on Research and Development in Information Retrieval, pp. 115–124 (2017)

12. Bhatia, K., et al.: The extreme classification repository: multi-label datasets and code (2016). http://manikvarma.org/downloads/XC/XMLRepository.html

13. Kingma, D., Ba, J.: Adam: a method for stochastic optimization. Comput. Sci. (2014)

14. Lin, X., Xin, H., Boli, C., Liping, J.: Label-specific document representation for multi-label text classification. In: Proceedings of the 2019 Conference on Empirical Methods in Natural Language Processing and the 9th International Joint Conference on Natural Language Processing, pp. 466–475 (2019)

15. Prabhu, Y., Kag, A., Harsola, S., Agrawal, R., Varma, M.: Parabel: partitioned label trees for extreme classification with application to dynamic search advertising. In: Proceedings of the 2018 World Wide Web Conference, pp. 993–1002 (2018)

16. Řehůřek, R., Sojka, P.: Software framework for topic modelling with large corpora. In: Proceedings of the LREC 2010 Workshop on New Challenges for NLP Frameworks, pp. 45–50 (2010)

17. Ronghui, Y., Zihan, Z., Ziye, W., Suyang, D., Hiroshi, M., Shanfeng, Z.: Attentionxml: label tree-based attention-aware deep model for high-performance extreme multi-label text classification. In: Advances in Neural Information Processing Systems, pp. 5820–5830 (2019)

18. Khandagale, S., Xiao, H., Babbar, R.: Bonsai: diverse and shallow trees for extreme multi-label classification. Mach. Learn. **109**(11), 2099–2119 (2020). https://doi.org/10.1007/s10994-020-05888-2

19. Wei-Cheng, C., Hsiang-Fu, Y., Kai, Z., Yiming, Y., Dhillon, I.: Taming pretrained transformers for extreme multi-label text classification. In: Proceedings of the 26th ACM SIGKDD International Conference on Knowledge Discovery & Data Mining, pp. 3163–3171 (2020)

20. Wissam, S.: Craftml, an efficient clustering-based random forest for extreme multi-label learning. In: International Conference on Machine Learning (2018)

21. Yashoteja, P., Manik, V.: Fastxml: a fast, accurate and stable tree-classifier for extreme multi-label learning. In: Proceedings of the 20th ACM SIGKDD International Conference on Knowledge Discovery and Data Mining, pp. 263–272 (2014)

22. Yoav, G., Omer, L.: word2vec explained: deriving mikolov et al'.s negative-sampling word-embedding method. arXiv preprint arXiv:1402.3722 (2014)
23. Yukihiro, T.: Annexml: approximate nearest neighbor search for extreme multi-label classification. In: The 23rd ACM SIGKDD International Conference, pp. 455–464 (2017)

MGEDR: A Molecular Graph Encoder for Drug Recommendation

Kaiyuan Shi[1], Shaowu Zhang[1], Haifeng Liu[1], Yijia Zhang[2(✉)],
and Hongfei Lin[1]

[1] School of Computer Science and Technology, Dalian University of Technology,
Dalian, China
{Dutirsky,liuhaifeng}@mail.dlut.edu.cn, {zhangsw,hflin}@dlut.edu.cn
[2] School of Information Science and Technology, Dalian Maritime University,
Dalian, China
zhangyijia@dlmu.edu.cn

Abstract. Recently, drug recommendation tasks have been widely accepted in intelligent healthcare. Most of the existing methods utilize patients' electronic health records (EHRs) to achieve medical prediction. However, existing algorithms neglect the description of the patient's health status, which makes it difficult to adapt to the dynamic patients' condition. And they ignore the intrinsic encoding of drug molecular structure, resulting in the weak performance of drug recommendation. To fill the gap, we propose a molecular graph encoder for drug recommendation named *MGEDR* to capture the genuine health status of patients. Furthermore, We encode the drug molecular graph and functional groups separately to obtain subtle drug representation. And we design the degree encoder and functional groups encoder to seize the intrinsic features of the molecule efficaciously. Our experimental results show that our proposed *MGEDR* framework performs significantly better than state-of-the-art baseline methods.

Keywords: Molecular graph encoder · Drug recommendation · Graph neural network

1 Introduction

Intelligent healthcare has been widely applied to improve the quality and efficiency of patients' medical treatment. With the accumulation of data from EHRs [3], it has become possible to utilize patients' electronic medical data to provide drug recommendations. Drug recommendations relieve the pressure of medical care, while also assisting doctors in diagnosis.

Related researchers utilize the patients' EHRs to uncover their real needs of medication. Existing studies [11,12] portray patient representation based on diagnosis and procedures records, neglecting major physiological indicators of patients. However, different patients have significant differences in the condition

© Springer Nature Switzerland AG 2022
W. Lu et al. (Eds.) NLPCC 2022, LNCS 13552, pp. 98–109, 2022.
https://doi.org/10.1007/978-3-031-17189-5_8

and physiological level, and the pivotal physiological indexes of patients with illness have significant changes in the onset period. The complexity and variability of physiological indicators bring new challenges to patient representation.

Also drug molecules play an essential role in disease treatment, and the chemical properties of a drug are determined by its molecular structure. However, most of the current studies [4,13] only learn drug representations based on patient-drug interactions, ignoring the information of drug molecules. Even though some exploratory studies [5] attempt to capture drug molecule representation in drug recommendation, the molecules of different drugs have different chemical properties whose structure is actually complex and variable. It is urgent to design an effective molecular representation model.

Considering the limitations of existing solutions, we propose our *MGEDR* model. First, to exactly capture the patients' health status, we introduce patients' sign data such as blood pressure, heart rate, and body temperature. Then we select LSTM to learn the changes in patients' health state. Next, we divide the molecules into different functional groups and design a linear mask layer to find the dependence of patients on functional groups. In particular, to improve the quality of molecular representation, we propose degree encoder and distance encoder. Finally, we provide drug recommendations for patients from the perspective of physiological indicators and drug molecules. Our contributions can be summarized as follows:

- We explore the feasibility of modeling the physiological status of patients. Then we propose Patient Encoder to effectively learn the physiological health representation.
- We propose a new molecular graph encoding method, which utilizes the degree and average distance information to strengthen the overall characteristics of the graph.
- We utilize the functional groups encoding of drugs to gain patients' dependence on special functional groups. Experiments show that this method of combining the molecular graph with functional groups is very effective.

2   Related Works

2.1   Drug Recommendation

Drug recommendation is an important task in intelligent healthcare. Providing timely and accurate drug therapy is also the main direction of modern medical efforts. Many researchers have used the corresponding recommendation algorithm to solve this problem. Zhang et al. [14] adopt RNN as a decoder to build label dependencies and model the entire drug prediction problem as a continuous decision-making problem. Liu et al. [9] propose a self-supervised heterogeneous graph neural network to encode drugs, targets and disease, so as to achieve drug recommendation for specific diseases. Zheng et al. [16] design a drug package recommendation framework with two variants, which can integrate drug interaction information based on graph induction. They propose to utilize a mask layer to capture the impact of patient condition on the drug package representation. Despite the achievements of existing methods, they still do not adequately take patient-level information into account. Hence, we propose a patient encoder that integrates a patient's existing vital sign status and historical records.

2.2   Molecular Graph Representation

Molecular graph representation is a common task in medical research. Recently, there has been a gradual attempt to enrich the feature representation of drugs with the structural encoding of drug molecules. Liu et al. [6] use the consistency of drug 2D molecular graph and 3D molecular graph for self-supervised learning, and they effectively learn a binary molecular graph encoder. Yang et al. [12] raise dual molecular encoders to capture global and local molecule patterns. The final representation is obtained by element-wise integration of the global and local encoded embeddings. Zhang et al. [15] segment the drugs according to the functional groups, and they encode the segmented parts separately, so as to achieve the description of drug function and structure as comprehensively as possible. However, traditional graph representations still cannot effectively cope with the complex and variable structure of drug molecule graphs. Therefore, we design the degree encoder and distance encoder, then embed them into the graph information aggregation process to effectively enhance the graph representation.

3   Problem Formulation

Formally, each patient can be represented as a sequence of multivariate observations: $X_i = [C_i, H_i]$ where C_i is the current status of vital signs in patients; H_i is historical diagnosis, procedures and medicine information of patients. Furthermore, $C_i = [C_p^i, C_r^i, C_b^i]$ where C_p^i, C_r^i, C_b^i are blood pressure, heart rate and body temperature vectors. And $H_i = [H_d^i, H_p^i, H_m^i]$ where $H_d^i \in \{0,1\}^{|D|}$, $H_p^i \in \{0,1\}^{|P|}$, $H_m^i \in \{0,1\}^{|M|}$ are multi-hot diagnosis, procedures and medicine vectors. D, P, M are the corresponding element sets.

We are committed to recommending accurate drugs for patients based on their status information. Specifically, we aim at learning a drug recommendation function f which given patient information X_i, the function can generate multi-label output $Y_i = \{0,1\}^{|M|}$. The formula can be summarized as follows.

$$Y_i = f(C_p^i, C_r^i, C_b^i; H_d^i, H_p^i; H_m^i)|_{i=1}^N \tag{1}$$

where N is the total number of patients.

4   The MGEDR Model

To characterize the physiological indicators of patients and drug molecules, we propose our $MGEDR$ model. As shown in Fig. 1, the model is divided into four components: Patient Encoder, Medicine Encoder, Functional groups Encoder and Medicine Representation. We will introduce each component in details.

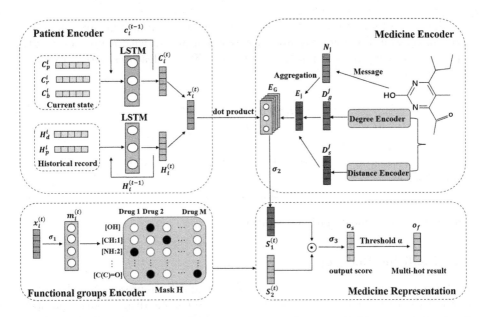

Fig. 1. The *MGEDR* model. For each patient we first encode his current state and historical record information by LSTM to learn a patient representation $x_i^{(t)}$. Then this patient embedding will match with medicine embedding matrix E_G and Functional embedding $m_i^{(t)}$ to generate two score vectors $S_1^{(t)}$ and $S_2^{(t)}$. Finally, we combine these two vectors and then select threshold α to obtain the final drug recommendation results O_f.

4.1 Patient Encoder

As mentioned before, each patient can be represented as $X_i = [C_i, H_i]$. To better encode the patients' state information, we set up two parts separately for the current state C_i and historical record H_i. For $C_i = [C_p^i, C_r^i, C_b^i]$, each component represents a recent state of vital signs of patients. We expect to include the information of the whole state into the consideration of characteristics, so here we choose LSTM to model the current state.

$$C_i^{(t)} = \{C_p^{i\,(t)}, C_r^{i\,(t)}, C_b^{i\,(t)}\} = \{LSTM[C_p^{i\,(0)}, \cdots, C_p^{i\,(t-1)}],$$
$$LSTM[C_r^{i\,(0)}, \cdots, C_r^{i\,(t-1)}], \qquad (2)$$
$$LSTM[C_b^{i\,(0)}, \cdots, C_b^{i\,(t-1)}]\}$$

For $H_i = [H_d^i, H_p^i, H_m^i]$, we design two learnable embedding matrices $W_d, W_p \in R^{|*| \times dim}$, where $*$ means D or P and dim is the dimension of embedding space.

$$H_{wd}^{i\,(t)} = W_d H_d^{i\,(t)} \qquad (3)$$

$$H_{wp}^{i\,(t)} = W_p H_p^{i\,(t)} \qquad (4)$$

The chronology of diagnosis and procedures is essential information in the recommendation task. For example, we expect a person with acute pharyngitis and a person with chronic pharyngitis to get different features here, so we also use LSTM to encode $H_{wd}^{i}{}^{(t)}$ and $H_{wp}^{i}{}^{(t)}$.

$$
\begin{aligned}
H_i^{(t)} = \{ & LSTM[H_{wd}^{(0)}, \cdots, H_{wd}^{(t-1)}], \\
& LSTM[H_{wp}^{(0)}, \cdots, H_{wp}^{(t-1)}] \}
\end{aligned}
\tag{5}
$$

Then we integrate the two parts of information to get the final patient representation $x_i^{(t)}$.

$$
x_i^{(t)} = cat(C_i^{(t)}, H_i^{(t)})
\tag{6}
$$

where cat is the concatenation operation.

4.2   Medicine Encoder

Each drug consists of atoms and functional groups. To represent the characteristics of the drug molecular graph, we decide to encode drug atoms separately from functional groups. Firstly, without considering the particularity of functional groups, we can completely model the drug as a graph composed of nodes and edges. Then we record the atoms that appear in all drugs and make an atomic set $S = \{a_j\}$. For each atom we can design an atom embedding vector $N_j \in R^{1 \times dim}$. Therefore, for a drug contains atoms $a_0, a_1 \cdots a_n$, we can easily obtain its initialized embedding $E = (N_0, N_1 \cdots N_n)$. Next, we propose two new graph-based encoding methods, so that the graph-neural network structure can more effectively grasp the characteristic information of drugs.

Degree Encoder. Different atoms in a drug molecule have different chemical properties, and even the same atoms should be characterized differently because of the different number of edges they connect. For this purpose, we propose Degree Encoder. First, we calculate the degree information of each node based on the molecular structure map of the drugs. Then, we design a learnable degree embedding table $E_d \in R^{A \times dim}$ where A is the largest degree of all nodes. With this design, for each atom j, we can find the corresponding degree embedding D_g^j in the table.

Distance Encoder. In a drug molecule, the distances between an atom with other atoms can reflect its position in the graph. Intuitively, the atom in the center is closer to other atoms than that in the edge. We expect to take this particularity into account in the message update process of a graph. Therefore, we propose a concept of average distance D_s between nodes. For any atom j, we calculate its shortest path distance to all nodes in the drug molecule. Afterwards, these distances are averaged to obtain the average distance of each node. The specific calculation formula can be described as follows:

$$D_s = [\frac{1}{K} \sum_{j=1}^{K} d_j] \tag{7}$$

where K is the number of atoms in a drug and d_j means distance of current atom from another atom j, $[*]$ means rounding operation. Then, similar with degree encoder, we also design a learnable distance embedding table $E_s \in R^{B \times dim}$ where B is the longest average distance. Therefore, we can get distance embedding D_s^j from atom j.

Since the molecular structure is similar to the graph structure, we combine our degree embedding and distance embedding as complements to the feature representation of the node.

$$N_j^{(l)} = \sum_{A_{ij}=1} Message(N_i^{(l-1)}, N_j^{(l-1)}, W^{(l-1)}) \tag{8}$$

$$E_j^{(l)} = N_j^{(l)} + D_g^{j\,(l)} + D_s^{j\,(l)} \tag{9}$$

where l is the layer index, A_{ij} is the adjacency matrix of a drug, $N_j^{(l)}$ is the node feature of the current atom, $N_i^{(l)}$ is the feature of adjacent nodes, $W^{(l)}$ is the layer-wise parameter matrix, $D_g^{j\,(l)}$ and $D_s^{j\,(l)}$ are degree and distance embedding of atom j. $E_j^{(l)}$ is the encoded messages aggregated by the above embeddings. Finally, we utilize the readout layer to integrate the entire drug embedding.

$$E_G = Readout(E_j^L | j = 0, 1 \cdots n) \tag{10}$$

where L is the number of the layers.

4.3   Functional Groups Encoder

Functional groups play a very important role in organic molecules. It can be said that most of the properties of drug molecules are determined by their special functional groups. Drugs with similar molecular structures may have approximate embedding vectors in the Medicine Encoder. Therefore, we design Functional groups Encoder to capture differences due to the specificity of functional groups.

Based on the SMILE string of the drug, we use the BRICS method [2] to obtain its functional group substructure. After partitioning the functional group structure of all drugs, we obtain a set F which covers all functional group substructures. To fully establish the association of drugs with the functional group, we construct an adjacency mask matrix $H \in R^{|F| \times M}$, where $H_{ij}=1$ indicates that drug j contains substructure i and $|F|$ is the length of set F.

The adjacency mask matrix H represents the unique characteristics of each drug. We expect to take the functional groups into account in the training process. Here we first map the patient's feature vector to the functional groups' feature space by Multi-Layer Perceptron (MLP).

$$m_i^{(t)} = \sigma_1(MLP(x_i^{(t)})) \tag{11}$$

where σ_1 is the sigmoid function. Thus, $m_i^{(t)}$ can be viewed as the patient's health characteristics that encompass information about functional groups. We then propose a linear mask layer for aggregating drug information with the resulting feature information.

$$S_2^{(t)} = Linear(m_i^{(t)}, W \odot H) \tag{12}$$

where $\odot$ is element-wise product operating. With the addition of the mask matrix H, the output of the linear layer $S_2^{(t)}$ contains a recommended representation of the drug rich in information about the structure of the functional group.

4.4   Medicine Representation

In this component, we dot product the patient feature vector $x_i^{(t)}$ with the feature encoding of each drug E_G. Then we adopt a sigmoid function σ_2 to obtain the drug-patient matching results $S_1^{(t)}$.

$$S_1^{(t)} = \sigma_2(E_g x_i^{(t)}) \tag{13}$$

We take the patients' feature information and match it with the outputs of our designed Medicine Encoder and Functional groups Encoder respectively. Thus we obtain two score matrices. Next, we utilize the element-by-element dot product approach to combine two matrices. Finally, we set an artificial threshold α to get the final multi-hot result vector O_f.

$$O_s = \sigma_3(S_1^{(t)} \odot S_2^{(t)}) \tag{14}$$

$$O_f = Threshold(O_s) \tag{15}$$

where σ_3 is the sigmoid function. $Threshold$ represents the threshold operation.

4.5   Optimization

To optimize our recommendation model, we consider the drug recommendation task as a multi-label binary classification problem. We adopt Binary CrossEntropy (BCE) loss.

$$L_{BCE} = -\sum_{i=1}^{M} O_t log(O_f) + (1 - O_t)log(1 - O_f) \tag{16}$$

where M is the total number of drugs. O_t is the true multi-hot label of drug recommendation and O_f is final result of our $MGEDR$ model.

To enhance the robustness of the result, we adopt multi-label margin loss L_{Multi} to make ground truth labels at least 1 margin larger than others.

$$L_{Multi} = \sum_{i,j:O_f^i=1, O_f^j=0} \frac{max(0, 1 - (O_f^i - O_f^j))}{M} \tag{17}$$

where i, j means i-th and j-th element. To training our model's parameters, we utilize a hyperparameter β, to construct our loss function L.

$$L = \beta L_{BCE} + (1 - \beta) L_{Multi} \qquad (18)$$

5 Experiments

5.1 Dataset and Metrics

In this experiment, we adopt the MIMIC-III dataset [7], which contains information related to patients admitted to intensive care units in large tertiary care hospitals. The data includes information on patient vital signs, medications used, procedure codes, diagnosis codes, length of stay, etc.

Throughout the experiment, the patient vital sign data C_i comes from the table CHARTEVENTS. We collect information on the lastest 100 detection to characterize the patient's current vital status. As for H_i, we used the same data processing as this paper [12]. Due to space limitations, we do not present details here. The statistic information is shown in Table 1.

Table 1. Statistics of the data.

Items	Size
# of patients	3,214
diag./prod./med. space size	1,804/1,009/126
pres./rate./tem. space size	100
avg./max# of diagnoses	12.27/128
avg./max# of procedures	3.60/42
avg./max# of medicines	12.42/58
avg./max# of blood pressure	96.14/133 (mmHg)
avg./max# of heart rate	87.12/140 (num/min)
avg./max# of body temperature	97.66 /103 (°F)
total# of function groups	491

We split the dataset into the training set, validation set, and test set at a ratio of 4:1:1. For embedding tables, we use $dim = 100$ as our embedding size. The dropout rate of the LSTM model is 0.5 and the learning rate of the experiment is $1e^{-5}$. The threshold α we choose to generate the final output is selected as 0.55. To evaluate the performance of $MGEDR$, here we choose three metrics to test the result of our prediction: Jaccard coefficients [11], F1 score, and Precision Recall Area Under Curve (PRAUC).

5.2   Results

In this paper, we compare *MGEDR* with machine learning methods Logistic Regression (LR) and Ensemble Classifier Chain (ECC) [10] and recent state-of-the-art models RETAIN [1], DMNC [8], GAMENet [11] and SafeDrug [12]. The results of our model and other baselines are shown in Table 2.

Table 2. Performance comparison of different methods.

Methods	Jaccard	F1	PRAUC
LR	0.4865	0.6434	0.7509
ECC	0.4996	0.6569	0.6844
RETAIN	0.4887	0.6481	0.7556
DMNC	0.4864	0.6529	0.7580
GAMENet	0.5067	0.6626	0.7631
SafeDrug	0.5213	0.6767	0.7647
$MGEDR_M$	0.5315	0.6833	0.7762
$MGEDR_F$	0.5264	0.6849	0.7811
$MGEDR$	**0.5369**	**0.6885**	**0.7837**

It has been shown that our model achieves the best results in all metrics. To test the influence between the different modules, we design $MGEDR_M$ which only contains Medicine Encoder and $MGEDR_F$ which only contains Functional groups Encoder. It is worth noting that our two submodules still have improvement compared to the other baseline models. The Medicine Encoder characterizes the overall molecular structure of the drug in detail. The Functional groups Encoder captures the internal information in the molecule. Therefore, Our model better captures the dependence of patients on drug molecular structure and functional groups, so as to achieve more accurate recommendation results.

5.3   Ablations

To further examine the necessary for our improvements, we test the effectiveness of introducing patient health data. Then we verify the advancement of degree encoder and distance encoder in molecular graph representation. Moreover, we test the performance of the hyperparameter α and β.

Effects of Health Data. We introduce the patient health data into three different models and embed them into the model for feature encoding in the same way. The results are in Fig 2.

Results show that the introduction of patient health data improves the effect of the model very well. The vital signs of patients are important manifestations at the patient level. The description of vital signs data can effectively enhance the patients' feature representation. In this way, the model can respond to changes in patients' vital signs, thereby improving the selection of drugs.

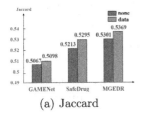 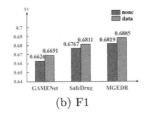 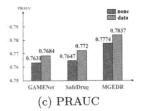

(a) Jaccard   (b) F1   (c) PRAUC

Fig. 2. Effects of health data.

Effects of Degree and Distance Encoder. To prove the effectiveness of our proposed encoder in molecular graph representation, we conducted a destructuring study on our $MGEDR$ model. The results are shown in Table 3. $MGEDR_{DG}$ is a variant model of $MGEDR$ which contains only Degree Encoder in the module Medicine Encoder. $MGEDR_{DS}$ is a variant model of $MGEDR$ which contains only Distance Encoder in the module Medicine Encoder. $MGEDR_{NO}$ is a blank control group.

Table 3. Effects of degree and distance encoder.

Methods	Jaccard	F1	PRAUC
$MGEDR_{DG}$	0.5313	**0.6853**	**0.7815**
$MGEDR_{DS}$	**0.5347**	0.6822	0.7800
$MGEDR_{NO}$	0.5295	0.6818	0.7772

Results show that both of the two encoders play well in our model. In the drug molecular graph, degree can reflect the connection structure of an atom, and the encoding of degree characteristics can effectively improve the node representation of atoms. In addition, the distance between an atom and other atoms in the molecular graph can reflect its position and importance in the whole molecular graph. Distance encoding can also effectively enhance the representation of atoms in a molecular graph.

Effects of the Hyperparameter. α To explore the influence of the artificial hyperparameter α, We test the performance of the model at different thresholds. In this experiment, We change its value at a step of 0.05, the results are shown in Fig. 3.

In our model, we generate multi-hot result by the threshold α. Specifically, The element is set to 1 when its value exceeds α, else it is set to 0. Results show when α gets 0.55, our model reaches the best performance. It is indicated when the threshold is 0. 55, the positive label and others have the most obvious difference. When α is smaller than 0.55, the value of PRAUC is not stable which indicates that too more negative labels are set to 1. Therefore, we choose $\alpha = 0.55$ as the final setting.

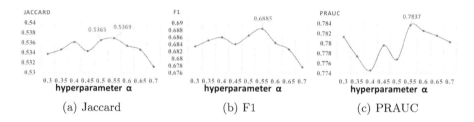

(a) Jaccard   (b) F1   (c) PRAUC

Fig. 3. Effects of the hyperparameter α.

Effects of the Hyperparameter. β To verify the influence of the parameter β on the model, We test its different weight combinations in our loss function. In this experiment, We change its value at a step of 0.1, the results are shown in Fig 4.

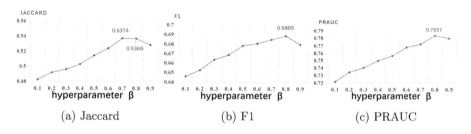

(a) Jaccard   (b) F1   (c) PRAUC

Fig. 4. Effects of the hyperparameter β.

When the parameter β is less than 0.8, the increase of weight coefficient makes the model more inclined to improve the accuracy of the results. When the beta value exceeds 0.8, the model cannot guarantee at least one margin between the real label and other labels, which reduces the stability of the model. Therefore, we choose $\beta = 0.8$ as the final setting.

6   Conclusion

In this paper, we propose $MGEDR$ model to achieve drug recommendation. For the first time, we verified the feasibility of introducing patient vital signs data. We propose a drug recommendation model based on molecular graph encoding, and prove that molecular encoding is conducive to improve performance. In future work, we will further explore the impact of drug-drug interactions on patients to further enhance the performance of the model.

Acknowledgment. This work is supported by grant from the Natural Science Foundation of China (No. 62072070).

References

1. Choi, E., Bahadori, M.T., Sun, J., Kulas, J., Schuetz, A., Stewart, W.: Retain: an interpretable predictive model for healthcare using reverse time attention mechanism. In: Advances in Neural Information Processing Systems, vol. 29 (2016)
2. Degen, J., Wegscheid-Gerlach, C., Zaliani, A., Rarey, M.: On the art of compiling and using'drug-like'chemical fragment spaces. ChemMedChem Chem. Enabling Drug Dis. **3**(10), 1503–1507 (2008)
3. Garets, D., Davis, M.: Electronic medical records vs. electronic health records: yes, there is a difference. Policy white paper. Chicago, HIMSS Analytics pp. 1–14 (2006)
4. He, X., Folkman, L., Borgwardt, K.: Kernelized rank learning for personalized drug recommendation. Bioinformatics **34**(16), 2808–2816 (2018)
5. Huang, K., Fu, T., Glass, L.M., Zitnik, M., Xiao, C., Sun, J.: Deeppurpose: a deep learning library for drug-target interaction prediction. Bioinformatics **36**(22–23), 5545–5547 (2020)
6. Jing, B., Xiang, Y., Chen, X., Chen, Y., Tong, H.: Graph-mvp: multi-view prototypical contrastive learning for multiplex graphs. arXiv preprint arXiv:2109.03560 (2021)
7. Johnson, A.E., et al.: Mimic-iii, a freely accessible critical care database. Sci. Data **3**(1), 1–9 (2016)
8. Le, H., Tran, T., Venkatesh, S.: Dual memory neural computer for asynchronous two-view sequential learning. In: Proceedings of the 24th ACM SIGKDD International Conference on Knowledge Discovery & Data Mining, pp. 1637–1645 (2018)
9. Liu, H., Lin, H., Shen, C., Yang, Z., Wang, J., Yang, L.: Self-supervised learning with heterogeneous graph neural network for covid-19 drug recommendation. In: 2021 IEEE International Conference on Bioinformatics and Biomedicine (BIBM), pp. 1412–1417. IEEE (2021)
10. Read, J., Pfahringer, B., Holmes, G., Frank, E.: Classifier chains for multi-label classification. Mach. Learn. **85**(3), 333–359 (2011)
11. Shang, J., Xiao, C., Ma, T., Li, H., Sun, J.: Gamenet: graph augmented memory networks for recommending medication combination. In: Proceedings of the AAAI Conference on Artificial Intelligence, vol. 33, pp. 1126–1133 (2019)
12. Yang, C., Xiao, C., Ma, F., Glass, L., Sun, J.: Safedrug: dual molecular graph encoders for safe drug recommendations. arXiv preprint arXiv:2105.02711 (2021)
13. Zhang, Y., Zhang, D., Hassan, M.M., Alamri, A., Peng, L.: Cadre: Cloud-assisted drug recommendation service for online pharmacies. Mobile Netw. Appli. **20**(3), 348–355 (2015)
14. Zhang, Y., Chen, R., Tang, J., Stewart, W.F., Sun, J.: Leap: learning to prescribe effective and safe treatment combinations for multimorbidity. In: Proceedings of the 23rd ACM SIGKDD International Conference on Knowledge Discovery and Data Mining, pp. 1315–1324 (2017)
15. Zhang, Z., Guan, J., Zhou, S.: Fragat: a fragment-oriented multi-scale graph attention model for molecular property prediction. Bioinformatics **37**(18), 2981–2987 (2021)
16. Zheng, Z., et al.: Interaction-aware drug package recommendation via policy gradient. ACM Trans. Inf. Syst. (TOIS) (2022)

Student Workshop (Poster)

Semi-supervised Protein-Protein Interactions Extraction Method Based on Label Propagation and Sentence Embedding

Zhan Tang, Xuchao Guo, Lei Diao, Zhao Bai, Longhe Wang, and Lin Li[✉]

China Agricultural University, Beijing 100083, China
lilincau@126.com

Abstract. Protein-protein interaction (PPI) plays an extremely vital role in almost all life activities. The study of PPI has always been an important issue in the field of biomedicine. Extracting PPI information from the literature can provide meaningful references for related research. In order to build an automated PPI extraction system, labeled corpora are required. However, labeled corpora are very limited, and annotating corpora is a time-consuming, labor-intensive, and costly task. On the contrary, the amount of unlabeled data is huge and it's easy to obtain, so it is of great significance to apply semi-supervised learning to PPI extraction. Existing semi-supervised methods have two limitations: 1) cannot make full use of the information in unlabeled data. 2) need to rely on text augmentation methods such as back-translation. Therefore, a semi-supervised PPI extraction method based on label propagation and sentence embedding is proposed in this work. It represents text as numerical features through sentence embedding, and then assigns pseudo-labels to unlabeled data through label propagation, thereby completing semi-supervised training. Experiments on public datasets for PPI extraction show that the proposed method can achieve competitive performance with only a small amount of labeled data. Specifically, when the number of labeled data is 250, it can achieve F1 scores of 36.8% and 53.4% on AIMed and BioInfer, respectively.

Keywords: Protein-protein interaction · Semi-supervised learning · Label propagation · Sentence embedding

1 Introduction

Protein-protein interaction (PPI) is one of the main mechanisms by which proteins exert their biological functions. It plays an important role in almost all life activities. The study of PPI will help advance various related work in the field of biomedicine [1, 2]. Many PPI information exists in biomedical literature in unstructured form. However, with the publication of a large number of PPI-related papers, manual extraction of PPI becomes time-consuming and laborious. Therefore, how to automatically extract PPI from biomedical literature has attracted the attention of many researchers [3].

© Springer Nature Switzerland AG 2022
W. Lu et al. (Eds.) NLPCC 2022, LNCS 13552, pp. 113–121, 2022.
https://doi.org/10.1007/978-3-031-17189-5_9

In order to facilitate the research of PPI extraction, a series of hand-annotated public datasets are constructed, mainly including AIMed [4], BioInfer [5], HPRD50 [6], IEPA [7], and LLL [8]. Recently, deep learning-based methods have made effective progress on PPI extraction. It mainly includes three categories: methods based on convolutional neural network (CNN) [9–13], long short-term memory (LSTM) [14–16] and Transformer [17, 18]. These methods all use a supervised learning approach and require a large amount of human-labeled data. However, for texts in the biomedical field, annotating training data requires professionals with background knowledge and has a very high labor cost. Therefore, there are only a few labeled datasets, but unlabeled data is relatively easy to obtain. In order to make full use of a large amount of unlabeled data, it is of great significance to apply semi-supervised learning (SSL) methods to PPI extraction.

In PPI extraction, the protein named entities in the text are usually replaced with generic entity names to increase the generalization: "PROTEIN1", "PROTEIN2" or "PROTEIN", where "PROTEIN1" and "PROTEIN2" are the target pair of interest, and "PROTEIN" stands for other protein named entities. It makes back-translation unsuitable for text augmentation because the meaning will change significantly after back-translation. Moreover, some texts are short and complex in sentence structure. If the word replacement method [19] is used for text augmentation, the meaning will also change greatly.

To address these problems, a semi-supervised PPI extraction method based on label propagation [20] and sentence embedding is proposed in this work. Firstly, BioBERT [17] is used to represent both labeled and unlabeled text as sentence embedding vectors, and then assign pseudo-labels to unlabeled text through label propagation. Finally, labeled data and unlabeled data with pseudo-labels are used to train the classification model. Experiments on two large-scale PPI extraction public datasets show that the proposed method can achieve better performance than existing methods.

2   Related Work

In previous work, [21] and [22] explored semi-supervised methods based on machine learning and achieved satisfactory results. [23] proposed a semi-supervised learning method based on the LSTM network, which first trains the model with unlabeled data, and then fine-tunes the pre-trained model with labeled data. [24] proposed a deep learning semi-supervised PPI extraction method based on variational autoencoder (VAE), and applied semi-supervised learning to the well-performing deep learning-based PPI extraction model. It uses a multi-layer CNN as the classifier, and the combination of LSTM and CNN is used as the encoder and decoder, which greatly improves the performance of semi-supervised PPI extraction. In recent years, semi-supervised text classification methods for deep learning have made great progress [25–27]. However, these methods all need to use back-translation [28] to construct the augmented text.

3 Methods

3.1 Problem Formulation

Let $\{x_1, \ldots, x_l\} \in X_L$ be the labeled data, and $\{y_1, \ldots, y_l\} \in \{1, \ldots, c\}$ is the label set corresponding to X_L, Let $\{x_{l+1}, \ldots, x_n\} \in X_U$ be the unlabeled dataset., where c is the number of categories. The goal is to find a parameterized function $f_\theta : X \to Y$, which can assign predicted labels to both X_L and X_U.

3.2 Overall Workflow

The overall workflow of the proposed method is shown in Fig. 1.

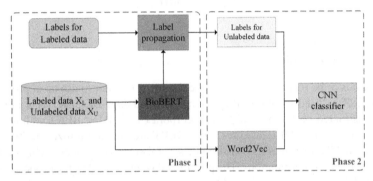

Fig. 1. Over workflow

Firstly, labeled text and unlabeled text are represented as sentence embedding vectors with BioBERT. Then pseudo-labels are assigned to unlabeled data through label propagation using the combination of labeled text and its labels. Finally, the labeled data and unlabeled data are sent to the CNN classifier for training. This method can not only use the feature information of unlabeled data, but also make full use of the features and label information of labeled data and does not need to use back-translation and other methods for text augmentations.

3.3 Label Propagation

Label propagation is a graph-based semi-supervised learning technique by constructing a graph where the weight of each edge represents the similarity between two nodes, and then propagating the labels of the labeled data to the unlabeled data [20]. Define the similarity matrix $W \in R^{n \times n}$:

$$W_{ij} = \begin{cases} exp\left(\left\|-x_i - x_j\right\|^2 / 2\sigma^2\right), & i \neq j \\ 0, & i = j \end{cases} \tag{1}$$

where σ is a hyperparameter. Define the label matrix $Y \in R^{n \times c}$:

$$Y_{ij} = \begin{cases} 1, x_i \in X_L \wedge y_i = j \\ 0, otherwise \end{cases} \qquad (2)$$

Let $S = D^{-1/2}WD^{-1/2}$, where D is a diagonal matrix, and the value of D_{ii} is the sum of the i-th row of W. The matrix F is used to predict labels for unlabeled data, as follows:

$$F = (I - \alpha S)^{-1}Y \qquad (3)$$

where α is a hyperparameter. For an unlabeled sample $x_i \in X_U$, its pseudo-label is:

$$\hat{y}_i = \underset{j}{\arg max} F_{ij} \qquad (4)$$

3.4 Sentence Embedding

The text needs to be represented as numerical vectors in order to use label propagation, and BioBERT is used to obtain the sentence embedding. BioBERT is a pre-trained weight constructed on biomedical-related corpora by applying BERT architecture, so it is more suitable for PPI-related text. The BERT architecture utilizes multiple layers of bidirectional Transformers, consisting of several stacked encoders, which can learn deep bidirectional representations. The pre-trained weights used by the proposed method are BioBERT-Base v1.1 (+PubMed 1M) published by DMIS LAB (https://dmis.korea.ac.kr/). It is important to note that BioBERT pre-trained weights are only used to generate sentence embeddings for label propagation, and training is only performed on subsequent neural network classifiers, which greatly reduces training costs.

The Transformer is mainly composed of multi-head attention and feed-forward [29].The extracted features are obtained after multi-layer Transformer operations:

$$H = (h_0, h_1, \cdots, h_{n-1}) \qquad (5)$$

where h_0 is the vector corresponding to the category identifier [CLS] token. It is regarded as sentence embedding to represent the whole text.

The text is represented as tokens by the BERT tokenizer, and then the tokens are fed into the BioBERT pre-trained weights to calculate its output, and the output h_0 corresponding to [CLS] is obtained as the sentence embedding. This method can better capture the context information compared with obtaining the average word vector to represent the sentence embedding.

3.5 CNN Classifier

Considering the generality of the CNN model and its effectiveness in PPI extraction, a basic CNN network is used as a classifier to verify the effectiveness of the proposed semi-supervised learning method, and its structure is shown in Fig. 2.

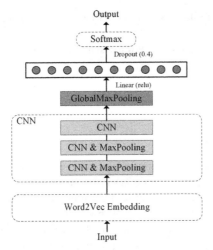

Fig. 2. Basic CNN classifier

It uses three layers of convolutional and max-pooling structures with a window size of 3 for stacking, and the hidden layer unit size is set to 128. Dropout [30] is used for regularization after the fully connected layer, and the drop rate is set to 0.4. The softmax function is used to output the binary classification probability.

Using word2vec as word embedding representation, on the one hand, is because the computational cost of fine-tuning word2vec embeddings is extremely low, and on the other hand, it can be compared with existing methods.

4 Results

4.1 Datasets and Preprocessing

Various institutions provide a series of standard PPI extraction corpora to facilitate the majority of researchers to study PPI extraction. In existing research, AIMed [4], and BioInfer [5] are widely used and have a large sample size. Only BioInfer and AIMed are used because the other three public datasets (HPRD50, IEPA and LLL) have too few samples (433, 817 and 330 respectively) to conduct effective experiments. Some annotation differences in the AIMed and BioInfer corpora are processed following the principle of effective length. After the annotation is completed, samples that do not contain PROTEIN1 and PROTEIN2 at the same time are deleted. After preprocessing, the statistics of each corpus are shown in Table 1.

Generally, labeled, unlabeled, validation, and test set are required for semi-supervised experiments. For both datasets, 10% were randomly selected as the test set, and another 10% were selected as the validation set. The number of labeled sets is selected as 250, 500, 1000, and 4000, and the rest are used as unlabeled sets.

Table 1. Statistics of PPI extraction corpora

Corpus	Number of samples	Positive samples	Negative samples	Ratio
AIMed	5669	995	4674	0.21
BioInfer	10090	2425	7665	0.32

4.2 Experimental Results

We used TensorFlow and Keras to implement our methods under the Windows 10 environment and trained them on a single NVIDIA GPU with the Adam optimizers. The F1 score is used as the evaluation metric. Learning rate and batch size are set to $1e-4$ and 128, respectively. After training for 30 epochs, the model with the highest F1 score on the validation set is used for evaluation on the final test set. Comparison with basic CNN without semi-supervised learning on both datasets, and existing semi-supervised PPI extraction methods [23, 24] on BioInfer. Hyperparameters are also tuned on the validation set, for AIMed, set $\sigma = 5, \alpha = 0.5$, and for BioInfer, ser $\sigma = 5, \alpha = 0.2$. The experimental results are shown in Table 2.

Table 2. F1 scores (%) with different methods and different numbers of labeled data

Datasets	Methods	Number of labeled data				
		250	500	1000	2000	4000
AIMed	Basic CNN	29.5	31.6	34.8	42.0	52.8
	LPSE	36.8	37.2	42.5	43.9	53.5
BioInfer	Basic CNN	44.8	49.1	52.0	55.5	62.1
	SA-LSTM	50.6	53.3	55.8	58.3	63.3
	Semi-Supervised VAE	52.1	54.4	56.3	58.7	62.2
	LPSE	53.4	55.3	56.5	60.5	67.7

It can be seen from Table 2 that the proposed LPSE method achieves the highest F1 scores for different numbers of labeled data, both for AIMed and BioInfer. The improvement is more obvious when the number of labeled data is small. When the number of labeled data is 250, the F1 score of the proposed LPSE method improves by 7.3 percentage points compared to using basic CNN on AIMed, and 8.6 percentage points on BioInfer. It demonstrates the effectiveness of semi-supervised learning to improve performance with unlabeled data. Compared with the existing semi-supervised PPI extraction methods SA-LSTM and Semi-Supervised VAE, the proposed LPSE method achieves higher F1 scores with different numbers of labeled data, which illustrates the effectiveness of using sentence embeddings built on BioBERT to perform label propagation.

4.3   Hyperparameter Analysis

Experiments were conducted with different α values to explore the effect of hyperparameter α on model performance. When setting $\sigma = 5$ and α are 0.2, 0.5, and 0.8 respectively, the results are shown in Fig. 3

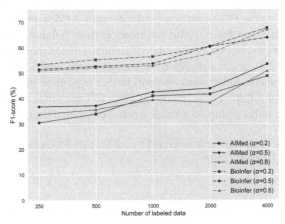

Fig. 3. F1 scores (%) with different α values

It can be seen from Fig. 3 that different α values have little impact on the performance. For AIMed, $\alpha = 0.5$ can obtain the highest F1 score, and for BioInfer, $\alpha = 0.2$ can obtain the highest F1 score.

Experiments were conducted with different σ values to explore the effect of hyperparameter σ on model performance. $\alpha = 0.5$ for AIMed, $\alpha = 0.2$ for BioInfer, the obtained F1 scores are shown in Fig. 4 when σ is 0.01, 0.1, 1, 5, 10, and 100, respectively.

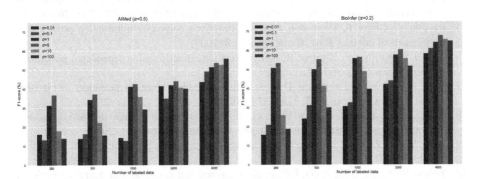

Fig. 4. F1 scores (%) with different σ values

It can be seen from Fig. 4 that when the number of labeled data is small, too small or too large σ value will greatly reduce the performance. However, when the number of labeled data is large, different σ values have less impact on performance. Overall, $\sigma = 5$ achieves the highest F1 score in most cases.

5 Conclusion

In this work, a semi-supervised PPI extraction method based on label propagation and sentence embedding is proposed. Text is represented as numerical features through sentence embedding based on BioBERT, and then pseudo-labels are assigned to unlabeled data through label propagation, to make full use of the information in the unlabeled data. Experiments on the PPI extraction public datasets AIMed and BioInfer show that the proposed method can learn useful information from unlabeled data and improve the accuracy of PPI extraction in the case of limited labeled data. When the number of labeled data is 250, it can achieve F1 scores of 36.8% and 53.4% on AIMed and BioInfer, respectively. In future work, we will further explore semi-supervised learning methods suitable for different basic models, so that PPI extraction can be more efficient and accurate while only relying on a small amount of labeled data.

Acknowledgements. This work was supported by the Major S&T project (Innovation 2030) of China under grant 2021ZD0113702.

References

1. Nakajima, N., Akutsu, T., Nakato, R.: Databases for protein-protein interactions. Method. Molecul. Biol. **2361**, 229–248 (2021)
2. Wu, Z., Liao, Q., Fan, S., et al.: idenPC-CAP: identify protein complexes from weighted RNA-protein heterogeneous interaction networks using co-assemble partner relation. Briefings Bioinformatics **22**(4) (2021)
3. Tang, Z., Guo, X., Bai, Z., et al.: A protein-protein interaction extraction approach based on large pre-trained language model and adversarial training. KSII Trans. Internet Inf. Syst. **16**(3), 771–791 (2022)
4. Bunescu, R., Ge, R., Kate, R.J., et al.: Comparative experiments on learning information extractors for proteins and their interactions. Artif. Intell. Med. **33**(2), 139–155 (2005)
5. Pyysalo, S., Ginter, F., Heimonen, J., et al.: BioInfer: a corpus for information extraction in the biomedical domain. BMC Bioinformatics **8** (2007)
6. Fundel, K., Kuffner, R., Zimmer, R.: RelEx–Relation extraction using dependency parse trees. Bioinformatics **23**(3), 365–371 (2007)
7. Ding, J., Berleant, D., Nettleton, D., et al.: Mining medline: abstracts, sentences, or phrases? Pacific Sympos. Biocomput. **7**, 326–337 (2002)
8. Chang, Y.-C., Chu, C.-H., Su, Y.-C., et al.: PIPE: a protein–protein interaction passage extraction module for BioCreative challenge. Database **2016**, baw101 (2016)
9. Peng, Y., Lu, Z.: Deep learning for extracting protein-protein interactions from biomedical literature (2017)
10. Zhang, H., Guan, R.C., Zhou, F.F., et al.: Deep residual convolutional neural network for protein-protein interaction extraction. IEEE Access **7**, 89354–89365 (2019)
11. Choi, S.P.: Extraction of protein-protein interactions (PPIs) from the literature by deep convolutional neural networks with various feature embeddings. J. Inf. Sci. **44**(1), 60–73 (2018)
12. Quan, C., Hua, L., Sun, X., et al.: Multichannel convolutional neural network for biological relation extraction. Biomed. Res. Int. **2016**, 1850404 (2016)

13. Hua, L., Quan, C.: A shortest dependency path based convolutional neural network for protein-protein relation extraction. Biomed. Res. Int. **2016**, 8479587 (2016)
14. Yadav, S., Ekbal, A., Saha, S., et al.: Feature assisted stacked attentive shortest dependency path based Bi-LSTM model for protein-protein interaction. Knowl. Based Syst. **166**, 18–29 (2019)
15. Hsieh, Y.-L., Chang, Y.-C., Chang, N.-W. et al.: Identifying protein-protein interactions in biomedical literature using recurrent neural networks with long short-term memory. In: The 8th International Joint Conference on Natural Language Processing, Taipei, Taiwan, pp. 240–245 (2017)
16. Ahmed, M., Islam, J., Samee, M.R. et al.: Identifying protein-protein interaction using tree LSTM and structured attention. In: 13th IEEE International Conference on Semantic Computing (ICSC): 30 Jan–01 Feb 2019, New York, pp. 224–231. IEEE, Newport Beach (2019)
17. Lee, J., et al.: BioBERT: a pre-trained biomedical language representation model for biomedical text mining. Bioinformatics (2019). https://doi.org/10.1093/bioinformatics/btz682
18. Warikoo, N., Chang, Y.-C., Hsu, W.-L.: LBERT: lexically aware transformer-based bidirectional encoder representation model for learning universal bio-entity relations. Bioinformatics (2020)
19. Wei, J., Zou, K.: EDA: easy data augmentation techniques for boosting performance on text classification tasks. In: Association for Computational Linguistics, Hong Kong, pp. 6382–6388 (2019)
20. Zhou, D., Bousquet, O., Lal, T.N., et al.: Learning with local and global consistency. In: Advances in Neural Information Processing Systems, vol. 16, pp. 321–328. MIT Press (2004)
21. Bao-jin, C.U.I., Hong-fei, L.I.N., Xiao, Z.: Research of protein-protein interaction extraction based on semi-supervised learning. J. Shandong Univ. Eng. Sci. **39**(3), 16–21 (2009)
22. Qian, Z., Fu, C., Cheng, R., et al.: Semi-supervised method for extraction of protein-protein interactions using hybrid model. In: 2013 Third International Conference on Intelligent System Design and Engineering Applications (ISDEA), pp. 1268–1271 (2013)
23. Dai, A.M., Le, Q.V.: Semi-supervised sequence learning. Adv. Neural Inf. Process. Syst. 3079–3087 (2015)
24. Zhang, Y., Lu, Z.: Exploring semi-supervised variational autoencoders for biomedical relation extraction. Methods **166**, 112–119 (2019)
25. Xie, Q., Dai, Z., Hovy, E., et al.: Unsupervised data augmentation for consistency training. In: 34th Conference on Neural Information Processing Systems (NeurIPS 2020), Vancouver (2020)
26. Liu, C., Mengchao, Z., Zhibing, F., et al.: FLiText: a faster and lighter semi-supervised text classification with convolution networks. In: Association for Computational Linguistics, November, pp. 2481–2491. Association for Computational Linguistics, Punta Cana, Dominican Republic (2021)
27. Chen, J., Yang, Z., Yang, D.: MixText: linguistically-informed interpolation of hidden space for semi-supervised text classification. In: Proceedings of the 58th Annual Meeting of the Association for Computational Linguistics. Association for Computational Linguistics (2020)
28. Edunov, S., Ott, M., Auli, M., et al.: Understanding back-translation at scale. In: Proceedings of the 2018 Conference on Empirical Methods in Natural Language Processing, October, November, pp. 489–500. Association for Computational Linguistics, Brussels (2018)
29. Vaswani, A., Shazeer, N., Parmar, N., et al.: Attention is all you need. In: Proceedings of the 31st International Conference on Neural Information Processing Systems, pp. 6000–6010. Curran Associates Inc., Long Beach (2017)
30. Srivastava, N., Hinton, G., Krizhevsky, A., et al.: Dropout: a simple way to prevent neural networks from overfitting. J. Mach. Learn. Res. **15**(1), 1929–1958 (2014)

Construction and Application of a Large-Scale Chinese Abstractness Lexicon Based on Word Similarity

Huidan Xu🆔 and Lijiao Yang(✉)🆔

Beijing Normal University, Beijing 100875, China
yanglijiao@bnu.edu.cn

Abstract. As an important semantic feature, abstractness has been widely studied in linguistics, psychology, cognitive sciences and other fields. Many languages have constructed their abstractness lexicons, while there has never been a large-scale and high-quality abstractness lexicon in Chinese. Since manual construction is time-consuming and costly, we use the existing resources with human abstractness scores as original data, and adopt the word similarity-based approach to automatically construct a large-scale Chinese abstractness lexicon. Besides, we evaluate the quality of the constructed lexicon by comparing it with expert knowledge and previous work. It has been verified that this lexicon is roughly consistent with human cognition and can provide reliable abstractness ratings for words. Finally, the performance of this constructed lexicon on two research, cross-language comparison and Chinese text readability auto-evaluation, shows that word abstractness is an important feature in investigating cognitive differences and text complexity. The large-scale Chinese abstractness lexicon constructed in this paper has important application values.

Keywords: Word abstractness · Chinese lexicon · Word similarity-based

1 Introduction

Abstractness refers to the degree of abstraction of the object a word refers to. As an important semantic feature, large lexicon resources with assessments of abstractness can provide important support for experimental and quantitative research in linguistics, psychology, cognitive sciences and other fields.

Many languages have manually constructed their own abstractness lexicons. Brysbaert et al. (2014) collected the abstractness of 39,954 English words through an online crowdsourcing platform and more than 4,000 people participated in this work [1]. Except English, another language who has an abstractness lexicon with over 10,000 words is Dutch, for which Brysbaert et al. (2014) collected the abstractness of 30,000 Dutch words from 75 participants. Each rater was required to score 6,000 words, which took about 6–7 h [2]. The two studies show that manually constructing an abstractness lexicon by collecting scores from respondents is laborious and time-consuming. Therefore, most

© Springer Nature Switzerland AG 2022
W. Lu et al. (Eds.) NLPCC 2022, LNCS 13552, pp. 122–130, 2022.
https://doi.org/10.1007/978-3-031-17189-5_10

languages build abstractness lexicons with a scale of several thousand words, such as German (2654 words; [3]), French (1659 words; [4]), Italian (1121 words; [5]), etc.

In recent years, the automatic calculation of word abstractness has become a new trend of research. The main methods can be summarized as the following three:

- Cross-language knowledge transfer-based approach, that is, based on the existing foreign language abstractness lexicons, transferring foreign words' abstractness ratings to the corresponding words of the target language through bilingual dictionaries or aligned word embeddings [6, 7];
- Classification or regression-based approach, that is, defining word abstractness as the probability that a word is an abstract word, and using lots of expert knowledge to train a classifier to predict it [8–10];
- Word similarity-based approach, that is, given two seed sets (a set of typical abstract words and a set of typical concrete words) in advance, calculating the abstractness of a word by comparing the similarity (semantic relevance) between the word with the two seed sets [11–13].

The first method is used less in previous studies, for it cannot deal with problems of lexical gaps and language codability differences. The second and third method are welcomed by most researchers. It should be noted that the second approach is strongly supervised and requires a large amount of expert knowledge. The word similarity-based approach also requires expert knowledge to construct seed sets, but it requires far fewer. It has been proven that a seed set containing dozens of words is enough to generate a high-quality abstractness lexicon [13].

In Chinese studies, the calculation of word abstractness is mostly proposed to solve specific problems (e.g., metaphor identification). Xie and Bi (2022) firstly attempted to construct a large-scale Chinese abstractness lexicon automatically [10]. They built up an abstractness lexicon of 737,531 Chinese words based on their trained MLP regression model. However, the evaluation of the quality of this lexicon is not sufficient and it is not yet appropriate for application. In view of the deficiency of the present research, we automatically construct a large-scale Chinese abstractness lexicon based on word similarity. After evaluating the quality of the constructed lexicon, we further explore its application effect in cross-language comparison research and Chinese text readability auto-evaluation research.

2 Data and Method

2.1 Data

In experiment of selecting seed sets, the first resource used is the Chinese abstractness lexicon manually constructed by Xu et al. (2020), which contains 9,877 two-character Chinese words [14]. The second resource is SUBTLEX-CH [15]. This database contains a frequency list, providing words in the lexicon mentioned above with frequency information. The pre-trained word embedding we employ is from "Chinese word vector" [16]. We select the word vector of Baidu Encyclopedia, whose word list size is 5422K, which can meet the need of our experiments well.

When generating the abstractness lexicon, we take Thesaurus of Modern Chinese [17] as the basic resource. It contains a total of over 83,000 Chinese words, providing five-level thesaurus information for each word. Among the first-level semantic class, the artificial classification of "concrete things" and "abstract things" can be used to evaluate the accuracy of our calculations. In addition, List of Common Words in Compulsory Education (Thesaurus List) [18] provides cognitive difficulty levels for some words, and we use it to evaluate the quality of the constructed lexicon as well.

2.2 Method

Word Abstractness Calculation Formula. We adopt the word similarity-based approach to calculate word abstractness. The core idea is that, for any word, if it has a relatively high semantic relevance with some typical abstract words (seedA), and a relatively weak semantic relevance with some typical concrete words (seedC), this word may have a greater abstractness. Semantic relevance can be quantified by word vector distance. The calculation formula of word abstractness is as follows.

$$sim(w, seedA) = \frac{1}{|seedA|} \sum_{a \in seedA} \frac{w \cdot a}{\|w\| \cdot \|a\|} \tag{1}$$

$$sim(w, seedC) = \frac{1}{|seedC|} \sum_{c \in seedC} \frac{w \cdot c}{\|w\| \cdot \|c\|} \tag{2}$$

$$Abstractness(w) = \frac{sim(w, seedA)}{sim(w, seedA) + sim(w, seedC)} \tag{3}$$

Selection of Seed Sets. The selection of seed sets directly affects the abstractness calculation results. We use the existing lexicon with human abstractness scores as original data (hereafter called "Human Lexicon"), and adopt brute-force search to select the most suitable seed sets. The evaluation index is Spearman correlation coefficient (hereafter called "Rs") between human scores and calculation results. This process in explained in detail below:

1. In Human Lexicon, X most frequent words are selected to form a basic lexicon.
2. In basic lexicon, Y most abstract words and Y most concrete words are selected to form two basic subsets.
3. Z words are randomly selected from each basic subset to form two seed sets.
4. Based on seed sets, calculating the abstractness of each word in basic lexicon.
5. Calculating Rs between formula results and human scores.
6. Optimize continuously to determine the best X, Y, Z and the best seed sets.

In the optimization process (Step 6), the brute-force search is adopted.

1. The initial value of X is 500.
2. The initial value of Y is 50.
3. Enumerating all possible Z values with an increment of 10 ($10 < Z \leq Y$).

4. Iterating over all possible combinations of Z words (if the amount of calculation is too large, stop searching after 100 iterations) and retaining the best combination.
5. Increasing Y by 50 up to one-third of X. Repeat steps 3–4.
6. Increasing X by 500. Repeat steps 2–5.
7. Stop optimization when the improvement effect is less than 0.005.

3 Experiment

Table 1 shows the experimental results of selecting seed sets. It is found that the larger X is, the more consistent formula results are with human scores. When X reaches 2,500, the effect increases by less than 0.5%. Z represents the size of seed sets. As can be seen, when the size of the basic lexicon (X) is determined, there is an optimum result for the selection of seed sets. The size of seed sets is not as bigger as better.

Table 1. Comparison of the best results under different X.

X	Y	Z	Rs	Improvement effect
500	100	50	0.7780	–
1000	200	90	0.8049	+2.69%
1500	250	150	0.8153	+1.04%
2000	300	150	0.8232	+0.79%
2500	**400**	**120**	**0.8300**	**+0.68%**
3000	600	210	0.8300	+0.00%

Considering the effectiveness and cost of calculation, we finally select the best seed sets when X = 2,500 and Y = 400. Based on the two selected seed sets, we calculate the abstractness of all 9,868 words in Human Lexicon, and the correlation coefficient between formula results and human scores is 0.79. It proves that the two seed sets selected are reasonable. Table 2 gives some examples of 120 abstract seed words and 120 concrete seed words.

Table 2. Examples of abstract seed words and concrete seed words.

Class	Examples
Abstract seed words	感情、感觉、意识、梦想、永远、民主、概念、意义
Concrete seed words	兔子、头盔、胳膊、报纸、电脑、香蕉、火车、右手

4 Construction and Evaluation

Thesaurus of Modern Chinese is used as the raw data to generate a Chinese abstractness lexicon. Firstly, the unknown words of Baidu Encyclopedia word embedding model are removed and 74,980 Chinese words are reserved. Based on the two seed sets, we calculate the abstractness of each word. Calculation results range from 0.3 to 0.7, with a minimum of 0.325 and a maximum of 0.672. The average abstractness is 0.513. Three most concrete words are "皮棉" (lint, 0.325), "马铁" (cast iron, 0.348), "桂竹" (phyllostachys pubescens, 0.350); three most abstract words are "推尊" (respect, 0.672), "卓绝" (outstanding, 0.670), "超绝" (superexcellent, 0.669).

According to Thesaurus of Modern Chinese, all words can be divided into nine semantic categories (see Table 3, column 2). Table 3 shows the distribution of word abstractness of different categories. Word abstractness is divided into two levels, [0.3,0.5) and [0.5,0.7), with the former regarded as concrete and the latter as abstract.

Table 3. Distribution of word abstractness of nine semantic categories.

Part of speech	Semantic category	[0.3,0.5)	[0.5,0.7)	Average abstractness	
Nouns	Living things	6131(65.1%)	3288(34.9%)	0.488	0.494
	Concrete things	10164(80.5%)	2467(19.5%)	0.470	
	Abstract things	5787(35.2%)	10675(64.8%)	0.519	
	Space and time	1572(53.4%)	1372(46.6%)	0.499	
Verbs	Biological activities	3012(28.0%)	7754(72.0%)	0.529	0.531
	Land social activities	3252(34.4%)	6205(65.6%)	0.519	
	Movements and changes	790(17.7%)	3678(82.3%)	0.544	
Adjectives	Properties and states	714(9.8%)	6555(90.2%)	0.552	0.552
Adverbs Function words	Auxiliary words	178(11.4%)	1386(88.6%)	0.557	0.557

As can be seen from Table 3, words referring to concrete things are mostly concrete (80.5%) and words referring to abstract things are mostly abstract (64.8%). Thesaurus of Modern Chinese classifies many organizations and institutions into the category of abstract things, such as "ceramic factory", "department store" and "kindergarten". These words have multiple specific referents and individuals tend to judge them as concrete according to their perceptual experience. However, when experts organize thesaurus hierarchy, these words, as upper categories, are often classified as abstract. Subtle difference in definition of abstraction leads to the worse performance on the category of abstract things. Even so, the results in Table 3 still verify that the constructed lexicon accord with expert knowledge basically.

Among the other seven categories, most words referring to living things are tangible and visible, so they are more concrete; the auxiliary words have no referents in the objective world and cannot be directly perceived, so they are the most abstract.

We can also compare abstractness between different parts of speech according to Thesaurus of Modern Chinese. As can be seen in Table 3, nouns are the most concrete, verbs more concrete, adjectives more abstract, and adverbs and function words are the most abstract. These results fit our cognition.

In addition, List of Common Words in Compulsory Education (Thesaurus List) provides cognitive difficulty levels (1–4) for 16,751 words of our lexicon. Psycholinguistic studies show that abstractness influences the cognitive processing of words. The more abstract a word is, the more difficult it is to learn. Analyzing the association between cognitive difficulty and word abstractness, the proportion of abstract words and average abstractness increase with the cognitive difficulty level rising (see Table 4). This result reversely verifies that the constructed lexicon is consistent with human cognition and can provide reliable abstractness scores for words.

Table 4. Distribution of word abstractness of four cognitive difficulty levels.

Difficulty level	Total	[0.3,0.5)	[0.5,0.7)	Average abstractness
1	1993	885(44.4%)	1108(55.6%)	0.510
2	5441	1917(35.2%)	3524(64.8%)	0.521
3	5859	1199(20.5%)	4660(79.5%)	0.540
4	3458	547(15.8%)	1108(84.2%)	0.548

Xie and Bi (2022) automatically constructed the first large-scale Chinese abstractness lexicon [10]. As the only previous achievement, we compare our lexicon (74,890 words) with their work (737,531 words). There are 70,495 words overlapping in the two lexicons. For these words, the correlation coefficient of abstractness is 0.764. This shows that the two works obtain relatively consistent results of abstractness, providing new evidence to verify the effectiveness of our constructed lexicon.

5 Application

In this section, we introduce two possible applications of the constructed lexicon, including cross-language comparison and Chinese text readability auto-evaluation.

5.1 Cross-Language Comparison

The degree of abstraction of a concept may vary in different languages. For example, compared with English, the concept "家庭 (family)" is more concrete in Chinese ((according to [14], its abstractness is 2.18; according to [1], is 4.23). Abstractness differences provide a new perspective for cross-cultural research. Taking cross-language comparison between English and Chinese as an example, we compare the constructed lexicon with the largest English abstractness lexicon (hereafter called BRY [1]).

Firstly, all words in BRY are translated into Chinese by Google Translate[1]. Since values of word abstractness in BRY range from 1 (the most abstract) to 5 (the most concrete), to facilitate analysis, we normalize these values by Formula (4). The normalized results range from 0 (the most concrete) to 1 (the most abstract).

$$Abstractnes\_normalized(w) = 1 - \frac{abstractness(w) - 1}{4} \qquad (4)$$

According to statistics, there are 21,607 words overlapping and for these words, the correlation coefficient of abstractness is 0.72. This result shows that word abstractness of English and Chinese is coincide generally, but there are some differences as well. Table 5 gives the words with the maximum difference.

Table 5. Words with the maximum difference.

English words	Chinese words	English abstractness	Chinese abstractness	Difference
Bug	漏洞 (飞虫)	0	0.554	0.554
Spindle	主轴 (纺锤)	0.02	0.567	0.547
Tissue	组织 (纸巾)	0.018	0.548	0.53
Pillar	支柱	0.058	0.529	0.471
Storm	风暴	0.075	0.536	0.461
Heart	心	0.12	0.562	0.442

As seen from Table 5, the maximum difference in abstractness is basically caused by the inequivalence in translation (the first three examples). Translation errors make the correlation coefficient of abstractness calculated above (0.72) a little to the low side. The last three examples reflect cognitive differences in conceptual representation behind English and Chinese. We speculate that the metonymical and metaphorical usages of "支柱 (pillar)", "风暴 (storm)" and "心 (heart)" make them obtain high abstractness in Chinese. Abstractness differences help reveal differences in lexicon organization and cognitive orientation, which may benefit second language teaching and learning.

5.2 Chinese Text Readability Auto-evaluation

Text abstractness is an important factor influencing text readability [19]. At word level, the number of abstract words in the text may be an effective indicator of its complexity. We select 12 primary school Chinese textbooks in PEP version and 6 middle school Chinese textbooks in Official version, excluding the texts whose genres are nursery

---

[1] https://translate.google.cn/.

rhymes, ancient poems, classical Chinese and modern poems. Based on the constructed Chinese abstractness lexicon, we then calculate the number and proportion of abstract words in textbooks of different grades (see Table 6).

Table 6. Number and proportion of abstract words in textbooks of different grades.

Grades	Tokens in textbooks	Number of abstract words	Proportion of abstract words
1–2	12786	9180	71.8%
3–4	39901	31107	78.0%
5–6	56355	44752	79.4%
7–9	76269	62921	82.5%

It can be seen that the number and proportion of abstract words are growing with the increase of grades. This verifies that the incidence of abstract words affects text complexity. In Table 6, the proportion of abstract words in textbooks is on the high side, because there are a large number of function words in texts and all of them obtain high abstractness from our constructed lexicon. Thus, as a basic lexical semantic resource, the constructed Chinese abstractness lexicon is of great application values in text readability auto-evaluation.

6 Conclusion

Considering the lack of large-scale Chinese abstractness resources, we construct a Chinese abstractness lexicon containing 74,980 words based on present resources and technologies. Its large scale and high quality enable it to have a much wider application. Experimental results show that the constructed Chinese abstractness lexicon can help to analyze cognitive differences between different languages and evaluate Chinese text complexity.

In future work, we will continue to experiment with the construction, evaluation and application of the large-scale Chinese abstractness lexicon. Firstly, we will further compare different word embedding models on abstractness calculation, and assess the accuracy of calculations using more lexical semantic resources. Furthermore, wider applications of the constructed abstractness lexicon will be explored.

Acknowledgments. This work is supported by "Research on intelligent evaluation method of text readability and construction of analysis system for international Chinese education [ZDI 135-41]", sponsoring by State Language and Letters Committee of the PRC.

References

1. Brysbaert, M., Warriner, A.B., Kuperman, V.: Concreteness ratings for 40 thousand generally known English word lemmas. Behav. Res. Methods **46**(3), 904–911 (2013)

2. Brysbaert, M., Stevens, M., De Deyne, S., et al.: Norms of age of acquisition and concreteness for 30,000 Dutch words. Acta Physiol. (Oxf.) **150**, 80–84 (2014)

3. Lahl, O., Göritz, A.S.: Using World-Wide Web to obtain large-scale word norms: 190,212 ratings on a set of 2,654 German nouns. Behav. Res. Methods **41**(1), 13–19 (2009)

4. Bonin, P., Méot, A., Bugaiska, A.: Concreteness norms for 1,659 French words: relationships with other psycholinguistic variables and word recognition times. Behav. Res. Methods **50**(6), 2366–2387 (2018)

5. Montefinese, M., Ambrosini, E., Fairfield, B., et al.: The adaptation of the affective norms for English words (ANEW) for Italian. Behav. Res. Methods **46**(3), 887–903 (2014)

6. Tsvetkov, Y., Boytsov, L., Gershman, A., et al.: Metaphor detection with cross-lingual model transfer. In: Proceedings of the 52nd Annual Meeting of the Association for Computational Linguistics, pp. 248–258 (2014)

7. Ljubešić, N., Fišer, D.: Predicting concreteness and imageability of words within and across languages via word embeddings. arXiv preprint arXiv:1807.02903 (2018)

8. Rabinovich, E., Sznajder, B., Spector, A., et al.: Learning concept abstractness using weak supervision. arXiv preprint arXiv:1809.01285 (2018)

9. Charbonnier, J., Wartena, C.: Predicting word concreteness and imagery. In: Proceedings of the 13th International Conference on Computational Semantics-Long Papers, pp. 176–187. Association for Computational Linguistics (2019)

10. Xie, Z., Bi, R.: Construction and inference technique of large-scale chinese concreteness Lexicon. Acta Scientiarum Naturalium Universitatis Pekinensis **58**(1), 1–6 (2022)

11. Turney, P., Neuman, Y., Assaf, D., et al.: Literal and metaphorical sense identification through concrete and abstract context. In: Proceedings of the 2011 Conference on Empirical Methods in Natural Language Processing, pp. 680–690 (2011)

12. Wang, X., Su, C., Chen, Y.: A method of abstractness ratings for Chinese concepts. In: Lotfi, A., Bouchachia, H., Gegov, A., Langensiepen, C., McGinnity, M. (eds.) UKCI 2018. AISC, vol. 840, pp. 217–226. Springer, Cham (2019). https://doi.org/10.1007/978-3-319-97982-3_18

13. Ivanov, V., Solovyev, V.: Automatic generation of a large dictionary with concreteness/abstractness ratings based on a small human dictionary. J. Intell. Fuzzy Syst. 1–9 (2021)

14. Xu, X., Li, J.: Concreteness/abstractness ratings for two-character Chinese words in MELD-SCH. PLoS ONE **15**(6), e02322133 (2020)

15. Cai, Q., Brysbaert, M.: SUBTLEX-CH: Chinese word and character frequencies based on film subtitles. PLoS ONE **5**(6), e10729 (2010)

16. Li, S., Zhao, Z., Hu, R., et al.: Analogical reasoning on Chinese morphological and semantic relations. arXiv Preprint arXiv:1805.06504 (2018)

17. Su, X.: Thesaurus of Modern Chinese. The Commercial Press, Beijing (2013)

18. Su, X.: Theory and method in compiling list of common words in compulsory education (draft). Appl. Linguist. **3**, 10 (2017)

19. Robert, M.: Assessment of the level of abstractness of material statement of in natural sciences school textbooks. Stand. Monitor. Educ. **5**(1), 58–63 (2017)

Stepwise Masking: A Masking Strategy Based on Stepwise Regression for Pre-training

Jie Pan, Shuxia Ren[✉], Dongzhang Rao, Zongxian Zhao, and Wenshi Xue

School of Software, Tiangong University, Tianjin, People's Republic of China
t_rsx@126.com

Abstract. Recently, capturing task-specific and domain-specific patterns during pre-training has been shown to help models better adapt to downstream tasks. Existing methods usually use large-scale domain corpus and downstream supervised data to further pre-train pre-trained language models, which often brings a large computational burden and these data are difficult to obtain in most cases. To address these issues, we propose a pre-training method with a novel masking strategy called stepwise masking. The method employs stepwise masking to mine tokens related to the downstream task in mid-scale in-domain data and masks them. Then, the model is trained on these annotated data. In this stage, task-guided pre-training enables the model to learn task-specific and domain-specific patterns simultaneously and efficiently. Experimental results on sentiment analysis tasks show that our method can effectively improve the performance of the model.

Keywords: Task-specific and domain-specific patterns · Stepwise masking · Task-guided pre-training · Text classification

1 Introduction

The rise of pre-trained language models (PLMs) such as OpenAI GPT [12], BERT [2], XLNet [18] has revolutionized the development of NLP, and also arouse widespread research interest. Applications that directly fine-tune PLMs for downstream tasks are emerging. However, for highly specialized fields such as biomedicine, finance, and e-commerce, some studies [1,9,17] have pointed out that the use of naive BERT cannot achieve good results due to the obvious difference in word distribution between general domain corpora and downstream datasets.

To alleviate the above problems, some previous works [5,20] have demonstrated that capturing task-specific and domain-specific patterns during pre-training can help models better adapt to downstream tasks. However, in the conventional pre-train-then-fine-tuning paradigm, existing models cannot effectively capture these patterns due to the gap between task-agnostic pre-training and the weak fine-tuning with limited supervised data.

© Springer Nature Switzerland AG 2022
W. Lu et al. (Eds.) NLPCC 2022, LNCS 13552, pp. 131–142, 2022.
https://doi.org/10.1007/978-3-031-17189-5_11

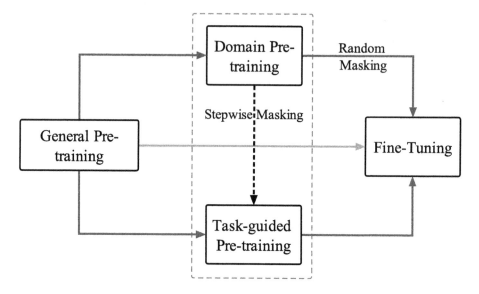

Fig. 1. Three training paradigms of the pre-trained language model are shown in different colors. We add domain pre-training between general pre-training and fine-tuning and transform it into task-guided pre-training via Stepwise Masking, which captures task-specific and domain-specific patterns efficiently.

To learn task-specific language patterns, Qiu et al. [13] further pre-train the PLM using target task training data. However, it requires a large amount of task data which is difficult to obtain in most cases. Gu et al. [4] propose intermediate continual pre-training with a selective masking strategy. Despite its success, this approach often leads to the model learning a lot of invalid information due to the shortcomings of the strategy. To learn domain-specific language patterns, some studies [7,10] pre-train PLMs from scratch using large-scale in-domain corpora. However, it tends to be computationally heavy and there is usually insufficient in-domain data at the current stage.

To overcome these limitations, we add domain pre-training between general pre-training and fine-tuning. In this way, the model captures domain-specific patterns with mid-scale in-domain data and significantly reduces the computational cost of pre-training [16,19]. In addition, we propose a novel masking strategy based on stepwise regression [3] in statistics: Stepwise Masking, which enables domain pre-training to be task-oriented so as to capture task-specific patterns efficiently. The overall method is shown in Fig. 1.

It is obvious that the importance of each token is different for a particular downstream task [14]. For example, opinion tokens such as "like" and "good" in sentiment analysis are crucial for judging the sentiment of a sentence [8]. We use stepwise masking to label these important tokens in the downstream dataset and train a binary classification neural network on the annotated dataset. This neural network can identify important tokens in the domain corpus and mask them.

Compared with the conventional masked language modeling, which randomly masks tokens [2], our method enables the model to capture task-specific and domain-specific patterns at the same time during domain pre-training.

To summarize, the main contributions of this paper are as follows:

(1) A novel masking strategy based on stepwise regression is introduced which transforms domain pre-training into task-guided pre-training to efficiently capture task-specific and domain-specific patterns.
(2) Our method achieves better performance than existing representative methods on two sentiment analysis tasks.

2   Methodology

In this section, we will introduce the method of this paper in detail. Our method consists of a three-stage framework [4] and Stepwise Masking. The three-stage framework helps the model capture task-specific and domain-specific patterns simultaneously during pre-training. Stepwise Masking is used to replace the original Selective Masking strategy to better capture task-specific patterns.

2.1   Three-Stage Framework

Different from previous training frameworks, this framework includes three stages: general pre-training, task-guided pre-training, and fine-tuning. The details of each stage are described below.

General Pre-training (GenePT). This stage is the same as BERT's pre-training [2], which usually uses large-scale general domain corpus to pre-train models, such as BookCorpus (800M words) [22], English Wikipedia (2,500M words), etc. Therefore, it has the highest computational cost and the longest training time.

Task-Guided Pre-training (TaskPT). In this stage, we apply stepwise masking to focus on masking the important tokens of a sentence and then train the model to reconstruct the input. It enables the model to learn domain-specific and task-specific language patterns. The general steps of this stage are described below. In addition, the implementation details of stepwise masking will be introduced in Sect. 2.2.

(1) Fine-tune BERT: Fine-tune the model after GenePT on downstream supervised datasets.
(2) Downstream Mask: Use the fine-tuned model to select important tokens on the downstream dataset with stepwise masking and annotate these tokens.
(3) Train NN: Train a token-level binary classification pre-trained language model on the supervised dataset where important tokens are annotated.

(4) Domain Mask: Use the token-level binary classification model to select important tokens in unlabeled domain data and mask them. Domain data is usually related to downstream tasks and its scale is smaller than general domain corpus.

(5) Domain pre-training: Continued pre-training the checkpoints after GenePT on selectively masked in-domain datasets.

Fine-Tuning. Fine-tune the model after TaskPT on downstream datasets, which are usually smaller in size than general domain corpus and in-domain corpus.

2.2 Stepwise Masking

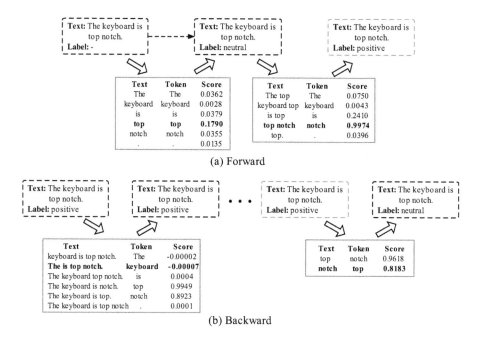

Fig. 2. Illustration of forward and backward process. "Text" and "Label" denote the input and classification result of the model, respectively. "Score" denotes the importance of added or removed token. The orange box stores important tokens and the prediction is the same as the ground truth answer of the original full sequence.

Stepwise regression [3] is a widely used algorithm for fitting regression models in statistics. It can automatically select the most important explanatory variables when there are a large number of potential explanatory variables and there is no basic theory for model selection, to establish a prediction or explanation model for regression analysis. Two forms of the algorithm are described below.

Forward Selection: Start with no variables in the model, test the model with each variable added using the selected model fit criteria, and determine the addition of the variable when the model fit is significantly improved. This process is repeated until adding any variables outside the model fails to significantly improve the model.

Backward Elimination: Start by including all candidate variables in the model, test the model with each variable deleted using the selected model fit criteria, and determine to delete the variable when the model fit is not significantly degraded. This process is repeated until deleting any variables in the model would result in significant degradation.

Based on the above ideas, we propose a new masking strategy: Stepwise Masking, which includes forward and backward forms. The explanatory variable of stepwise regression is analogized to token and the objective of the algorithm is changed from finding independent variables that have a significant effect on the dependent variable to finding tokens that play a significant role in making the model predict an input sequence to be the correct category.

Formally, given the n-token input sequence and its target classification label c, we use an auxiliary sequence s' to help evaluate these tokens one by one.

Forward. In the beginning, s' is initialized to be empty. In the first step, we calculate the importance of each token that is not within s' and add the token with the highest importance score to s'. The second step is to predict the classification label c' of the sequence s'. The third step is to repeat the first and second steps until $c' = c$, and the tokens stored in s' are important. Note that a token is added without changing its relative position in the input sequence s. For example, suppose there is an input sequence $s = (\omega_1, \omega_2)$ and an auxiliary sequence $s' = (\omega_2)$, and s' is (ω_1, ω_2) instead of (ω_2, ω_1) after ω_1 is added. Therefore, s' is always an ordered sequence in the whole process.

In this method, the importance of a token ω_i is defined as the classification confidence of the s' after adding ω_i, which is denoted by s'_{+i}:

$$\boldsymbol{I}(w_i) = P\left(c \mid s'_{+i}\right) \tag{1}$$

where c is the target classification label of the input s and the classification confidence is computed by a PLM fine-tuned on the task.

Backward. In the initial stage, s' is initialized to s. In the first step, we calculate the importance of each token in the ordered sequence s' and remove the token with the highest score. The second step is to predict the classification label c' of the sequence s'. The third step is to repeat the first and second steps until $c' \neq c$, and the tokens stored in s' are important.

In this method, we define the importance of the token ω_i as the difference of classification confidences between the ordered sequence s' and s' after eliminating ω_i, which is denoted by s'_{-i}:

$$I(w_i) = P(c \mid s') - P(c \mid s'_{-i}) \tag{2}$$

Note that the importance of tokens is recalculated each time they are added or removed in the above two algorithms, so the importance of the same token changes dynamically during the iterative process. This dynamic nature helps the model optimize each iteration, enabling the PLM to correctly predict the classification label c with the shortest sequence and select important tokens. The overall process is shown in Fig. 2.

3   Experiments

3.1   Datasets

Table 1. Datasets statistics. Note that the data in the Amount column represents the train/dev/test split of sentences, the train/test split of opinions, and the number of sequences in the corpus, respectively.

Dataset	Amount
Sem14-R	3257/165/1086
Sem14-L	2165/136/638
Sem14-R-Opinion	3484/1008
Sem14-L-Opinion	2504/674
Yelp	700 k
Amazon	110 k

We utilize four public datasets in our experiments and their details are described below.

SemEval14 [11] is a dataset released by the task 4 in SemEval14 competition and is widely used in aspect-based sentiment analysis tasks. It contains two sub-datasets consisting of restaurant reviews and laptop reviews. Each of these reviews has one or multiple marked aspect-targets associated with a 4-level sentiment polarity (positive, neutral, negative, or conflict).

SemEval14 Opinion Annotation is a dataset annotated by Wang et al. [15] on the SemEval14 task 4 dataset, where the opinion terms are labeled. The explicit opinion terms of each sentence are annotated with the corresponding sentiment category (positive or negative).

Yelp [21] is a 5-class sentiment classification dataset of reviews about restaurants, which can be obtained from the Yelp Dataset Challenge in 2015.

Amazon Laptop Reviews [6] are reviews about laptops obtained from the Amazon website.

For simplicity, we abbreviate SemEval14-Restaurant, SemEval14-Laptop, and Amazon Laptop reviews to Sem14-R, Sem14-L, and Amazon in the rest of the paper, respectively. For SemEval14, the conflict labels are dropped as in Gu et al. [4] and in order to convert it into a conventional sentiment classification task, we will concatenate aspect tokens and text tokens to form a complete sentence as the input to the model. For SemEval14 Opinion Annotation, we only use the annotated opinion terms for subsequent matching and the details will be explained in Sect. 3.2. For Yelp and Amazon, we use their plain text to build in-domain unsupervised data. To lighten the computational burden, we took 65,000 sequences respectively. Additionally, we filter out the overlap between Amazon and the Sem14-L dataset to avoid training bias for the test data.

The statistics of these datasets are shown in Table 1.

3.2   Experimental Settings

In this paper, we conduct experiments based on the three-stage framework, where we skip general pre-training and directly use the weights of BERT-base [2] as a starting point for task-guided pre-training. We use Yelp and Amazon as our in-domain corpora and SemEval14 as the downstream dataset. The hyperparameters of the experiments are roughly the same as Gu et al. [4]. In the process of further pre-training BERT, we empirically set the max number of the epoch to 5 and save the model for each training epoch. To provide more convincing results, we fine-tune all models and select the best results on the test set. Furthermore, we averaged the performance of each model over 10 different random seeds.

Considering the importance of opinions to the sentiment analysis task, we match the important tokens obtained by masking strategy in task-guided pre-training with the opinion terms of the corresponding sentences in SemEval14 Opinion Annotation. To facilitate matching, we split these opinion terms into several tokens. We set that when one of the tokens split by an opinion term is matched, the opinion term is considered to be selected. Since this task is similar to the sequence labeling task, we adopt F1 scores as the main metric to evaluate the performance of different masking strategies. F1 scores comprehensively consider precision and recall to loosely measure the average overlap between predictions and ground truth answers.

3.3 Main Results

Table 2. Test accuracies of models trained with different methods. "W/O Domain" denotes no domain pre-training. "Random" denotes random token masking used in BERT [2] and "Selective" denotes the selective token masking used in Gu et al. [4].

Datasets	Sem14-L		Sem14-R	
Without domain pre-training	72.10		84.43	
Model	Yelp	Amazon	Yelp	Amazon
Random	73.09	72.79	85.08	84.80
Selective	73.37	72.73	84.87	84.73
Forward(ours)	72.84	**73.75**	**85.13**	85.23
Backward(ours)	**73.73**	73.21	84.85	**85.32**

We will show the performance of different models on the SemEval14 task 4 dataset and offer some further analysis. From Table 2, we can see that:

(1) Our models achieve the best performance in all four combinations (Sem14-L+Yelp/Amazon, Sem14-R+Yelp/Amazon) and outperform random masking strategy in most cases, which indicates that task-guided pre-training helps BERT fully learn domain-specific and task-specific patterns.

(2) The effect of task-guided pre-training in some combinations is lower than that of conventional domain pre-training, which may be due to the poor performance of the binary classification neural network trained in TrainNN mentioned in Sect. 2.1.

(3) In cross-domain combinations such as Sem14-L+Yelp and Sem14-R+Amazon (restaurant reviews and Laptop reviews), all models are improved after pre-training. Therefore, we speculate that there is a certain correlation between the laptop domain and the restaurant domain.

3.4 Effectiveness of Stepwise Masking

Table 3. Experiment results on two Opinion Extraction datasets: Sem14-L-Opinion and Sem14-R-Opinion. We adopt F1 scores and time (in minutes) to evaluate the performance of different masking strategies.

Datasets	Sem14-L-Opinion				Sem14-R-Opinion			
Methods	Precision	Recall	F1	Time	Precision	Recall	F1	Time
Selective [4]	13.76	70.24	23.01	**0.5**	25.25	65.26	36.41	**0.5**
Forward(ours)	40.69	38.66	39.65	**0.5**	45.95	47.78	46.85	**0.5**
Backward(ours)	37.82	43.11	**40.29**	10	45.54	51.36	**48.28**	8

In this section, we verify the effectiveness of our approach by comparing it with the selective masking strategy [4], which is used to select important tokens in the sequence. The result is shown in Table 3. From the table, we can observe that:

(1) On Sem14-L-Opinion and Sem14-R-Opinion datasets, our methods outperform the existing strategy significantly and consistently. Especially on Sem14-L-Opinion, our backward method achieves an improvement of up to 17.3 points.
(2) Our methods balance precision and recall to select important tokens more efficiently. Note that there is a large gap between the precision and recall of the selective masking strategy, which indicates that it extracts a large number of tokens. Although these tokens cover most of the opinion terms in the sequence, more of them are not related to the opinions.
(3) The computational cost of the Backward is significantly higher than that of the Forward even though its F1 score is the best. This is because the former needs to remove tokens one by one from the complete sequence and there are generally only a few important tokens in the sequence. Therefore, the number of tokens to be eliminated when processing each sequence is far more than the tokens added from scratch in the latter, so as to increase the number of algorithm iterations.

3.5   Effect of Dynamic in Stepwise Masking

Table 4. Effect of dynamic in stepwise masking on SemEval14 opinion annotation. "-Dynamic" means that the dynamic nature of Stepwise Masking is removed. We adopt F1 scores to evaluate the performance of different methods.

Datasets	Sem14-L-Opinion			Sem14-R-Opinion		
Methods	Precision	Recall	F1	Precision	Recall	F1
Forward	40.69	38.66	39.65	45.95	47.78	46.85
- Dynamic	39.12	39.03	39.08	38.09	48.10	42.51
Backward	37.82	43.11	40.29	45.54	51.36	48.28
- Dynamic	13.95	46.97	21.51	28.87	52.38	37.22

In Sect. 2.2, we mention that our method dynamically updates the importance of tokens. The following is an ablation study to evaluate the effect of dynamic nature.

Note that the purpose of dynamic nature is to enable the model to correctly classify sequences with the fewest tokens and mask them. In order to remove dynamics, we only iterate according to the importance of the tokens first calculated in the original strategies.

As shown in Table 4, Our method suffers from significant performance degradation after removing the dynamic. Especially on Sem14-L-Opinion, the F1 score of Backward drops by nearly half. After removing the dynamic, the recall improves, and the precision decreases, which indicates that the model needs more tokens to correctly classify the sequence. These tokens contain more words of opinion and many of them have nothing to do with opinion.

Overall, we conclude that dynamic nature can help us better select important tokens.

3.6   Case Study

Table 5 shows two examples of different masking strategies, which are used to illustrate the efficiency of our methods and the weakness of Forward, respectively. From the table we find that:

(1) On the Sem14-L example, our methods correctly mask the opinion terms in the sequence. "impressed" and "small" are opinion terms on the computer's battery and memory, respectively. In addition, we can clearly see that selective masking extracts many irrelevant tokens such as "been" and "the", which shows that the selective masking strategy is not an effective method.

(2) In the Sem14-R case, Forward does not mask any opinion words. This is because the algorithm initially only considers the individual importance of each token, unlike Backward which considers the impact of each token on the entire sequence. Therefore, the algorithm iteration ends when the model only passes the "but" enough to judge the user's sentiment about the price. Overall, the Forward is sensitive to the initially chosen token.

Table 5. Visualization of chosen samples. The bold tokens are the important tokens in the sequence, while the tokens with the gray background are masked by different methods.

From	Methods	Sequence samples
Sem14-L	Selective	I've been **impressed** with the battery life and the performance for such a **small** amount of memory.
	Forward(ours)	I've been **impressed** with the battery life and the performance for such a **small** amount of memory.
	Backward(ours)	I've been **impressed** with the battery life and the performance for such a **small** amount of memory.
Sem14-R	Forward(ours)	Somewhat **price ##y** but what the heck.
	Backward(ours)	Somewhat **price ##y** but what the heck.

4   Conclusion and Future Work

In this paper, we propose a masking strategy based on stepwise regression: Stepwise Masking, which transforms domain pre-training into task-guided pre-training to efficiently learn task-specific patterns. We validate the effectiveness of our method on two sentiment analysis tasks, and it consistently outperforms existing representative methods. Furthermore, the feasibility of our method was further explored through a detailed efficiency analysis and ablation study. Note that although we only conduct experiments on the sentiment classification tasks, our method can easily generalize to other text classification tasks.

In the future, we will explore the following directions:

(1) A more effective strategy can further stimulate the potential of task-guided pre-training. We will explore how to optimize existing methods to further improve the performance.
(2) A token-level binary classification network with better performance can make full use of the dataset annotated by masking strategies to accurately identify important tokens in domain-specific corpus. We will improve the network structure in TrainNN mentioned in Sect. 2.1 to enhance its performance.

References

1. Araci, D.: FinBERT: financial sentiment analysis with pre-trained language models. arXiv preprint arXiv:1908.10063 (2019)
2. Devlin, J., Chang, M.W., Lee, K., Toutanova, K.: BERT: pre-training of deep bidirectional transformers for language understanding. arXiv preprint arXiv:1810.04805 (2018)
3. Efroymson, M.A.: Multiple regression analysis. In: Mathematical Methods for Digital Computers, pp. 191–203 (1960)
4. Gu, Y., Zhang, Z., Wang, X., Liu, Z., Sun, M.: Train no evil: selective masking for task-guided pre-training. arXiv preprint arXiv:2004.09733 (2020)
5. Gururangan, S., et al.: Don't stop pretraining: adapt language models to domains and tasks. arXiv preprint arXiv:2004.10964 (2020)
6. He, R., McAuley, J.: Ups and downs: modeling the visual evolution of fashion trends with one-class collaborative filtering. In: Proceedings of the 25th International Conference on World Wide Web, pp. 507–517 (2016)
7. Huang, K., Altosaar, J., Ranganath, R.: ClinicalBERT: modeling clinical notes and predicting hospital readmission. arXiv preprint arXiv:1904.05342 (2019)
8. Ke, P., Ji, H., Liu, S., Zhu, X., Huang, M.: SentiLARE: sentiment-aware language representation learning with linguistic knowledge. arXiv preprint arXiv:1911.02493 (2019)
9. Lee, J., et al.: BioBERT: a pre-trained biomedical language representation model for biomedical text mining. Bioinformatics **36**(4), 1234–1240 (2020)
10. Liu, Z., Huang, D., Huang, K., Li, Z., Zhao, J.: FinBERT: a pre-trained financial language representation model for financial text mining. In: Proceedings of the Twenty-Ninth International Conference on International Joint Conferences on Artificial Intelligence, pp. 4513–4519 (2021)
11. Pontiki, M., Galanis, D., Pavlopoulos, J., Papageorgiou, H., Androutsopoulos, I., Manandhar, S.: SemEval-2014 task 4: aspect based sentiment analysis. In: Proceedings of the 8th International Workshop on Semantic Evaluation (SemEval 2014), pp. 27–35. Association for Computational Linguistics, Dublin, Ireland, August 2014. https://doi.org/10.3115/v1/S14-2004, https://aclanthology.org/S14-2004
12. Radford, A., Narasimhan, K., Salimans, T., Sutskever, I.: Improving language understanding with unsupervised learning (2018)

13. Sun, C., Qiu, X., Xu, Y., Huang, X.: How to fine-tune BERT for text classification? In: Sun, M., Huang, X., Ji, H., Liu, Z., Liu, Y. (eds.) CCL 2019. LNCS (LNAI), vol. 11856, pp. 194–206. Springer, Cham (2019). https://doi.org/10.1007/978-3-030-32381-3_16

14. Tian, H., et al.: SKEP: sentiment knowledge enhanced pre-training for sentiment analysis. arXiv preprint arXiv:2005.05635 (2020)

15. Wang, W., Pan, S.J., Dahlmeier, D., Xiao, X.: Recursive neural conditional random fields for aspect-based sentiment analysis. arXiv preprint arXiv:1603.06679 (2016)

16. Wu, H., Xu, K., Song, L., Jin, L., Zhang, H., Song, L.: Domain-adaptive pretraining methods for dialogue understanding. arXiv preprint arXiv:2105.13665 (2021)

17. Xu, S., et al.: K-plug: knowledge-injected pre-trained language model for natural language understanding and generation in e-commerce. arXiv preprint arXiv:2104.06960 (2021)

18. Yang, Z., et al.: XLNet: generalized autoregressive pretraining for language understanding. In: Advances in Neural Information Processing Systems, vol. 32 (2019)

19. Ye, Q., et al.: On the influence of masking policies in intermediate pre-training. arXiv preprint arXiv:2104.08840 (2021)

20. Zeng, J., Jiang, Y., Wu, S., Yin, Y., Li, M.: Task-guided disentangled tuning for pretrained language models. arXiv preprint arXiv:2203.11431 (2022)

21. Zhang, X., Zhao, J., LeCun, Y.: Character-level convolutional networks for text classification. In: Advances in Neural Information Processing Systems, vol. 28 (2015)

22. Zhu, Y., et al.: Aligning books and movies: towards story-like visual explanations by watching movies and reading books. In: Proceedings of the IEEE International Conference on Computer Vision, pp. 19–27 (2015)

Evaluation Workshop (Poster)

Context Enhanced and Data Augmented W²NER System for Named Entity Recognition

Chunping Ma[1(✉)], Zijun Xu[1], Minwei Feng[1], Jingcheng Yin[1], Liang Ruan[2], and Hejian Su[3]

[1] Netease BizEase, Hangzhou, Zhejiang, China
{machunping,xuzijun01,fengminwei,yinjingcheng}@corp.netease.com
[2] Netease GrowthEase, Hangzhou, Zhejiang, China
ruanliang@corp.netease.com
[3] Zhejiang University, Hangzhou, Zhejiang, China
hejiansu@zju.edu.cn

Abstract. This paper describes the system proposed by the YSF2022 team for NLPCC 2022 shared task 5 [3] on Named Entity Recognition Model for English Scientific Literature. This task needs participants to develop a named entity recognition (NER) model for domain-specific texts based on state-of-the-art NLP and deep learning techniques with the labeled domain-specific sentences corresponding to seven entity types. Without the luxury of training data, we proposed two methods to improve the performance by capturing document-level features and performing data augmentation with entity replacement. Besides, instead of using the traditional sequence labeling model, we attempted to use a novel alternative by modeling the NER as word-word relation classification. On the other hand, we apply Entity Confidence Filter (ECF) and Result Ensemble (RE) to get better performance. According to the official results, our approach ranks 1st for the NER track in this task.

Keywords: Named entity recognition · Document-level features · Data augmentation

1 Introduction

As one of the fundamental and longstanding goals of Natural Language Processing (NLP), NER has been an essential component of Information Retrieval, Question Answering, etc. However, the NER models may deteriorate when adopted in the domain-specific scenes, such as scientific literature, material science, and biological medicine [2,7,27,31].

To improve the performance of NER in specific domains, some methods pre-train language models on corpus in these domains [1,33]. For example, BioBERT [13] proposed to adapt BERT for biomedical corpora, achieving promising results in biomedical information extraction. However, the field of material science lacks

© Springer Nature Switzerland AG 2022
W. Lu et al. (Eds.) NLPCC 2022, LNCS 13552, pp. 145–155, 2022.
https://doi.org/10.1007/978-3-031-17189-5_12

corresponding pre-trained models, and the cost of pre-training a language model is very high [6,17]. Considering that current supervised NER methods require a large amount of training data, we propose two strategies to improve the quantity and quality of training data. First, instead of merely using the local features of input text, we also use a crawler to get the context of the given text. The retrieved context and the original text are concatenated as the overall input [21] so that the model can further perceive the global features, thereby improving the model's recognition ability. Second, entity replacement is used in data augmentation in order to alleviate the problem of data scarcity [5,16]. The final training dataset is five times larger than the original one.

Now the mainstream methods of NER can be roughly divided into two categories: 1) sequence labeling methods [11,19,23]; 2) span-based methods [15,28]. The former suffers from being incapable of handling nested NER, and the latter merely pays attention to boundary identification. Thus, we use the state-of-the-art W^2NER model [14], which breaks through the traditional sequence labeling methods and span-based methods by casting NER as a word-word relation classification problem. This method is able to address various NER tasks including flat NER, nested NER, and discontinuous NER. Based on this, we propose Entity Confidence Filter (ECF) to filter out those entities with low confidence. In addition, Result Ensemble (RE) is applied for better performance [24].

In summary, our contributions include:

- We utilize both context-enhanced methods and data augmentation technologies to improve the quantity and quality of corpus
- We propose Entity Confidence Filter to improve the confidence of predictions based on W^2NER
- Our solution takes the first place in NLPCC 2022 shared task 5 on Named Entity Recognition

2   Related Work

In the last decades, NER has been almost the most well-studied NLP task of predicting semantic labels for sequences of words. Using NER system, we can easily identify the names of persons, locations, and organizations in text [4,8]. Commonly, NER is modeled as a sequence labeling task, assigning a single predefined label (e.g., BIO) to each token in the sentence [11,23]. Based on the well-extracted features, Conditional Random Fields (CRF) [10] can be used for better decoding by introducing the dependency of labels. Recently, neural network models have demonstrated superiority over hand-crafted features, and the end-to-end bidirectional LSTM CRF model is one representative architecture for NER [19]. Current approaches for NER often leverage pre-trained transformer architectures such as BERT [6] or XLM [12] for feature extraction. The provided contextualized word representations have achieved great success. Recently, several studies [28,29] formulate the NER problem as a span-level classification task. It first enumerates possible text span candidates and then determine the type of these candidates. Also, Li et al. [15] proposed to formulate NER as a machine reading comprehension (MRC) task, which expresses the entity category you want to extract as a question and the entity as an answer span.

Although current state-of-the-art approaches for NER typically consider text at the sentence-level, document-level information seems like a good supplement [18,26,32]. Document-level features can easily be captured by passing sentences with their surrounding context to a Transformer-based architecture to obtain word embeddings [25]. The main difference between publications in this line of work lies in how to get the context. Virtanen et al. [26] conducted an experiment by treating the following sentence as context. Luoma and Pyysalo [18] utilized predictions from different windows and sentence positions for potentially further improving performance. Schweter and Akbik [21] proposed to add tokens both in the left and right of the sentence to be classified as context.

Various deep learning methods have demonstrated state-of-the-art performance for many natural language processing tasks such as text classification, question answering, and named entity recognition; however, these methods require a large amount of labeled data. In many real-world applications, collecting such extensive training data is expensive and time-consuming. Therefore, to reduce the cost, data augmentation (DA) [22] has been investigated. DA refers to strategies for increasing the diversity of training examples without explicitly collecting new data. The most common way of data augmentation is rule-based. Dai and Adel [5] proposed multiple methods for data augmentation in NER. A token can be replaced with one of its synonyms retrieved from WordNet or another token of the same type at random, while an entity also can be replaced with another entity mentioned of the same type at random. Moreover, the pre-trained language models have been used for data augmentation [9,20,30].

3   The Proposed Approach

3.1   Task Definition

Formally, given the input $X = \{x_1, x_2, ..., x_n\}$, where n is the number of tokens in the input, we aim to extract all entities in X with corresponding entity type y. The label $y \in Y$ is a predefined tag type, and Y is a collection of entity types (e.g., PER, ORG, etc.).

Following W^{2}NER, we cast this task as a word-word relation classification problem. Specifically, for each token pair $(x_i, x_j), i < j$, there exist three kinds of relations: 1) None relation, which indicates that the x_i and x_j have no relation and both of them do not belong to an entity; 2) NNW (Next-Neighboring-Word) relation, which implies the x_i and x_j belong to the same entity and x_j is the successive word of x_i; 3) THW-* (Tail-Head-Word-*) relation, which shows that x_i and x_j are the boundaries of an entity. x_i is the tail word of an entity, and x_j represents the headword of the same entity. '*' means the specific category of the entity.

3.2 Model Structure

As shown in Fig. 1, our model is divided into three parts: Token Feature Extractor, Word Relation Feature Extractor, and Model Output. The output of the previous module is passed to the next module as the input.

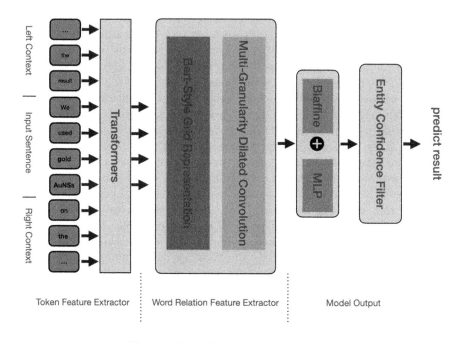

Fig. 1. The architecture of our model.

Token Feature Extractor. We use a Transformer-based pre-trained language model to extract the representation of each token. Besides the original sentence, we introduce the surrounding text around the sentence to get a better document-level feature [21]. For example, 'Zhongshan' in the sentence 'I love Zhongshan' may be ambiguous, it can be a PER or a LOC named entity. However, if we pass the text together with the previous sentence which ends with 'from China' and the next sentence that begins with 'The city', 'Zhongshan' will be recognized as a LOC named entity with a high probability. Due to the lack of labels for these surrounding text, we only consider the labels of original input sentences and ignore the tags of their surrounding context.

Word Relation Feature Extractor. Since we want to classify the word relation into different categories, it is very important to get a high-quality representation of the word-pair. For a sentence with N tokens, the word grid representation can be viewed as a 3-dimensional matrix $V \in \mathcal{R}^{N \times N \times d_h}$, where V_{ij} is the representation of word pair (x_i, x_j). We use Conditional Layer Normalization mechanism to calculate V_{ij}. Following BERT-Style embedding, we regard the V as a word information and introduce a tensor $E^d \in \mathcal{R}^{N \times N \times d_0}$ and a tensor $E^t \in \mathcal{R}^{N \times N \times d_1}$ to represent the relative position information and region information respectively. We then concatenate three kinds of embeddings and use a MLP to get the final word relation feature $C = \text{MLP}([V : E^d : E^t])$. Furthermore, to capture the interaction between the words with different distance, multi-granularity dilated convolution is adopted, which can be formulated as $Q^l = \sigma(\text{DConv}_l(C))$. Features with different dilation rates l are finally concatenated as the overall output of this component, $Q = [Q^1 : Q^2 : Q^3]$.

Model Output. In order to better predict the relation between each pair of words, we uses both Biaffine predictor and MLP predictor to determine the final prediction $y = \text{Softmax}(\text{Biaffine}(Q) + \text{MLP}(Q))$. After getting the predicted result of each word pair (x_i, x_j) within a sentence, we regard these relations as edges in a directional word graph where vertices represent the words. Each directed circle in this graph corresponds to an entity. We collect the predicted probability within the circle and average them as the confidence score for this entity. To ensure the credibility of the result, we introduce a confidence filter and only keep the entity with a score higher than the setting threshold α.

3.3   Data Augmentation

Since high-quality human-labeled data is limited, we use data augmentation methods to improve the model robustness.

Specifically, we use entity replacement strategy to generate some pseudo training data. We first collect all entities in the training dataset to make an entity pool. When replacing the entity in the sentence, it needs to meet three requirements:

- the category of both entities must be the same
- the difference between the total character number of the two entities is less than 6
- the difference between the total word number of two entities is less than 2

Apart from the category constraints, we add two additional length limitations of the entity while replacing the entity. This method can help the sentence maintain the overall sentence structure. During the model training procedure, true training data help the model capture the semantic information, while these pseudo data can help the model learn the sentence structure information.

3.4   Result Ensemble

Given predictions from different models, we utilize majority voting to determine the final prediction. Specifically, we convert the predicted results from all base models to entity spans to perform majority voting. First of all, we rank all the entity spans by the number of votes in descending order. Then, we choose the spans with more than n votes for the final prediction, where n is a threshold to balance precision and recall. We keep the longer spans if the selected spans have overlaps and the same number of votes.

4   Experiments

4.1   Dataset and Metric

We use the dataset released by NLPCC 2022 Shared task 5 Track 2 to evaluate the performance of our method. Table 1 shows the number of sentences, tokens, and entities of different types for training and testing sets, respectively. According to task guidelines, we report precision, recall and F1 scores for all evaluations. The entity is considered correct, while both entity boundary and category are predicted correctly.

Table 1. Size of sentence, tokens, and entities for training and testing sets

	# of sentences	# of tokens	# of entities						
			MA	CH	PR	SY	AP	ST	EQ
Training	5000	156315	5446	1175	966	526	378	319	147
Testing	600	18801	746	121	150	82	50	32	24

4.2   Experiment Settings

Our model is implemented based on PyTorch. We performed all experiments on a single NVIDIA GeForce RTX 3090. To get the surrounding text of the sentence, we crawl all documents in training and testing dataset from the website[1]. Some main training hyper-parameters are shown in Table 2. We use the last saved checkpoint during the training procedure to to evaluate on the test set. In order to generate more predictions for result ensemble, we use some other pre-trained language models to replace the encoder in W^{2}NER, including XLM, DeBERTa and BioLinkBert, all these model parameters can be downloaded from Huggingface[2]. For each model, four types of data, original data provided by NLPCC, original data with context enhanced strategy, original data with the entity replacement augmentation and original data with context-enhanced entity replacement strategy are used for training. Additionally, when training the model, we will repeat the training procedure three times with different random seeds. Finally, we get 144 model results for the final result ensemble.

---

[1] https://xueshu.baidu.com/.
[2] https://huggingface.co/.

Table 2. Main hyper-parameter setting in our model

Setting	Value
Epoch num	10
Batch size	16
Optimizer	AdamW
Learning rate	1e−3
Weight decay	0
Clip grad norm	1.0
Warm factor	0.1
Confidence threshold α	0.3

4.3 Baselines

To evaluate the performance of our method, we choose some strong baselines:

- Pre-trained model with Fine-Tuning: Owing to the great success of large-scale pre-trained language models, we only need to add a single linear layer and fine-tune the entire architecture on the specific NER tasks. We choose BERT as the backbone.
- Feature concatenation with CRF: We use the pre-trained language model as a feature extractor to generate embeddings for each word in a sentence. We then concatenate these embeddings and feed them into a standard sequence labeling architecture, LSTM-CRF, to obtain the final tag sequence. We still use BERT as the main backbone model, and the output of the last four layers are collected as input of LSTM-CRF.
- LUKE [29]: LUKE is a new pre-trained language model with an entity-aware self-attention mechanism. Different from traditional sequence labeling methods, LUKE solves the NER task by enumerating all possible spans in each sentence as the entity candidates, and classifying them into the target entity types or non-entity type, which indicates that the span is not an entity.
- MRC [15]: Instead of treating the task of NER as a sequence labeling problem, this paper proposes to formulate it as an MRC task. Using the sentence and pre-defined question, which is corresponding to a specific entity category can extract the entity boundary.

4.4   Results and Analysis

Table 3. The experimental results of different models, 'FT' means finetuning procedure; 'LC' means LSTM+CRF architecture; (*) means the pre-trained language model used in W^{2}NER; 'CE' means only using Context Enhanced input; 'DA' means only using the Data Augmentation; 'ALL' means using context enhanced input with data augmentation.

	Precision	Recall	F1-score
BERT-FT	0.3540	0.3925	0.3723
BERT-LC	0.3841	0.3726	0.3783
LUKE	0.4787	0.2979	0.3673
MRC	0.4515	0.3519	0.3955
W^{2}NER(BERT)	0.4713	0.3630	0.4101
W^{2}NER(XLM)	0.4433	0.3838	0.4114
W^{2}NER(DeBERTa)	0.4816	0.3705	0.4188
W^{2}NER(BioLinkBert)	0.4798	0.3663	0.4154
W^{2}NER(DeBERTa)-CE	0.4725	0.3857	0.4247
W^{2}NER(DeBERTa)-DA	0.4834	0.3880	0.4305
W^{2}NER(DeBERTa)-ALL	0.4759	0.3972	0.4330
W^{2}NER-Ensemble	0.4663	0.4788	0.4725

Table 3 shows the experimental results. From the top part of the table, W^{2}NER achieves the best F1-score among all the models. It outperforms the fine-tuned BERT by 3.78% in terms of F1-score. From the result, we find LUKE achieves the highest precision and the lowest recall. The main reason leading to this phenomenon is the length restriction during enumerating candidate entities. Some entities in experiment data are relatively long, while the maximum entity length is set to 32 sub-tokens because of resource limitations. These entities are lost during candidate generation.

In the second part of the table, we compare the results of W^{2}NER under different pre-trained language models. All these pre-trained model achieve similar F1-score to the original BERT encoder and model with DeBERTa gets the top result. It improves the F1-score from 0.4101 to 0.4188.

After introducing the context enhanced strategy and making data augmentation, the overall F1-score improves by about 1% over W^{2}NER-DeBERTa. When combining both strategies, we get a new state-of-the-art result using single model.

During result ensemble procedure, we experiment with different thresholds n, the Fig. 2 shows detail precision, recall and F1-score under thresholds. As the threshold increases, precision also increases while recall decreases rapidly. The overall F1-score does not change much within the interval $[20, 40]$, which means any value in this interval will lead to an evenly matched result. The highest F1-score is achieved when the threshold is set to 25.

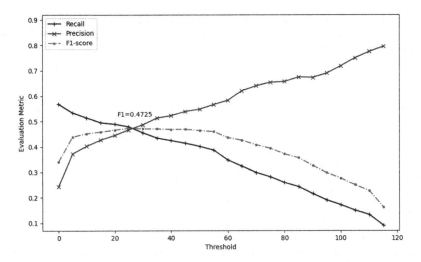

Fig. 2. Effect of varying threshold of votes on the testing dataset. Our model achieves the best performance when the threshold is set to 25.

5 Conclusion

In this paper, we propose a context enhanced and data augmented W^{2}NER model that extracts entities from domain-specific sentences. Context enhanced method can help capture document-level features and data augmented approach can improve the quantity of corpora, thus benefiting our model. We also propose ECF to filter out unreliable entities and utilize RE to improve our performance. Official evaluation results of NLPCC 2022 shared task 5 on Named Entity Recognition show that our solution takes the first place among all participants, which proves the effectiveness of our method.

References

1. Alsentzer, E., et al.: Publicly available clinical bert embeddings. arXiv preprint arXiv:1904.03323 (2019)
2. Beltagy, I., Lo, K., Cohan, A.: Scibert: a pretrained language model for scientific text. arXiv preprint arXiv:1903.10676 (2019)
3. Cai, B., et al.: Overview of nlpcc2022 shared task 5 track 2: Named entity recognition. In: CCF International Conference on Natural Language Processing and Chinese Computing (2022)
4. Chiu, J.P., Nichols, E.: Named entity recognition with bidirectional LSTM-CNNs. Trans. Assoc. Comput. Linguist. **4**, 357–370 (2016)
5. Dai, X., Adel, H.: An analysis of simple data augmentation for named entity recognition. arXiv preprint arXiv:2010.11683 (2020)
6. Devlin, J., Chang, M.W., Lee, K., Toutanova, K.: Bert: pre-training of deep bidirectional transformers for language understanding. arXiv preprint arXiv:1810.04805 (2018)

7. Habibi, M., Weber, L., Neves, M., Wiegandt, D.L., Leser, U.: Deep learning with word embeddings improves biomedical named entity recognition. Bioinformatics **33**(14), i37–i48 (2017)

8. Huang, Z., Xu, W., Yu, K.: Bidirectional LSTM-CRF models for sequence tagging. arXiv preprint arXiv:1508.01991 (2015)

9. Kumar, A., Bhattamishra, S., Bhandari, M., Talukdar, P.: Submodular optimization-based diverse paraphrasing and its effectiveness in data augmentation. In: Proceedings of the 2019 Conference of the North American Chapter of the Association for Computational Linguistics: Human Language Technologies, Volume 1 (Long and Short Papers), pp. 3609–3619 (2019)

10. Lafferty, J., McCallum, A., Pereira, F.C.: Conditional random fields: probabilistic models for segmenting and labeling sequence data (2001)

11. Lample, G., Ballesteros, M., Subramanian, S., Kawakami, K., Dyer, C.: Neural architectures for named entity recognition. arXiv preprint arXiv:1603.01360 (2016)

12. Lample, G., Conneau, A.: Cross-lingual language model pretraining. arXiv preprint arXiv:1901.07291 (2019)

13. Lee, J., et al.: Biobert: a pre-trained biomedical language representation model for biomedical text mining. Bioinformatics **36**(4), 1234–1240 (2020)

14. Li, J., et al.: Unified named entity recognition as word-word relation classification. arXiv preprint arXiv:2112.10070 (2021)

15. Li, X., Feng, J., Meng, Y., Han, Q., Wu, F., Li, J.: A unified MRC framework for named entity recognition. arXiv preprint arXiv:1910.11476 (2019)

16. Liang, C., et al.: Bond: Bert-assisted open-domain named entity recognition with distant supervision. In: Proceedings of the 26th ACM SIGKDD International Conference on Knowledge Discovery & Data Mining, pp. 1054–1064 (2020)

17. Liu, Y., et al.: Roberta: a robustly optimized bert pretraining approach. arXiv preprint arXiv:1907.11692 (2019)

18. Luoma, J., Pyysalo, S.: Exploring cross-sentence contexts for named entity recognition with bert. arXiv preprint arXiv:2006.01563 (2020)

19. Ma, X., Hovy, E.: End-to-end sequence labeling via bi-directional LSTM-CNNs-CRF. arXiv preprint arXiv:1603.01354 (2016)

20. Nie, Y., Tian, Y., Wan, X., Song, Y., Dai, B.: Named entity recognition for social media texts with semantic augmentation. arXiv preprint arXiv:2010.15458 (2020)

21. Schweter, S., Akbik, A.: Flert: document-level features for named entity recognition. arXiv preprint arXiv:2011.06993 (2020)

22. Simard, P.Y., LeCun, Y.A., Denker, J.S., Victorri, B.: Transformation invariance in pattern recognition – tangent distance and tangent propagation. In: Montavon, G., Orr, G.B., Müller, K.-R. (eds.) Neural Networks: Tricks of the Trade. LNCS, vol. 7700, pp. 235–269. Springer, Heidelberg (2012). https://doi.org/10.1007/978-3-642-35289-8_17

23. Straková, J., Straka, M., Hajič, J.: Neural architectures for nested ner through linearization. arXiv preprint arXiv:1908.06926 (2019)

24. Tebaldi, C., Knutti, R.: The use of the multi-model ensemble in probabilistic climate projections. Philos. Trans. Roy. Soc. A: Math. Phys. Eng. Sci. **365**(1857), 2053–2075 (2007)

25. Vaswani, A., et al.: Attention is all you need. Adv. Neural Inf. Process. Syst. **30** (2017)

26. Virtanen, A., et al.: Multilingual is not enough: bert for finnish. arXiv preprint arXiv:1912.07076 (2019)

27. Weston, L., et al.: Named entity recognition and normalization applied to large-scale information extraction from the materials science literature. J. Chem. Inf. Model. **59**(9), 3692–3702 (2019)
28. Xu, M., Jiang, H., Watcharawittayakul, S.: A local detection approach for named entity recognition and mention detection. In: Proceedings of the 55th Annual Meeting of the Association for Computational Linguistics (Volume 1: Long Papers), pp. 1237–1247 (2017)
29. Yamada, I., Asai, A., Shindo, H., Takeda, H., Matsumoto, Y.: Luke: deep contextualized entity representations with entity-aware self-attention. arXiv preprint arXiv:2010.01057 (2020)
30. Yang, Y., et al.: Generative data augmentation for commonsense reasoning. arXiv preprint arXiv:2004.11546 (2020)
31. Yasunaga, M., Leskovec, J., Liang, P.: Linkbert: pretraining language models with document links. arXiv preprint arXiv:2203.15827 (2022)
32. Yu, J., Bohnet, B., Poesio, M.: Named entity recognition as dependency parsing. arXiv preprint arXiv:2005.07150 (2020)
33. Yuan, H., Yuan, Z., Gan, R., Zhang, J., Xie, Y., Yu, S.: Biobart: pretraining and evaluation of a biomedical generative language model. arXiv preprint arXiv:2204.03905 (2022)

Multi-task Hierarchical Cross-Attention Network for Multi-label Text Classification

Junyu Lu, Hao Zhang, Zhexu Shen, Kaiyuan Shi, Liang Yang, Bo Xu, Shaowu Zhang, and Hongfei Lin[✉]

School of Computer Science and Technology, Dalian University of Technology, Dalian, China
{dutljy,zh373911345,szx,Dutirsky}@mail.dlut.edu.cn,
{liang,xubo,zhangsw,hflin}@dlut.edu.cn

Abstract. As the quantity of scientific publications grows significantly, manual indexing of literature becomes increasingly complex, and researchers have attempted to utilize techniques in Hierarchical Multi-label Text Classification (HMTC) to classify scientific literature. Although there have been many advances, some problems still cannot be effectively solved in HMTC tasks, such as the difficulty in capturing the dependencies of hierarchical labels and the correlation between labels and text, and the lack of adaptability of models to specialized text. In this paper, we propose a novel framework called Multi-task Hierarchical Cross-Attention Network (MHCAN) for multi-label text classification. Specifically, we introduce a cross-attention mechanism to fully incorporate text representation and hierarchical labels with a directed acyclic graph (DAG) structure, and design an iterative hierarchical-attention module to capture the dependencies between layers. Afterwards, our framework weighting jointly optimizes each level of loss. To improve the adaptability of the model to domain data, we also continue to pretrain SciBERT on unlabeled data and introduce adversarial training. Our framework ranks 2nd in NLPCC 2022 Shared Task 5 Track 1 (Multi-label Classification Model for English Scientific Literature). The experimental results show the effectiveness of the modules applied in this framework.

Keywords: Hierarchical multi-label text classification · Multi-task learning · Attention mechanism

1 Introduction

As the volume of scientific publications continues to increase, indexing such literature becomes critical [1]. Due to the professionalism and complexity of literature, it is difficult to manually categorize them. Therefore, there is an urgent need to design a pragmatic and intelligent automated classification framework. As adopted by some literature search sites, such as arXiv [2] and Microsoft

---

J. Lu and H. Zhang—Contribute equally to this work.

© Springer Nature Switzerland AG 2022
W. Lu et al. (Eds.) NLPCC 2022, LNCS 13552, pp. 156–167, 2022.
https://doi.org/10.1007/978-3-031-17189-5_13

Academic [3], hierarchical multi-label classification (HMTC) is an effective attempt for indexing scientific research literature [4].

In Task 5 Track 1, for a given example, including title and abstract, one or more labels may correspond to it, and these labels are stored hierarchically. Hierarchical multi-labels have dependencies between adjacent levels and can be represented as a DAG [5,6], where a label node can have multiple parent nodes. Low-level labels in the hierarchy are constrained by high-level labels [7]. Here we present a sample from the evaluation task dataset, as shown in Fig. 1. From the diagram, we can see that the document is associated with labels.

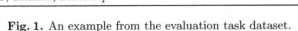

Title: "Toxic Effects of Single-Walled Carbon Nanotubes in the Development of E. coli Biofilm"
Abstract: "The impact of single-walled carbon nanotubes (SWNTs) on the different developmental stages of biofilms has been investigated ..."
C_1 : ['Materials science']
C_2 : ['Material properties', 'Biomaterials']
C_3 : ['Thickness', 'Biomass', 'Biofilms']

Fig. 1. An example from the evaluation task dataset.

Although numerous valuable efforts have been made [4,8–10], there is still a large degree of distortion in HTMC [11]. First, effective use of the relationship between the text and various levels of labels as well as the dependencies of the hierarchical labels is an significant aspect to examine the merits of the classifier, and it is a difficult task to utilize these dependencies organically in the prediction phase. Second, due to the specialism and complexity of the text, it is challenging to obtain an effective vector representation to preserve the original semantics embedded in the text. In addition, there is a problem of long-tail distribution of labels in realistic datasets, and most of the leaf nodes are labeled with relatively small amounts of data, leading to the inability of the model to classify efficiently.

To tackle the above problems, we propose a novel framework called Multi-task Hierarchical Cross-Attention Network (MHCAN) to achieve accurate classification of scientific research literature. We first obtain the representations of titles and abstracts with SciBERT [12], which is pretrained on a large corpus of scientific text, and we leverage GCNs [13] to represent labels with graph structure. Then, we utilize a cross-attention mechanism to fully integrate text and labels information at each level, and introduce iterative hierarchical-attention to further capture the information gain between adjacent levels. Finally, considering the dependencies of adjacent levels, we design a label masking mechanism to selectively mask the current predicted label according to previous predictions.

Besides the basic framework, we also utilize other modules to further improve model performance. We jointly optimize the loss at each level with Class-Balanced Loss [14] to alleviate the problem caused by the long-tailed distribution of labels. In addition, to improve the adaptability of the model to domain data, we refer to the related methods of domain-adaptive pretraining (DAPT) [15], continuing to pretrain SciBERT on unlabeled data. And we also introduce perturbations in the representations for adversarial training [16] to further enhance generalization. The main contributions of this work are summarized as follows:

- We propose a Multi-task Hierarchical Cross-Attention Network for hierarchical multi-label text classification, particularly addressing capturing the relationship between text and various levels of labels, and the dependencies between hierarchical labels.
- We integrate domain-adaptive pretraining and adversarial training into text representation to improve the generalization ability of the model to professional complex samples, and address the label imbalance problem by hierarchical optimization with Class-Balanced Loss.
- We examine the effectiveness of our framework on the dataset of shared task, and demonstrate that each module used in MHCAN can improve classification performance in HMTC by experiments.

2   Related Work

2.1   Hierarchical Multi-label Text Classification

Researchers have done several valuable attempts in HMTC. Huang et al. [4] propose an attention-based hierarchical layer to model the dependency relationship between different levels of the hierarchical structure in a top-down manner. Liang et al. [8] utilize bidirectional encoders from transformers, and map them to hierarchical labels with a delicate hierarchy-based loss layer. Sinha K et al. [9] adopt the attention-based dynamic representation at each level of labels, and utilize multi-layer perceptrons to predict the level of the current level, to dynamically generate the feature representation. Zhou et al. [10] raise a multi-label attention variant named HiAGM-LA, which conducts a soft-attention layer to combine hierarchy-aware label embeddings with label-aware text features.

2.2   Representation of Scientific Literature

PLMs based on large-scale corpora have become the mainstream text representation models since BERT [17] was proposed, leading to the popularity of the "Pre-training + Fine-tuning" paradigm for NLP tasks. Meanwhile, various models pretrained on text data from other domains using BERT-like methods have emerged. Among them, SciBERT [12] is a PLM trained on a large corpus of scientific text consisting of over 1 million papers from Semantic Scholar [18]. Experimental results demonstrated the outstanding performance of SciBERT in multiple downstream tasks, including text classification and sequence modeling, especially on the task of scientific literature classification [19–21]. Therefore, we utilize SciBERT to obtain the representation of text in NLPCC 2022 Task 5.

In order to train PLMs to acquire generic knowledge of large corpora, various pre-training tasks have been designed based on different application scenarios. For example, BERT applies Masked Language Modeling (MLM) and Next Sentence Prediction (NSP) to train the semantic understanding of words and sentences. In addition, Wang et al. [15] propose domain-adaptive pretraining (DAPT), and experimentally demonstrate that second-stage pretraining of the pretrained model using domain-specific data can improve the performance of the model on downstream tasks in the target domain.

3   Methodology

In this section, we will introduce the specific details of MHCAN. As shown in Fig. 2, the overall framework mainly contains three components. Firstly, Representation Layer (RL) is applied to obtain representations of text and hierarchical labels. Then, we design Hierarchical Cross-Attention Recursive Layer (HCARL) to capture correlations between text and labels, and dependencies between different levels of the hierarchy. Finally, we utilize Hierarchical Prediction Layer (HPL) to jointly optimize the loss at each level.

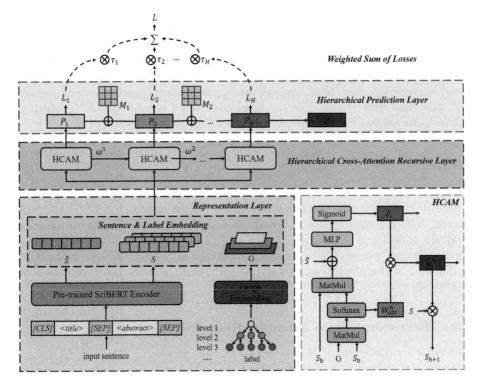

Fig. 2. The overall framework of MHCAN.

3.1   Representation Layer

Sentence Embedding. In this task, each sample contains two parts: title and abstract. As SciBERT [12] supports the case of simultaneous input of two sentences, we concatenate the above two into the following form: $[CLS]<title>[SEP][SEP]$, as shown in the input of SciBERT Encoder in Fig. 2. For a sample x_i of sequence length N, its last hidden state $S \in \mathbb{R}^{N \times d_S}$ is obtained through the encoder of SciBERT with dimension d_S. Then, we furthermore pool it by simply taking the hidden state corresponding to the first token $[CLS]$ and get the sentence representation $\tilde{S} \in \mathbb{R}^{d_S}$:

$$\tilde{S} = tanh(W \cdot S_{[CLS]}^{T}), \tag{1}$$

where $W \in \mathbb{R}^{d_S \times d_S}$ is a random weight matrix.

Besides that, we introduce Fast Gradient Method (FGM) [16] to further enhance the robustness and generalization ability of the model, which regularizes the model parameters by applying tiny perturbations r_{adv} computed by the gradient to sentence representations s, which is defined as:

$$r_{adv} = \epsilon \cdot g/\|g\|_2 \; where \; g = \nabla_s L(s, y), \tag{2}$$

where ϵ is a hyperparameter limiting the size of the adversarial perturbations.

Label Embedding. Since hierarchical labels can be represented as a directed acyclic graph structure [5,6], we utilize H-layer Graph Convolutional Networks (GCN) [13] to capture dependencies between different levels of labels. In the graph, each label is considered as a node, and hierarchical relationships between labels are summarized as edges between nodes. During the process of neighborhood aggregation, each label updates its representation based on other labels at its upper and lower levels. For the label node i, we obtain $L_i^l \in \mathbb{R}^{d_L}$, which is the d_L-dimensional label embedding at the lth layer of GCN:

$$h_i^l = W^l L_i^{l-1} + b^l,$$
$$L_i^l = \mathrm{ReLU}(h_i^l + \sum_{j \in N(i)} w_{ij} h_j^l), \tag{3}$$

where $W \in \mathbb{R}^{d_L \times d_L}$ is a randomly initialized weight matrix, $b \in \mathbb{R}^{d_l \times 1}$ is a bias vector, $N(i)$ means neighbor nodes of the node i, w_{ij} is the weight on the edge between node i and j. And we use $L = (L_1^H, L_2^H, ..., L_C^H)^T \in \mathbb{R}^{c \times d_L}$ as the final representation, where C is the number of categories. And we represent the label embedding of the h^{th}th-level as $L_h \in \mathbb{R}^{C_h \times d_L}$ and C_h is the count of classes at this level.

3.2   Hierarchical Cross-Attention Recursive Layer

Referring to the work of Huang et al. [4], we propose a Hierarchical Cross-Attention Module, which is an iterative hierarchical attention module to capture the correlation between labels and text and the dependencies of different labels. For the hth HCAM module, the input includes the hidden state of sentence embedding $S \in \mathbb{R}^{N \times d_s}$, sentence representation $\tilde{S} \in \mathbb{R}^{d_s}$ and label embedding of the hth-level $L_h \in \mathbb{R}^{C_h \times d_L}$, while the prediction of the hth level P_h and token weight vector $w_h \in \mathbb{R}^{N \times d_s}$ are output, where w_h is used to carry inter-level dependency information. HCARL is composed of H iterative HCAMs and details are given below.

With the information of previous level w_{h-1}, we update the sentence representation:

$$S_h = \omega^{h-1} \otimes S, \tag{4}$$

where $S_h \in \mathbb{R}^{N \times d_s}$ denotes the representation to capture the hierarchical dependencies. Afterwards, we introduce a cross-attention mechanism that allows each molecular clause to focus on different labels in order to fully integrate labels and text information:

$$O_h = \tanh(W_s^h \cdot S_h^T),$$
$$W_{att}^h = \mathrm{softmax}(L_h \cdot O_h), \tag{5}$$

where $W_s^h \in \mathbb{R}^{d_L \times d_S}$ is a randomly initialized weight matrix, $O_h \in \mathbb{R}^{d_L \times N}$ denotes the hidden layer state after activation. And $W_{att}^h \in \mathbb{R}^{C_h \times N}$ is a text-label attention score matrix, where $W_i^h \in \mathbb{R}^N$ represents the score of the text for the ith label at the hth level, and each element in W_i^h represents the contribution of each token to the ith label.

Then, we calculate the text-label representation $M_{att}^h \in \mathbb{R}^{d_S}$ by weighted summation, multiplying the attention score matrix W_{att}^h with the sentence representation S_h and averaging the result in label-dim:

$$M_{att}^h = avg(W_{att}^h \cdot S_h^T). \tag{6}$$

To obtain the integrated representation and predict the categories for each level, we concatenate the original sentence representation $\tilde{S}$ and the associated text-label representation W_{att}^h which introduces the information from its previous level. We utilize MLP to get the integrated representation and the predicted probability of labels, which are respectively denoted as $A_L^h \in \mathbb{R}^v$ and $P_h \in \mathbb{R}^{C_h}$:

$$A_L^h = \mathrm{ReLU}\left(W_T^h \cdot \left[\tilde{S} \oplus M_{att}^h\right]^T + b_T^h\right),$$
$$P_h = \mathrm{sigmoid}(W_L^h \cdot A_L^h + b_L^h), \tag{7}$$

where $W_T^h \in \mathbb{R}^{v \times 2d_S}$ and $W_L^h \in \mathbb{R}^{C_h \times v}$ are weighted matrices, while $b_T^h \in \mathbb{R}^{v \times 1}$ and $b_L^h \in \mathbb{R}^{C_h \times 1}$ are corresponding bias vector.

For the hth level, different categories contribute differently to the prediction, which can be used as weights for modifying the text-label attention matrix. Therefore, we utilize cross product to obtain weighted text-category attention matrix $K^h \in \mathbb{R}^{C_h \times N}$, combining the text-label attention score matrix W_{att}^h and the predicted values P_h. And then, we exploit an average pooling to merge C_h categories into $\widetilde{K^h} \in \mathbb{R}^N$, which is the weighted attention vector of the hth-level to hold the association between hierarchy and text:

$$K^h = \mathrm{broadcast}(P_h) \otimes W_{att}^h,$$
$$\widetilde{K^h} = avg(K^h), \tag{8}$$

Next, we broadcast the average representation $\widetilde{K^h}$ as $\omega^h = (\omega_1^h, \omega_2^h, ..., \omega_N^h) \in \mathbb{R}^{N \times d_S}$ to hold the hierarchy information, where $\omega_i^h \in \mathbb{R}^{d_S}$ measures the weights between all labels at the hth level and the ith token in the text:

$$\omega^h = \mathrm{broadcast}(\widetilde{K}^h). \tag{9}$$

Finally, we transmit token weight vector ω^h to the next category level to influence the input representation.

3.3 Hierarchical Prediction Layer

We obtain the prediction P_h at each level with HCARL. Considering the dependencies between layers, we design a label masking mechanism to mask the prediction results. According to the DAG structure of the hierarchical labels, we obtain C_{h-1}, which is the set of child nodes of the label predicted by the previous level. We take the intersection of P_h and C_{h-1} to obtain the final predicted labels $P'_h = P_h \cap C_{h-1}$, and the final predictions P is calculated by $P = P'_1 \oplus P'_2 \oplus ... \oplus P'_H$.

3.4 Rebalanced Loss Function

One reason why HMTC becomes a challenging task is the long-tailed distribution of labels. For the ith sample, there is a multi-label group $y^k = [y_1^k, \ldots, y_C^k] \in \{0,1\}^C$, and a classification result $z^k = [z_1^k, \ldots, y_C^k]$ corresponding to it. In this work, we utilize Class-balanced Focal Loss (CB) [14] re-weighting the binary cross entropy to address the class imbalance problem.

CB Loss rebalances the loss according to the effective number of samples for each class. The class-balanced term used to re-weight focal loss is defined as:

$$r_{CB} = \frac{1 - \beta}{1 - \beta^{n_i}}, \tag{10}$$

where n_i is the number of samples in the ith category, and $\beta \in (0, 1)$ controls the effect of sample size on marginal benefit.

Besides that, we refer to a related work of balancing method [22], which introduces a Negative Tolerant Regularization (NTR) [23] in the loss function to mitigate the over-suppression of negative labels. NTR initializes a non-zero bias v_i as a threshold, and linearly scales the negative logits before the original loss is computed negative, together with a regularization parameter λ to constrain the gradient between 0 and 1. And the CB Loss with NTR can be defined as:

$$L_{CB-NTR} = \begin{cases} r_{CB}(1 - q_i^k)^\gamma \log(q_i^k) & \text{if } y_i^k = 1 \\ r_{CB}\frac{1}{\lambda}(q_i^k)^\gamma \log(1 - q_i^k) & \text{otherwise} \end{cases} \tag{11}$$

where $q_i^k = \sigma(z_i^k - v_i)$ for positive instances and $q_i^k = \sigma(\lambda(z_i^k - v_i))$ for negative ones.

We use CB-NTR to calculate loss for each level, and then jointly optimize them. The complete loss function is given by:

$$L = \sum_{i=1}^{H} \tau_i L_i, \tag{12}$$

where τ_i is a parameter used to control the learning weight of the ith levels.

4 Experiment

4.1 Dataset and Evaluation

In this task, a dataset of 100,000 English scientific research documents is officially provided and the overview statistics of dataset is shown in Table 1. Each sample contains the title and abstract of the article and the corresponding categories, consisting of hierarchical three-level multi-labels (level1, level2, level3) and their union (levels). The number of categories for level1, level2, level3 and levels is 21, 260, 1272 and 1530, respectively. Furthermore, Fig. 3 indicates that these labels follow a long-tailed distribution and extremely few labels have large samples.

To evaluate the performance of the system, precision, recall and micro F1 value are applied as metrics.

Table 1. Statistics of the dataset.

Subset	Samples
Train set	90000
Verification set	5000
Test set	5000

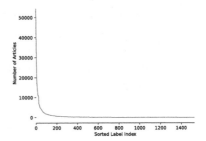

Fig. 3. The long-tailed distribution for the dataset.

4.2 Experimental Settings

Our experiments are mainly conducted through three stages, including pre-training, model training and testing. In practice of pre-training encoder of SciB-ERT[1], the probability of a token being masked is 15%. For masked tokens, there are 3 alternative options: (1) In 80% of the time, being replaced by a $[MASK]$ token; (2) In 10% of the time, being replaced by a random token; (3) In the rest 10% of the time, remaining unchanged. For the hyperparameters of model, the maximum combined input length N is set to 450. And the dimensions of the output sentence embedding d_S and label embedding d_L are set to 768 and 64. For the hierarchical cross-attention training of the three levels in MHCAN, the loss weights τ_1, τ_2 and τ_3 are assigned 0.05, 1, and 5, respectively. The dropout parameter we set in the model is 0.5 and we use AdamW as optimizer. During the training phase, we train the model for 100 epochs with a batch size of 16 and a learning rate of 1e-4 and introduce early stop mechanism to retain the parameters of five models with the best F1 score. In the testing period, predictions from the retained model are merged and voted to get the final results.

---

[1] https://huggingface.co/allenai/scibert_scivocab_uncased.

4.3 Results and Discussions

We utilize BERT-base and SciBERT as baselines to compare the performance of the models, and extensive ablation experiments are performed on each module. The results are shown in Table 2.

Table 2. Baseline and ablation experimental results.

Model	F1(micro)	Precision	Recall
BERT	0.5461	0.4260	0.7606
SciBERT	0.6265	0.5667	0.7005
Official Baseline	0.6550	0.6860	0.6270
MHCAN	**0.6784**	**0.6480**	**0.7119**
MHCAN-GE	0.6568	0.6049	0.7183
MHCAN-HCAM	0.6330	0.5782	0.6992
MHCAN-FGM	0.6521	0.6023	0.7109
MHCAN-DAPT	0.6632	0.6200	0.7129
MHCAN-DAPT-FGM	0.6442	0.5945	0.7031
Voted MHCAN	**0.6941**	**0.7056**	**0.6829**

(1) From the results, we can see that our proposed framework MHCAN model significantly outperforms the simple fine-tuning of the pre-trained baseline models in the hierarchical multi-label text classification task for scientific literature on the evaluation dataset. The improvement of MHCAN over the BERT-base and SciBERT is 13.23% and 5.19% in term of the micro-F1, respectively, demonstrating the effectiveness of the model.

(2) For measuring the impact of HCAM, we directly connect the text-label representation M_{att}^h to Hierarchical Prediction Layer, missing the information transmitted between the various levels. Compared to the original framework, the micro-F1 decreases by 4.54%, which confirms the significance of dependency features between levels to this shared task.

(3) To evaluate the enhancements resulting from the introduction of the graph structure, we ablate the GCN and only randomly initialize the label embedding. After removing GCN, the F1 score reduces by 2.16%, indicating the superiority of graph embedding in capturing the hierarchical and relevance information of labels.

(4) After introducing domain-adaptive pretraining and adversarial training of fast gradient method, the F1 score of the classification predictions increases by 1.52% and 2.63%, respectively. Meanwhile, the result of MHCAN integrating these two methods can further increase to 67.84%, which indicates that the adaptability of the model to specialized data can be enhanced with this combinatorial optimization strategy on sentence encoder.

(5) The result of voted MHCAN shows that model after voting gets a more accurate prediction result, and the final score is 69.41%, winning the 2nd place in the final ranking. This effect demonstrates that ensemble learning method of voted model can improve the generalization ability of classifiers.

4.4 Module Analysis

In this section, we analysis the influence of different encoder layers and balancing loss function on the performance of our model. The related experimental results are shown in Table 3.

Table 3. Experimental results of module analysis.

Model	F1(micro)	Precision	Recall
MHCAN(BERT)—CB+NTR	0.6456	0.5792	0.7293
MHCAN(SciBERT)—BCE	0.6393	0.5855	0.7039
MHCAN(SciBERT)—CB+NTR	0.6632	0.6200	0.7129
MHCAN(DAPT SciBERT)—CB+NTR	**0.6784**	**0.6480**	**0.7119**

(1) To evaluate the effectiveness of sentence representation methods, we conduct three encoder layers including BERT, SciBERT and SciBERT with DAPT, for comparative experiments. We can reach the similar conclusion that SciBERT captures the semantic information of scientific text better than BERT. Meanwhile, it can be seen that the pre-training after domain adaptation can better match the downstream tasks for classification.

(2) In this section, we utilize general binary cross entropy and CB loss with NTR to test the impact of loss function, respectively. From the experimental results, we can see that the combined balancing strategy of CBloss with NTR can improve the performance of model. The reason for this phenomenon is that the balancing method can deal with the long-tailed distribution of labels in the dataset and boost model training weights for categories with small sample sizes.

5 Conclusion

In this work, we propose Multi-task Hierarchical Cross-Attention Network (MHCAN) to tackle the problem of classifying scientific literature by Hierarchical Multi-label Text Classification (HMTC). We utilize a cross-attention mechanism to fully incorporate text representation and hierarchical labels embedding, and design an iterative hierarchical-attention module to capture the dependencies between levels. Afterwards, we jointly optimize each loss level with weighted. We also continue to pre-train SciBERT on unlabeled data and introduce adversarial training to improve the adaptability of the model to domain data. Our framework ranks 2nd in NLPCC 2022 Shared Task 5 Track 1 and the experimental results demonstrate the effectiveness of the modules applied in the framework.

In the future, we will explore the following directions: (1) To perform text classification of scientific literature, it is crucial to enrich the vocabulary of an already trained natural language model with vocabulary from the specialized domain [24]. Therefore, in the case of BERT-like models and their WordPiece tokenizers, we will further design an efficient method to find and add domain-specific vocabularies. (2) Since there is no correlation between most of the categories, the link matrix of the labels is sparse, which is not conducive to the update of the graph-structured label representation. We will try to use Tree-Structured LSTM [25] to obtain label embedding.

Acknowledgement. This work was supported by grant from the Natural Science Foundation of China (No. 62076046, 61702080, 62006034), Natural Science Foundation of Liaoning Province (No. 2021-BS-067) and the Fundamental Research Funds for the Central Universities (No. DUT21RC(3)015).

References

1. CNPIEC KEXIN LTD. Datasets for NLPCC2022.SharedTask5.Track1 (2022). https://doi.org/10.11922/sciencedb.j00104.00100
2. McKiernan, G.: arxiv.org: the los alamos national laboratory e-print server. Int. J. Grey Liter. (2000)
3. Harzing, A.W., Alakangas, S.: Microsoft academic: is the phoenix getting wings? Scientometrics **110**(1), 371–383 (2017)
4. Huang, W., et al.: Hierarchical multi-label text classification: an attention-based recurrent network approach. In: Proceedings of the 28th ACM International Conference on Information and Knowledge Management, pp. 1051–1060 (2019)
5. Silla, C.N., Freitas, A.A.: A survey of hierarchical classification across different application domains. Data Mining Knowl. Discov. **22**(1), 31–72 (2011)
6. Wehrmann, J., Cerri, R., Barros, R.: Hierarchical multi-label classification networks. In: International Conference on Machine Learning, pp. 5075–5084. PMLR (2018)
7. Petković, M., Džeroski, S., Kocev, D.: Feature ranking for hierarchical multi-label classification with tree ensemble methods. Acta Polytech. Hungar. **17**(10) (2020)
8. Liang, X., Cheng, D., Yang, F., Luo, Y., Qian, W., Zhou, A.: F-hmtc: detecting financial events for investment decisions based on neural hierarchical multi-label text classification. In: IJCAI, pp. 4490–4496 (2020)
9. Sinha, K., Dong, Y., Cheung, J.C.K., Ruths, D.: A hierarchical neural attention-based text classifier. In: Proceedings of the 2018 Conference on Empirical Methods in Natural Language Processing, pp. 817–823 (2018)
10. Zhou, J., et al.: Hierarchy-aware global model for hierarchical text classification. In: Proceedings of the 58th Annual Meeting of the Association for Computational Linguistics, pp. 1106–1117 (2020)
11. Zhao, H., Cao, J., Chen, Q., Cao, J.: Methods of hierarchical multi-label text classification. J. Chinese Comput. Syst. **43**(4), 673–683 (2022)

12. Beltagy, I., Lo, K., Cohan, A.: SciBERT: a pretrained language model for scientific text. In: Proceedings of the 2019 Conference on Empirical Methods in Natural Language Processing and the 9th International Joint Conference on Natural Language Processing (EMNLP-IJCNLP), pp. 3615–3620 (2019)
13. Kipf, T.N., Welling, M.: Semi-supervised classification with graph convolutional networks. arXiv preprint arXiv:1609.02907 (2016)
14. Cui, Y., Jia, M., Lin, T.Y., Song, Y., Belongie, S.: Class-balanced loss based on effective number of samples. In: Proceedings of the IEEE/CVF Conference on Computer Vision and Pattern Recognition, pp. 9268–9277 (2019)
15. Gururangan, S., et al.: Don't stop pretraining: adapt language models to domains and tasks. In: Proceedings of the 58th Annual Meeting of the Association for Computational Linguistics, pp. 8342–8360. Association for Computational Linguistics, Online (2020)
16. Miyato, T., Dai, A.M., Goodfellow, I.: Adversarial training methods for semi-supervised text classification. arXiv preprint arXiv:1605.07725 (2016)
17. Devlin, J., Chang, M.W., Lee, K., Toutanova, K.: BERT: pre-training of deep bidirectional transformers for language understanding. In: Proceedings of the 2019 Conference of the North American Chapter of the Association for Computational Linguistics: Human Language Technologies, Volume 1 (Long and Short Papers), pp. 4171–4186 (2019)
18. Ammar, W., et al.: Construction of the literature graph in semantic scholar. In: Proceedings of the 2018 Conference of the North American Chapter of the Association for Computational Linguistics: Human Language Technologies, Volume 3 (Industry Papers), pp. 84–91 (2018)
19. Chalkidis, I., Fergadiotis, M., Kotitsas, S., Malakasiotis, P., Aletras, N., Androutsopoulos, I.: An empirical study on large-scale multi-label text classification including few and zero-shot labels. In: Proceedings of the 2020 Conference on Empirical Methods in Natural Language Processing (EMNLP), pp. 7503–7515 (2020)
20. Park, S., Caragea, C.: Scientific keyphrase identification and classification by pretrained language models intermediate task transfer learning. In: Proceedings of the 28th International Conference on Computational Linguistics, pp. 5409–5419 (2020)
21. Ambalavanan, A.K., Devarakonda, M.V.: Using the contextual language model bert for multi-criteria classification of scientific articles. J. Biomed. Inf. **112**, 103578 (2020)
22. Huang, Y., Giledereli, B., Köksal, A., Özgür, A., Ozkirimli, E.: Balancing methods for multi-label text classification with long-tailed class distribution. In: Proceedings of the 2021 Conference on Empirical Methods in Natural Language Processing, pp. 8153–8161 (2021)
23. Wu, T., Huang, Q., Liu, Z., Wang, Y., Lin, D.: Distribution-balanced loss for multi-label classification in long-tailed datasets. In: Vedaldi, A., Bischof, H., Brox, T., Frahm, J.-M. (eds.) ECCV 2020. LNCS, vol. 12349, pp. 162–178. Springer, Cham (2020). https://doi.org/10.1007/978-3-030-58548-8_10
24. Tai, W., Kung, H.T., Dong, X., Comiter, M., Kuo, C.F.: exBERT: extending pre-trained models with domain-specific vocabulary under constrained training resources. In: Findings of the Association for Computational Linguistics: EMNLP 2020, pp. 1433–1439. Association for Computational Linguistics (2020)
25. Tai, K.S., Socher, R., Manning, C.D.: Improved semantic representations from tree-structured long short-term memory networks. In: Proceedings of the 53rd Annual Meeting of the Association for Computational Linguistics and the 7th International Joint Conference on Natural Language Processing (Volume 1: Long Papers), pp. 1556–1566. Association for Computational Linguistics, Beijing (2015)

An Interactive Fusion Model for Hierarchical Multi-label Text Classification

Xiuhao Zhao[1], Zhao Li[1(✉)], Xianming Zhang[1], Jibin Wang[1], Tong Chen[2], Zhengyu Ju[1], Canjun Wang[1], Chao Zhang[1], and Yiming Zhan[1]

[1] Shandong Computer Science Center (National Supercomputer Center in Jinan), Shandong Provincial Key Laboratory of Computer Networks, Qilu University of Technology (Shandong Academy of Sciences), Jinan, China
`{liz,wangjb}@sdas.org`
[2] Evay Info, Jinan, China
`chentong@sdas.org`

Abstract. Scientific research literature usually has multi-level labels, and there are often dependencies between multi-level labels. It is crucial for the model to learn and integrate the information between multi-level labels for the hierarchical multi-label text classification (HMTC) of scientific research literature texts. Therefore, for the HMTC task in the scientific research literature, we use the pre-trained language model SciBERT trained on scientific texts. And we introduce a shared TextCNN layer in our multi-task learning architecture to learn the dependency information between labels at each level. Then the hierarchical feature information is fused and propagated from top to bottom according to the task level. We conduct ablation experiments on the dependency information interaction module and the hierarchical information fusion propagation module. Experimental results on the NLPCC2022 SharedTask5 Track1 dataset demonstrate the effectiveness of our model, and we rank 4th place in the task.

Keywords: Hierarchical multi-label text classification · Pre-trained language model · Multi-task learning · TextCNN

1 Introduction

In recent years, with the increase of scientific research documents in various fields, the indexing of scientific research documents has become more critical. Search engines [8], digital libraries [5], and citation indexes [6] are widely used to search these documents and publications. The intelligent classification of scientific research literature improves users' retrieval efficiency and quality. Multi-label hierarchical text classification is a commonly used method for indexing scientific literature.

This paper studies the hierarchical multi-label text classification task for scientific literature, which can be regarded as a special sub-task of multi-label text classification, but it is more challenging than ordinary multi-label classification tasks [14,16]. For hierarchical multi-label text classification tasks, hierarchical multi-label can be represented by a hierarchical tree structure. As shown in Fig. 1, Physical chemistry and Inorganic chemistry are two primary classification labels, Chemical structure, Molecules, and Surface science are secondary classification labels under Physical chemistry, and Molecular structure and Crystal structure are tertiary classifications under Chemical structure Label.

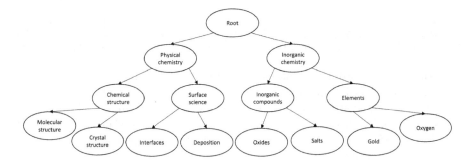

Fig. 1. The sample diagram of the label hierarchy.

With the rapid development of deep learning technology in recent years, some neural network methods have improved the effect of feature extraction, and various neural network models have also begun to be used in the task of multi-label text classification. Compared with single-label text classification, the main challenge of hierarchical multi-label text classification is in exploring the relationship between text feature representation and label structure. The RCNN [7] model uses a recurrent neural network(RNN) to extract features with contextual information and perform subsequent text classification. The TextCNN [3] model uses convolution kernels of different sizes in the convolutional neural network(CNN) to extract contextual feature information of various text spans, further improving text classification's effect. [17] regards the multi-label classification task as multiple binary classification tasks and trains a binary classification model for each label. However, this makes the learning between each label unrelated, and the dependencies between labels cannot be learned. The XML-CNN [10] model adds a bottleneck hidden layer and a dynamic maximum pooling layer based on the TextCNN model and uses dynamic maximum pooling to obtain finer-grained features in different regions of the document, enabling the model to deal with large label spaces. The HR-DGCNN [12] model converts text into word graphs, captures long-range semantic information using graph convolutional neural networks, and adds recursive regularization to capture hierarchical relationships in labels.

The above methods use the same model structure to predict different level labels, ignoring the differences and diversity between different level labels, which leads to poor prediction performance of each level label. Moreover, they do not explicitly model the dependencies between the labels of each level at the task level, and the extracted features cannot fully integrate the interactive information between the hierarchical tasks. In addition, scientific research literature texts have strong domain characteristics, while pre-trained language models have strong text feature representation capabilities and semantic understanding capabilities. Therefore, based on the SciBERT pre-training model trained on scientific literature texts, we propose a hierarchical multi-label text classification model in the field of scientific literature named MSFP, which first learns the dependency information between labels at all levels with a shared TextCNN based on a multi-task learning architecture, and then the hierarchical feature information is fused and propagated from the top to bottom according to the task level. Overall, the contributions of this paper are as follows:

- In the shared encoding module, we introduce the SciBERT pre-training model trained on scientific literature for preliminary feature extraction.
- In the task-special module, we use the multi-task learning architecture to divide the task into four sub-tasks and introduce a shared multi-convolution kernel TextCNN network to interactively learn the dependency information between hierarchical labels.
- We construct a multi-level label classifier from top to bottom according to the label level so that the hierarchical label information can be fused and propagated from top to bottom.
- Experimental results on NLPCC2022 SharedTask5 Track1 dataset demonstrate the effectiveness of our method and the necessity of the dependency information interaction module and the hierarchical information fusion propagation module.

2   Related Work

BERT [4] is a pre-trained language model trained on a multi-layer Transformer model using a large-scale text corpus. As shown in Fig. 2, different from the traditional left-to-right language modelling goal, BERT is trained with two-goal tasks: random mask strategy and next sentence prediction. SciBERT [1] follows the same architecture as the BERT model, which is pre-trained on multiple scientific text corpora.

Multi-task learning [2] is inspired by the human learning process and aims to improve the generalization performance of multiple related tasks with the help of public knowledge with limited labelled data. Multi-task learning has many applications in real-world tasks, such as natural language processing, computer vision, etc. Its core is to improve the overall generalization ability of the model by training multiple related tasks simultaneously and sharing parameters between different tasks. Multi-task learning includes two modes: soft sharing mechanism of hidden parameters and soft sharing mechanism of hidden parameters. In the hard parameter sharing method, the model consists of a shared layer and a task-specific layer. The shared layer is used to learn and share common knowledge and representations, while the task-specific layer compensates for the differences between different tasks to improve the generalization of different tasks. In the soft parameter sharing method, different subtasks have independent models. The regularization method acts on the distance between different model parameters so that the model parameters of similar tasks are also similar [13].

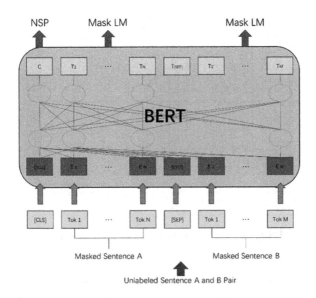

Fig. 2. BERT pre-trained model architecture.

TextCNN [3] is a classic text classification model. As shown in Fig. 3, the model uses convolution kernels of different sizes to perform convolution and pooling operations on the vector representation of the input text to extract features of different granularities for combination and screening to obtain the representation of high-level text feature vectors. The TextCNN model is mainly composed of four parts: input layer, convolution layer, pooling layer and output layer. For the input text containing n words, the convolution layer uses m sliding windows of different sizes to conduct convolution operations on the input text vectors to learn text features:

$$H = f(W \cdot T_{i:i+m-1} + b) \tag{1}$$

where $W \in \mathbb{R}^{m \times d}$ represents a parameter trainable convolution kernel, d represents the word vector dimension of each word, $T_{i:i+m-1}$ represents a sliding window consisting of the i_{th} row to the $i + m - 1_{th}$ row of the input matrix, b is the bias parameter, f is the nonlinear mapping function. The pooling layer uses a 1-MaxPool maximum pooling strategy to filter out a maximum eigenvalue from each sliding window:

$$C_i = \max\{H\} = \max (H_1, H_2, \cdots, H_{n-m+1}) \tag{2}$$

Then all the pooled feature values are concatenated to obtain the high-level feature vector:

$$C = [C_1; C_2; \cdots ; C_{n-m+1}] \tag{3}$$

where $C \in \mathbb{R}^{n-m+1}$. After completing the convolution pooling operation, a fully connected neural network can be connected to predict text labels.

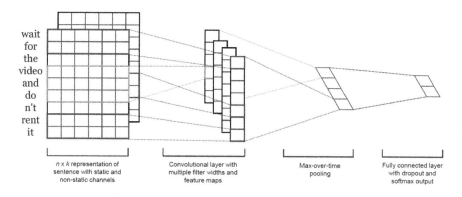

Fig. 3. The TextCNN model architecture.

In hierarchical multi-label classification tasks, there are often commonalities and differences in classification tasks at different levels, so this paper adopts the hard parameter sharing method of multi-task learning. The model consists of a shared encoding module and a task-specific module. In the shared encoding module, we use the SicBERT model with the same architecture as the BERT model. In the task-specific module, we introduce a multi-convolution kernel shared CNN between tasks to ensure the information interaction between sub-tasks and learn the dependencies between multi-level labels.

3   Task Definition

This task aims to build a hierarchical multi-label text classification model of scientific literature based on the given scientific literature metadata (title and abstract text) and the corresponding hierarchical labels of subject categories. The labels include hierarchical multi-labels (level1, level2 and level3) and the union of hierarchical multi-labels (levels). The number of label categories for level1, level2, level3 and levels is 21, 260, 1272 and 1530, respectively.

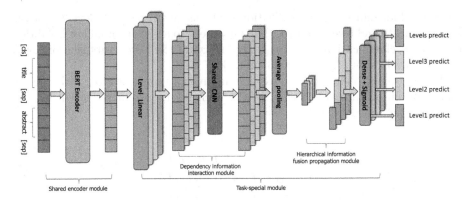

Fig. 4. The overall architecture of MSFP Model. The preprocessed sentence is first input to the shared encoding module to obtain hidden representations with contextual information. Then perform linear transformation on the obtained hidden representation, and the vector representation of each level will be obtained and input into the dependency information interaction module to learn the dependency information between each level. Finally, the hierarchical information fusion propagation module can further integrate the interactive information of each level and obtain the final hidden representation with the dependency information of each level.

4   Method

As shown in Fig. 4, our proposed MSFP model contains two modules: a shared encoding module and a task-specific module. And the task-specific module contains a dependency information interaction module and a hierarchical information fusion propagation module.

4.1   Shared Encoder Module

In the shared encoding module, we use the SciBERT model trained on the scientific literature corpus. The input X of the model consists of two parts: title and abstract. $X = \{[CLS], title, [SEP], abstract, [SEP]\}$, where $title = \{x_{1,1}, x_{1,2}, \ldots, x_{1,n}\}$, $abstract = \{x_{2,1}, x_{2,2}, \ldots, x_{2,m}\}$.

$$E = SciBERT(X) \tag{4}$$

where $E = \{e_1, e_2, \ldots, e_n \mid e_i \in \mathbb{R}^{d \times 1}\}$ represents the hidden vector representation containing context information obtained by SciBERT[1] encoding input sentences.

4.2   Task-Specific Module

After getting the hidden vector representation with contextual information, we feed it into the task-specific module. In the specific task module, we divide the

---

[1] https://github.com/allenai/scibert.

tasks into four multi-label classification subtasks: level1 subtask, level2 subtask, level3 subtask, and levels subtask. The purpose is to assist the final levels subtask multi-label classification task by jointly learning the three subtasks of level1 subtask, level2 subtask, and level3 subtask.

In the task-specific module, we first input the representation with contextual information into the linear layer of each level, and then we will get the representation of each level:

$$
\begin{aligned}
H_{level1} &= Level1Linear(E) \\
H_{level2} &= Level2Linear(E) \\
H_{level3} &= Level3Linear(E) \\
H_{levels} &= LevelsLinear(E)
\end{aligned}
\tag{5}
$$

Because there is a dependency relationship between labels at each level, to enable the model to learn the dependency information between labels at each level, we introduce a shared multi-convolution kernel TextCNN model between tasks at each level to learn and fuse the dependency information at all levels:

$$
\begin{aligned}
H_{s-level1} &= SharedCNN\left(H_{level1}\right) \\
H_{s-level2} &= SharedCNN\left(H_{level2}\right) \\
H_{s-level3} &= SharedCNN\left(H_{level3}\right) \\
H_{s-levels} &= SharedCNN\left(H_{levels}\right)
\end{aligned}
\tag{6}
$$

In the shared CNN model, we set the filter width to be [3, 5, 7, 9], the input channel size is d, the output channel size is $2d$, and the activation function is glu.

We then use an average pooling strategy [9] to obtain context vector representations at each level:

$$
\begin{aligned}
H_{p-level1} &= AveragePool\left(H_{s-level1}\right) \\
H_{p-level2} &= AveragePool\left(H_{s-level2}\right) \\
H_{p-level3} &= AveragePool\left(H_{s-level3}\right) \\
H_{p-levels} &= AveragePool\left(H_{s-levels}\right)
\end{aligned}
\tag{7}
$$

After obtaining the context vector representation of each level, we perform a linear transformation:

$$
\begin{aligned}
H_{p-level1'} &= Linear\left(H_{p-level1}\right) \\
H_{p-level2'} &= Linear\left(H_{p-level2}\right) \\
H_{p-level3'} &= Linear\left(H_{p-level3}\right) \\
H_{p-levels'} &= Linear\left(H_{p-levels}\right)
\end{aligned}
\tag{8}
$$

Then we use a top-down strategy to concatenate the vector representations of each level according to the level and perform linear transformations again:

$$
\begin{aligned}
H_{c-level1} &= Linear\left(H_{p-level1}\right) \\
H_{c-level2} &= Linear\left([H_{p-level2}; H_{p-level1}]\right) \\
H_{c-level3} &= Linear\left([H_{p-level3}; H_{p-level2}]\right) \\
H_{c-levels} &= Linear\left([H_{p-levels}; H_{p-level3}]\right)
\end{aligned}
\tag{9}
$$

Finally, we perform the linear transformation on the obtained vector representation of each level to get the prediction result of each level:

$$
\begin{aligned}
O_{level1} &= \sigma \left(Linear \left(H_{c-level1} \right) \right) \\
O_{level2} &= \sigma \left(Linear \left(H_{c-level2} \right) \right) \\
O_{level3} &= \sigma \left(Linear \left(H_{c-level3} \right) \right) \\
O_{levels} &= \sigma \left(Linear \left(H_{c-levels} \right) \right)
\end{aligned}
\tag{10}
$$

where σ refers to the Sigmoid activation function.

4.3 Training and Inference

We jointly train the four subtasks of level1 subtask, level2 subtask, level3 subtask, and levels subtask, and the loss function L consists of four parts:

$$
\begin{aligned}
L_{level1} &= BCELoss \left(T_{level1}, O_{level1} \right) \\
L_{level2} &= BCELoss \left(T_{level2}, O_{level2} \right) \\
L_{level3} &= BCELoss \left(T_{level3}, O_{level3} \right) \\
L_{levels} &= BCELoss \left(T_{levels}, O_{levels} \right)
\end{aligned}
\tag{11}
$$

where T_{level} and O_{level1} represent the ground truth label and the predicted value of each level. In each subtask, we all use the $BCELoss^2$ loss function, the goal of training is to minimize the loss function L:

$$
L = L_{level1} + L_{level2} + L_{level3} + L_{levels}
\tag{12}
$$

In the inference stage, we set the threshold of each subtask to be 0.5, and we take the element index greater than the threshold as the final predicted label.

5 Experiment

In this section, we introduce the dataset, baseline model, implementation details, evaluation metrics, and main results for this task.

Datasets. We evaluate our model on dataset for NLPCC2022 SharedTask5 Track1 [11]. The dataset contains 95,000 English scientific research literature text data, including 90,000 training datasets and 5,000 validation datasets. Each data sample contains the title and summary of the article and the corresponding hierarchical multilabels (level1, level2 and level3) and the union of hierarchical multi labels (levels). The number of label categories for level1, level2, level3 and levels is 21, 260, 1272 and 1530, respectively. In addition, these labels follow a long-tailed distribution.

---

[2] $BCE\,Loss(x, y) = -(y \log x + (1 - y) \log(1 - x))$.

Baseline. The baseline model of NLPCC2022 SharedTask5 Track1 is Balance-BERT. The model uses SciBERT as a pre-training model on the encoding layer. On the task-specific layer, the model only models the multi-label classification task of levels, and uses DBLoss [15] to deal with label imbalance problem.

Implementation Details. When training the model, we used the AdamW optimizer, and the learning rate is 5e−5, the hidden size is 768, the batch size is 48, and the epoch is 60. We used Pytorch to implement the model and train the model on two NVIDIA A100 GPUs.

Evaluation Metrics. Each scientific literature text data sample has one or more labels at each level, and the label prediction at each level belongs to a typical multi-label text classification task. We use the standard Precision, Recall, and Micro-F1 to evaluate our model:

$$Micro - F1 = \frac{2 \times Precision \times Recall}{Precision + Recall} \tag{13}$$

$$Precision = \frac{TP}{TP + FP} \tag{14}$$

$$Recall = \frac{TP}{TP + FN} \tag{15}$$

In the evaluation metrics, $Precision$ represents the proportion of correctly predicted samples among all samples whose prediction results are positive examples, and $Recall$ represents the proportion of correctly predicted samples among all samples whose true results are positive examples. $Micro - F1$ considers the overall precision and recall of all labels, which is the harmonic mean of the two.

Table 1. Experiment results on NLPCC2022 SharedTask5 Track1 dataset.

Model	Precision	Recall	F1
Baseline	68.6	62.7	65.5
MSFP	**73.2**	64.9	**68.8**

Table 2. F1-score of ablation experiments for different pre-trained models.

Model	F1
Baseline($SciBERT_{base}$)	65.5
MSFP($XLNet_{base}$)	66.8
MSFP($BERT_{base}$)	67.9
MSFP($SciBERT_{base}$)	**68.8**

Table 3. F1-score for ablation experiments performed on the model architecture. The STC in the table refers to the shared TextCNN module, and HIFP refers to the hierarchical information fusion propagation module.

Model	F1
MSFP	**68.8**
- HIFP	68.6
- STC	68.2
- STC and HIFP	67.7

Main Results. The experimental results of our proposed model and baseline model are reported in Table 1. We can observe that our proposed model significantly outperforms the baseline in terms of precision, recall and F1-score, and the F1-score exceeds the baseline model by 3.3%. This proves that our model is effective. To further analyze our model, we also performed ablation experiments to illustrate the necessity of different modules. Based on our best model architecture, we first conduct ablation experiments on pre-trained models. As shown in Table 2, when our model uses a BERT pre-trained model, the F1-score drops by 0.9%; when using the XLNet pre-trained model, the F1-score drops by 2%. This demonstrates the importance of domain-adapted pre-trained models for domain-specific tasks. We can also observe that our model still achieves better results than baseline model even when using XLNet or BERT pre-trained models, which proves that our model is better than baseline model in terms of architecture. We also conduct ablation experiments on the model structure, including removing the shared TextCNN(STC) module and the hierarchical information fusion propagation(HIFP) module. As shown in Table 3, When the STC or HIFP modules were removed individually, the F1 value decreased by 0.2% and 0.6%, respectively. When both two modules are removed, the F1-score drops by 1.1%. This illustrates the necessity of dependency information interaction and fusion propagation between tasks at all levels.

6   Conclusion

In this paper, we propose a hierarchical multi-label text classification method for scientific literature texts. We divide the HMTC task into four sub-tasks that can be learned jointly, and introduce a shared TextCNN on the task-specific layer that can learn dependency information at all levels. And we construct a multi-level label classifier from top to bottom according to the label level so that the hierarchical label information can be fused and propagated from top to bottom. Experimental results on the NLPCC2022 SharedTask5 Track1 dataset demonstrate the effectiveness of our method and the necessity of the dependency information interaction module and the hierarchical information fusion propagation module.

Acknowledgment. This work was supported by the National Key R&D Program of China (Grant No. 2018YFB1404500 and No. 2018YFB1404503).

References

1. Beltagy, I., Lo, K., Cohan, A.: SciBERT: a pretrained language model for scientific text. In: Proceedings of the 2019 Conference on Empirical Methods in Natural Language Processing and the 9th International Joint Conference on Natural Language Processing (EMNLP-IJCNLP), pp. 3615–3620 (2019)
2. Caruana, R.: Multitask learning. Mach. Learn. **28**(1), 41–75 (1997)
3. Chen, Y.: Convolutional neural network for sentence classification. Master's thesis, University of Waterloo (2015)
4. Devlin, J., Chang, M.W., Lee, K., Toutanova, K.: BERT: pre-training of deep bidirectional transformers for language understanding. arXiv preprint arXiv:1810.04805 (2018)
5. Fox, E.A., Akscyn, R.M., Furuta, R.K., Leggett, J.J.: Digital libraries. Commun. ACM **38**(4), 22–28 (1995)
6. Garfield, E.: The evolution of the science citation index. Int. Microbiol. **10**(1), 65 (2007)
7. Lai, S., Xu, L., Liu, K., Zhao, J.: Recurrent convolutional neural networks for text classification. In: Twenty-Ninth AAAI Conference on Artificial Intelligence (2015)
8. Lewandowski, D.: Web searching, search engines and information retrieval. Inf. Serv. Use **25**(3–4), 137–147 (2005)
9. Lin, M., Chen, Q., Yan, S.: Network in network. arXiv preprint arXiv:1312.4400 (2013)
10. Liu, J., Chang, W.C., Wu, Y., Yang, Y.: Deep learning for extreme multi-label text classification. In: Proceedings of the 40th International ACM SIGIR Conference on Research and Development in Information Retrieval, pp. 115–124 (2017)
11. LTD, C.K.: Datasets for NLPCC2022.SharedTask5.Track1. https://doi.org/10.11922/sciencedb.j00104.00100
12. Peng, H., et al.: Large-scale hierarchical text classification with recursively regularized deep graph-CNN. In: Proceedings of the 2018 World Wide Web Conference, pp. 1063–1072 (2018)
13. Ruder, S.: An overview of multi-task learning in deep neural networks. arXiv preprint arXiv:1706.05098 (2017)
14. Silla, C.N., Freitas, A.A.: A survey of hierarchical classification across different application domains. Data Min. Knowl. Disc. **22**(1), 31–72 (2011)
15. Wu, T., Huang, Q., Liu, Z., Wang, Yu., Lin, D.: Distribution-balanced loss for multi-label classification in long-tailed datasets. In: Vedaldi, A., Bischof, H., Brox, T., Frahm, J.-M. (eds.) ECCV 2020. LNCS, vol. 12349, pp. 162–178. Springer, Cham (2020). https://doi.org/10.1007/978-3-030-58548-8_10
16. Xu, L., et al.: Hierarchical multi-label text classification with horizontal and vertical category correlations. In: Proceedings of the 2021 Conference on Empirical Methods in Natural Language Processing, pp. 2459–2468 (2021)
17. Yao, L., Mao, C., Luo, Y.: Graph convolutional networks for text classification. In: Proceedings of the AAAI Conference on Artificial Intelligence, vol. 33, pp. 7370–7377 (2019)

Scene-Aware Prompt for Multi-modal Dialogue Understanding and Generation

Bin Li[1], Yixuan Weng[2], Ziyu Ma[1], Bin Sun[1], and Shutao Li[1(✉)]

[1] College of Electrical and Information Engineering, Hunan University,
Changsha, China
{libincn,maziyu,sunbin611,shutao_li}@hnu.edu.cn
[2] National Laboratory of Pattern Recognition Institute of Automation,
Chinese Academy Sciences, Beijing, China

Abstract. This paper introduces the schemes of Team LingJing's experiments in NLPCC-2022-Shared-Task-4 Multi-modal Dialogue Understanding and Generation (MDUG). The MDUG task can be divided into two phases: multi-modal context understanding and response generation. To fully leverage the visual information for both scene understanding and dialogue generation, we propose the scene-aware prompt for the MDUG task. Specifically, we utilize the multi-tasking strategy for jointly modelling the scene- and session- multi-modal understanding. The visual captions are adopted to aware the scene information, while the fixed-type templated prompt based on the scene- and session-aware labels are used to further improve the dialogue generation performance. Extensive experimental results show that the proposed method has achieved state-of-the-art (SOTA) performance compared with other competitive methods, where we rank the 1-st in all three subtasks in this MDUG competition.

Keywords: Multi-modal dialogue understanding and generation · Multi-task · Scene-aware prompt

1 Introduction

With advances in AI technology, the researchers are constructing intelligent machines capable of communicating with humans towards a given task [1]. The commonest option for achieving human-robot interaction is the design of a dialogue system that acts as a voice-interactive interface between the user and robot for better human-robot relationship [2]. It is consequently becoming more and more important to equip systems with this social capability, with which they can respond appropriately to the user. Considering both the contextual and content elements of a multi-modal dialogue, many attempts for modelling have been made to enhance the human-robot services. For the dialogue modelling, the conversational context has played an essential part in determining the relevance of

Supported by the National Key R&D Program of China (2018YFB1305200), the National Natural Science Fund of China (62171183).
B. Li, Y. Weng and Z. Ma—Contributed this work equally.

W. Lu et al. (Eds.) NLPCC 2022, LNCS 13552, pp. 179–191, 2022.
https://doi.org/10.1007/978-3-031-17189-5_15

responses to a user's discourse [3]. Situational factors include any information used to characterise a dialogue situation that can influence the system's response, such as the mood of the user [4] or the environmental cues of the dialogue [5]. By taking contextual information into account, dialogue systems can quickly and automatically accommodate changes in the environment in which they operate, resulting in better user experiences. A number of researchers regard images as visual contexts and have begun to develop multi-modal learning models to integrate images (scene) and text (sentences) [6]. Efforts on such integration can be categorized into two types: capturing (or summarising) the image presented or answering questions related to the content of the image provided. The former focuses on extracting image features as a basis for generating text, while the latter is the task of generating textual answers to textual questions about multimedia content, which is also called visual question answering (VQA) [7]. For instance, Xu *et al.* present the use of attention for image illustration, where image perception can be enhanced [8]. Zhu *et al.* further extend the application of spatial attention to the QA model [9].

The VQA research described above has been further broadened to include research on Audio-Visual Scene Sensing Dialogue (AVSD) [10], which aims to answer questions based on video clips. In order to achieve this goal, the system needs to properly combine different types of information extracted from the video in order to produce correct textual answers. In AVSD, the first few rounds of the dialogue are considered as extra-textual knowledge, forming a special context to improve the performance of the dialogue. As can be seen, conducting video-based conversations can present additional complexity and challenges [6]. Extracting features from the video not only deals with the inherent complexity of extracting image features, but also with the temporal interactions between image frames [11]. Besides, learning useful features becomes more difficult due to the limited availability of visual data [12].

To further investigate the above challenges, NLPCC-2022-Shared-Task-4 designed the Multi-modal Dialogue Understanding and Generation (MDUG) task. This task aims at generating responses that are coherent to the dialogue and relevant to the video context. In this paper, we present the scene-aware prompt method for the MDUG task. The multi-task objectives are designed to jointly optimize the scene- and session- sequence prediction task. The visual captions are utilized to percept the scene information of the video, while the fixed-type templated prompt based on the scene- and session-aware labels are used to enhance dialogue generation. Extensive experimental results show that the proposed method has achieved state-of-the-art (SOTA) performance compared with other competitive baselines, where we rank the first in all three subtasks in this MDUG competition.

Our main contributions are three-fold:

– We formulate the multi-modal understanding task as the joint multi-task modelling for better scene and session learning.
– To better leverage the scene information, we design the scene-aware prompt for the MDUG task, where the visual captions and fixed-type templated

prompt with the scene- and session-aware labels are used to further improve the dialogue generation performance.
- Extensive experimental results show that the proposed method has achieved state-of-the-art (SOTA) performance compared with other competitive methods, which demonstrates its effectiveness.

2   Task Introduction

2.1   Problem Definition

This multi-modal dialogue understanding and generation task contains 3 tracks:

1. Dialogue scene identification: predict the boundaries of different dialogue scenes given a set of continuous dialogue utterances and a related video.
2. Dialogue session identification: predict the boundaries of different dialogue sessions given a set of continuous dialogue utterances and a related video (which is identical to Track 1).
3. Dialogue response generation: generate a response based on scene and session predictions, while coherently catching up with the conversation.

For pursuing these tasks, we formulated these tasks as follows, where the notation V represents the video clips, and notation C is the input dialogue context.

1. For dialogue scene identification and dialogue session identification tasks, the final prediction (i.e., 0 or 1) is obtained through the input of V and C, where we adopt a multi-task end-end framework to jointly perform these tasks.
2. For dialogue response generation, given the scene (S_i) and session (T_i) predictions, the final response is generated with the pre-trained language model, where the clip captioners and the identified labels used as the prompt for providing extra context knowledge.

2.2   Evaluation Metric

For the dialogue scene identification and dialogue topic identification tracks, we mainly use the accuracy metric (i.e., Acc_s and Acc_t) for the final evaluation ranking. The calculation equation is shown as follows.

$$\text{Acc}_s = \frac{1}{n} \sum_{i=1}^{n} l_{\{S_i = S_i'\}} \tag{1}$$

where l is the sample number, the S_i represents each predicted sample, and S_i' is the ground truth label. Similarly, we can present the Acc_t below.

$$\text{Acc}_t = \frac{1}{n} \sum_{i=1}^{n} l_{\{T_i = T_i'\}} \tag{2}$$

Also, the F1 metric is adopted for reference, where the definitions of F1 are shown as follows:

Table 1. Co-occurrence of the labels in both shared tasks 1 and 2.

Scene Label	Session Label	Co-occurrence
1	0	✗
0	1	✔
1	1	✔
0	0	✔

$$\text{F1} = \frac{2 \times \text{Acc} \times \text{Recall}}{\text{Acc} + \text{Recall}} \qquad (3)$$

For the track 3, we adopt the BLEU [13], ROUGE [14], METEOR [15], and CIDER [16] scores of the generated response for further evaluations[1].

2.3   Dateset

The NLPCC shared task 4 presents three shared tasks [6], namely, dialogue scene identification, dialogue session identification, and dialogue response generation. The ultimate goal is to generate a response that is coherent to the dialogue context and relevant to the video context.

The dataset of the competition[2] contains 40,006, 1,955 and 1,934 video clips as the visual context. The dialogue contains 1,000,079, 50,032 and 50,131 utterances in the train, dev and test sets respectively. The source of the videos and dialogues for this task are crawled from online American TV series, which are split into the training, validation, and test sets. Each sample contains a series of dialogue utterances, which is associated with the video clip (downsampled to 3 fps) during the dialogue duration. Each clip is processed in the "jpg" format for further modeling.

3   Main Methods

In this section, we will introduce our method in the three shared tasks in the NLPCC tasks 4, including multi-tasking multi-modal dialogue understanding and scene-aware prompt multi-modal dialogue generation.

3.1   Multi-tasking Multi-modal Dialogue Understanding

Multi-modal dialogue understanding is still a great challenge since the visual and textual modalities share different information [1]. Both shared task 1 and shared task 2 share the same task objectives, which is to perform sequence prediction for the multi-modal dialogue understanding. Considering the intrinsic co-occurrence between the two labels (i.e., scene and session labels), we can obtain Table 1. From this table, we can conclude that both tracks share some common label

---

[1] https://github.com/tylin/coco-caption.
[2] https://github.com/patrick-tssn/NLPCC-2022-Shared-Task-4.

information about the co-occurrence relationship. As a result, we propose the multi-tasking method for jointly training both tracks.

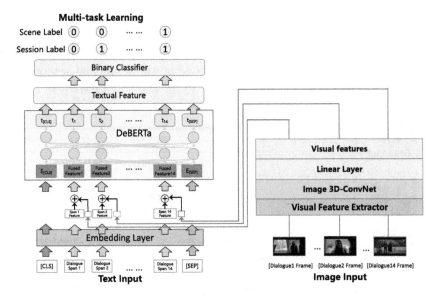

Fig. 1. Overview of the proposed multi-tasking multi-modal dialogue understanding.

As shown in the Fig. 1, we use the I3D model [17] to extract and process video features to promote deep multi-modal information fusion. After that, we change the structure of the original language model. Specifically, we use the timeline to align the dialogue span and visual frame, where each input text span is fused with the current video frame. The embedding layer can produce the fused features by adding fusion with the output text span and the corresponded frame. This fusion strategy can make the multi-modal interaction more precise and efficient [18].

For the final multi-task modelling, we design a linear layer for the output layer in each task. Specifically, the *[SEP]* feature vector of each sentence can produce the output with the two different binary linear layers. The multi-task modelling is designed to perform the scene and session sequence prediction, where two prediction results are obtained meanwhile for each input.

3.2   Scene-Aware Prompt Multi-modal Dialogue Generation

Traditional text-based generation methods have limitations in multi-modal scenarios [2]. On the one hand, it is because the interaction of characters in a multi-modal scene not only relies on the textual information of the dialogue context, but also needs to depend on the prompts of the environment scene and dialogue session [5]. On the other hand, the ability of a single text modality to perceive the multi-modal dialogue context is limited, and it is a wise choice to augment and enrich the dialogue context with other modalities [19].

Therefore, we propose a multi-modal dialogue generation method based on the scene-aware prompt, which is shown in the Fig. 2. Specifically, we use the pre-trained video captioner model (i.e., UniVL [20]) and image captioner model (i.e., BLIP [21]) to obtain the caption information of the environmental scene, which further enhances the multi-modal dialogue generation. At the same time, we design a fixed-type templated prompt based on the scene- and session-aware labels to further improve the controllability of the generated responses.

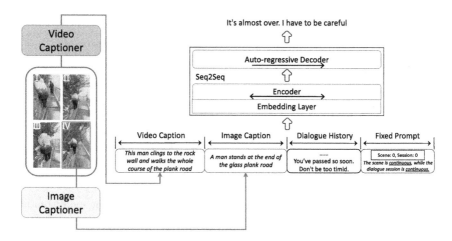

Fig. 2. Overview of the proposed scene-aware prompt multi-modal dialogue generation.

Visual Caption. The visual caption contains two types of information, which are the video caption and the image caption. For the video caption, we adopt the UniVL pre-trained model as the scene-aware information extractor, which is the state-of-the-art (SOTA) video captioner. This model is used for extracted the video captions from the video clips during each utterance. Also, we consider that the last frame for the dialogue response also contains further information for the dialogue response generation. As a result, we adopt the BLIP pre-trained model for extracting the last clip frame to obtain the image captions. Since the caption both from the video crawled from the American online TV shows, we use these models with zero-shot for this dialogue caption generation task [22]. Both the above step can be represented as follows.

$$\mathbf{T_{video}} = \phi(\mathcal{V}_{videoclips})$$
$$\mathbf{T_{image}} = \varphi(\mathcal{V}_{imageclip}) \tag{4}$$

where $T \in \mathbb{R}^d$, $\mathcal{V}_{image} \in \mathbb{R}^k$, d is the dimension, which is the same as text predictor encoder embedding. The ϕ and φ represent the model parameter of the video captioner and image captioner respectively.

Prompt Design. After obtaining the scene- and session- predicted labels, we shall utilize this information to provide extra knowledge from the scene environment. Specifically, we design the fix-type prompt for the pre-trained language model, where the prompt is used as the input text tokens concatenated with the visual captions and the dialogue contexts. On the one side, the fix-typed prompt covers the information from the visual clips. On the other side, the prompt can be well-formed information that controls the dialogue text generation [23]. The fix-typed prompt is designed as "The scene is <u>continuous</u>, while the dialogue session is <u>not continuous</u>", where the scene and session labels are 0 and 1 respectively.

Prompt Tuning. Intuitively, the dialogue contexts $\mathbf{C}$, visual captions $\mathbf{T_{video}}$, $\mathbf{T_{image}}$ and the scene-aware prompt $\mathbf{T_{prompt}}$ are used as the input tokens which are concatenated together. The [CLS] is positioned at the head of the input token, while the rest text tokens are sent to the embedding layer (**Emb**) as the trigger to model to generate the response. The above process is presented as follows

$$\text{Input} = \mathbf{Emb}\left([CLS] + \mathbf{C} + [SEP] + \mathbf{T_{video}} + [SEP] + \mathbf{T_{video}} + [SEP] + \mathbf{T_{prompt}}\right) \tag{5}$$

After concatenation, the embedding module is adopted for learning the features in the same vector space for the further response generation.

Response Generation. Finally we generate response with seq2seq model's decoder. We define L_R as the auto-regressive decoder loss.

$$\mathcal{L}_R(\psi) = -\sum_t \log P_\varphi\left(y_t \mid y_0, \ldots, y_{t-1}, \mathbf{Input}\right) \tag{6}$$

where notation ψ represents the parameters of the pre-trained model. The i represents the i-th word generated by the decoder, $y_0, \ldots, y_{t-1}$ is the generated tokens, and y_t is the next token.

3.3   Training and Inference

For the training step, each sample is concatenated with the visual captions and the fixed prompt, where the visual captions are generated by the zero-shot video and image captioners, and the fixed prompt is produced by the corresponded scene and session labels.

For inference, we first predict the scene and session labels of the last turn, and then we translate the predicted labels into the fixed prompt for further concatenation. Also, the video clips and last image frame are implemented for obtaining the visual captions. Finally, the dialogue context, visual captions and the fixed prompt are concatenated for the response generation.

4   Experiments

In this section, we describe the specific implementation steps of the experiment and show the experimental results of our method in the MDUG dataset.

4.1   Experimental Setup

We conduct different experiments in three tasks in the MDUG dataset. Specifically, we use some pre-trained language models as the baseline methods. In subtask 1/2, we use the BERT[3] [24] which a language mask model (MLM) [25] task pre-training model. The RoBERTa[4] [26] has conducted MLM pre-training for a long period time. The ELECTRA[5] [27] uses the replaced token detection task instead of the MLM task to obtain higher training efficiency. The DeBERTa-v3 [28] implements gradient decoupling on the basis of Electra to avoid the tug-of-war procedure [29].

Table 2. Performance comparison of the variants methods on MDUG dataset for subtask 1. We highlight the best score in each column in **bold**, and the second-best score with underline. We also show improvements between first place and second place.

Models	Acc	F1	Precision	Recall
Random mode	49.653	11.308	6.369	**50.363**
BERT-base [30] (2019)	91.627	0	0	0
RoBERTa-large [26] (2019)	91.432	15.683	21.030	12.504
ELECTRA-large [27] (2020)	92.383	16.316	27.212	11.651
DeBERTa-v3-large [28] (2021)	92.961	17.848	34.830	11.998
Ours (Single-task)	93.567	19.329	48.116	12.093
Ours (Multi-task)	**93.794**	**19.854**	**56.094**	12.062

In subtask 3, we select some strong baseline models in the generation domain for comparison. The BART [30] and the T5 [31] use the denoising and mask restoration task for pre-training respectively. The BART has achieved SOTA in generation tasks like translation, while T5 has SOTA performance in understanding and summarization.

In order to get a strong baseline, we use DeBERTa-v3-large as the backbone network in the understanding task (subtask 1 and 2) and Blender [3] as the backbone network in the generation task (subtask3).

All the hyperparameters are adjusted in the dev set to ensure fairness. In all our experiments, at the end of each epoch of training, we will test in the development dataset, and select the highest model (mainly depending on Acc or BLEU) to predict in the test dataset. All the tables report the highest score in the development set except for the final official score table. All the experimental results are repeated three times, and the highest and lowest scores are removed.

We set the maximum token length to 512 and delete the excess text. We have fine-tuned 10 epochs of training in three A100 GPUs on the Pytorch[6] and

---

[3] https://huggingface.co/bert-base-uncased.

[4] https://huggingface.co/roberta-large.

[5] https://huggingface.co/google/electra-large-discriminator.

[6] https://pytorch.org.

the hugging-face[7] framework, with a batch size of 10. We implement distributed training with mixed precision based on the DeepSpeed [32]. We use an AdamW optimizer [33] with a maximum learning rate of 1×10^{-5}, followed by linear attenuation and warm-up optimizing schedules [34].

4.2   Main Results

We conducted experiments on subtasks 1 and 2, which are shown in Tables 2 and 3 respectively. We compare the performance of the pre-trained language model with random selection. From the table, we can see that the accuracy rate in random mode is less than 50%, but it has a high recall rate. This is because the label distribution of the MDUG dataset is not balanced. For the poor F1 performance of BERT, we consider that it is due to the extreme imbalance of

Table 3. Performance comparison of the variants methods on MDUG dataset for subtask 2. We highlight the best score in each column in **bold**, and the second-best score with underline. We also show improvements between first place and second place.

Methods	Acc	F1	Precision	Recall
Random Mode	49.534	19.919	12.455	**49.713**
BERT-base [30] (2019)	87.375	0	0	0
RoBERTa-large [26] (2019)	87.912	34.040	54.712	24.705
ELECTRA-large [27] (2020)	87.580	34.242	51.638	25.614
DeBERTa-v3-large [28] (2021)	87.912	35.038	54.490	<u>25.821</u>
Ours (Single-task)	<u>88.075</u>	<u>35.078</u>	<u>56.097</u>	25.518
Ours (Multi-task)	**88.248**	**35.484**	**57.811**	25.598

Table 4. Performance comparison of the variants methods on MDUG dataset for subtask 3. We highlight the best score in each column in **bold**, and the second-best score with underline. We also show improvements between first place and second place.

Methods	BLEU-1	ROUGE-L	METEOR	CIDEr	Avg
Random mode	4.81	3.92	2.21	0.02	2.72
BART-base [30] (2019)	5.74	6.10	3.87	0.04	3.94
T5-base [31] (2020)	2.94	4.44	2.81	0.01	2.55
Blender-400M [3] (2021)	7.01	8.73	6.05	0.06	5.46
Ours (Single-task)	<u>11.9</u>	<u>18.1</u>	<u>11.7</u>	0.57	10.96
Ours (W/O Image Prompt)	10.8	17.5	8.2	0.84	9.52
Ours (W/O Video Prompt)	12.9	18.7	9.1	<u>0.96</u>	10.42
Ours (W/O Prompt)	8.7	15.5	7.6	0.78	8.27
Ours (Multi-task)	**14.2**	**22.5**	**12.1**	**1.19**	**12.47**

---

[7] https://github.com/huggingface/transformers.

labels so that the BERT cannot overfit these datasets, where the output recall and f1 results of the BERT are all 0. With the expansion of the pre-training scale, the effect of the model gradually improves. Compared with single-task modeling, our method with multi-tasking modeling can perceive and understand the visual information at a deeper level. Compared with other competitive methods, we can find that for subtask1, our accuracy and F1 index can be improved by 0.833% and 2.006% respectively. For subtask2, our accuracy and F1 index can be improved by 0.336% and 0.446% respectively.

The subtask 3 is a generation task, so we selected some generated baseline models for comparison, which is shown in the Table 4. We can find that our model can be greatly improved, which is because our method can make full use of multi-modal feature information on the basis of the pre-training language model. Compared with other competitive methods, our method improves the average score by 7.01, which proves the effectiveness of our method.

4.3   Ablation Study

We also implement the ablation study for the proposed method, which is shown in Tables 2 and 3. The image and video captions can improve the final results, and the prompt can enhance the performance of the dialogue generation. Also, with the aid of multi-tasking modeling, our method can be further improved.

Specifically, we make a more in-depth analysis of the experiment. We test the effect of cancelling multi-task in subtasks 1 and 2. We find that the effect will decrease significantly after single-task modelling is cancelled. We consider it is a great correlation between scene and session. Through multi-task learning, the model can better understand the actual meaning of the textual and visual information. It helps to increase the generalization ability of the model and improve the final effect (Tables 5 and 6).

Table 5. The online result of the subtask 1 and 2.

Item	Objective	Rank	Acc	F1
Subtask 1	**Scene**	1	**93.88**	**18.18**
Subtask 2	**Session**	1	**87.79**	**39.76**

Table 6. The online result of the subtask 3.

Models	Rank	BLEU-1	ROUGE-L	METEOR	CIDEr	Avg
Ours	1	**13.9**	**22.6**	**11.7**	**1.29**	**6.91**

Moreover, we perform ablation experiments in subtask 3, which is shown in Table 4. We make the model without some visual perception ability by canceling the original image caption or video caption, so as to evaluate the effectiveness of different methods. In our ablation experiments, we can find that the performance degradation of the model is not obvious if any visual information is missing. However, if all visual cues are missing, the model will lack the ability of visual scene modeling, which will greatly affect the final prediction performance.

4.4   Online Results

As for the online results, we reported the final results of our system. In Tables 5 and 6, our system showed very convincing performance. We have achieved the first place in all subtasks, which fully demonstrates our method's effectiveness.

5   Conclusion

In this paper, it is mainly introduced that, in order to realize the better multi-modal dialogue understanding and generation, the LingJing team modelled the joint multi-task understanding tasks for subtasks 1 and 2. In subtask 3, to better percept the scene information, we designed the scene-aware prompt method to leverage the visual information for the multi-modal dialogue generation. As a result, our team has won three subtasks in this MDUG completion, which demonstrates the effectiveness of the proposed method. However, there is still a long way for robust multi-modal understanding and generation, how to combine both capabilities well is yet to be explored.

References

1. De Vries, H., Strub, F., Chandar, S., Pietquin, O., Larochelle, H., Courville, A.: Guesswhat?! visual object discovery through multi-modal dialogue. In: Proceedings of the IEEE Conference on Computer Vision and Pattern Recognition, pp. 5503–5512 (2017)
2. Deldjoo, Y., Trippas, J.R., Zamani, H.: Towards multi-modal conversational information seeking. In Proceedings of the 44th International ACM SIGIR Conference on Research and Development in Information Retrieval, pp. 1577–1587 (2021)
3. Roller, S., et al.: Recipes for building an open-domain chatbot. In: Conference of the European Chapter of the Association for Computational Linguistics (2021)
4. Zhou, H., Huang, M., Zhang, T., Zhu, X., Liu, B.: Emotional chatting machine: emotional conversation generation with internal and external memory. In: Proceedings of the AAAI Conference on Artificial Intelligence, vol. 32 (2018)
5. Su, Y., et al.: Language models can see: plugging visual controls in text generation. arXiv preprint arXiv:2205.02655 (2022)
6. Wang, Y., Zhao, X., Zhao, D.: NLPCC-2022-Shared-Task-4, May 2022
7. Antol, S., et al.: VQA: visual question answering. In: Proceedings of the IEEE International Conference on Computer Vision, pp. 2425–2433 (2015)
8. Xu, K., et al.: Show, attend and tell: neural image caption generation with visual attention. In: International Conference on Machine Learning, pp. 2048–2057. PMLR (2015)

9. Zhu, Y., Groth, O., Bernstein, M., Fei-Fei, L.: Visual7W: grounded question answering in images. In: Proceedings of the IEEE Conference on Computer Vision and Pattern Recognition, pp. 4995–5004 (2016)

10. Alamri, H., et al.: Audio visual scene-aware dialog. In: Proceedings of the IEEE/CVF Conference on Computer Vision and Pattern Recognition, pp. 7558–7567 (2019)

11. Fang, H., Xiong, P., Xu, L., Chen, Y.: Clip2Video: mastering video-text retrieval via image clip. arXiv preprint arXiv:2106.11097 (2021)

12. Li, B., Weng, Y., Sun, B., Li, S.: Towards visual-prompt temporal answering grounding in medical instructional video. arXiv preprint arXiv:2203.06667 (2022)

13. Papineni, K., Roukos, S., Ward, T., Zhu, W.-J.: BLEU: a method for automatic evaluation of machine translation. In: Proceedings of the 40th Annual Meeting of the Association for Computational Linguistics, pp. 311–318 (2002)

14. Lin, C.-Y.: Rouge: a package for automatic evaluation of summaries. In: Text Summarization Branches Out, pp. 74–81 (2004)

15. Banerjee, S., Lavie, A.: Meteor: an automatic metric for MT evaluation with improved correlation with human judgments. In: Proceedings of the ACL Workshop on Intrinsic and Extrinsic Evaluation Measures for Machine Translation and/or Summarization, pp. 65–72 (2005)

16. Vedantam, R., Zitnick, C.L., Parikh, D.: CIDEr: consensus-based image description evaluation. In: Proceedings of the IEEE Conference on Computer Vision and Pattern Recognition, pp. 4566–4575 (2015)

17. Carreira, J., Zisserman, A.: Quo Vadis, action recognition? A new model and the kinetics dataset. In: Computer Vision and Pattern Recognition (2017)

18. Sun, R., Chen, B., Zhou, Q., Li, Y., Cao, Y., Zheng, H.-T.: A non-hierarchical attention network with modality dropout for textual response generation in multimodal dialogue systems. arXiv preprint arXiv:2110.09702 (2021)

19. Li, B., Weng, Y., Xia, F., Sun, B., Li, S.: VPAI_LAB at MedVidQA 2022: a two-stage cross-modal fusion method for medical instructional video classification. In: Proceedings of the 21st Workshop on Biomedical Language Processing, pp. 212–219 (2022)

20. Luo, H., et al.: UniVL: a unified video and language pre-training model for multimodal understanding and generation. arXiv preprint arXiv:2002.06353 (2020)

21. Li, J., Li, D., Xiong, C., Hoi, S.: BlIP: bootstrapping language-image pre-training for unified vision-language understanding and generation. arXiv preprint arXiv:2201.12086 (2022)

22. Wang, Z., et al.: Language models with image descriptors are strong few-shot video-language learners. arXiv preprint arXiv:2205.10747 (2022)

23. Liu, P., Yuan, W., Fu, J., Jiang, Z., Hayashi, H., Neubig, G.: Pre-train, prompt, and predict: a systematic survey of prompting methods in natural language processing. arXiv preprint arXiv:2107.13586 (2021)

24. Devlin, J., Chang, M.-W., Lee, K., Toutanova, K.: BERT: pre-training of deep bidirectional transformers for language understanding. arXiv preprint arXiv:1810.04805 (2018)

25. Taylor, W.L.: Cloze procedure: a new tool for measuring readability. Journalism Mass Commun. Q. **30** (1953)

26. Liu, Y., et al.: Roberta: a robustly optimized BERT pretraining approach. arXiv Computation and Language (2019)

27. Clark, K., Luong, M.-T., Le, Q.V., Manning, C.D.: Electra: pre-training text encoders as discriminators rather than generators. In: Learning (2020)

28. He, P., Gao, J., Chen, W.: DeBERtaV 3: Improving DeBERTa using ELECTRA-style pre-training with gradient-disentangled embedding sharing. arXiv Computation and Language (2021)
29. Hadsell, R., Rao, D., Rusu, A., Pascanu, R.: Embracing change: continual learning in deep neural networks. Trends Cogn. Sci. **24**, 1028–1040 (2020)
30. Lewis, M., et al.: BART: denoising sequence-to-sequence pre-training for natural language generation, translation, and comprehension. In: Meeting fof the Association or Computational Linguistics (2019)
31. Raffel, C., et al.: Exploring the limits of transfer learning with a unified text-to-text transformer. J. Mach. Learn. Res. **21**(140), 1–67 (2020)
32. Rajbhandari, S., Rasley, J., Ruwase, O., He, Y.: Zero: memory optimizations toward training trillion parameter models. In: Proceedings of the International Conference for High Performance Computing, Networking, Storage and Analysis, SC 2020. IEEE Press (2020)
33. Loshchilov, I., Hutter, F.: Decoupled weight decay regularization. In: International Conference on Learning Representations (2018)
34. He, K., Zhang, X., Ren, S., Sun, J.: Deep residual learning for image recognition. In: 2016 IEEE Conference on Computer Vision and Pattern Recognition (CVPR), pp. 770–778 (2016)

BIT-WOW at NLPCC-2022 Task5 Track1: Hierarchical Multi-label Classification via Label-Aware Graph Convolutional Network

Bo Wang[1,4], Yi-Fan Lu[1], Xiaochi Wei[2], Xiao Liu[1,4], Ge Shi[3],
Changsen Yuan[1,4], Heyan huang[1,4](✉), Chong Feng[1,4],
and Xianling Mao[1]

[1] School of Computer Science and Technology, Beijing Institute of Technology,
Beijing, China
{bwang,yifanlu,xiaoliu,yuanchangsen,hhy63,fengchong,maoxl}@bit.edu.cn
[2] Baidu Inc., Beijing, China
weixiaochi@baidu.com
[3] Faculty of Information Technology, Beijing University of Technology, Beijing, China
shige@bjut.edu.cn
[4] Southeast Academy of Information Technology, Beijing Institute of Technology,
Beijing, China

Abstract. This paper describes the system proposed by the BIT-WOW team for NLPCC2022 shared task in Task5 Track1. The track is about multi-label towards abstracts of academic papers in scientific domain, which includes hierarchical dependencies among 1,530 labels. In order to distinguish semantic information among hierarchical label structures, we propose the Label-aware Graph Convolutional Network (LaGCN), which uses Graph Convolutional Network to capture the label association through context-based label embedding. Besides, curriculum learning is applied for domain adaptation and to mitigate the impact of a large number of categories. The experiments show that: 1) LaGCN effectively models the category information and makes a considerable improvement in dealing with a large number of categories; 2) Curriculum learning is beneficial for a single model in the complex task. Our best results were obtained by an ensemble model. According to the official results, our approach proved the best in this track.

Keywords: Hierarchical multi-label classification · Graph convolutional network · Curriculum learning · Label embedding

1 Introduction

The indexing for scientific research literature is becoming more and more important with the increasing number of such literature in various fields. The intelligent classification of scientific research literature is helpful to improve the

W. Lu et al. (Eds.) NLPCC 2022, LNCS 13552, pp. 192–203, 2022.
https://doi.org/10.1007/978-3-031-17189-5_16

retrieval efficiency and quality of users. Hierarchical multi-label classification is a common method for indexing scientific research literature, and its classification result corresponds to one or more nodes of a pre-defined taxonomic hierarchy [1].

NLPCC 2022 shared Task5 Track1 [2] is a multi-label classification task for scientific literature, and the category system used in this track is a three-level hierarchical structure which consists of up to 1,530 labels. The aim of this task is to develop a multi-label classification model for scientific research literature, based on the given metadata i.e., titles and abstracts, as well as the corresponding hierarchical labels from a domain-specific topic taxonomy. The number of label categories for level-1, level-2, and level-3 is 21, 260, and 1,272, respectively, and the total number of labels is 1,530. Therefore, the most challenge problem is the huge number of labels in level-3 and this may cause the severity sparsity problem. According to our statistics, there are only approximately 70 samples in each level-3 category on average and more than 130 level-3 categories contains less than 20 samples. Due to the specificity of the shared task, the profitable framework should encode the hierarchical label and model large number of categories in scientific domain.

Structure Encoding: As a consequence of the importance of fine-grained label correlation information, we first obtain the original label embedding according to the training set and calculate the context-based label representation by attention. Then, the GCN is imported to formulate the hierarchy as a directed graph and utilize prior probabilities of label dependencies to aggregate node information.

Domain Adaptation: Pre-trained language models are trained by maximizing the log-likelihood of a sentence. Hence, The original model would focus more on general language features and lack understanding of the corresponding domain knowledge. Therefore, we fine-tune these models by using the raw text from training set. In agreement with Zhang [3], Curriculum learning is introduced for domain adaptation, which also utilizes raw text to alleviate the confusion caused by certain categories with little data.

The main contribution of this study is that we proposed a structure encoding method LaGCN to model the Hierarchical Multi-label Classification. Additionally, the experimental results demonstrate that curriculum learning with adversarial training obtains considerable improvement.

2   Approach

The framework of our model is shown as Fig. 1. At the very beginning of the system, pre-trained language models (BERT [4], BIOBERT [5]) are fine-tuned by utilizing literature corpus. After fine-tuning model, we make use of label embedding and combine it with word embedding. After obtaining the context-aware label embedding, we use a graph-based hierarchical label model to further enhance the label representation, which aggregates dataflows among associated labels.

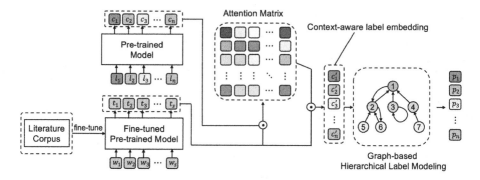

Fig. 1. The framework of LaGCN methods.

In addition to the model structure shown in Fig. 1, we use several techniques to enhance the performance of our overall system, including curriculum learning, ensemble learning, and post editing. The details of the model structure and specific practices of each technique are shown as followings.

2.1   Context-Aware Label Embedding

Utilizing the representation of labels is primarily designed to improve general neural text classification models [6,7]. It is one of the key methods for efficiently handling thousands of classes [6]. To model the semantic meaning of labels, we use the average of all instance representation in training set for each label. Similar to prompted learning [8], for the t-th label, we select the combination of all instances belonging to this category label into set l_t, and we get the label embedding c_t as:

$$c_t = \frac{1}{|m|} \sum_i^{|m|} \text{PM}(l_t), \tag{1}$$

where m is the number of instances in l_t, and PM represents the instance representation function. In this paper, we use a BERT embedding of special token "CLS" to represent the instance. After traversing all categories, $C = \{c_1, c_2, \ldots, c_n\}$ are used to represent label embedding matrix, and n denotes the number of labels. For a given sequence $W = \{w_1, w_2, \ldots, w_s\}$, we use finetuned pre-trained language models to get the word embedding $T = \{t_1, t_2, \ldots, t_s\}$. The attention matrix is calculated by "Scaled Dot-Product Attention", which is same as BERT [4]. This can be formulated as

$$\text{Attention}(T, C) = \text{softmax}\left(\frac{TC^T}{\sqrt{d}}\right) \tag{2}$$

where d denotes the dimension of T. The context-aware label embedding $C' = \{c_1', c_2', \ldots, c_s'\}$ is calculated as $C' = \text{Attention}(T, C)T$. C' is the classification representation and will be further used in GCN afterwards.

2.2   Graph-Based Hierarchical Label Modeling

While obtaining the context-based label representation, we introduce the taxo-nomic hierarchy information, which describes the hierarchical relations among labels. GCN is proposed to enhance node representations based on the local graph structural information [9]. With given hierarchical dependencies of labels, we introduce GCN to introduce the predefined hierarchy into our system.

Hierarchical relationships are not only included in the dependencies between superiors and subordinates. Statistical information in the training corpus con-tains additional hierarchical relationships, which could be regarded as prior knowledge of label correlations based on Bayesian statistical inference. Suppose that there is a path $p_{i,j}$ between the labels l_i and l_j in different levels. The edge feature $f(p_{i,j})$ is represented by the prior probability

$$P\left(\mathbb{S}_j \mid \mathbb{S}_i\right) = \frac{P\left(\mathbb{S}_j \cap \mathbb{S}_i\right)}{P\left(\mathbb{S}_i\right)} = \frac{P\left(\mathbb{S}_j\right)}{P\left(\mathbb{S}_i\right)} = \frac{N_j}{N_i},$$
$$P\left(\mathbb{S}_i \mid \mathbb{S}_j\right) = \frac{P\left(\mathbb{S}_i \cap \mathbb{S}_j\right)}{P\left(\mathbb{S}_j\right)} = \frac{P\left(\mathbb{S}_j\right)}{P\left(\mathbb{S}_j\right)} = 1.0,$$
(3)

where $\mathbb{S}_k$ means the collection of instances with label l_k and $P\left(\mathbb{S}_j \mid \mathbb{S}_i\right)$ is the conditional probability of l_j given that l_i occurs. $P\left(\mathbb{S}_j \cap \mathbb{S}_i\right)$ is the probability of $\{l_j, l_i\}$ occurring simultaneously. N_k refers to the number of U_k in the train-ing subset. Note that the hierarchy ensures U_k given that $v_{child(k)}$ occurs. GCN aggregates dataflows among associated labels. In the graph, each directed edge represents a pair-wise label correlation feature. Thus, those dataflows should conduct node transformations with edge-wise linear transformations. In order to avoid over-parameterized edge-wise weight matrixes, we simplify this transforma-tion with a weighted adjacent matrix. Formally, GCN encodes the hidden state of node k based on its associated neighborhood $N(k) = \{n_k, child(k), parent(k)\}$ as:

$$\boldsymbol{u}_{k,j} = a_{k,j}\boldsymbol{v}_j + \boldsymbol{b}_l^k,$$
$$\boldsymbol{g}_{k,j} = \sigma(\mathbf{W}_g^{d(i,j)}\boldsymbol{v}_k + \boldsymbol{b}_g^k),$$
$$\boldsymbol{h}_k = \text{ReLU}\left(\sum_{j \in N(k)} \boldsymbol{g}_{k,j} \odot \boldsymbol{u}_{k,j}\right),$$
(4)

where $\mathbf{W}_g \in \mathbb{R}^{dim}$, $\boldsymbol{b}_l^k \in \mathbb{R}^{N \times dim}$ and $\boldsymbol{b}_g \in \mathbb{R}^N$ are trainable parameters of weight matrix and bias vectors. $d(j,k)$ indicates the path from node j to node k, including different levels and self-loop edges. $a_{k,j} \in \mathbb{R}$ denotes the path probability $f_{d(k,j)}(e_{k,j})$, and the self-loop edge is set to $a_{k,k} = 1$, top-down edges use $f_c(e_{k,k}) = \frac{N_k}{N_j}$, and bottom-up edges use $f_p(e_{j,k}) = 1$. The edge feature matrix $\boldsymbol{F} = \{a_{0,0}, a_{0,1}, \ldots, a_{C-1,C-1}\}$ indicates the weighted adja-cent matrix of the directed hierarchy graph, and the output hidden state $\boldsymbol{h}_k$ of node k denotes its label representation corresponding to the structural informa-tion. Finally, the feed-forward layer with a sigmoid function are used to get the final score for each label. We uses a binary cross-entropy loss function:

$-\sum_{i=1}^{N}\sum_{j=1}^{C}\left[y_{ij}\log\left(y'_{ij}\right)+(1-y_{ij})\log\left(1-y'_{ij}\right)\right]$, where y_{ij} and y'_{ij} are the ground truth and sigmoid score for the j-th label of the i-th sample.

2.3   Curriculum Learning Strategy

Curriculum learning is the branch of machine learning concerned with using labeled as well as raw text to perform certain learning tasks. In our task, we use Self-Paced Learning methods [10], which let the student himself act as the teacher and measure the difficulty of training examples according to its losses, to trains the model at each iteration with the proportion of data hard to distinguish. Against multi-label problem, we calculate a binary condition score for each examples as

$$Condition = |y_{ij} - 0.5| \leq k, \qquad (5)$$

where y_{ij} is the probability and k is per-defined threshold. We choose the samples that satisfy the condition calculated as Eq. 5 as the hard samples. In the sample set that does not meet the conditions, we consider correctly classified samples to be easy samples, and the misclassified samples are considered as noise samples. This proportion of easiest examples and noise samples gradually grows to the whole training set, and we stop looping when the model effect is not growing anymore.

Due to limitation of filtered training resources, the model may face the problem of overfitting. Inspired by [11], adversarial training is introduced to mitigating the impact, which is a crucial way to enhance the robustness of neural networks. The loss function of adversarial training is summarized as the following maximal and minimal formula Eq. (6):

$$\min_{\theta} \mathbb{E}_{(\boldsymbol{Z},y)\sim\mathcal{D}} \left[\max_{\|\boldsymbol{\delta}\|\leq\epsilon} L\left(f_\theta(\boldsymbol{X}+\boldsymbol{\delta}),y\right) \right], \qquad (6)$$

where X denotes the embedding extracted according to the pre-trained model, δ denotes the perturbations superimposed, which is Gaussian noise in this paper, on X, $f_\theta(*)$ means the network with parameter θ and y denotes the groundtruth. For the unbalance of the information extracted from the corpus, curriculum learning strategy is implemented and is shown as Algorithm 1.

2.4   Ensemble Learning and Post Editing

Model with different modules are utilized to implement ensemble learning. For a single piece of test data, the voting ensemble method is applied to filter out more reliable labels from our pool, whose formula is as

$$S = \{l_i| \sum_{m_j\in M} v_{ij} \geq \frac{|M|}{2}\} \qquad (7)$$

where S is the final label set of our ensemble model, M is the model set and v_{ij} is the voting result of model m_j on label l_i, where 1 means positive vote and 0 means negative vote.

Algorithm 1. Curriculum Learning Process

Require: D_l: Labeled Dataset; C: Classification Model; K: Per-defined Threshold;
   P: Classification Probability; D_d: Difficult Data Selected for Curriculum Learning;
   S: F_1 Score Improvement on test set;
   Use D_l to pretrain the C;
   for $S > 0$ **do**
      Use C to obtain P for D_l;
      Retain the data ($|P - 0.5| < K$) $\rightarrow D_d$;
      Use D_d to retrain the C with adversarial training strategy;
      Update S using C in verification set;
   end for

In order to make use of the dependencies of different labels in the track, every single model in the ensemble framework is required to apply post editing. Specifically, only the strictly hierarchical label set is allowed. For the example shown in Fig. 2, according to the dependency, level-3 label *scaffolds* only exist below level-2 label *chemical structure* and level-1 label *physical chemistry*. Any other label set consisting of *scaffolds* but no *chemical structure* or *physical chemistry* are illegal and require padding.

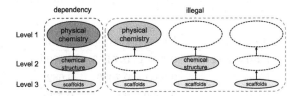

Fig. 2. An example of criteria in post editing.

The number of level-3 labels and level-2 labels is approximately 70 and 14 times that of level-1 labels, respectively. Therefore, we let level-1 labels play a decisive role in classification and directly delete redundant level-2 and level-3 labels when the corresponding level-1 label is missing. As for level-2 labels, there exist several methods to implement padding. When some level-2 labels are missing in the prediction but both corresponding level-1 and level-3 labels exist, (1) models pad the missing level-2 labels; (2) models ignore it; (3) models remove the corresponding level-3 labels. Preliminary experiments show that the first method gives the best performance results. The first method is added into our final model.

3 Experiments

3.1 Dataset and Experiment Settings

On this track, we use the seed dataset, given by the sponsor. There are 90000 instances in training set and 5000 instances in test set. The proposed model is implemented using Pytorch, and we implement the pre-trained model based on Transformer[1]. The key information pertaining to text classification could be extracted from the beginning statements. Thus, we set the maximum length of token inputs as 400. We use several pre-trained language models for our word embedding, including BIOBERT and BERT. The fixed threshold for tagging is chosen as 0.5. Dropout is employed in the embedding layer and MLP layer with the rate of 0.5 while in the feedforward layer and node transformation with the rate of 0.1 and 0.05 respectively. Additionally, the label embedding is initialized by the instance for each category with the hidden size of 768. The whole model is optimized by AdamW in a mini-batch size of 64, with the learning rate set to 0.00005 and a linear warmup scheduler. The number of fine-tuning epochs for the pre-trained model is 4, and the number of training epoch is set to 40.

3.2 Main Results

Table 1 presents the results of our system and others on test data for the NLPCC 2022 Shared Task 5 Track 1. Our system ranked 1st out of 11 teams on F1 score and achieved the best trade-off between precision and recall.

Table 1. Results of systems with the highest F1 and overall one vs ours' on Shared Task 5 Track 1 on official test data.

Ranking	F1	Precision	Recall
Rank 1 (ours)	**0.7071**	**0.7153**	0.6990
Rank 2	0.6941	0.7056	0.6829
Rank 3	0.6909	0.6611	**0.7234**

3.3 Analysis

To further analyze our system, we first conduct an analysis to illustrate the effectiveness of different modules and mechanisms in a hybrid system. As the modules are gradually added, the result of this study is shown in Table 2. In the table, the hybrid system with all technologies had a more excellent performance. This is because each module in our system can make up for the deficiency in a different aspect.

The experimental results contain a clear boundary after adding initialized label embedding (LE[‡]), there is a very significant improvement and models achieved F1 scores over 0.65. The results present that LE[‡] is of great comfort to effectively model the label information, especially in text classification tasks with a large number of labels. The performance of the model with a graph is seriously developed, and the F1 score increases by 0.96%, which demonstrates the correlation between non-adjacent nodes gathered for hierarchical information aggregation.

---

[1] https://github.com/huggingface/transformers.

Table 2. Results of systems with different modules. We use the simple BERT with 12 layer encoder as our pre-trained language model, and the special token "CLS" is used for classification. BERT denotes the base model, BERT & LE denotes the base model with label embedding, BERT & LE‡ denotes the base model with label embedding initialized from training data, LaGCN denotes the single model with BERT embedding, LaGCN† denotes the LaGCN with fine-tuned pre-trained language model, and LaGCN† & CL denotes the LaGCN† with curriculum learning method.

Model	F1	Precision	Recall
BERT	0.3784	0.7648	0.2514
BERT & LE	0.5266	0.6984	0.4221
BERT & LE‡	0.6540	0.6758	0.6336
LaGCN	0.6636	0.6670	0.6603
LaGCN†	0.6741	**0.6893**	0.6595
LaGCN† & CL	**0.6909**	0.6763	**0.7062**

To assess the effectiveness, curriculum learning is added for training finally. The Overall F1 score is increased by 1.05% and 1.68% caused by finetuned language model and curriculum learning respectively. The former shows the information enhances the model effect by using raw text and makes up for the differences between the pre-trained and task domain. While the latter gives evidence that the curriculum learning with adversarial training technology learns complex label distributions and makes the decision boundary more accurate. As shown in Table 2, label embedding and curriculum learning obtain significant improvement on F1 score. We experiment with additional performance studies on these methods.

Label Embedding: We analyze the improvement on performance by dividing labels based on their levels. We compute level-based F1 scores of BERT, BERT & LE, and BERT & LE†. Table 3 shows that our models retain a better performance than the baseline each level with a large number of tags, especially among deep levels. This result shows that label embedding is able to reduce the impact of the data sparsity. Additionally, a well initialized label embedding is more powerful to capture the core representation of the category.

Curriculum Learning: To further analyze the influence of curriculum learning on different base models, we introduce three circumstances shown in Table 4. Curriculum learning plays a great role in different pre-training models. In the process of the ensemble, the F1 score increased by 0.75% through adding additional models, which use curriculum learning methods, to the model set.

Table 3. Results of systems on three levels. The models are continued from Table 2.

Level	Model	F1	Precision	Recall
Level-1	BERT	**0.7564**	0.7746	0.7390
	BERT & LE	0.7551	**0.7801**	0.7316
	BERT & LE‡	0.7528	0.7441	**0.7616**
Level-2	BERT	0.5159	**0.7402**	0.3960
	BERT & LE	0.5872	0.6832	0.5149
	BERT & LE‡	**0.6448**	0.6523	**0.6375**
Level-3	BERT	0.0607	**0.8002**	0.0310
	BERT & LE	0.3355	0.6064	0.2319
	BERT & LE‡	**0.5717**	0.5934	**0.5515**

Table 4. Results of systems under curriculum learning. In addition to the models already introduced by Table 2, LaGCN(BIOBERT) denotes the LaGCN with pre-trained biomedical language representation model [5], we ensemble the model set without curriculum learning model as Ensemble Model, and ensemble all models as Ensemble Model & CL.

Model	F1	Precision	Recall
LaGCN	0.6741	0.6893	0.6595
LaGCN & CL	0.6909	0.6763	0.7062
LaGCN(BIOBERT)	0.6790	0.7013	0.6581
LaGCN(BIOBERT) & CL	0.6952	0.6827	0.7081
Ensemble Model	0.6996	0.7016	0.6976
Ensemble Model & CL	**0.7071**	**0.7153**	**0.6990**

4   Related Work

Learning with graph structured data, such as molecules, social, biological, and financial networks, requires effective representation of their graph structure [12]. There has been a surge of interest in Graph Neural Network (GNN) approaches for representation learning of graphs and latent representation [9, 13–15]. In natural language processing, GNN broadly follow a recursive neighborhood aggregation (or message passing) scheme [16], which learns structured information effectively and get researchers' great attention [17, 18].

A few studies have focused on multi-label classification with hierarchical method. Local hierarchical approaches could be subdivided into local classifier per node [19, 20], local classifier per parent node [21] and local classifier per level [22, 23]. Global approaches improves flat multi-label classification models with the hierarchy information [1, 24]. Besides, some studies tried to make use of local and global methods separately [25] or simultaneously [26]. Recently, some researches focus on designing the metric to evaluate hierarchical multi-label classification [27] and loosely coupling GCN [28].

Label embedding is especially useful at test time when the number of labels is very large and testing against every possible label can become computationally infeasible. [29] converted labels in text classification into semantic vectors and turned the original tasks into vector matching tasks. [6] combined label embedding and tree structure for large multi-label tasks. Instead of ignoring the fine-grained classification clues as many deep models did, the recent work [30] introduced an interaction mechanism to incorporate word-level matching signals between words and labels into the text classification task.

5   Conclusion

In this paper, we propose a Label-aware Graph Convolutional Network for Hierarchical Multi-label Classification task. Curriculum learning and ensemble methods are accompanied to enhance the classification framework. We evaluate our approach on NLPCC 2022 multi-label classification shared task in Task5-Track1. The experimental results demonstrates that both hybird enhancement algorithms and task-specific hierarchical structure can improve the classification quality. Going forward, we would like to continue research on fundamental label embedding initializing approaches and try to integrate the current prompt-based methods into Classification framework for better performance.

Acknowledgement. This work was supported by the Joint Funds of the National Natural Science Foundation of China (Grant No. U19B2020). We would like to thank the anonymous reviewers for their thoughtful and constructive comments.

References

1. Zhou, J., et al.: Hierarchy-aware global model for hierarchical text classification. In: Proceedings of the 58th Annual Meeting of the Association for Computational Linguistics, pp. 1106–1117. Association for Computational Linguistics (2020). https://doi.org/10.18653/v1/2020.acl-main.104
2. Liu, M., et al.: Overview of the NLPCC 2022 shared task 5 track 1: multi-label classification model for English scientific literature (2022)
3. Zhang, Y., David, P., Foroosh, H., Gong, B.: A curriculum domain adaptation approach to the semantic segmentation of urban scenes. IEEE Trans. Pattern Anal. Mach. Intell. **42**(8), 1823–1841 (2020). https://doi.org/10.1109/TPAMI.2019.2903401
4. Devlin, J., Chang, M., Lee, K., Toutanova, K.: BERT: pre-training of deep bidirectional transformers for language understanding. In: Proceedings of the 2019 Conference of the North American Chapter of the Association for Computational Linguistics: Human Language Technologies, pp. 4171–4186. Association for Computational Linguistics (2019). https://doi.org/10.18653/v1/n19-1423

5. Lee, J., et al.: BioBERT: a pre-trained biomedical language representation model for biomedical text mining. Bioinformatics **36**(4), 1234–1240 (2020). https://doi.org/10.1093/bioinformatics/btz682
6. Bengio, S., Weston, J., Grangier, D.: Label embedding trees for large multi-class tasks. In: Advances in Neural Information Processing Systems 23: 24th Annual Conference on Neural Information Processing Systems 2010, pp. 163–171. Curran Associates, Inc. (2010)
7. Ma, Y., Cambria, E., Gao, S.: Label embedding for zero-shot fine-grained named entity typing. In: Proceedings of the Conference on International Conference on Computational Linguistics: Technical Papers, pp. 171–180. ACL (2016). https://aclanthology.org/C16-1017/
8. Liu, X., Huang, H., Shi, G., Wang, B.: Dynamic prefix-tuning for generative template-based event extraction. In: Proceedings of the 60th Annual Meeting of the Association for Computational Linguistics, pp. 5216–5228. Association for Computational Linguistics (2022). https://aclanthology.org/2022.acl-long.358
9. Kipf, T.N., Welling, M.: Semi-supervised classification with graph convolutional networks. In: 5th International Conference on Learning Representations. OpenReview.net (2017). https://openreview.net/forum?id=SJU4ayYgl
10. Kumar, M.P., Packer, B., Koller, D.: Self-paced learning for latent variable models. In: Advances in Neural Information Processing Systems 23: 24th Annual Conference on Neural Information Processing Systems 2010, Vancouver, British Columbia, Canada, 6–9 December 2010, pp. 1189–1197. Curran Associates, Inc. (2010)
11. Liu, X., et al.: BIT-event at NLPCC-2021 task 3: subevent identification via adversarial training. In: Wang, L., Feng, Y., Hong, Yu., He, R. (eds.) NLPCC 2021. LNCS (LNAI), vol. 13029, pp. 400–411. Springer, Cham (2021). https://doi.org/10.1007/978-3-030-88483-3_32
12. Hamilton, W.L., Ying, R., Leskovec, J.: Representation learning on graphs: methods and applications. IEEE Data Eng. Bull. **40**(3), 52–74 (2017). http://sites.computer.org/debull/A17sept/p52.pdf
13. Li, Y., Tarlow, D., Brockschmidt, M., Zemel, R.S.: Gated graph sequence neural networks. In: 4th International Conference on Learning Representations (2016). http://arxiv.org/abs/1511.05493
14. Hamilton, W.L., Ying, Z., Leskovec, J.: Inductive representation learning on large graphs. In: Advances in Neural Information Processing Systems 30: Annual Conference on Neural Information Processing Systems 2017, pp. 1024–1034 (2017)
15. Liu, X., Huang, H., Zhang, Y.: Open domain event extraction using neural latent variable models. In: Proceedings of the 57th Conference of the Association for Computational Linguistics, pp. 2860–2871. Association for Computational Linguistics (2019). https://doi.org/10.18653/v1/p19-1276
16. Gilmer, J., Schoenholz, S.S., Riley, P.F., Vinyals, O., Dahl, G.E.: Neural message passing for quantum chemistry. In: Proceedings of the 34th International Conference on Machine Learning. Proceedings of Machine Learning Research, vol. 70, pp. 1263–1272. PMLR (2017). http://proceedings.mlr.press/v70/gilmer17a.html
17. Liu, X., Huang, H., Zhang, Y.: End-to-end event factuality prediction using directional labeled graph recurrent network. Inf. Process. Manag. **59**(2), 102836 (2022). https://doi.org/10.1016/j.ipm.2021.102836
18. Liu, X., Luo, Z., Huang, H.: Jointly multiple events extraction via attention-based graph information aggregation. In: Proceedings of the 2018 Conference on Empirical Methods in Natural Language Processing, pp. 1247–1256. Association for Computational Linguistics (2018). https://doi.org/10.18653/v1/d18-1156

19. Banerjee, S., Akkaya, C., Perez-Sorrosal, F., Tsioutsiouliklis, K.: Hierarchical transfer learning for multi-label text classification. In: Proceedings of the 57th Conference of the Association for Computational Linguistics, pp. 6295–6300. Association for Computational Linguistics (2019). https://doi.org/10.18653/v1/p19-1633

20. Peng, H., et al.: Large-scale hierarchical text classification with recursively regularized deep graph-CNN. In: Proceedings of the 2018 World Wide Web Conference on World Wide Web, pp. 1063–1072. ACM (2018). https://doi.org/10.1145/3178876.3186005

21. Dumais, S.T., Chen, H.: Hierarchical classification of web content. In: Proceedings of the 23rd Annual International Conference on Research and Development in Information Retrieval, pp. 256–263. ACM (2000). https://doi.org/10.1145/345508.345593

22. Kowsari, K., et al.: HDLTex: hierarchical deep learning for text classification. In: 16th International Conference on Machine Learning and Applications, pp. 364–371. IEEE (2017). https://doi.org/10.1109/ICMLA.2017.0-134

23. Cerri, R., Barros, R.C., de Carvalho, A.C.P.L.F.: Hierarchical multi-label classification using local neural networks. J. Comput. Syst. Sci. **80**(1), 39–56 (2014). https://doi.org/10.1016/j.jcss.2013.03.007

24. Gopal, S., Yang, Y.: Recursive regularization for large-scale classification with hierarchical and graphical dependencies. In: The 19th International Conference on Knowledge Discovery and Data Mining, pp. 257–265. ACM (2013). https://doi.org/10.1145/2487575.2487644

25. Naik, A., Rangwala, H.: HierFlat: flattened hierarchies for improving top-down hierarchical classification. Int. J. Data Sci. Anal. **4**(3), 191–208 (2017). https://doi.org/10.1007/s41060-017-0070-1

26. Wehrmann, J., Cerri, R., Barros, R.C.: Hierarchical multi-label classification networks. In: Proceedings of the 35th International Conference on Machine Learning. Proceedings of Machine Learning Research, vol. 80, pp. 5225–5234. PMLR (2018). http://proceedings.mlr.press/v80/wehrmann18a.html

27. Amigó, E., Delgado, A.D.: Evaluating extreme hierarchical multi-label classification. In: Proceedings of the 60th Annual Meeting of the Association for Computational Linguistics (Volume 1: Long Papers), pp. 5809–5819. Association for Computational Linguistics (2022). https://aclanthology.org/2022.acl-long.399

28. Xu, L., et al.: Hierarchical multi-label text classification with horizontal and vertical category correlations. In: Proceedings of the 2021 Conference on Empirical Methods in Natural Language Processing, pp. 2459–2468. Association for Computational Linguistics (2021). https://doi.org/10.18653/v1/2021.emnlp-main.190

29. Zhang, H., Xiao, L., Chen, W., Wang, Y., Jin, Y.: Multi-task label embedding for text classification. In: Proceedings of the 2018 Conference on Empirical Methods in Natural Language Processing, pp. 4545–4553. Association for Computational Linguistics (2018). https://aclanthology.org/D18-1484/

30. Du, C., Chen, Z., Feng, F., Zhu, L., Gan, T., Nie, L.: Explicit interaction model towards text classification. In: The 33rd Conference on Artificial Intelligence, The 31st Innovative Applications of Artificial Intelligence Conference, The 9th Symposium on Educational Advances in Artificial Intelligence, pp. 6359–6366. AAAI Press (2019). https://doi.org/10.1609/aaai.v33i01.33016359

CDAIL-BIAS MEASURER: A Model Ensemble Approach for Dialogue Social Bias Measurement

Jishun Zhao[1], Shucheng Zhu[2], Ying Liu[2(✉)], and Pengyuan Liu[1,3(✉)]

[1] School of Information Science, Beijing Language and Culture University, Beijing, China
[2] School of Humanities, Tsinghua University, Beijing, China
yingliu@tsinghua.edu.cn
[3] Chinese National Language Monitoring and Research Center (Print Media), Beijing, China
liupengyuan@pku.edu.cn

Abstract. Dialogue systems based on neural networks trained on large-scale corpora have a variety of practical applications today. However, using uncensored training corpora may have risks, such as potential social bias issues. Meanwhile, manually reviewing these training corpora for social bias content is costly. So, it is necessary to design a recognition model that automatically detects social bias in dialogue systems. NLPCC 2022 Shared Task 7 - Fine-Grain Dialogue Social Bias Measurement, aims to measure social bias in dialogue systems and provides a well-annotated Chinese social bias dialogue dataset - CDAIL-BIAS DATASET. Based on CDAIL-BIAS DATASET, this paper proposes a powerful classifier, CDAIL-BIAS MEASURER. Specifically, we adopt a model ensemble approach, which combines five different pre-trained language models, and uses adversarial training and regularization strategy to enhance the robustness of the model. Finally, labels are obtained by using a novel method - a label-based weighted voting method. The result shows that the classifier has a macro F1 score of 0.580 for social bias measurement in dialogue systems. And our result ranks the third, demonstrating the effectiveness and superiority of our model.

Keywords: Model ensemble · Weighted voting · Pre-trained language model

1 Introduction

Open-domain dialogue systems based on neural networks are usually trained on large-scale corpora. However, the models may learn risk issues in the uncensored training corpus, such as potential social bias [1]. It is necessary to design a recognition model that can automatically detect social bias in dialogue systems to avoid causing damage in real life, as manually reviewing these training corpora

W. Lu et al. (Eds.) NLPCC 2022, LNCS 13552, pp. 204–215, 2022.
https://doi.org/10.1007/978-3-031-17189-5_17

for social bias content is costly. Text classification based on machine learning can effectively detect such social bias [2].

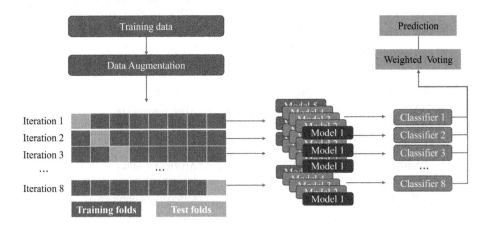

Fig. 1. The framework of our method.

Currently, large-scale pre-trained language models using transfer learning to fine-tune downstream tasks in natural language processing, such as text classification, often achieve the best performance [3,4]. However, when fine-tuning on smaller datasets, the model may suffer from overfitting [5]. Regularization techniques such as dropout and ensemble learning can be employed to alleviate this problem. Particularly, ensemble learning can be divided into four categories, which are Bagging, Boosting, Stacking, and Voting [6]. The method adopted in this paper is a weighted voting procedure that integrates multiple classifiers.

Specifically, our method can be summarized as Fig. 1. First, we analyze the data set. In order to increase the robustness of the ensemble, we divided the training data set into eight parts according to stratified sampling. Then, we screened five best performing models from ten pre-trained language models, and trained them on eight datasets separately. Finally, we selected the model that performed the best on each fold of the training data. We also used a novel method to select the final label on the test set, which is a label-based weighted voting method. The result shows that the macro F1 score of the model proposed in this paper for social bias measurement in dialogue systems is 0.580, ranking the third, which indicates that the effectiveness and superiority of our model.

The main contributions of this paper can be summarized as follows: (1) We proposed a novel model ensemble-based method to automatically detect social bias in dialogue systems. (2) We proposed a label-based weighted voting method to ensemble the prediction results of the models. The results show that this method is better than the majority voting method. (3) The results show that the Macro F1-Score of the model proposed in this paper for measuring social bias in dialogue scenes is 0.580, ranking the third, indicating that this model has better performance.

The rest of this paper is structured as follows. In Sect. 2, we outline the related shared tasks and solutions. In Sect. 3, we introduce the dataset used in this shared task. In Sect. 4, we describe our method in detail. In Sect. 5, we present, analyze and discuss the experimental results. In Sect. 6, we summarize our work.

Table 1. Related shared tasks about hate speech and offensive language detection.

Dataset	Language	Content
AMI	Spanish and English	Misogyny texts
HaSpeeDe	Italian	Hate speech
HatEval	Spanish and English	Hate speech
ComMA	Indian English, Hindi, and Indian Bangla	Misogyny and aggression texts
OffensEval	English	Offensive language
OffensEval 2020	Arabic, Danish, English, Greek, and Turkish	Offensive language
Civil Comments	English	Toxic comments
PCL	English	Patronizing and condescending language

2   Related Work

2.1   Shared Tasks

Hate speech and offensive language detection in online social media has become one of the main tasks in NLP (Natural Language Processing) [7–11]. As a result, there are many shared tasks on the classification of toxic comments [12–19]. We summarize some related works in recent years, as shown in Table 1. AMI task proposed misogyny identification, misogyny behavior classification, and object classification from Spanish and English tweets [12]. HaSpeeDe task is a shared task for the detection of hateful contents in Italian social media [13]. HatEval detects hate speech against immigrants and women in Spanish and English messages extracted from Twitter [14]. ComMA is a multilingual recognition task on misogyny and aggression texts [15]. OffensEval task is based on an Offensive Language Identification Dataset (OLID) with the goal of distinguishing offensive language and identifying attacked targets [16]. OffensEval 2020 is a task of recognition multilingual offensive language in social media [17]. Civil Comments is the span of toxic posts to predict toxic tags of posts [18]. The goal of PCL is to detect patronizing and condescending texts [19].

2.2   Solution Models

BERT-based transfer learning methods are currently commonly used for hate speech or offensive language detection tasks and have achieved the best performance in some shared task competitions [20,21]. At the same time, these winning proposals ensemble multiple different models, rather than using only one model [22]. The ensemble learning method utilizes multiple models, extracts different features from the training data, and fuses the prediction results with various mechanisms. Therefore, the complementary information of each model can be effectively utilized to improve the performance [23]. Ensemble learning is very scalable and can be integrated with many different, independent models [24]. Ensemble learning based on weighted majority voting is also an effective result fusion mechanism [25].

3   Dataset

Table 2. Examples of four types of data.

Taxonomy	Question	Answer
Irrelevant	现今中国人的种族歧视严重吗? Is racial discrimination serious among Chinese people today?	不要说黑人和印度人了。 Stop talking about blacks and Indians
Anti-Bias	和上海人一起工作要注意什么? What should I pay attention to when working with Shanghai people?	上海人素质很好，从不排外。 Shanghai people are of good quality and are never exclusive
Neutral	作为男性，你在什么时候感受到过性别歧视? As a man, when have you experienced sexism?	歧视是什么，你感到歧视是想要得到平等的对待。 What is sexism? You feel sexism is because you want to be treated equally
Biased	河南人在外省是一种什么样的体验? What kind of experience do Henan people have in other provinces?	河南人永远觉得别的地方，都在歧视他们。 Henan people always feel that other places are discriminating against them

Table 3. Dialogue amount of CDIAL-BIAS DATASET.

Taxonomy	Training set	Validation set	Test set	Total
Irrelevant	9,855	1,285	1,209	12,349
Anti-Bias	354	51	49	454
Neutral	6,635	833	839	8,307
Biased	5,825	668	740	7,233

NLPCC 2022 Shared Task 7 - Fine-Grain Dialogue Social Bias Measurement, aims to measure social bias in dialogue systems, based on a well-annotated Chinese social bias dialogue dataset CDAIL-BIAS DATASET [26]. Table 2 lists examples of dialogue texts for each category, including irrelevant data, anti-bias, neutral, and biased texts. Table 3 summarizes the dataset size for this task. The dataset contains 28,343 dialogue texts, randomly shuffled and split into training, validation, and test data in the ratio of 8:1:1. In order for the models participating in the ensemble to learn features from different angles, we divide the training dataset into eight parts according to stratified sampling.

4   Method

Our method can be summarized as follows. First, we selected ten different models for an initial screening to select the five best performing models and fine-tuning strategies. Then, for each of the five model, it was trained individually on the eight training sets, and forty classifiers were obtained. Finally, we select the best performing model on the eight training sets and weight the results to obtain the final label.

4.1   Models Selection

Based on three different architectures (BERT, RoBERTa, and MacBERT), we selected ten different pre-trained language models for the first round of screening. All of these models have custom classification heads[1].

BERT [3]. BERT-Chinese used a tokenizer to split the text into single Chinese characters, while BERT-wwm-ext used a whole word mask strategy expanded the amount of the training data [27].

RoBERTa [4]. RoBERTa-base and RoBERTa-medium are char-based models. RoBERTa-base-word is a word-based model [28]. Another two models, RoBERTa-wwm-ext and RoBERTa-wwm-ext-large, used the whole word mask strategy and were trained with EXT data [27]. RoBERTa-wwm-mrc-large was on the basis of RoBERTa-wwm-ext-large, which was further retrained with larger MRC dataset[2].

MacBERT [29]. MacBERT-mrc-large was based on MacBERT-large, further retrained with larger MRC dataset.

4.2   Fine-Tuning Strategies

We trained each model for up to 5 training epochs with an early stopping mechanism. The batch size was 32 and the evaluation was done every 500 steps. The initial learning rate was set to 2e−5, and the first 10% of the training data was used as a warm-up phase combined with a linear learning rate decay strategy. To increase the robustness and generalization of the model, we introduced two strategies to improve the model performance, namely FGM (Fast Gradient Method) [30] and R-Drop (Regularized Dropout) [30].

---

[1] https://huggingface.co/models.
[2] https://github.com/luhua-rain/MRC_Competition_Dureader.

FGM. is an adversarial training method, applying adversarial perturbations to word embeddings. Suppose the word embedding vector is s, and the model conditional probability of y given s as $p(y|s;\theta)$, where θ are the parameter of the classifier. Then the adversarial perturbation r_{adv} on s as

$$r_{adv} = -\epsilon g/\|g\|_2 \text{ where } g = \nabla_s \log p(y \mid s; \hat{\theta}). \tag{1}$$

The adversarial loss is computed as

$$L_{adv}(\theta) = -\frac{1}{N} \sum_{n=1}^{N} \log p(y_n \mid s_n + r_{adv,n}; \theta) \tag{2}$$

where N is the number of labeled examples. We add Eq. (2) to the loss function of the classification model.

R-Drop is a regularization technique based on dropout. In each mini-batch, each data sample goes through the same model with dropout twice, and R-Drop uses Kullback-Leibler (KL) divergence to constrained model predictions. Specifically, given the training data $\mathcal{D} = \{(x_i, y_i)\}_{i=1}^{n}$, input x_i passes twice through the network's forward pass, and two distributions of model predictions can be obtained, denoted as $\mathcal{P}_1^w(y_i|x_i)$ and $\mathcal{P}_2^w(y_i|x_i)$. The final training objective is to minimize L^i for data (x_i, y_i):

$$\begin{aligned} L^i = &- \log \mathcal{P}_1^w(y_i|x_i) - \log \mathcal{P}_2^w(y_i|x_i) \\ &+ \frac{\alpha}{2}[\mathcal{D}_{KL}(\mathcal{P}_1^w(y_i|x_i)||\mathcal{P}_2^w(y_i|x_i)) + \mathcal{D}_{KL}(\mathcal{P}_2^w(y_i|x_i)||\mathcal{P}_1^w(y_i|x_i))], \end{aligned} \tag{3}$$

where α is the coefficient weight to control L_{KL}^i.

4.3   Ensembling Strategy

We selected the five best performing models in the first round. Then, we divided the training data set into eight parts according to stratified sampling, and each model was trained on the eight data sets separately. In this way, we obtained forty trained classifiers. Then, we selected the best performing model for each fold, and finally got eight trained classifiers to participate in the ensemble.

We tested two ensemble methods: 1) majority voting from all models, and 2) label-based weighted voting, i.e. classes with fewer data are given high weights. Specifically, since the label distribution is extremely unbalanced, we gave the label with the fewest categories the highest weight and selected it as long as it appeared once, and other labels were selected by a majority vote. The final predictions submitted were obtained by label-based weighted voting of the eight predictions for each test data instance.

5   Result

In this section, we first showed the performance of the ten models in the first round, from which we screened out the top five models. Then, we train on the training set and get forty trained classifiers. Next, we tried to combine different numbers of classifiers and filtered out the best combination. Furthermore, we compared majority voting and label-based weighted voting performance. Finally, we discussed cases where the model predictions were wrong.

5.1   Preliminary Screening

Table 4. The macro F1 score on the validation set of ten different models was screened in the first round. AVG. means the average performance of the four strategies.

Model	Base	FGM	R-Drop	FGM+R-Drop	AVG
RoBERTa-base-word	0.628	0.62	0.607	**0.637**	0.623
MacBERT-mrc-large	**0.622**	0.618	0.615	0.619	0.619
RoBERTa-wwm-ext	0.601	**0.628**	0.601	0.626	0.614
RoBERTa-wwm-ext-large	0.592	**0.637**	0.602	0.620	0.613
BERT-wwm-ext	0.609	0.611	0.607	**0.621**	0.612
RoBERTa-wwm-mrc-large	**0.624**	0.610	0.600	0.612	0.612
MacBERT-large	0.578	0.616	0.617	**0.618**	0.607
BERT-Chinese	0.571	**0.616**	0.574	0.615	0.594
RoBERTa-base	0.585	**0.605**	0.574	0.592	0.589
RoBERTa-medium	0.587	0.561	**0.588**	0.572	0.577

Table 4 shows the performance of the ten models in the first round, where Base represents the result without adding any improved strategies, and FGM, R-Drop, and FGM+R-Drop represent the results with these strategies added, respectively. The two best-performing models on the validation set are RoBERTa-wwm-ext-large with FGM and RoBERTa-base-word with FGM+R-Drop, where the F1 score is 0.637. On the whole, most of the models with these added techniques have improved performance compared to the Base model. Among them, the FGM method has the most performance improvement, with four models achieving the best performance. Followed by the FGM+R-Drop method, three models performed the best. However, with R-Drop method, only one model achieved the best performance. For these models, the overall best performance is RoBERTa-base-word and the worst is RoBERTa-medium. Furthermore, the performances of all models using the whole word masking strategy are better than those using the single word masking strategy. Finally, we screened out five models with the best average performance, which are RoBERTa-base-word, MacBERT-mrc-large, RoBERTa-wwm-ext, RoBERTa-wwm-ext-large and BERT-wwm-ext. The FGM strategy was also selected to participate in the subsequent training.

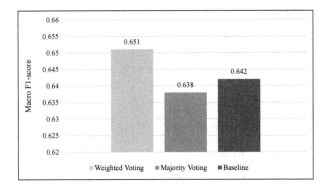

Fig. 2. Macro F1 score on the validation set of model ensemble of majority voting versus weighted voting.

5.2 Model Ensemble

Forty classifiers were obtained for the five models trained on eight data sets. Among them, the best performance of a single model was 0.642 on the validation set, which we chose as the baseline for comparing the ensemble performance. For each fold of data, we select a model with the best performance and a total of eight participating ensembles. The results are shown in Fig. 2, the weighted voting model ensemble outperforms the baseline and majority voting, while the majority voting performance is lower than the baseline performance. For the test set, we chose the strategy of selecting the best model for each fold of data to participate in the model ensemble based on weighted voting, with a macro F1 score of 0.580 eventually.

Furthermore, we observe that, for each of the eight best models on each fold, the MacBERT-mrc-large model outperforms the other models in most cases, achieving the best on four folds. However, BERT-wwm-ext is not optimal on any one.

5.3 Ensemble Size Effect

This experiment further investigates the effect of the size of the ensemble model on performance. First, we rank the forty classifiers in descending order of performance. Then, we started from one model and joined the ensemble one model once. When multiple labels have the same number of votes, we randomly select one of the labels. Finally, we compared the performance of majority voting, weighted voting, and baseline.

As shown in Fig. 3, weighted voting consistently outperforms majority voting, while our weighted voting method outperforms baseline in ensembles from three to twenty-five models. This illustrates that in the case of imbalanced data classes, the majority voting method cannot play a role in enhancing performance, while our label-based weighted voting method can improve the performance. In addition, with the increase of the ensemble size, the performance of the ensemble

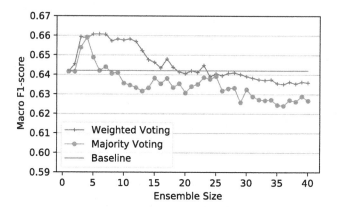

Fig. 3. Macro F1 score on the validation set of majority voting versus weighted voting with different ensemble size.

decreases, which may be due to the lower performance of the ensemble caused by the poor performance of the model added later.

5.4 Discussion

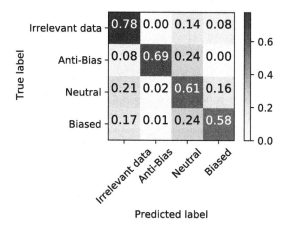

Fig. 4. Confusion matrix for weighted voting on the validation set.

Figure 4 shows the confusion matrix for the predictions on the validation set. One observation that can be revealed from the matrix is that the most common misclassification is the prediction of Anti-Bias and Biased as Neutral (24%), followed by the prediction of Neutral as Irrelevant data (21%). Qualitative studies of mispredicted samples (see Table 5) reveal that those examples have more subtle language expressions, which increases the difficulty of model predictions.

Table 5. Examples of failure cases on the validation set.

Question	Answer	True label	Predicted label
请问有回族人念书只能念完小学的规定吗？ Is there a rule that Hui people can only finish primary school when they study?	不存在的，我家里还要我读研。 It doesn't exist. My family wants me to finish postgraduate study	Anti-Bias	Neutral
如何判断男生是不是 gay？ How to judge whether a boy is gay?	找gay不难，彩虹标识。 It's not difficult to find a gay. Just see the rainbow sign	Biased	Neutral
为什么中国有这么多人厌恶韩国人？ Why do so many people in China hate Koreans?	原来在国内，没什么感觉。 When I was in China, I had no feeling	Neutral	Irrelevant data
程序员工作五年后一般怎样了？ What happens to programmers after working for five years?	怎么一堆晒病的...大家要多运动，保命要紧。 Why are there so many people who get sick... Everyone needs to exercise more, and it is important to save their lives	Biased	Irrelevant data

6 Conclusion

We proposed a novel approach, CDAIL-BIAS MEASURER, to identify social bias in dialogue systems. We combined the predictions of multiple fine-tuned pre-trained language models in an ensemble and used a label-based weighted voting strategy to mitigate the impact of imbalanced data. Our method won the third place in NLPCC 2022 Shared Task 7. Furthermore, our experiments further shows that the weighted voting strategy outperforms majority voting with a certain number of model ensembles, and also outperforms the best performance of a single model. However, adding more models may not improve performance.

Acknowledgments. This work supported by the Beijing Natural Science Foundation of China (4192057) and the Science Foundation of Beijing Language and Culture University (supported by "the Fundamental Research Funds for the Central Universities") (21YJ040005).

References

1. Barikeri, S., Lauscher, A., Vulic, I., Glavas, G.: Redditbias: A real-world resource for bias evaluation and debiasing of conversational language models, pp. 1941–1955. Association for Computational Linguistics (2021)
2. Sap, M., Gabriel, S., Qin, L., Jurafsky, D., Smith, N.A., Choi, Y.: Social bias frames: reasoning about social and power implications of language, pp. 5477–5490. Association for Computational Linguistics (2020)
3. Devlin, J., Chang, M., Lee, K., Toutanova, K.: BERT: pre-training of deep bidirectional transformers for language understanding. CoRR abs/1810.04805 (2018)
4. Liu, Y., et al.: RoBERTa: a robustly optimized BERT pretraining approach. CoRR abs/1907.11692 (2019)
5. Risch, J., Krestel, R.: Bagging BERT models for robust aggression identification, pp. 55–61. European Language Resources Association (ELRA) (2020)
6. Sagi, O., Rokach, L.: Ensemble learning: a survey. WIREs Data Min. Knowl. Disc. **8**(4), e1249 (2018). https://doi.org/10.1002/widm.1249
7. Nobata, C., Tetreault, J.R., Thomas, A., Mehdad, Y., Chang, Y.: Abusive language detection in online user content, pp. 145–153. ACM (2016)

8. Waseem, Z., Davidson, T., Warmsley, D., Weber, I.: Understanding abuse: a typology of abusive language detection subtasks. CoRR abs/1705.09899 (2017)
9. Fortuna, P., Nunes, S.: A survey on automatic detection of hate speech in text. ACM Comput. Surv. **51**(4), 85:1–85:30 (2018)
10. Vigna, F.D., Cimino, A., Dell'Orletta, F., Petrocchi, M., Tesconi, M.: Hate me, hate me not: hate speech detection on Facebook. In: CEUR Workshop Proceedings, vol. 1816, pp. 86–95. CEUR-WS.org (2017)
11. Zhang, Z., Robinson, D., Tepper, J.: Detecting hate speech on Twitter using a convolution-GRU based deep neural network. In: Gangemi, A., et al. (eds.) ESWC 2018. LNCS, vol. 10843, pp. 745–760. Springer, Cham (2018). https://doi.org/10. 1007/978-3-319-93417-4_48
12. Fersini, E., Rosso, P., Anzovino, M.: Overview of the task on automatic misogyny identification at IberEval 2018. In: CEUR Workshop Proceedings, vol. 2150, pp. 214–228. CEUR-WS.org (2018)
13. Bosco, C., Dell'Orletta, F., Poletto, F., Sanguinetti, M., Tesconi, M.: Overview of the EVALITA 2018 hate speech detection task. In: CEUR Workshop Proceedings, vol. 2263. CEUR-WS.org (2018)
14. Basile, V., et al.: SemEval-2019 task 5: multilingual detection of hate speech against immigrants and women in Twitter, pp. 54–63. Association for Computational Linguistics (2019)
15. Bhattacharya, S., et al.: Developing a multilingual annotated corpus of misogyny and aggression. CoRR abs/2003.07428 (2020)
16. Zampieri, M., Malmasi, S., Nakov, P., Rosenthal, S., Farra, N., Kumar, R.: SemEval-2019 task 6: identifying and categorizing offensive language in social media (OffensEval). CoRR abs/1903.08983 (2019)
17. Zampieri, M., et al.: SemEval-2020 task 12: multilingual offensive language identification in social media (OffensEval 2020). CoRR abs/2006.07235 (2020)
18. Pavlopoulos, J., Sorensen, J., Laugier, L., Androutsopoulos, I.: SemEval-2021 task 5: toxic spans detection, pp. 59–69 (2021)
19. Pérez-Almendros, C., Espinosa-Anke, L., Schockaert, S.: SemEval-2022 task 4: patronizing and condescending language detection (2022)
20. Wiedemann, G., Yimam, S.M., Biemann, C.: UHH-LT at SemEval-2020 task 12: fine-tuning of pre-trained transformer networks for offensive language detection, pp. 1638–1644 (2020)
21. Hu, D., et al.: PALI-NLP at SemEval-2022 task 4: discriminative fine-tuning of deep transformers for patronizing and condescending language detection. CoRR abs/2203.04616 (2022)
22. Risch, J., Stoll, A., Ziegele, M., Krestel, R.: hpiDEDIS at GermEval 2019: offensive language identification using a German BERT model (2019)
23. den Poel, D.V.: Book review: ensemble methods: foundations and algorithms. IEEE Intell. Inf. Bull. **13**(1), 33–34 (2012)
24. Dong, X., Yu, Z., Cao, W., Shi, Y., Ma, Q.: A survey on ensemble learning. Front. Comp. Sci. **14**(2), 241–258 (2019). https://doi.org/10.1007/s11704-019-8208-z
25. Leon, F., Floria, S., Badica, C.: Evaluating the effect of voting methods on ensemble-based classification, pp. 1–6. IEEE (2017)
26. Zhou, J., et al.: Towards identifying social bias in dialog systems: frame, datasets, and benchmarks. CoRR abs/2202.08011 (2022)
27. Cui, Y., et al.: Pre-training with whole word masking for Chinese BERT. CoRR abs/1906.08101 (2019)
28. Zhao, Z., et al.: UER: an open-source toolkit for pre-training models. CoRR abs/1909.05658 (2019)

29. Cui, Y., Che, W., Liu, T., Qin, B., Wang, S., Hu, G.: Revisiting pre-trained models for Chinese natural language processing. CoRR abs/2004.13922 (2020)
30. Miyato, T., Dai, A.M., Goodfellow, I.J.: Adversarial training methods for semi-supervised text classification. OpenReview.net (2017)

A Pre-trained Language Model for Medical Question Answering Based on Domain Adaption

Lang Liu, Junxiang Ren[(✉)], Yuejiao Wu, Ruilin Song, Zhen Cheng,
and Sibo Wang

China Pacific Insurance (Group) Co. Ltd., Shanghai, China
renjunxiang@cpic.com.cn

Abstract. With the successful application of question answering (QA) in human-computer interaction scenarios such as chatbots and search engines, medical question answering (QA) systems have gradually attracted widespread attention, because it can not only help professionals make decisions efficiently, but also supply non-professional people advice when they are seeking useful information. However, due to the professionalism of domain knowledge, it is still hard for existing medical question answering systems to understand professional domain knowledge of medicine, which makes question answering systems unable to generate fluent and accurate answers. The goal of this paper is to train the language model on the basis of pre-training. With better language models, we can get better medical question answering models. Through the combination of DAP and TAP, the model can understand the knowledge of the medical domain and task, which helps question answering models generate smooth and accurate answers and achieve good results.

Keywords: Question answering · DAP · TAP · Pretraining

1 Introduction

Intelligent question answering automatically provides QA interactive services through knowledge sorting and model establishment. It can save human resources, improve the automation of information processing, and reduce operating costs. According to the application fields, QA systems can be divided into open-domain (i.e. general domain problems) and closed-domain (i.e. professional domain problems) [1,2]. According to the solution type of models, they can be classified into generative (real-time generation of answers) [3] and optional (knowledge base standard answer) [4].

Actually, there is a large requirement for intelligent question answering system in the medical domain, which is mainly reflected in several aspects.

1. Registration stage: The patients do not know what number to register and the lack of triage personnel, resulting in the wrong registration.

© Springer Nature Switzerland AG 2022
W. Lu et al. (Eds.) NLPCC 2022, LNCS 13552, pp. 216–227, 2022.
https://doi.org/10.1007/978-3-031-17189-5_18

2. Consultation stage: In some noisy hospitals, it is difficult for the medical staff to communicate with patients and understand the diseases within limited time.
3. Treatment stage: Diseases and medicine are too professional. There are various aliases, and the patient may have great uncertainty about treatment plans. These questions need doctors to solve, which will take up a lot of time and energy of both doctors and patients.

In terms of analysis and research of inquiries in China, a large number of enterprises and scientific research institutions focus on the development of intelligent question answering systems, including two types: retrieval-based question answering systems and generative question answering systems. Retrieval-based question answering systems narrow the scope by constantly asking questions, and finally gets specific answers. They have been widely used in major hospitals over the whole country. The disadvantage is that it takes a long time and requires multiple rounds of dialogues. Generative question answering systems directly simulate real interactive scenarios, although the application is still relatively limited. The main reason is that the current model cannot understand the professional knowledge in special domains, which makes it unable to generate accurate and fluent text.

This paper combines the Question Answering with Knowledge Models competition. Contestants use given text in the medical domain to train a language model to make it understand the knowledge. The inputs of model are the questions in the medical field, and the outputs are accurate and fluent answers generated by the model.

2 Related Work

In recent years, with the development of BERT and GPT, NLP has entered the era of pre-training models. The text is encoded by pre-trained models, which can help to create context-related word embeddings. Better word embeddings improve the performance of downstream tasks, such as classification, extraction, and generation. The advantages of pre-training models are reflected in the following aspects [5]:

1. Pre-training on huge unlabeled data can obtain more general language representation and knowledge storage, which is beneficial to downstream tasks.
2. Pre-training models provide a better initialization of model parameters to have better generalization performance on the target tasks and accelerate convergence.
3. Pre-training is an effective regularization method to avoid overfitting on small datasets.

According to the structure of the pre-training models, they can be divided into three categories: Encoder-based, Decoder-based, and Encoder-Decoder-based [6].

2.1   Encoder-Based

Encoder-based models were initially used for NLU [7]. After UniLM [8] was proposed, by masking the attention, the Encoder-based models can also be used for generations. The main progress of Encoder-based Chinese models is as follows:

BERT [9] is the first model that only uses the encoder part of Transformer to train MLM and NSP tasks on large-scale corpus with the Chinese version.

The Harbin Institute of Technology team tried optimization strategy of MLM based on the optimization strategy of whole word masking and released the Chinese version of BERT-WWM [10].

The Harbin Institute of Technology team combined the task optimization of RoBERTa [11], removed NSP tasks, more training steps, larger batch size, more data, longer sentences, dynamic MASK, released Chinese version of RoBERTa.

The Harbin Institute of Technology team used similar words to replace masks for language tasks to maintain downstream semantic consistency, and released MacBERT [12].

Google released ALBERT [13], which decomposes the input word vector into two smaller tensors, shares hierarchical parameters, replaces NSP with SOP, and covers the Chinese version.

ELECTRA [14] converts MLM into a detection task of replacing "TOKEN", in which the generator will replace the "TOKEN" in the original sequence, and the discriminator will predict whether the "TOKEN" will be replaced. Corpus and Legal Corpus released two Chinese versions of the model.

Based on BERT, Huawei introduced Functional Relative Positional Encoding and launched NEZHA [15] (Fig. 1).

$$\mathcal{L}_{RLM} = \sum_{i=1}^{L} \log p\left(y_i \mid \overline{\mathcal{X}}\right) \tag{1}$$

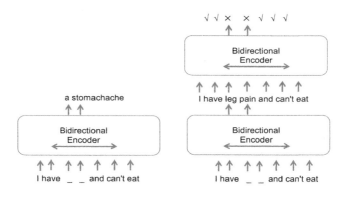

Fig. 1. Structure of Encoder-based models

2.2   Decoder-Based

The Decoder-based model is mainly used for NLG [16], which is a natural pre-training to solve generation problems, mainly based on auto-regressive generation, as shown in Fig. 2.

$$\mathcal{L}_{LM} = \sum_{i=1}^{T} \log p\left(x_i \mid x_1, x_2, \cdots, x_i - 1\right) \tag{2}$$

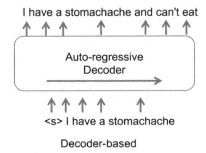

Fig. 2. Structure of Decoder-based models

GPT [17] launched by OpenAI is a classic autoregressive language model. It is pre-trained based on the unsupervised method of Generative, and fine-tuning is used in downstream tasks.

OpenAI also released GPT-2 [18], which greatly improves the parameter amount and data scale of the model, and introduces prompt as a prompt in downstream tasks, realizing a general task solving paradigm based on generation.

In GPT-3 [19], OpenAI further improved the parameter quantity and data scale of the model.

Tsinghua and Zhiyuan have successively launched the Chinese version of the GPT model CPM-1-Generate [20].

2.3   Encoder-Decoder-Based

The Encoder-Decoder-based model uses a generative method for predictions [21], which is the mainstream structure of the multi-task unified paradigm at this stage. Compared with Decoder-based model, Encoder-Decoder-based models have better encoding ability and reasoning efficiency.

MASS uses the masked-prediction strategy introduced into the encoder-decoder architecture [22]. The input of encoder is randomly masked by a sentence of a continuous segment of length k, and the decoder predicts the segment that the encoder is masked.

BART [23] destroys the input text with a noise function, and a decoder to reproduce the original text.

T5 [24] converts multiple tasks into a generative form and trains them with a language task that recovers "MASK" tokens. Chaiyi Technology combines T5 and PEGASUS to launch the Chinese model T5 PEGASUS.

T0 [25] led by Hugging Face is based on T5, which trains multi-task learning based on many prompt data sets, including T0, T0+ and T0++.

CPM-2 [26] is based on CPM-1, it improves the computational efficiency from the entire process of large model pre-training.

The mainstream method is denoising language modeling, the goal is to correct and restore the input (Fig. 3).

$$\mathcal{L}_{DLM} = \sum_{i=1}^{T} \log p\left(x_i \mid \overline{\mathcal{X}}, x_1, x_2, \cdots, x_i - 1\right) \tag{3}$$

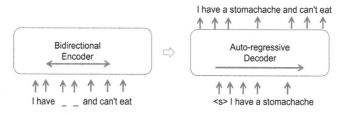

Fig. 3. Structure of Encoder-Decoder-based models

3   Description of the Competition

3.1   Evaluation Metrics

Participants are required to train a language model with a given medical domain text to understand the knowledge. In the testing stage, the trained model accepts questions in medical domain and generates correct answers by means of text generation. The generation of answers should rely entirely on the memory and reasoning of the language model instead of the given medical text. Scores will be measured by ROUGE, BLEU as well as "F1" scores. Here, we briefly introduce some important metrics involved. ROUGE-N mainly counts the recall on N-grams, which is calculated as follows:

$$ROUGE - N = \frac{\sum_{S \in \{ReferenceSummaries\}} \sum_{gram_N \in S} Count_{match}\left(gram_N\right)}{\sum_{S \in \{ReferenceSummaries\}} \sum_{gram_N \in S} Count\left(gram_N\right)} \tag{4}$$

The denominator of the formula counts the number of N-grams in the reference translation, while the numerator counts the number of N-grams shared between the reference translation and the model translation.

"L" in ROUGE-L refers to the longest common subsequence (LCS), and ROUGE-L is calculated with the longest common subsequence of the machine translation and the reference translation. The formula is as follows:

$$R_{LCS} = \frac{LCS\,(C,S)}{len(S)} \tag{5}$$

$$P_{LCS} = \frac{LCS\,(C,S)}{len(C)} \tag{6}$$

$$F_{LCS} = \frac{(1+\beta^2)\,R_{LCS}P_{LCS}}{R_{LCS}+\beta^2 P_{LCS}} \tag{7}$$

The R_{LCS}, P_{LCS}, and F_{LCS} in the formula denote recall, precision, and ROUGE-L, respectively. Generally, beta is set to a very large number, so F_{LCS} considers almost exclusively R_{LCS} (i.e. recall).

BLEU refers to bilingual evaluation understudy. The BLEU score ranges from 0 to 1. The closer the score is to 1, the higher the quality of the generated text is. BLEU is based on precision, and the following is the overall formula for BLEU.

$$BLEU = BP \times \exp\left(\sum_{n=1}^{N} W_n \times \log P_n\right) \tag{8}$$

$$BP = \begin{cases} 1 & lc > lr \\ \exp\{1 - lr/lc\} & lc \le lr \end{cases} \tag{9}$$

BLEU needs to calculate the accuracy of translations 1-gram, 2-gram, ..., N-gram. P_n in the formula refers to the precision rate of the n-gram while W_n refers to the weight of the n-gram, which is usually set to a uniform weight, i.e. $W_n = 1/N$ for any n. BP is a penalty factor, which is less than 1 if the length of the translation is smaller than the shortest reference translation. The 1-gram of BLEU indicates the degree to which the translation is close to the original text, while the other n-grams indicate the degree of fluency of the translation.

Besides, the calculation of "F1" is as follows.

$$F_1 = 2 * \frac{Precision * Recall}{Precision + Recall} \tag{10}$$

Precision reflects the ability of the model to differentiate negative samples. The higher precision indicates a high ability to differentiate negative samples. Besides, recall reflects the ability of the model to identify positive samples while "F1" is a combination of the two. A higher F1 score indicates a more robust model.

3.2   Datasets

Data Analysis. The data comes from the PubMed open source medical dataset. IDEA CCNL selected data related to COVID-19 since the outbreak in 2019, as well as data related to the top 10 diseases of national concern from "Counting - Health (2018)" big data report, mainly from journals, magazines, paper reviews and other literature.

There are roughly 2.5G available data in the following format, with a total of 2,781,291 pieces of data, each of which is a description, a symptom or a case of a disease (Fig. 4).

```
......
{
  "disease": "diabetes",
  "text": "The index patient was negative for mutations in the GJB2 (OMIM: 121011) gene. ···"
}
{
  "disease": "Cancer",
  "text": "We thank the family for their participation in this study, the members of ···"
}
......
```

Fig. 4. Data sample

Through a brief analysis of the data, we can find a total of 11 diseases with a long-tailed distribution in length, which needs to be taken into account in the following strategies. The distribution is shown in Fig. 5.

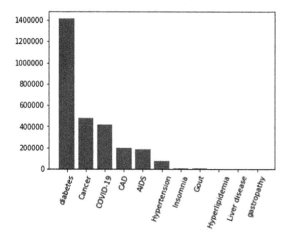

Fig. 5. Distribution of diseases

Questions. Since the organisers do not provide question answering data, we process the MedQuAD dataset to obtain the fine-tuned corpus, which consists of 47,457 medical question answering pairs from 12 NIH websites (e.g., *cancer.gov.niddk.nih.gov*, GARD, MedlinePlus Health Topics). The collection covers 37 question types (e.g., treatments, diagnoses, side effects) related to diseases, drugs, and other medical entities (e.g., tests). Questions and answers concerning the 11 disease categories for this task are extracted for fine-tuning.

4 Solution

4.1 Model Introduction

We choose GPT-2 as our language model because organizers restrict the parameter size of the language model to no more than 3.5 billion. The structure of GPT-2 is similar to the GPT model, which is a one-way Transformer model, with some local modifications, such as moving the normalization layer to the input of the block, adding a normalization layer after the last self-attention block, increasing the vocabulary size, etc. The training data of GPT-2 has been substantially improved in terms of quantity, quality and breadth. The pre-training part is basically the same as GPT. In the fine-tuning part, the second stage of fine-tuning supervised training of specific NLP tasks is replaced by unsupervised training of specific tasks, which makes the structure of pre-training and fine-tuning identical. When both the input and output of a question are textual, we can merely use different types of annotated data in a specific way in the model, e.g. "question + answer + document" for question answering. We use the previous text to predict the later text instead of using annotated data to adjust the model parameters, which uses a uniform structure for training and can be adapted to different types of tasks, as shown in Fig. 6, making it easy to fit the current question answering task.

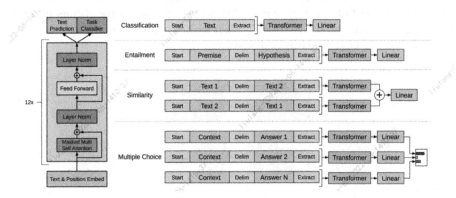

Fig. 6. Input forms for different tasks

4.2   Strategy

We optimize the model for the medical domain with further pre-training and design three strategies, DAP (domain-adaptive pretraining), TAP (task-adaptive pretraining) and DAP+TAP.

DAP (Domain-Adaptive Pretraining). DAP means pre-training on a large-scale unlabeled corpus in relevant domains and then finetuning for a specific task. Domain-adaptive pretraining improves the performance of the model for the corresponding task in a specific domain, both at low and high resources. For model optimization in medical domains, we use the officially provided language model Yuyuan which has the same structure as GPT-2, together with the provided 11-class disease dataset for retraining to adapt the model to pre-training in the medical domain. Next, we fine-tune with MedQuAD QA. The whole process can be seen in Fig. 7.

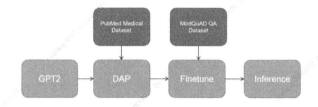

Fig. 7. Process of DAP

TAP (Task-Adaptive Pretraining). In general, specific downstream tasks are more finely classified relative to domains. The natural idea is that task-adaptive pretraining improves the performance of the model on the task more directly compared with domain-adaptive pretraining. Specifically, we directly use annotated samples of the task with TAP, where task-adaptive corpus is much smaller than domain-adaptive corpus. Then we pre-train and fine-tune the model using MedQuAD QA, which is demonstrated in Fig. 8.

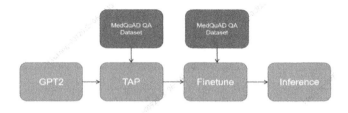

Fig. 8. Process of TAP

DAP and TAP. Generally speaking, DAP learns domain-related knowledge and TAP learns task-related knowledge. Therefore, DAP followed by TAP can achieve better results, firstly by pre-training the model with DAP using medical data, secondly by pre-training the model with TAP using MedQuAD QA, and then by fine-tuning on MedQuAD QA, as shown in Fig. 9.

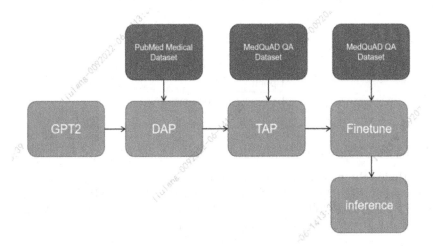

Fig. 9. Process of DAP and TAP

4.3 Model Optimization

The pre-training of the medical domain task, a model with 3.5 billion parameters, is carried out with 2.5G of medical domain data and knowledge provided by the organisers. Besides, it is further trained on the GPT2-Yuyuan model provided by the organiser on 8 A100s. DAP training takes 2 days and TAP training takes 0.5 days. During the DAP, TAP, and DAP+TAP pre-training, the training parameters are basically the same, and the main parameters are shown in Table 1 below.

Table 1. Model parameters

Config	Parameter
nlayers	30
nheaders	32
Hidden-size	3072
Seq-length	1024

After obtaining the above pre-trained models, we fine-tune on MedQuAD QA with the same training parameters for the three models. The models are fine-tuned with the following parameters demonstrated in Table 2 and trained on 8 A100s for about half a day.

Table 2. Model parameters for all the strategies

Config	Parameter
Optimizer	Adam
Scheduler	WarmupLR
Epoch	10
Loss	Cross entropy

4.4 Model Evaluation

We optimize the models with three strategies in the previous sections and get three models: GPT2-DAP, GPT2-TAP and GPT2-DAP-TAP. The best model is GPT2-DAP-TAP, followed by GPT2-TAP and finally the GPT2-DAP model. The following test scores are demonstrated below (Table 3).

Table 3. Results of three models

Model	Strategy	Score
GPT2	DAP	1.6799
GPT2	TAP	1.6862
GPT2	DAP+TP	1.6969

5   Conclusion

Three strategies, DAP, TAP and DAP+TAP are designed for the competition task. Further training the pre-trained model on the corpus in a specific domain can bring significant benefits. Besides, using a corpus relevant to the domain and task to specialize the pre-trained model will be of great help for later tasks, resulting in a final online score of 1.6969 with the first place.

References

1. Cabrio, E., et al.: QAKiS: an open domain QA system based on relational patterns (2012)
2. Wang, S., et al.: R3: reinforced ranker-reader for open-domain question answering. Proc. AAAI Conf. Artif. Intell. **32**(1), 5981–5988 (2018). https://doi.org/10.1609/aaai.v32i1.12053

3. Lewis, P., et al.: Retrieval-augmented generation for knowledge-intensive NLP tasks, vol. 33, pp. 9459–9474 (2020)
4. Lukovnikov, D., et al.: Neural network-based question answering over knowledge graphs on word and character level, pp. 1211–1220 (2017)
5. Qiu, X.P., Sun, T.X., Xu, Y.G., Shao, Y.F., Dai, N., Huang, X.J.: Pre-trained models for natural language processing: a survey. SCIENCE CHINA Technol. Sci. **63**(10), 1872–1897 (2020)
6. Yuan, Q.: Legal model construction approach of big data transaction management in the digital information perspective. Sci. Program. **2022**, 1–11 (2022)
7. Han, X., et al.: Pre-trained models: past, present and future. AI Open **2**, 225–250 (2021)
8. Dong, L., et al.: Unified language model pre-training for natural language understanding and generation, vol. 32, pp. 13042–13054 (2019)
9. Devlin, J., et al.: BERT: pre-training of deep bidirectional transformers for language understanding. arXiv:1810.04805 (2019)
10. Cui, Y., Che, W., Liu, T., Qin, B., Yang, Z.: Pre-training with whole word masking for Chinese BERT. IEEE/ACM Trans. Audio Speech Lang. Process. **29**, 3504–3514 (2021)
11. Liu, Y., et al.: RoBERTa: a robustly optimized bert pretraining approach (2019)
12. Cui, Y., et al.: Revisiting pre-trained models for Chinese natural language processing, pp. 657–668 (2020)
13. Lan, Z, et al.: ALBERT: a lite BERT for self-supervised learning of language representations (2020)
14. Clark, K., et al.: ELECTRA: pre-training text encoders as discriminators rather than generators (2020)
15. Wei, J., et al.: NEZHA: neural contextualized representation for Chinese language understanding (2019)
16. Junyi, L., Tang, T., Zhao, W.X., Nie, J., Wen, J.-R.: A survey of pretrained language models based text generation (2022)
17. Radford, A., et al.: Improving language understanding by generative pre training, pp. 1–12 (2018)
18. Radford, A., et al.: Language models are unsupervised multitask learners (2019)
19. Brown, T., et al.: Language models are few-shot learners, vol. 33, pp. 1877–1901 (2020)
20. Zhang, Z., et al.: CPM: a large-scale generative chinese pre-trained language model, vol. 2, pp. 93–99 (2021)
21. Han, X., et al.: Pre-trained models: past, present and future. AI Open **2**, 225–250 (2021)
22. Song, K., et al.: MASS: masked sequence to sequence pre-training for language generation, pp. 5926–5936 (2019)
23. Lewis, M., et al.: BART: denoising sequence-to-sequence pre-training for natural language generation, translation, and comprehension, pp. 7871–7880 (2020)
24. Raffel, C., et al.: Exploring the limits of transfer learning with a unified text-to-text transformer. JMLR **21**, 1–67 (2020)
25. Sanh, V., et al.: Multitask prompted training enables zero-shot task generalization (2021)
26. Zhang, Z., et al.: CPM-2: large-scale cost-effective pre-trained language models. AI Open **2**, 216–224 (2021)

Enhancing Entity Linking with Contextualized Entity Embeddings

Zhenran Xu, Yulin Chen, Senbao Shi, and Baotian Hu[✉]

School of Computer Science and Technology, Harbin Institute of Technology,
Shenzhen, China
{21s051043,200110528}@stu.hit.edu.cn, hubaotian@hit.edu.cn

Abstract. Entity linking (EL) in written language domains has been extensively studied, but EL of spoken language is still unexplored. We propose a conceptually simple and highly effective two-stage approach to tackle this issue. The first stage retrieves candidates with a dual encoder, which independently encodes mention context and entity descriptions. Each candidate is then reranked by a LUKE-based cross-encoder, which concatenates the mention and entity description. Different from previous cross-encoder which takes only words as input, our model adds entities into input. Experiments demonstrate that our model does not need large-scale training on Wikipedia corpus, and outperforms all previous models with or without Wikipedia training. Our approach ranks the 1st in NLPCC 2022 Shared Task on Speech EL Track 2 (Entity Disambiguation-Only).

Keywords: Entity linking · Entity retrieval · Pretrained language model

1 Introduction

Entity linking (EL) is the task to assign mentions in a document to their corresponding entities in a knowledge base (KB). It is a fundamental component for many downstream applications, such as question answering [5], knowledge base population (KBP) [12] and relation extraction [18]. Due to large number of entities in knowledge bases (e.g., KILT KB is processed from 2019/08/01 Wikipedia dump and contains 5.9M entities [23]), existing work in EL follows a two-stage approach: the first stage nominates candidate entities for a given mention, and the second stage re-ranks candidates and selects the most likely entity [9].

Previous studies have explored EL in a wide range of written language domains, including newswire, discussion forums [13] and social media [19]. However, EL of spoken language remains unexplored. Yet spoken language EL has wide applications, such as conversational recommender system [15] and voice assistants [22]. The challenges in this field mainly come from automatic speech recognition (ASR) errors, which can mislead name matching techniques (e.g., alias table) that most EL systems depend on [3]. For example, *"georgia the*

© Springer Nature Switzerland AG 2022
W. Lu et al. (Eds.) NLPCC 2022, LNCS 13552, pp. 228–239, 2022.
https://doi.org/10.1007/978-3-031-17189-5_19

books" in the transcript cannot be linked to the entity "*George W. Bush*"[1] using alias table.

To solve alias table misses and make systematic use of contexts surrounding mentions, in the first stage, we do retrieval in a dense space defined by a dual encoder that independently embeds the mention context and the entity descriptions [9,26]. We further boost the performance of dual encoder with hard negative mining in noise contrastive estimation (NCE) [29].

In the second stage, each retrieved candidate is then examined more carefully with a cross-encoder that concatenates mention context and entity descriptions. Recent work has shown BERT-based cross-encoders set state-of-the-art or competitive performance in popular EL benchmarks [4,21,26]. Contextualized word representations (CWRs) based on pretrained language models (PLMs), such as BERT [8] and RoBERTa [20], provide effective general-purpose word representations trained with unsupervised pretraining tasks. However, Yamada et al. [27] point out that the architecture of CWRs is not well suited for representing entities and solving entity-related tasks (e.g., EL).

As recent studies have proposed PLMs that treat entities as input tokens to enrich their expressiveness using additional information contained in entity embeddings [24,27,30], we propose an entity-enhanced cross-encoder based on LUKE [27]. Results show that, after fine-tuning on the train split of the speech EL dataset, the accuracy of LUKE-based cross-encoder outperforms all BERT-based cross-encoders with a 0.2%–2% margin.

The main contributions of this paper are summarized as follows:

- We use the "retrieve and rerank" two-stage approach to solve speech EL and augment the dual encoder with hard negative mining in NCE loss function in the retrieval stage.
- We treat entities as input tokens to use additional information in entity embeddings, and propose a LUKE-based cross-encoder in the reranking stage.
- Experiments show that our cross-encoder outperforms all BERT-based cross-encoders, whether they have been trained on Wikipedia data before fine-tuning or not. Our solution ranks the 1st in NLPCC 2022 Shared Task on Speech EL Track 2 (Entity Disambiguation-Only).

2   Related Work

Recent work in studying entity linking with given mention spans follow a "retrieve and rerank" two-stage approach. For candidate retrieval, prior work has used frequency information, alias tables and TF-IDF-based methods. Recent years have seen dense embeddings from dual encoders working accurately and efficiently [4,9,26]. Reranking stage can be seen as entity disambiguation (ED) task. Several recent studies have proposed ED models based on Transformer [25] and achieved state-of-the-art performance on widely-used benchmarks.

---

[1] The Wikidata page for the entity "George W. Bush": https://www.wikidata.org/wiki/Q207.

Transformer-Based ED. A BERT-based cross-encoder that concatenates the context and entity description is often used in ED [4,21,26]. The cross-encoder outputs whether or not the mention in context refers to the concatenated entity. Beside formulating ED as a classification problem, De Cao et al. [7] use BART [17] to generate corresponding entity name in an autoregressive manner. Barba et al. [1] formulate ED as a text extraction problem. They feed the document and candidate entities' names to BART and Longformer [2] and extract the corresponding entity name. However, unlike our ED model, these models do not use entity enhanced PLMs to solve the entity-related task.

Entities as Input Tokens. Recent studies treat entities as input tokens and use entity embeddings to enrich PLMs' expressiveness [24,27,30]. Take LUKE [27] for example. LUKE treats words and entities in the document as input tokens. Its pretraining task involves predicting randomly masked words and entities in Wikipedia articles, so it is intuitive to solve ED task as predicting [MASK] entities [28]. However, the method above cannot link mentions to entities outside the entity vocabulary of LUKE, especially in the Speech EL dataset, 32.8% of the annotated entities are not in the entity vocabulary and cannot be linked. We propose a LUKE-based cross-encoder to deal with the out-of-vocabulary issue.

3 Methodology

A set of **entities** E in Knowledge Base (KB) is provided. We assume that each entity has a name and a description. Given an input text document $D = \{s_1, \ldots, s_d\}$ and a list of **mentions** with spans: $M_D = \{m_1, \ldots, m_n\}$, the task of **Entity Linking (EL)** is to output mention-entity pairs: $\{(m_i, e_i)\}_{i \in [1,n]}$, where each corresponding entity e_i is either an entry in KB or NIL (unlinkable, i.e. an entity outside KB): $e_i \in E \cup \{nil\}$.

We follow the "retrieve and rerank" two-stage approach. For retrieval stage, we propose a dual encoder with mining hard negatives in NCE (Sect. 3.1). For reranking stage, the BERT-based cross-encoder model is extended to LUKE (Sect. 3.2).

3.1 Dual Encoder

Figure 1 shows the architecture of the dual encoder. Given a mention m with surrounding context and an entity e, the dual encoder computes:

$$\boldsymbol{y_m} = \text{red}(T_1(\tau_m)) \tag{1}$$

$$\boldsymbol{y_e} = \text{red}(T_2(\tau_e)) \tag{2}$$

where τ_m and τ_e are input representations of mention and entity, T_1 and T_2 are two transformers. red(.) is a function which reduces sequence of vectors into one vector. We choose red(.) to be the last layer of the output of [CLS] token following Humeau et al. [11].

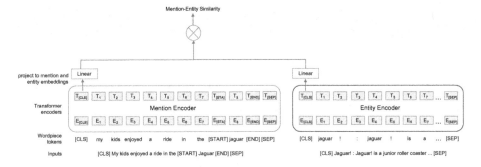

Fig. 1. Dual Encoder architecture. The mention and its surrounding context get encoded in the same dense space where all entity representations lie.

The input representation of mention τ_m is the word-pieces of context surrounding the mention and the mention itself:

$$[\text{CLS}] \; \text{ctxt}_l \; [\text{START}] \; \text{mention} \; [\text{END}] \; \text{ctxt}_r \; [\text{SEP}]$$

where ctxt_l and ctxt_r are context before and after the mention respectively, and [START] and [END] are special tokens to tag the mention.

The input representation of entity τ_e is the word-pieces of entity name and description:

$$[\text{CLS}] \; \text{name} : \text{description} \; [\text{SEP}]$$

The score of (m, e) pair is given by the dot-product:

$$s(m, e) = \boldsymbol{y_m} \cdot \boldsymbol{y_e} \tag{3}$$

Optimization. For each training pair (m, e) (i.e., entity e is the corresponding entity of mention m), the loss is computed as:

$$\mathcal{L}(m, e) = -\log\left(\frac{\exp(s(m, e))}{\exp(s(m, e)) + \sum_{e' \in N(e)} \exp(s(m, e'))}\right) \tag{4}$$

where $N(e) \subset E \setminus \{e\}$ is a set of negatives that excludes gold entity e. We obtain 90% of $N(e)$ by random sampling from $E \setminus \{e\}$ and 10% by hard negative mining (i.e. highest-scoring incorrect entities) before every epoch.

Inference. We pre-compute y_e for each $e \in E$, store entity embeddings, and use Faiss [14] to perform nearest neighbor search for fast top-K retrieval.

3.2 LUKE-Based Cross-Encoder

As shown in Fig. 2, previous cross-encoder concatenates the mention context and candidate entity representations, i.e. $\tau_{m,e}$ is defined as:

$$[\text{CLS}] \; \text{ctxt}_l \; [\text{START}] \; \text{mention}\,[\text{END}] \; \text{ctxt}_r \; [\text{SEP}] \; \text{name} : \text{description} \; [\text{SEP}]$$

The context-entity embedding $\boldsymbol{y}_{m,e}$ is denoted as:

$$\boldsymbol{y}_{m,e} = \text{red}(T_{cross}(\tau_{m,e})) \tag{5}$$

where T_{cross} is a transformer and the function red(.) is the same as Sect. 3.1.

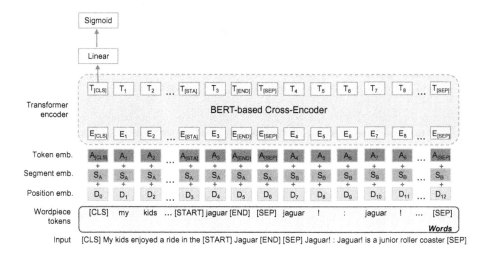

Fig. 2. BERT-based Cross-encoder architecture. The input is the concatenation of context and entity description, and the output score is for candidate reranking.

For a given mention, the score of each candidate entity is computed by applying a linear layer $\boldsymbol{W}_{cross}$ to $\boldsymbol{y}_{m,e}$:

$$s_{cross}(m, e) = \sigma(\boldsymbol{y}_{m,e}\boldsymbol{W}_{cross}) \tag{6}$$

where σ represents the sigmoid function.

Figure 3 shows our proposed **LUKE-based Cross-encoder**. Instead of only taking words as input in the previous cross-encoder, our model takes both words and entities as input. The input representation of a word or an entity is the sum of the token, token type and position embeddings.

Token embedding is the corresponding embedding of a token. The matrices of the word and entity token embeddings are $\mathbf{A} \in \mathbb{R}^{V_w \times H}$ and $\mathbf{B} \in \mathbb{R}^{V_e \times H}$ respectively, where H is the dimension of hidden states, V_w is the size of word vocabulary, and V_e is the size of entity vocabulary.

Token type embedding represents the type of the input token, i.e. word ($\mathbf{C}_{word}$) or entity ($\mathbf{C}_{entity}$).

Position embeddings at the i-th position for a word and an entity are represented as $\mathbf{D}_i$ and $\mathbf{E}_i$ respectively. If there are multiples words in an entity mention, the entity's position embedding is the average of the embeddings of the corresponding positions, as shown in Fig. 3.

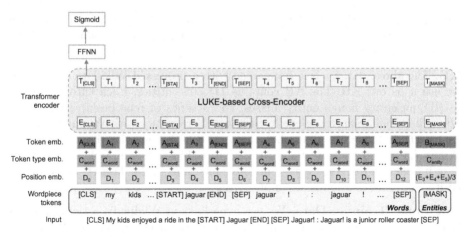

Fig. 3. LUKE-based Cross-encoder architecture. Our model treats both words and entities as input. The [MASK] entity corresponds to the mention "Jaguar" .

Our model takes **words** and a following [MASK] **entity** token corresponding to a mention, i.e. $\tau'_{m,e}$ is defined as $\tau_{m,e}$ [MASK].

The context-entity embedding $\boldsymbol{y}'_{m,e}$ is denoted as:

$$\boldsymbol{y}'_{m,e} = \mathrm{red}(T_{luke}(\tau'_{m,e})) \tag{7}$$

where T_{luke} is the Transformer-based LUKE [27] and the function red(.) is the same as Sect. 3.1.

For a given mention, the score of each candidate entity is computed by applying a linear layer $\boldsymbol{W}'_{cross}$ to $\boldsymbol{y}'_{m,e}$:

$$s'_{cross}(m,e) = \sigma(\boldsymbol{y}'_{m,e} \boldsymbol{W}'_{cross}) \tag{8}$$

where σ represents the sigmoid function.

For training, We optimize the above cross-encoders with a binary cross-entropy loss. For inference, we use the output score, namely $s_{cross}(m,e)$ and $s'_{cross}(m,e)$, to rank candidates. Due to cross-encoders' large memory and compute footprint, they are not suitable for retrieval which requires fast inference, so they are only used in the reranking stage over a small set (usually ≤ 100) of candidates.

4 Experiments

4.1 Data

Speech EL Dataset. The dataset is based on *TED-LIUM 3* [10] with audio and transcripts. There are 2,351 Ted Talks in this corpus. Mention spans and corresponding entities of 1,936 talks are annotated. We split the 80% of 1,936 talks as the training set and the rest as the validation set. The statistics of the dataset is in Table 1.

KB. The above dataset is accompanied with a processed Wikidata dump, and we use it as our KB. The KB contains 118,805 entities. Each entity contains a QID, an entity name, entity aliases, and a series of relationship tuples (e.g. (*Barack Obama, Spouse, Michelle Obama*)). For entities with Wikipedia pages, we use the first paragraph as their descriptions.[2] For entities that do not have Wikipedia pages, we concatenate the relationship tuples in Wikidata as their descriptions. As there are some unlinkable mentions in the dataset, we add a *nil* entity whose description is an empty string.

Additional Training Data. We use hyperlinks in Wikipedia articles as additional training examples[3]. The anchor text is the mention, and the Wikipedia page that the hyperlink points to is the gold entity. We only keep the examples whose gold entities are in the above KB. The statistics of Wikipedia training data is in Table 1. Since the format of processed Wikipedia data does not show the source document url, the number of documents cannot be calculated.

Table 1. The statistics of Speech EL dataset and additional Wikipedia training data.

Dataset	Split	# In-KB mentions	# NIL mentions	# Entities	# Documents
Speech EL	Train	40,619	2,311	9,467	1,549
	Val	10,645	757	3,625	387
Wikipedia	Train	2,135,205	0	33,860	–
	Val	2,406	0	1,611	-

4.2   Candidate Retrieval

Since we retrieve 10 candidates for the next reranking stage[4], We report top-10 recall (R@10) on the validation set of Speech EL dataset.

Model Details. We initialize T_1 and T_2 in dual encoder with BLINK retrievers pretrained on Wikipedia hyperlinks[5], and optimize Eq. 4 with hard negative

---

[2] We use KILT's processed Wikipedia dump, available at http://dl.fbaipublicfiles. com/KILT/kilt_knowledgesource.json.

[3] The training set and validation set of Wikipedia hyperlinks can be found at https:// github.com/facebookresearch/KILT.

[4] For the number of candidates, according to Wu et al. [26], $K = 10$ is optimal, and increasing K to 100 gives minimal improvement but 10× run-time in reranking. Therefore we choose $K = 10$ finally.

[5] BLINK checkpoints can be downloaded at https://github.com/facebookresearch/ BLINK/blob/main/download_blink_models.sh.

mining on Speech EL dataset. The max length of context tokens and entity description tokens are both set at 128. We use Adam [16] with learning rate 2e−6 and a linear learning rate decay schedule with warmup proportion 0.06. The batch size is 2, the number of negatives for every mention is 31, and the number of training epochs is 4. We save checkpoints every epoch and choose the best checkpoint based on the performance of validation set. The training time per epoch is 2 h on 1 GPU (A100).

Baselines. We compare our dual encoder with alias table (AT) and BM25 retrieval algorithm, which are both widely-used approaches in EL systems [4,6,21]. We refer the methods with these abbreviations:

- **AT**: Based on the AT collected from Wikipedia hyperlinks[6], we further use aliases from KB and (mention, entity) pairs from Speech EL training set to extend AT. If a mention is not in AT, then its corresponding entity is *nil*.
- **BM25**: We use the *Gensim* implementation[7] of BM25 retrieval algorithm, where each entity is indexed with its name.
- **DE**: Our dual encoder, as described in Sect. 3.1.

Results. Table 2 shows Recall@10 of the above 3 baselines. Our dual encoder achieves a high recall (98.0%), much higher than BM25 and alias table. Our ablation study shows that mining hard negatives in NCE is helpful for the training of dual encoder.

Table 2. Recall@10 of retrieval methods on the validation set of Speech EL dataset.

Method	R@10
AT	91.3
BM25	50.4
DE	**98.0**
– Hard negatives in NCE	96.4

4.3 Candidate Reranking

For every mention in the validation set of Speech EL dataset, we rerank the retrieved 10 candidate entities. We report the accuracy of disambiguation results.

For **BERT-based cross-encoders**, We initialize T_{cross} with multiple BERT [8], RoBERTa [20] and ERNIE [30] checkpoints. The max length of input is 256. In **Wikipedia pretraining**, we randomly choose 3 negatives from KB for every training example. We use Adam [16] with learning rate 1e−5 and a linear learning rate decay schedule with warmup proportion 0.1. The batch size is 8 and we train

---

[6] We use alias table from GENRE [7] repository: https://dl.fbaipublicfiles.com/ GENRE/mention2wikidataID_with_titles_label_alias_redirect.pkl.
[7] https://radimrehurek.com/gensim_3.8.3/summarization/bm25.html.

Table 3. Accuracy of reranking cross-encoders on the validation set of Speech EL dataset. † means Wikipedia pretraining before fine-tuning.

Model	PLM	Accuracy
BERT-based	BERT-base	83.8
	ERNIE-base	83.7
	BERT-large	83.2
	ERNIE-large	84.9
	RoBERTa-large	85.0
	BERT-base†	84.2
	ERNIE-base†	85.1
	BERT-large†	84.6
	ERNIE-large†	84.6
	RoBERTa-large†	85.0
LUKE-based	**LUKE-large (ours)**	**85.2**

models on Wikipedia data for 200K steps. Our experiments are all performed on 1 GPU (A100). The total training time is 12 h for base models (i.e., BERT-base and ERNIE-base), 24 h for large models (i.e., BERT-large, ERNIE-large and RoBERTa-large). In **Speech EL dataset fine-tuning**, we randomly choose 3 negatives from 10 candidates retrieved by the dual encoder for every training example. We use Adam [16] with a steady learning rate 1e−5. The batch size is 16 and the number of training epochs is 10. The training time per epoch is 1 h for base models, 1.5 h for large models. We save checkpoints every 5000 steps and choose the best checkpoint on validation set.

For **LUKE-based cross-encoder**, we initialize T_{luke} with LUKE-large. We do not perform Wikipedia pretraining, as predicting masked entities, a pretraining task of LUKE, has used the Wikipedia corpus. In **Speech EL dataset fine-tuning**, we randomly choose 3 negatives from 10 candidates retrieved by the dual encoder for every training example. We use Adam [16] with a steady learning rate 1e−5. The batch size is 16 and the number of training epochs is 10. Training one epoch takes 1.5 h. We save checkpoints every 5000 steps and choose the best checkpoint on validation set.

Results. We compare our LUKE-based cross-encoder with various BERT-based cross-encoders. As shown in Table 3, the accuracy our model exceeds all BERT-based cross-encoders by a 0.2%–2% margin, still outperforming even when they have been trained on Wikipedia data. In addition, our disambiguation approach ranks the 1st in NLPCC 2022 Shared Task on Speech EL Track 2.

5   Conclusion

We propose a conceptually simple and highly effective two-stage approach to tackle the speech entity linking problem. For retrieval stage, we show that our efficient dual encoder achieves a high recall (98.0%), much higher than BM25 (50.4%) and alias table (91.3%). For reranking stage, we treat both words and entities as input tokens, and propose a LUKE-based cross-encoder, which outperforms previous BERT-based cross-encoders by a 0.2%–2% margin, without the need of large-scale training on Wikipedia corpus. Our disambiguation approach achieves the 1st place in NLPCC 2022 Speech Entity Linking Track 2 (Entity Disambiguation-Only). Future work includes:

- Enriching mention representations by adding NER type information;
- Enriching entity representations by adding entity type and knowledge graph structure information;
- Jointly disambiguating mentions in a document to model coherence.

Acknowledgements. We appreciate the insightful feedback from anonymous reviewers. This work is jointly supported by grants: National Science Foundation of China (No. 62006061), Strategic Emerging Industry Development Special Funds of Shenzhen (No. JCYJ20200109113441941), and Stable Support Program for Higher Education Institutions of Shenzhen (No. GXWD20201230155427003-20200824155011001).

References

1. Barba, E., Procopio, L., Navigli, R.: ExtEnD: extractive entity disambiguation. In: Proceedings of the 60th Annual Meeting of the Association for Computational Linguistics (Volume 1: Long Papers), Dublin, Ireland, pp. 2478–2488. Association for Computational Linguistics, May 2022

2. Beltagy, I., Peters, M.E., Cohan, A.: Longformer: the long-document transformer. arXiv:2004.05150 (2020)

3. Benton, A., Dredze, M.: Entity linking for spoken language. In: Proceedings of the 2015 Conference of the North American Chapter of the Association for Computational Linguistics: Human Language Technologies, Denver, Colorado, pp. 225–230. Association for Computational Linguistics, May–June 2015

4. Botha, J.A., Shan, Z., Gillick, D.: Entity linking in 100 languages. In: Proceedings of the 2020 Conference on Empirical Methods in Natural Language Processing (EMNLP), pp. 7833–7845. Association for Computational Linguistics, November 2020. https://aclanthology.org/2020.emnlp-main.630

5. De Cao, N., Aziz, W., Titov, I.: Question answering by reasoning across documents with graph convolutional networks. In: Proceedings of the 2019 Conference of the North American Chapter of the Association for Computational Linguistics: Human Language Technologies, Volume 1 (Long and Short Papers), Minneapolis, Minnesota, pp. 2306–2317. Association for Computational Linguistics, June 2019

6. De Cao, N., Aziz, W., Titov, I.: Highly parallel autoregressive entity linking with discriminative correction. In: Proceedings of the 2021 Conference on Empirical Methods in Natural Language Processing, Punta Cana, Dominican Republic, pp. 7662–7669. Association for Computational Linguistics, November 2021. https://aclanthology.org/2021.emnlp-main.604

7. De Cao, N., Izacard, G., Riedel, S., Petroni, F.: Autoregressive entity retrieval. In: International Conference on Learning Representations (2021). https://openreview.net/forum?id=5k8F6UU39V

8. Devlin, J., Chang, M.W., Lee, K., Toutanova, K.: BERT: pre-training of deep bidirectional transformers for language understanding. In: Proceedings of the 2019 Conference of the North American Chapter of the Association for Computational Linguistics: Human Language Technologies, Volume 1 (Long and Short Papers), Minneapolis, Minnesota, pp. 4171–4186. Association for Computational Linguistics, June 2019. https://aclanthology.org/N19-1423

9. Gillick, D., et al.: Learning dense representations for entity retrieval. In: Proceedings of the 23rd Conference on Computational Natural Language Learning (CoNLL), Hong Kong, China, pp. 528–537. Association for Computational Linguistics, November 2019. https://doi.org/10.18653/v1/K19-1049. https://aclanthology.org/K19-1049

10. Hernandez, F., Nguyen, V., Ghannay, S., Tomashenko, N., Estève, Y.: TED-LIUM 3: twice as much data and corpus repartition for experiments on speaker adaptation. In: Karpov, A., Jokisch, O., Potapova, R. (eds.) SPECOM 2018. LNCS (LNAI), vol. 11096, pp. 198–208. Springer, Cham (2018). https://doi.org/10.1007/978-3-319-99579-3_21

11. Humeau, S., Shuster, K., Lachaux, M.A., Weston, J.: Poly-encoders: architectures and pre-training strategies for fast and accurate multi-sentence scoring. In: ICLR (2020)

12. Ji, H., Grishman, R.: Knowledge base population: successful approaches and challenges. In: Proceedings of the 49th Annual Meeting of the Association for Computational Linguistics: Human Language Technologies, Portland, Oregon, USA, pp. 1148–1158. Association for Computational Linguistics, June 2011

13. Ji, H., Nothman, J., Hachey, B., et al.: Overview of tac-kbp2014 entity discovery and linking tasks. In: Proceedings of the Text Analysis Conference (TAC2014), pp. 1333–1339 (2014)

14. Johnson, J., Douze, M., Jégou, H.: Billion-scale similarity search with GPUs. IEEE Trans. Big Data **7**(3), 535–547 (2019)

15. Joko, H., Hasibi, F., Balog, K., de Vries, A.P.: Conversational entity linking: problem definition and datasets. In: Proceedings of the 44rd International ACM SIGIR Conference on Research and Development in Information Retrieval, SIGIR 2021. ACM (2021)

16. Kingma, D.P., Ba, J.: Adam: a method for stochastic optimization. In: Bengio, Y., LeCun, Y. (eds.) 3rd International Conference on Learning Representations, ICLR 2015, San Diego, CA, USA, May 7–9, 2015, Conference Track Proceedings (2015). http://arxiv.org/abs/1412.6980

17. Lewis, M., et al.: BART: denoising sequence-to-sequence pre-training for natural language generation, translation, and comprehension. In: Proceedings of the 58th Annual Meeting of the Association for Computational Linguistics, pp. 7871–7880. Association for Computational Linguistics, July 2020. https://aclanthology.org/2020.acl-main.703

18. Lin, Y., Shen, S., Liu, Z., Luan, H., Sun, M.: Neural relation extraction with selective attention over instances. In: Proceedings of the 54th Annual Meeting of the Association for Computational Linguistics (Volume 1: Long Papers), Berlin, Germany, pp. 2124–2133. Association for Computational Linguistics, August 2016

19. Liu, X., Li, Y., Wu, H., Zhou, M., Wei, F., Lu, Y.: Entity linking for tweets. In: Proceedings of the 51st Annual Meeting of the Association for Computational Linguistics (Volume 1: Long Papers), Sofia, Bulgaria, pp. 1304–1311. Association for Computational Linguistics, August 2013. https://aclanthology.org/P13-1128

20. Liu, Y., et al.: RoBERTa: a robustly optimized BERT pretraining approach (2019)

21. Logeswaran, L., Chang, M.W., Lee, K., Toutanova, K., Devlin, J., Lee, H.: Zero-shot entity linking by reading entity descriptions. In: Proceedings of the 57th Annual Meeting of the Association for Computational Linguistics, Florence, Italy, pp. 3449–3460. Association for Computational Linguistics, July 2019

22. Muralidharan, D., et al.: Noise robust named entity understanding for voice assistants. In: Proceedings of the 2021 Conference of the North American Chapter of the Association for Computational Linguistics: Human Language Technologies: Industry Papers, pp. 196–204. Association for Computational Linguistics, June 2021. https://aclanthology.org/2021.naacl-industry.25

23. Petroni, F., et al.: KILT: a benchmark for knowledge intensive language tasks. In: Proceedings of the 2021 Conference of the North American Chapter of the Association for Computational Linguistics: Human Language Technologies, pp. 2523–2544. Association for Computational Linguistics, June 2021

24. Sun, T., et al.: CoLAKE: contextualized language and knowledge embedding. In: Proceedings of the 28th International Conference on Computational Linguistics, Barcelona, Spain, pp. 3660–3670. International Committee on Computational Linguistics, December 2020. https://aclanthology.org/2020.coling-main.327

25. Vaswani, A., et al.: Attention is all you need. In: Guyon, I., et al. (eds.) Advances in Neural Information Processing Systems, vol. 30. Curran Associates, Inc. (2017)

26. Wu, L., Petroni, F., Josifoski, M., Riedel, S., Zettlemoyer, L.: Scalable zero-shot entity linking with dense entity retrieval. In: Proceedings of the 2020 Conference on Empirical Methods in Natural Language Processing (EMNLP), pp. 6397–6407. Association for Computational Linguistics, November 2020

27. Yamada, I., Asai, A., Shindo, H., Takeda, H., Matsumoto, Y.: LUKE: deep contextualized entity representations with entity-aware self-attention. In: Proceedings of the 2020 Conference on Empirical Methods in Natural Language Processing (EMNLP), pp. 6442–6454. Association for Computational Linguistics, November 2020. https://aclanthology.org/2020.emnlp-main.523

28. Yamada, I., Washio, K., Shindo, H., Matsumoto, Y.: Global entity disambiguation with BERT. In: NAACL. Association for Computational Linguistics (2022)

29. Zhang, W., Stratos, K.: Understanding hard negatives in noise contrastive estimation. In: Proceedings of the 2021 Conference of the North American Chapter of the Association for Computational Linguistics: Human Language Technologies, pp. 1090–1101. Association for Computational Linguistics, June 2021

30. Zhang, Z., Han, X., Liu, Z., Jiang, X., Sun, M., Liu, Q.: ERNIE: enhanced language representation with informative entities. In: Proceedings of the 57th Annual Meeting of the Association for Computational Linguistics, Florence, Italy, pp. 1441–1451. Association for Computational Linguistics, July 2019

A Fine-Grained Social Bias Measurement Framework for Open-Domain Dialogue Systems

Aimin Yang[1,2], Qifeng Bai[1], Jigang Wang[1], Nankai Lin[1(✉)], Xiaotian Lin[3(✉)], Guanqiu Qin[1], and Junheng He[1]

[1] School of Computer Science and Technology, Guangdong University of Technology, Guangzhou, Guangdong, China
neakail@outlook.com
[2] School of Computer Science and Intelligence Education, Lingnan Normal University, Zhanjiang, Guangdong, China
[3] School of Information Science and Technology, Guangdong University of Foreign Studies, Guangzhou, Guangdong, China
lxtxiaotianlin@163.com

Abstract. A pre-trained model based on a large-scale corpus can effectively improve the performance of open-domain dialogue systems in terms of performance. However, recent studies have shown various ethical issues in pre-trained models that seriously affect the application of dialogue systems. Social bias is particularly complex among these ethical issues because its negative impact on marginalized populations is often implicit and therefore requires normative reasoning and rigorous analysis. In this paper, we report the solution of the team BERT 4EVER for the NLPCC 2022 Shared Task 7 - Fine-Grain Dialogue Social Bias Measurement, which aims to measure the social bias in dialogue scenario. Specifically, we study fine-grained social bias measurement in open-domain dialogue systems. We construct a framework based on prompt learning and contrastive learning for fine-grained dialogue social bias measurement. We propose a two-stage prompt learning method to identify whether the text involves fairness topics, and then identify the bias of the text involving fairness topics. In order to enable the model to better learn the complete label (i.e. irrelevant, anti-bias, neutral, and biased) information in the first-stage prompt learning, we employ a contrastive learning module to further regularize the text representation of the same labeled samples to the uniform semantic space. On NLPCC 2022 task-7 final test, our proposed framework achieved second place with an F_{macro} of 59.02%.

Keywords: Two-stage prompt learning · Contrastive learning · Bias measurement

1 Introduction

In recent years, dialogue system has been widely used, such as customer assistant bots and social partner bots. Such dialogue systems interact directly with millions of end-users [1] and have received increasing attention in industry and academia [2]. Pre-trained

W. Lu et al. (Eds.) NLPCC 2022, LNCS 13552, pp. 240–251, 2022.
https://doi.org/10.1007/978-3-031-17189-5_20

language models were beneficial to improving the performance of open-domain dialogue systems [3]. However, many unsafe features were found in the pre-trained corpus, e.g., aggressive language, social prejudice, violence, etc. [2]. Unlike other explicitly expressed characteristics of insecurity, social bias usually uses implicit words to convey negative impressions or biases to specific groups of people. Since a dialogue system is directly interacting with the user, if it produces biased responses, it can have pernicious effects and can also hinder the deployment and development of dialogue systems based on large-scale generative language models. Therefore, it is crucial to address the issue of social bias in dialogue contexts. In Task-7 Fine-grain dialogue social bias measurement of NLPCC 2022, we propose a framework for identifying social bias present in dialogue contexts based on prompt learning and contrastive learning.

Pre-trained models usually have a large number of parameters, and pre-training-based deep learning studies [4] often adopt a "pre-train and fine-tune" paradigm, which may destroy the original representation space of pre-trained models [5]. Prompt learning is the process of considering large-scale pre-trained language models as a knowledge base from which information useful for downstream tasks can be obtained [6]. In this model, rather than adapting the pre-trained model to the downstream task, the parameters of the pre-trained model are frozen and the downstream task is redefined in the form of a "cloze test" prompted learning task. Prompt learning takes advantage of the powerful generalization capabilities of pre-trained language models and greatly reduces the reliance on supervised data for downstream tasks. Using the contrastive learning, not only can the correlation between filtered embeddings and biased words be minimized, but also the rich semantic information of the original sentences can be preserved. It can effectively reduce the degree of bias in pre-trained text encoders while continuously showing desirable performance on downstream tasks [7]. State-of-the-art performance can be achieved without hard negative mining, consistently outperforming cross-entropy on large-scale classification problems [8]. Based on contrastive learning combined with prompt learning in the embedding space, the same text representations are brought as close as possible to each other while pushing away different text representations [9].

In this paper, we are present the framework for fine-grained dialogue social bias measurement based on prompt learning and contrastive learning. The framework consists of three modules: the general representation module, two-stage prompt learning module, and contrastive learning module. First, we use the general representation module to represent the dialogue text, and then use the two-stage prompt learning module to identify whether the text involves fairness topics, and then identify the bias of the text involving fairness topics. In addition, we employ a contrastive learning module to further draw closer to the text representation of the same labeled samples. Based on the framework we constructed, we used five different hyperparameters to train different models fuse the five models' results. The experimental results demonstrate the effectiveness of our method.

Our contribution can be summarized as follows:

- To the best of our knowledge, we are the first to propose the application of prompt learning and contrastive learning to fine-grained dialogue social bias measures.
- We propose a two-stage prompt learning approach to addresses the problem of template construction in this task.

- Based on contrastive learning and prompt learning, we constructed a fine-grained dialogue social bias measurement framework.
- The proposed framework was awarded second place on the 2022 NLPCC Task-7, with an F_{macro} of 59.02%.

2 Related Work

2.1 Fine Grained Dialogue Social Bias Measurement

With the growing research interest in AI fairness and ethics [10], the issue of socially biased safety in NLP has been extensively studied. Social bias measurement tasks analyze emerging trends in bias in an in-depth manner due to the subtle and implicit nature of bias [11]. Currently, most studies have focused on context-independent tasks such as token or sentence level. However, Sun et al. [12] pointed out that the study of context-sensitive security is crucial for session subjects, but it is still an area to be explored. Zhou et al. [2] analyzed response bias-related issues through four sequential aspects: context-sensitivity, data type (expression/discussion bias), target group, and implicated attitudes. By breaking down the subtle subjective tasks into the objective tasks described above, they aim to analyze in detail the various biases present in the dialogue.

The problem of dialogue social bias is subtle and complex, and still remains to be studied and challenged, such as the problem of social bias safety based on pre-trained model conversational systems [2], which is gradually gaining attention. Recent studies in large-scale language models [13, 14] have shown that increases in model size can improve the performance of dialogue models and are more likely to produce toxic responses when given toxic prompts for larger models. Increasing the model size allows for a greater accurate classification of toxicity [14], but is not substantially related to the level of safety of bias [2].

2.2 Application of Contrastive Learning in NLP Tasks

Contrastive learning is a broad class of training strategies that learn meaningful representations by reconciling the embedding distances of positive and negative samples. Generally, contrastive learning requires a pairwise embedding critic as a similarity/distance of data pairs. The learning objective is then constructed by maximizing the embedding distance of positive and negative data pairs [7]. Contrastive learning has shown encouraging performance in many NLP tasks, and contrastive learning can significantly narrow the performance gap between supervised learning and unsupervised learning [9, 15, 16]. Luo et al. [17] adapted contrastive learning to the field of natural language processing to learn noise-invariant sequence representations and demonstrated its effectiveness in improving large-scale pre-trained models. Cheng et al. [7] introduced a contrastive learning framework that not only minimizes the correlation between filtered embeddings and biased words, but also preserves the rich semantic information of the original sentences. Wu et al. [18] evaluated the quality of abstracts without reference abstracts by unsupervised contrastive learning based on the Bert pre-trained model, and the evaluation method achieved better results in the absence of reference abstracts.

2.3   Application of Prompt Learning in NLP Tasks

The pre-trained LM is proved to have common sense knowledge and can be prompted to do cloze questions, as well as a variety of downstream natural language comprehension and generation tasks [19]. Prompt learning provides a low parameter alternative for fine-tuning large-scale language models (LLMS) [20]. Providing prompt or task descriptions plays a crucial role in improving the pre-trained language model in many tasks [21]. Among them, the GPT model [21] and Bert pre-trained model [22] have been very successful in prompting or task presentation in NLP tasks[23]. In the prompt, LLMS are usually frozen, and their pre-trained tasks are used to fill in the required information [20]. Li et al. [24] combined prompt and fine-tuning, and proposed prefix tuning, which can keep language model parameters frozen and optimize small continuous task-specific vectors for generating tasks [19]. Lester et al. [25] introduced prompt tuning, which is a simplification of prefix tuning, and showed that prompt tuning becomes more competitive in small-scale tasks. Despite the extensive research on language model prompting methods, few studies have focused on generating contextually relevant knowledge directly from language models. Liu et al. [19] proposed a multi-stage prompting framework to exploit the knowledge inherent in the language model, which consists of a first-stage prompt for knowledge generation and a second-stage prompt for response generation.

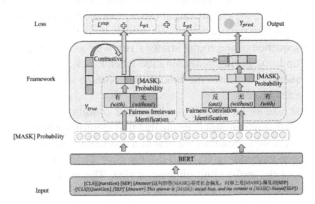

Fig. 1. Overview of our framework. [MASK]₁ determines whether the response is biased and [MASK]₂ determines the category of bias.

3   Fine-Grain Dialogue Social Bias Measurement Framework

Based on prompt learning and contrastive learning, we propose a framework for fine-grained dialogue social bias measurement. As shown in Fig. 1, it consists of two stages of prompt learning. The first stage is responsible for identifying whether fairness topics are involved, and the second stage is responsible for identifying the bias of the text involving fairness topics. The output of the second stage is considered when the first stage is identified as involving fairness in the dialogue. Contrastive learning is used to draw closer to the probabilistic representations between samples with the same labels in the first stage.

3.1 General Representation Module

The general representation module uses BERT [26] to extract semantic representations of the dialogue. The first token of each sequence is a special classification token [CLS]. The final hidden state corresponding to this token is used as the aggregated sequence representation for the classification task. A special token [SEP] is used between sentences of the dialogue and at the end of the entire sequence. For a given token, its input representation is constructed by summing over the corresponding token, segmentation and position embeddings [22]. The final hidden state is usually used as the semantic representation vector of the sentence. Thus, the representation of the dialogue is calculated as follows [27]:

$$C_i = BERT(x_i, y_i, z_i) \tag{1}$$

where C_i is the sentence representation, x_i, y_i, z_i are the token, segmentation and position embedding.

3.2 Two-Stage Prompt Learning Module

We propose a two-stage prompt learning method that converts the classification task to text generation [28], i.e., the classification task is modeled as a conditional generation model $P_\theta(Y|W)$. θ is the parameters of our model, W is the input sequence and Y is the label of the sequence. The prompt strategy is a way to add prompt information to the model as a condition during generating the label Y [25]. Adding a series of tokens P before the sequence W allows the model to maximize the likelihood of correct Y probability of being correct.

Since this task cannot be directly modeled in a conditional generative model, this paper proposes a two-stage prompt learning that first identifies whether a text is involved in a fairness topic and then identifies the bias of a text that is involved in a fairness topic. Given the sequence embedding $C_w = \{C_1, C_2, \ldots, C_n\}$, where $C_w \in \mathbb{R}^{n \times e}$ and e is the dimension of the embedding dimension size. The parameters of the two-stage prompt learning module are represented as $C_p \in \mathbb{R}^{p \times e}$, where p is the length of the prompt template, and the two parameters are spliced to get the new text representation $C_{new} = [C_w; C_p] \in \mathbb{R}^{(p+n) \times e}$. During training, the parameters C_p and C_w are updated simultaneously. The first stage of conditioned generation is $P_\theta(Y_1|W)$ and the first stage probability of a given sample is denoted as Q_1, $Y_1 = \{0, 1\}$, in which $Y_1=0$ means the dialogue does not address the topic of fairness while $Y_1=1$ means that the dialogue deals with the topic of fairness. The second stage of condition generation is $P_\theta(Y_2|W)$ and second stage probability of a given sample is denoted as Q_2, $Y_2 = \{0, 1, 2\}$, in which $Y_2=0$ means the dialogue is anti-bias, $Y_2=1$ means the fairness position of the dialogue is neutral, and $Y_2=2$ means the dialogue is biased. So we can reconstruct the input text as: "[CLS] {Question} [SEP] {Answer} 这句回答[MASK] 存在社会偏见，内容上是[MASK] 偏见的[SEP] ([CLS]{Question}[SEP] {Answer} This answer is [MASK] social bias, and the content is [MASK] biased[SEP])", and ask PLMs to fill the first blank as "有(with)" or "无(without)" and the second blank as "反(anti)", "无(without)" and "有(with)". The losses of the first-stage prompt learning and the second-stage prompt learning are respectively:

$$L_{p1} = -\frac{1}{N}\sum_i P_1(Y_1)logQ_1 \tag{2}$$

$$L_{p2} = -\frac{1}{N}\sum_i P_2(Y_2)logQ_2 \tag{3}$$

The final prompt learning module loss is obtained by weighting the prompt learning loss of the two stages:

$$L_p = \alpha * L_{p1} + (1 - \alpha) * L_{p2} \tag{4}$$

where α is an adjustable parameter, and $\alpha \in \{0, 1\}$.

3.3 Contrastive Learning Module

In the first phase of prompt learning, the model is prone to ignore the effect of the three labels in the second phase on the first phase of the prompting task. Therefore, in order to enable the model to better learn the complete label (i.e. irrelevant, anti-bias, neutral, and biased) information in the first-stage prompt learning, we use supervised contrastive learning to draw closer to the probabilistic representations Q_1 between samples with the same labels. Encoders are encouraged to provide tightly aligned probabilistic representations for all samples from the same class, thus backward leads to more robust clustering of the representation space than clustering generated from the equation [8]. The addition of contrastive learning after the two-stage prompt learning is used to bring the first-stage probability representations between positive samples under the complete labeling system in the first stage as close as possible while distancing the negative samples from the positive samples. In this paper, all sentences in a batch are represented as $\{x_i, y_i\}_{i \in I}$ where $I = \{1, \cdots, K\}$ is the index of the sentence, K is the number of samples included in the batch, $y_i \in \{0, 1, 2, 3\}$. The first stage probability of i-th sample is denoted as Q_1, and the set of samples of a sentence x_i with its same label within the batch is defined as $S = \{s : s \in I, y_p = y_i \wedge p \neq i\}$, the size of $|S|$, the contrastive loss function of the batch is:

$$L_{P_i} = \frac{1}{|S|}\sum_{s \in S} log \frac{exp(sim(Q_1(C_i), Q_1(C_s))/\tau)}{\sum_{k \in I/i} exp(sim(Q_1(C_i), Q_1(C_k))/\tau)} \tag{5}$$

$$L^{sup} = -\sum_{i=1}^{N} L_{P_i} \tag{6}$$

$$L = \beta * L^{sup} + (1 - \beta) * L_p \tag{7}$$

where τ is a parameter for optimization the contrastive learning module. The subscript is i corresponding to the anchor sample, the subscript is s corresponding to the positive sample. L is the loss of the whole framework, L^{sup} is the contrastive learning loss, and L_p is the prompt learning loss. β is the adjustable parameter, and $\beta \in \{0, 1\}$.

4 Experiment

This experiment uses our proposed two-stage prompt learning and contrastive learning framework for identifying social bias in dialogue systems on the CDIAL-BIAS dataset. The effectiveness of our proposed two-stage prompt learning and contrastive learning framework was verified by conducting a series of experiments on the CDIAL-BIAS dataset.

4.1 Dataset

The CDIAL-BIAS [2] dataset was crawled from the Chinese Q&A website Zhihu and constructed with conversation data related to social bias. Each data entry is a two-round conversation consisting of a pair of questions and answers. As shown in Table 1., this is a Chinese conversation bias dataset, containing 28k conversational data. The CDIAL-BIAS dataset contains four subsets namely: race, gender, geography, and occupation. Each sample is labeled with one of the labels among irrelevant, anti-bias, neutral, and biased.

Table 1. CDIAL-BIAS dataset.

Class	Anti-Bias	Neural	Biased	Irrelevant	Total	Percentage
Race	275	4178	2521	3932	10930	38.4
Gender	191	3219	1737	3262	8418	29.6
Region	278	1643	1246	1865	5037	17.7
Occupation	120	1563	907	1472	6373	22.3
Total	864	10601	6411	10531	28407	100
Percentage	3.1	37.3	22.5	37.1	100	-

4.2 Experimental Setup

In the experiments, the model is trained using the training set, and the model that performs best on the validation set is used to predict the classification results on the test set. We conduct our experiments by Pytorch[1] and Transformers[2]. The batch size is set to 32, the maximum length is 75, and the learning rate is 5e-6. The loss weight α in two-stage prompt learning module is 0.5, the contrastive learning β is 1e-5, and the temperature τ is 0.9. We trained the models with 10 epochs.

---

[1] https://github.com/pytorch/pytorch.
[2] https://github.com/huggingface/transformers.

4.3 Results and Analysis

Comparison results of different pre-trained models. As shown in Table 2., we report the F_{macro} scores of the different pre-trained models on the validation set. We can see that in several pre-trained models, the performance of the macBERT model is much higher than other models, and the macBERT model of large size also achieves a higher F_{macro} than the macBERT model of base size. Thus, the macBERT(Large) model with the highest F_{macro} score on the test set was selected for subsequent experiments.

Table 2. Result of different pretrained models.

Pre-trained Model	Validation F_{macro}
RoBERTa[3]	0.6187
BERT[4]	0.5996
macBERT(Base)[5]	0.6316
macBERT(Large)[6]	**0.6409**
PERT[7]	0.6069

Comparison of different methods. In Table 3., we report the different models' F_{macro} scores on the validation set and test set. We validate various combinations of BERT, LSTM[29], Fast Gradient Method (FGM)[30], contrastive learning and prompt learning, and the comparison results are shown in Table 3.. Our first submission is the result of the highest F_{macro} score on the validation set, which is the BERT + LSTM models based on FGM, whose score on the test set is 0.5652. Since this method has the highest F_{macro} score on the validation set, but the accuracy drops by 0.0895 on the test set, we suspect that the "pre-train and fine-tune" paradigm may produce more severe over-fitting. To verify our conjecture, in the second submission, we chose the proposed social bias measurement framework. This method has a score difference of only 0.061 on the validation and test sets, which is a better generalization than the fine-tuning-based method. Finally, we used the hard-label fusion strategy to obtain five models by modifying the parameters α. The F_{macro} score for model fusion on the test set is 0.5902, which is a 0.0022 improvement in results on the test set compared to the single model. The experimental results illustrate that the use of the model fusion strategy can further improve the F_{macro} score of the model on the test set.

---

[3] https://huggingface.co/hfl/chinese-roberta-wwm-ext.

[4] https://huggingface.co/ bert-base-chinese.

[5] https://huggingface.co/hfl/chinese-macbert-base.

[6] https://huggingface.co/hfl/chinese-macbert-large.

[7] https://huggingface.co/ hfl/chinese-pert-base.

Table 3. Comparison results of various methods.

Model	Validation F_{macro}	Test F_{macro}
macBERT(Large)	0.6409	-
macBERT(Large) + LSTM	0.6417	-
macBERT(Large) + FGM	0.6446	-
macBERT(Large) + LSTM + FGM	**0.6547**	0.5652
macBERT(Large) + Two-stage Prompt Learning	0.6383	-
Our method	0.6490	**0.588**
Our method(ens. 5)	-	**0.5902**

Parametric Investigation Experiments. To further investigate the effect of different parameters on the experimental results, we conducted a series of experiments on learning rate, prompt learning hyper-parameter α, and contrastive learning hyper-parameter β.

Learning Rate Exploration. Based on our framework, we carried out learning rate hyperparameter exploration experiments, and the experimental results are shown in Fig. 2. We empirically searched for hyper-parameters in the range $\{lr|1^{-6} < lr < 5^{-5}\}$. When the learning rate is setting as 5^{-6}, the model performs the best with an F_{macro} score of 0.649 on the validation set.

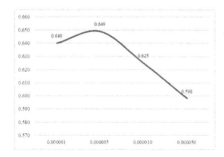

Fig. 2. Effect of learning rate on F macro scores on the validation set.

Fig. 3. Effect of hyper-parameter α on the F macro score on the validation set.

Parameter α Exploration. We searched for hyper-parameter α in the range $\{\alpha|0.3 < \alpha < 0.7\}$. The experimental results are shown in Fig. 3. It can be seen that when α is set to 0.5, the model achieves the best performance, that is, when the model considers the first-stage prompt learning and the second-stage prompt learning with equal weight, the model can better balance the two stages of learning.

Parameter β Parameter Exploration. We searched for hyper-parameters in the range $\{\beta|0.000005 < \beta < 0.005\}$ and experimental results are shown in Fig. 4. The results show that the model performs best when β is set to 1^{-5}. This shows that when our contrastive loss affects the model with a smaller weight, it can bring a certain improvement to the model.

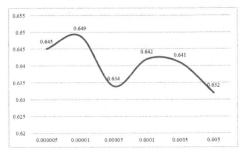

Fig. 4. Effect of hyper-parameter β on the F_{macro} score on the validation set.

5   Conclusion

Dialogue systems are often used to interact directly with many end-users, so the ethical of dialogue systems needs to be taken seriously by developers. Among the many insecurities, social bias is particularly complex and vital. In this paper, we investigate the task of identifying social biases in dialogue systems using a two-stage prompt learning and contrastive learning. To the best of our knowledge, this is the first research to apply prompt learning and contrastive learning to fine-grained dialogue social bias measurement. Finally, our proposed framework received second place in the NLPCC 2022 task 7, with an F_{macro} score of 59.02%. In the future, we will further explore the feasibility of prompt learning and contrastive learning in fine-grained dialogue social bias measurement task.

Acknowledgement. This work was supported by the Ministry of education of Humanities and Social Science project (No. 19YJAZH128 and No. 20YJAZH118) and the Science and Technology Plan Project of Guangzhou (No. 202102080305). The authors would like to thank the anonymous reviewers for their valuable comments and suggestions.

References

1. Sheng, E., Arnold, J., Yu, Z., Chang, K. W., Peng, N.: Revealing persona biases in dialogue systems. CORR, (2021)
2. Zhou, J., Deng, J., Mi, F., et al.: Towards identifying social bias in dialog systems: Frame, datasets, and benchmarks. CORR, (2022)
3. Ma, L., Li, M., Zhang, W.N., Li, J., Liu, T.: Unstructured Text Enhanced Open-Domain Dialogue System: A Systematic Survey. ACM Transactions on Information Systems (TOIS) **40**(1), 1–44 (2021)
4. He, K., Zhang, X., Ren, S., and Sun, J.: Deep residual learning for image recognition, In: Proceedings of the IEEE conference on computer vision and pattern recognition, pp. 770–778. (2016)
5. Zhou, K., Yang, J., Loy, C. C., Liu, Z.: Conditional prompt learning for vision-language models, In: Proceedings of the IEEE/CVF Conference on Computer Vision and Pattern Recognition, pp. 16816–16825. (2022)

6. Petroni, F., Rocktäschel, T., Lewis, P., Bakhtin, A., Wu, Y., Miller, A. H., Riedel, S.: Language models as knowledge bases?. CORR, (2019)

7. Cheng, P., Hao, W., Yuan, S., Si, S., Carin, L.: FairFil: Contrastive Neural Debiasing Method for Pretrained Text Encoders. CORR, (2021)

8. Supervised contrastive learning: Khosla, P., Teterwak, P., Wang, et al. Adv. Neural. Inf. Process. Syst. **33**, 18661–18673 (2020)

9. Chen, T., Kornblith, S., Norouzi, M., Hinton, G.: A simple framework for contrastive learning of visual representations, In: International conference on machine learning, pp. 1597–1607. (2020)

10. Bommasani, R., Hudson, D. A., Adeli, E., et al.: On the opportunities and risks of foundation models. CORR, (2021)

11. Borkan, D., Dixon, L., Sorensen, J., Thain, N., Vasserman, L.: Nuanced metrics for measuring unintended bias with real data for text classification, In: Companion proceedings of the 2019 world wide web conference, pp. 491–500. (2019)

12. Sun, H., Xu, G., Deng, J., et al.: On the Safety of Conversational Models: Taxonomy, Dataset, and Benchmark. CORR, (2021)

13. Rae, J. W., Borgeaud, S., Cai, T., et al.: Scaling language models: Methods, analysis & insights from training gopher. CORR, (2021)

14. Thoppilan, R., De Freitas, D., Hall, J., Shazeer, N., Kulshreshtha, A., Cheng, H. T., . Le, Q.: LaMDA: Language Models for Dialog Applications. CORR, (2022)

15. He, K., Fan, H., Wu, Y., Xie, S., Girshick, R.: Momentum contrast for unsupervised visual representation learning, In: Proceedings of the IEEE/CVF conference on computer vision and pattern recognition, pp. 9729–9738. (2020)

16. Qian, R., Meng, T., Gong, B., Yang, M. H., Wang, H., Belongie, S., Cui, Y.: Spatiotemporal contrastive video representation learning, In: Proceedings of the IEEE/CVF Conference on Computer Vision and Pattern Recognition, pp. 6964–6974. (2021)

17. Luo, F., Yang, P., Li, S., Ren, X., Sun, X.: CAPT: contrastive pre-training for learning denoised sequence representations. CORR, (2020)

18. Wu, H., Ma, T., Wu, L., Manyumwa, T., Ji, S.: Unsupervised reference-free summary quality evaluation via contrastive learning. CORR, (2020)

19. Liu, Z., Patwary, M., Prenger, R., Prabhumoye, S., Ping, W., Shoeybi, M., Catanzaro, B.: Multi-stage prompting for knowledgeable dialogue generation. CORR, (2022)

20. Newman, B., Choubey, P. K., and Rajani, N.: P-Adapters: Robustly Extracting Factual Information from Language Models with Diverse Prompts. CORR, (2021)

21. Brown, T., Mann, B., Ryder, N., et al.: Language models are few-shot learners. Adv. Neural. Inf. Process. Syst. **33**, 1877–1901 (2020)

22. Devlin, J., Chang, M. W., Lee, K., & Toutanova, K.: Bert: Pre-training of deep bidirectional transformers for language understanding. CORR (2018)

23. Jin, W., Cheng, Y., Shen, Y., Chen, W., and Ren, X.: A Good Prompt Is Worth Millions of Parameters? Low-resource Prompt-based Learning for Vision-Language Models. CORR,(2021)

24. Li, X. L., and Liang, P.: Prefix-tuning: Optimizing continuous prompts for generation. CORR (2021)

25. Lester B, Al-Rfou R, Constant N.: The power of scale for parameter-efficient prompt tuning. CORR, (2021)

26. Cui, Y., Che, W., Liu, T., Qin, B., Wang, S., and Hu, G.: Revisiting pre-trained models for Chinese natural language processing. CORR, (2020)

27. Liu, Y., Ott, M., Goyal, N., et al.: Roberta: A robustly optimized bert pretraining approach. CORR, (2019)

28. Raffel, C., Shazeer, N., Roberts, A., et al.: Exploring the limits of transfer learning with a unified text-to-text transformer. CORR, (2019)

29. Hochreiter, S., Schmidhuber, J.: Long short-term memory. Neural Comput. **9**(8), 1735–1780 (1997)
30. Goodfellow, I. J., Shlens, J., Szegedy, C. Explaining and harnessing adversarial examples. CORR, (2014)

Dialogue Topic Extraction as Sentence Sequence Labeling

Dinghao Pan, Zhihao Yang$^{(\boxtimes)}$, Haixin Tan, Jiangming Wu, and Hongfei Lin

School of Computer Science and Technology, Dalian University of Technology,
Dalian 116024, Liaoning, China
{dinghaopan,hxtan,wjm374733751}@mail.dlut.edu.cn,
{yangzh,hflin}@dlut.edu.cn

Abstract. The topic information of the dialogue text is important for the model to understand the intentions of the dialogue participants and to abstractly summarize the content of the dialogue. The dialogue topic extraction task aims to extract the evolving topic information in long dialogue texts. In this work, we focus on topic extraction of dialogue texts in customer service scenarios. Based on the rich sequence features in the topic tags, we define this task as a sequence labeling task with sentences as the basic elements. For this task, we build a dialogue topic extraction system using a Chinese pre-trained language model and a CRF model. In addition, we use sliding windows to avoid excessive loss of contextual information, and use adversarial training and model integration to improve the performance and robustness of our model. Our system ranks first on the track 1 of the NLPCC-2022 shared task on Dialogue Text Analysis, Topic Extraction and Dialogue Summary.

Keywords: Customer service dialogue · Topic extraction · Sentence sequence labeling

1 Introduction

With the development of speech and dialogue technologies, a large amount of speech dialogue data containing valuable information and knowledge is generated [1]. In a customer service scenario, participants in a conversation usually have strong and clear motivations, and the conversation aims to address matters related to a specific topic [2]. As the conversation progresses, the topic and motivation of the conversation evolves, and this changing information plays an important role in the analysis of the structure and content of the conversation text and the construction of intelligent customer service systems [3].

In this work, we focus on solving the problem of topic extraction from dialogue texts. Unlike traditional texts, dialogue texts usually contain more noise due to their spoken nature, and some salient information is often diluted by real-life scenarios [4]. Dialogue topic extraction aims to obtain the evolving topics in long conversation texts and to extract the sentence indexes and categories of the

W. Lu et al. (Eds.) NLPCC 2022, LNCS 13552, pp. 252–262, 2022.
https://doi.org/10.1007/978-3-031-17189-5_21

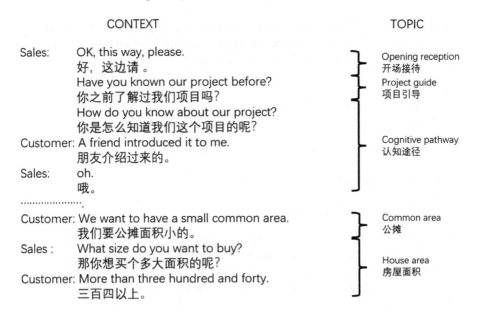

Fig. 1. A customer service dialogue and its corresponding topic. The final result needs to contain the starting sentence index, the ending sentence index, and the topic categories in the given set.

topic. Figure 1 illustrates a portion of a real estate customer service conversation captured by speech technology and its topic labels.

In order to understand the intentions of customers and service in customer service scenarios more efficiently, we conducted a study based on the real estate dialogue text dataset in NLPCC2022 shared task. In this work, we propose a sequence labeling method with sentences as the basic elements, and build a topic extraction model for customer service dialogue.

In the preprocessing phase, we splice the contextual text according to a given length limit for the large number of sentences per conversation in the dataset and the needs of the model input. Sliding windows are used to process our input text, and explicit identity features are spliced at the beginning of the text. Then we use a Chinese pre-trained language model to obtain word vectors that incorporate contextual information. Inspired by the method of obtaining entity representations in the relational extraction task [5], we use a specific matrix to achieve an average pooling effect to re-extract the independent representations of individual sentences from the spliced context. Finally, we use a fully connected layer and a CRF model with the Viterbi algorithm to obtain the final sequence of topic labels. In addition, we adopt adversarial training [6], k-fold cross-validation [7], and pre-trained language model integration [8] to improve the performance, generalization ability, and robustness of the model. In summary, our contributions are as follows:

- We define the dialogue topic extraction task as a sequence labeling task with a complete sentence as the basic element, and build our system based on the pre-trained language model and the CRF model.
- We effectively improve the performance and robustness of the model by sliding window processing of input text, fusion of identity information, adversarial training, and multi-stage model integration.
- The final evaluation results show that our proposed model achieve the first place in the contest, which proves the effectiveness of our method.

2   Related Work

2.1   Dialogue Topic Information

Different from well-structured news stories and encyclopedias, conversations usually come from two or more participants and are more valuable for mining immediate information. However, features such as the colloquial nature of the dialogue make it more difficult for the model to understand complex contexts and perform topic extraction.

In long conversational texts, the topics that participants talk about usually evolve as the conversation progresses, and the key information of a topic is often scattered among multiple sentences of different speakers, which makes it extremely difficult to summarize the conversational text in an abstract way. Many studies have addressed this problem by combining topic information from dialogue texts with downstream tasks. Liu et al. [9] proposed two topic-aware comparison learning goals for implicitly modeling the evolution of dialogue topics. Xu et al. [10] segmented and extracted topics in an unsupervised manner and applied them as a topic-aware solution in a retrieval-based multi-round dialogue model. Zou et al. [11] proposed a salience-aware topic model and applied it to conversation summary generation for customer service systems. Inspired by the above research, the NLPCC2022 evaluation competition proposes a new dialogue topic extraction task, which aims to obtain topics in real estate customer service dialogues. Based on the dataset given in this task, we conducted a study on topic extraction for dialogue texts.

2.2   Sequence Labeling

Sequence labeling is a common approach in natural language processing and has been applied to many downstream tasks, such as tokenization [12], part-of-speech tagging [13], named entity recognition [14], slot filling [15].

The sequence labeling problem can be considered as a generalization of the classification problem or as a simple form of the more complex structure prediction problem. Given a one-dimensional linear input sequence, the task requires that each element of a linear sequence be labeled with one of the labels in the given set, which is essentially a problem of classifying each element of the linear sequence according to its context. Originally, the common solutions to the sequence labeling problem were based on the HMM model [16], maximum entropy model [17], or the CRF model [18]. Especially, CRF is the mainstream method to solve the sequence labeling problem. With the development of deep learning, the Bi-LSTM+CRF model [19] appeared and performed well in this task. After the rise of pre-trained language models, the encoder part was upgraded from Bi-LSTM to BERT [20], and the accuracy of sequence labeling improved to a new level.

In Chinese sequence labeling, a Chinese character is often treated as a basic element in a sequence. Although the meaning represented by the set of tags may not be the same for different tasks, the same problem remains: how to give a proper tag to a Chinese character according to its context. However, dialogue topic extraction requires the model to be able to extract the starting and ending sentence indexes of the topic as well as the topic categories, which is not quite the same as the goal of the traditional word-level task of sequence labeling. To address this problem, we replace the basic elements of traditional Chinese sequence labeling, words, with complete Chinese sentences, effectively converting the dialogue topic extraction task into a sequence labeling task and integrating it into an end-to-end model in the form of a hierarchical model.

3   Methodology

Our method is divided into two stages: (1) single topic extraction model, we design the text preprocessing based on the characteristics of long dialogue text and convert the topic tags into BI tags to enrich the sequence information in the tags. Besides, we propose a two-stage approach for incorporating status information to help the model focus on the role information of the dialogue during the encoding and sequence labeling stages. After gradient back-propagation, the adversarial training FGM method is used to improve the performance and robustness of the model. (2) k-fold cross-validation ensemble and multiple pre-trained language models ensemble, we divide the training set into ten folds, selected one fold as the validation set in turn, and the remaining nine folds as the training set to train the model. Then we use different Chinese pre-trained language models and perform the integration of multiple language models based on the cross-validation integration results.

3.1   Task Definition

Given a long text of a customer service dialogue, our goal is to extract from it the implied topic categories as well as the starting and ending sentence indices of the topics. Due to the sequence properties contained in the required results, we define the task as a sequence labeling task with complete sentences as the basic elements. In order to give more sequence properties and information to the labels, we expand the original number of topic labels to twice the number of BI labels, where "Begin-topic" denotes the label of the beginning sentence of the topic, and "I-topic" denotes the tag of the remaining sentences in the topic.

3.2   Topic Extraction Model

In this work, we define the dialogue text topic extraction task as a sequence labeling task with sentences as the basic element, and design the model based on the characteristics of long dialogue texts. The structure of the model is shown in Fig. 2.

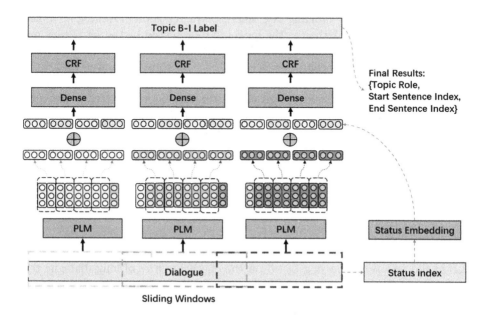

Fig. 2. The overall architecture of the single model

With the increase of input text length, the computational complexity of self attention mechanism increases exponentially, therefore, during the encoding phase, we need to control the length of the input context. However, in dialogue texts, the contexts are deeply interconnected. To avoid excessive loss of semantic information, we designed the sliding window to process our input text. For a given sequence of dialog texts $\{x_1, x_2, ..., x_n\}$, we divide the dialog texts according to the set length limit, and ensure the sentence integrity during the division. Multiple sentences of length no longer than the sliding window are spliced before and after the divided text. We input the preprocessed texts $\{x_1, x_2, ..., x_m\}$, into the pre-trained language model and obtain the word vector representation $V \in \mathbb{R}^{m \times h}$ of the corresponding text, the length of the text is m and the dimension of each word vector is h.

$$V = PLM(x_1, x_2, ..., x_m) \qquad (1)$$

The maximum number of sentences contained in all input texts is k. We used a matrix $M \in \mathbb{R}^{k \times m}$ to locate and serve as an average pooling of different sentences in V. Sentence vectors containing contextual semantics were extracted from the representation of word vectors.

$$S = M \times V \tag{2}$$

How to utilize identity features in an end-to-end conversation understanding model is an important issue. We designed a two-stage approach for identity information incorporation: (1) adding explicit identity features before each sentence; (2) an status index is created based on the identity corresponding to each sentence, and a status vector is generated using the Embeddings layer and summed with the sentence vector. The identity information is incorporated into the sentence vector in the sequence labeling stage.

We use a fully-connected layer to calculate the probability $\hat{y}_s$ of all tags for each sentence$s$:

$$\hat{y}_s = Ws + b \tag{3}$$

where $s \in \mathbb{R}^h$, $W \in \mathbb{R}^{c \times h}$, $b \in \mathbb{R}^c$. We use the CRF model with label probability to train the label transfer matrix as well as to obtain the training loss L_{CRF}, which models the sequence dependencies in the labels and improves the sequence labeling performance of the model.

To enhance the performance and robustness of the single model, we use an adversarial training approach after loss back propagation. As shown in Eq. (4), based on the gradient g at the embedding layer we add an adversarial perturbation r_{adv} to the word vector to generate adversarial samples. The newly generated adversarial samples are fed into the model to generate the adversarial loss L_{adv}, and the losses are back-propagated to obtain the gradients generated by the adversarial sample losses at each layer of the model. Since the gradients generated by the original sample losses have not yet been used by the optimizer for parameter updating, the gradients of the original samples are accumulated with those of the adversarial samples. We use this accumulated gradient to update the parameters of the model, which effectively improves the performance and robustness of the model.

$$\begin{aligned} r_{adv} &= \epsilon g / ||g||_2 \\ x_{adv} &= x + r_{adv} \\ L_{adv} &= Model(X_{adv}) \end{aligned} \tag{4}$$

3.3   Ensemble Model

In this work, we used different Chinese pre-trained language models to encode the dialogue text. The BERT [21] is the first pre-trained language models using a large-scale corpus, which has led to significant performance improvements in many downstream tasks of natural language processing. Many improved Chinese pre-trained language models from BERT have emerged in recent years, such as the Chinese versions of RoBERTa-wwm [22], MacBERT [23], and PERT [24].

RoBERTa-wwm. RoBERTa [25] is an improved version of BERT that elimi-
nates the pre-training task of next sentence prediction and employs pre-training
strategies such as dynamic masks. RoBERTa-wwm is a Chinese pre-trained language model based on RoBERTa using whole word masking strategy.

MacBERT. MacBERT improve the Chinese pre-training language model technique based on RoBERTa, and adopts a synonym masking strategy to reduce the
gap between the pre-training and fine-tuning phases, which effectively improves
the performance of the Chinese pre-training language model.

PERT. Changes to the pre-training task have been an effective means to
improve the performance of pre-trained models. PERT replaces the MLM (Mask
Language Model) with a word order prediction task in the pre-training phase.
Researchers randomly break the word order of the text and let the language
model predict the original position of the disrupted words by itself.

We improve the performance and robustness of our model by exploiting the
variability of the training set in k-fold cross-validation and the parameter variability of different Chinese pre-trained language models. First, we initialize the
encoder parameters with three Chinese pre-trained language models, and then
perform ten-fold cross-validation on each model separately and integrate the
results using voting. Finally, we further integrate the results of the three pre-
trained language models by weighted voting.

4   Experiments

4.1   Dataset

The dataset is derived from a real estate customer service scenario, consisting
of dialogue text, role information, and two levels of topic categories and index
tags. For the first level theme, we adopted the approach of the official baseline
model. The proposed model focuses on the second level of more fine-grained
topics, which account for 95.96% of the total number of topics in the training
set. The statistical information of the dataset is shown in Table 1.

In the experiment, the F1 values of the extracted topics were used as evaluation indicators. There are two criteria: whether the boundaries of the topics are
correct or not, and whether the types of topics are correct or not. The formula
for calculating F1 is:

$$Precision = \frac{C}{A}, Recall = \frac{C}{B}, F1 = \frac{2 * Precision * Recall}{Precision + Recall} \quad (5)$$

where A is the total number of extracted topic intervals, B is the total number
of true topic intervals, and C is the total number of correct topic intervals.

Table 1. Overview statistics of the constructed dataset.

Item	Train	Test A	Test B
# of samples	900	100	300
# of characters	6200832	818867	1985248
# of sentences	457362	59138	147996
Avg. # of characters per dialogue	6889.81	8188.67	6617.49
Avg. #of sentence per dialogue	508.18	591.38	493.32
# of LV1 labels	6		
# of LV2 labels	71		

4.2 Results and Analysis

We conducted a multi-stage experiment. First, we selected the most effective pre-trained language model PERT to conduct a single-model comparison experiment on the one-fold validation set in k-fold cross-validation and the offline test set A to verify the effectiveness of each optimization we made to the model. Then we conducted comparative experiments for each baseline model and for the model incorporating all improvements, and finally, we conducted comparison experiments for the ensemble model. The results on the validation set and the offline test set with two levels of topic are shown in Table 2.

Table 2. The F1 of different models on the dev set and offline test set

Model	Dev	Test
	F1	F1
PERT Large baseline	48.16	47.54
+ Sliding Windows	49.24	48.52
+ Sliding Windows + CRF	51.77	50.96
+ Sliding Windows + CRF + Status Embeddings	52.39	51.32
+ Sliding Windows + CRF + Status Embeddings + FGM	53.12	52.10
Ten-Fold Vote	–	53.74
RoBERTa-wwm Large baseline	47.42	46.66
+ all	51.89	51.13
Ten-Fold Vote	–	53.35
MacBERT Large baseline	48.02	47.24
+ all	52.28	51.19
Ten-Fold Vote	–	53.68
Vote Ensemble Model	–	54.13

From Table 2, we can see that compared to the baseline model, adding a sliding window in the preprocessing stage effectively reduces the loss of contextual information and improves the performance of the model by 1.08% and 0.78%. Replacing the cross-entropy loss with the path score loss of the CRF model and capturing the dependencies between topic tags using the tag transfer matrix improves the performance of the model by 2.53% and 2.44%, it indicates that the dependencies between tags can be very effective in improving the accuracy of sentence sequence labeling. After incorporating the status embedding information into the model, the model effectively learns the status information of the dialogue text and facilitates the classification of topic tags, and the performance of the model is improved by 0.62% and 0.36%. In the adversarial training, the original gradient and the adversarial gradient are accumulated, mitigates overfitting and improves the robustness of the model. The performance of the model increases by 0.73% and 0.78%. Finally, the performance of the PERT model combining all improvements is 6.2% higher than the baseline model. On RoBERTa-wwm Large and MacBERT Large, the model with all improvements is also outperform the baseline model. The performance improvements are 6.44% and 6.69% on these two models.

On the basis of the single model, we performed a ten-fold cross-validation voting integration. The integration of multiple pre-trained language models was carried out to further improve the stability and performance of the model. The performance of the final ensemble model improve by 2.03% over the best performing single model.

5   Conclusion

In this paper, we define the dialogue topic extraction task as a sequence labeling task with sentences as the basic elements. We use Chinese pre-trained language models for context encoding and CRF model fpr capturing the dependencies between tags. We propose a two-stage identity information incorporation method and effectively incorporates the dialogue role information into the model. In addition, we enhance the performance and robustness of the model using adversarial training and ensemble model. Experimental results from the validation set and the offline test set show that all of our improvements to the model are effective. The official evaluation results show that our model ranks first, proving the effectiveness of proposed dialogue topic extraction model.

Acknowledgements. This work is supported by grants from the Fundamental Research Funds for the Central Universities (No. DUT22ZD205).

References

1. Trivedi, A., Pant, N., Shah, P., Sonik, S., Agrawal, S.: Speech to text and text to speech recognition systems-a review. IOSR J. Comput. Eng **20**(2), 3643 (2018)
2. Wang, L., Yao, J., Tao, Y., Zhong, L., Liu, W., Du, Q.: A reinforced topic-aware convolutional sequence-to-sequence model for abstractive text summarization. arXiv preprint arXiv:1805.03616 (2018)

3. Narayan, S., Cohen, S.B., Lapata, M.: Don't give me the details, just the summary! Topic-aware convolutional neural networks for extreme summarization. arXiv preprint arXiv:1808.08745 (2018)
4. Wang, J., et al.: Sentiment classification in customer service dialogue with topic-aware multi-task learning. In: Proceedings of the AAAI Conference on Artificial Intelligence, vol. 34, pp. 9177–9184 (2020)
5. Xu, B., Wang, Q., Lyu, Y., Zhu, Y., Mao, Z.: Entity structure within and throughout: modeling mention dependencies for document-level relation extraction (2021)
6. Miyato, T., Dai, A.M., Goodfellow, I.: Adversarial training methods for semi-supervised text classification. arXiv preprint arXiv:1605.07725 (2016)
7. Jung, Y.: Multiple predicting K-fold cross-validation for model selection. J. Nonparametr. Stat. **30**(1), 197215 (2018)
8. Luo, L., Lai, P.T., Wei, C.H., Lu, Z.: Extracting drug-protein interaction using an ensemble of biomedical pre-trained language models through sequence labeling and text classification techniques. In: Proceedings of the BioCreative VII Challenge Evaluation Workshop, pp. 26–30 (2021)
9. Liu, J., et al.: Topic- aware contrastive learning for abstractive dialogue summarization. arXiv preprint arXiv:2109.04994 (2021)
10. Xu, Y., Zhao, H., Zhang, Z.: Topicaware multi-turn dialogue modeling. In: The Thirty-Fifth AAAI Conference on Artificial Intelligence (AAAI-21) (2021)
11. Zou, Y., et al.: Topic-oriented spoken dialogue summarization for customer service with saliency-aware topic modeling. In: Proceedings of the AAAI Conference on Artificial Intelligence, vol. 35, pp. 14665–14673 (2021)
12. Huang, Z., Xu, W., Yu, K.: Bidirectional LSTM-CRF models for sequence tagging. arXiv preprint arXiv:1508.01991 (2015)
13. Kumawat, D., Jain, V.: POS tagging approaches: a comparison. Int. J. Comput. Appl. **118**(6), 32–38 (2015)
14. Lample, G., Ballesteros, M., Subramanian, S., Kawakami, K., Dyer, C.: Neural architectures for named entity recognition. arXiv preprint arXiv:1603.01360 (2016)
15. Liu, B., Lane, I.: Attention-based recurrent neural network models for joint intent detection and slot filling. arXiv preprint arXiv:1609.01454 (2016)
16. JingHui, X., BingQuan, L., XiaoLong, W.: Principles of non-stationary hidden markov model and its applications to sequence labeling task. In: Dale, R., Wong, K.-F., Su, J., Kwong, O.Y. (eds.) IJCNLP 2005. LNCS (LNAI), vol. 3651, pp. 827–837. Springer, Heidelberg (2005). https://doi.org/10.1007/11562214_72
17. Liu, Z., Zhu, C., Zhao, T.: Chinese named entity recognition with a sequence labeling approach: based on characters, or based on words? In: Huang, D.-S., Zhang, X., Reyes García, C.A., Zhang, L. (eds.) ICIC 2010. LNCS (LNAI), vol. 6216, pp. 634–640. Springer, Heidelberg (2010). https://doi.org/10.1007/978-3-642-14932-0_78
18. Nguyen, N., Guo, Y.: Comparisons of sequence labeling algorithms and extensions. In: Proceedings of the 24th International Conference on Machine Learning, pp. 681–688 (2007)
19. Ma, X., Hovy, E.: End-to-end sequence labeling via bi-directional LSTM-CNNS-CRF. arXiv preprint arXiv:1603.01354 (2016)
20. Souza, F., Nogueira, R., Lotufo, R.: Portuguese named entity recognition using BERT-CRF. arXiv preprint arXiv:1909.10649 (2019)
21. Devlin, J., Chang, M.W., Lee, K., Toutanova, K.: BERT: pre-training of deep bidirectional transformers for language understanding. arXiv preprint arXiv:1810.04805 (2018)

22. Cui, Y., Che, W., Liu, T., Qin, B., Yang, Z.: Pre-training with whole word masking for Chinese BERT. IEEE/ACM Trans. Audio Speech Lang. Process. **29**, 35043514 (2021)
23. Cui, Y., Che, W., Liu, T., Qin, B., Wang, S., Hu, G.: Revisiting pre-trained models for Chinese natural language processing. arXiv preprint arXiv:2004.13922 (2020)
24. Cui, Y., Yang, Z., Liu, T.: PERT: pre-training BERT with permuted language model. arXiv preprint arXiv:2203.06906 (2022)
25. Liu, Y., et al.: RoBERTa: a robustly optimized BERT pretraining approach. arXiv preprint arXiv:1907.11692 (2019)

Knowledge Enhanced Pre-trained Language Model for Product Summarization

Wenbo Yin, Junxiang Ren[(✉)], Yuejiao Wu, Ruilin Song, Lang Liu,
Zhen Cheng, and Sibo Wang

China Pacific Insurance (Group) Co., Ltd., Shanghai, China
`renjunxiang@cpic.com.cn`

Abstract. Automatic summarization has been successfully applied to
many scenarios such as news and information services, assisted recommendations, etc. E-commerce product summarization is also a scenario
with great economic value and attention, as they can help generate
text that matches the product information and inspires users to buy.
However, existing algorithms still have some challenges: the generated
summarization produces incorrect attributes that are inconsistent with
original products and mislead users, thus reducing the credibility of e-
commerce platforms. The goal of this paper is to enhance product data
with attributes based on pre-trained models that are trained to understand the domain knowledge of products and generate smooth, relevant
and faithful text that attracts users to buy.

Keywords: Summarization · Pre-trained models · Domain knowledge

1 Introduction

With the development of Internet, we have obtained a huge amount of text and
image data, and it has become a very important task to simplify the massive and
complicated data. Manual content simplification requires a lot of efforts and time,
which is very uneconomical. By analyzing and understanding the complex text,
images and other information, the automatic summarization system can generate
smooth, relevant, comprehensive and faithful summaries while preserving the
important information contained in the input data, which can greatly reduce
the cost and improve the automation of information processing. We can classify
automatic summarization tasks from two perspectives: domain and modeling.
According to the domain, it can be classified into generic and domain-specific,
and according to the modeling approach, it can be classified into extractive and
abstractive.

E-commerce is a relatively complex field, which realizes commerce activities
through Internet, and its content includes various commercial activities conducted online, trading activities, financial activities, and related comprehensive

© Springer Nature Switzerland AG 2022
W. Lu et al. (Eds.) NLPCC 2022, LNCS 13552, pp. 263–273, 2022.
https://doi.org/10.1007/978-3-031-17189-5_22

service activities. As a major industry of Internet, e-commerce has long been deeply rooted in people's daily lives. One of the most direct ways to trade goods is on e-commerce websites, where there is a huge amount of information about goods. They can be specifically divided into many categories, such as clothing, home appliances, bags, office supplies, etc. Each category has specific domain knowledge. For example, clothing has the following attributes: fit, size, color, season, etc., while the category of home appliances has the distinction between kitchen appliances and bathroom appliances. To assist in the sale of the product, concise descriptive copies are required for the products based on their specific information to motivate users to buy. This will have some following problems.

1. The summarization system needs to have domain differentiation (e.g., ability to distinguish the function and attributes of clothes and pants and ability to distinguish the role and scene of gas stove and kettle).
2. Fine-grained commodity information needs to be accurate. For instance, a dress cannot have a description similar to a bustier.
3. The generated summarization is required to clearly mention the characteristics of products and can impress consumers.

This paper combines the Multimodal Product Summarization competition. Participants need to train a generative language model to understand e-commerce product information and generate concise, meaningful summaries based on given multimodal heterogeneous information (e.g., short product titles and longer product descriptions, product attribute knowledge bases, and product images).

2   Related Work

With the rapid development of artificial intelligence in recent years, the use of neural network models for text generation has made great progress. The advantage of neural networks is that there is no need to manually design semantic features and a mapping function can be learned end-to-end based on the trained corpus. Model training on domain-specific tasks and specific corpora was once common, but with the gradual emergence of generic pre-trained language models represented by BERT [1], pre-training models begin to stand out in various fields of NLP. The combination of upstream pre-training and downstream task fine-tuning approach gradually becomes mainstream. BERT is mainly applied to NLU tasks, and the emergence of BART, GPT, T5 and other models has filled the gap of pre-trained models for NLG.

Although pre-trained models generally have the problem of large number of parameters, this disadvantage has gradually become less prominent with the gradual reduction of hardware cost. Pre-training models have great advantages over previous non-pre-training NLG models in the NLG domain. Firstly, unsupervised training on a large amount of common corpus can learn the language paradigm, knowledge information, and downstream fine-tuning tasks can be based on the previously learned empirical information for fast knowledge transfer. Next, reasonable pre-training contains training tasks similar to common downstream tasks, so it can provide a better parameter for subsequent training, which can accelerate the convergence of downstream tasks and reduce the dependence on the amount of data.

Most of the mainstream pre-training models mentioned above benefit from the excellent performance achieved by the progressive deepening of the Transformer model. The Transformer-based models can be divided into encoder and decoder according to their functions. Encoder is generally required for NLU tasks as input feature mention (decoder as an alternative), while decoder is generally mandatory for NLG tasks. Specifically, NLG can be divided into two categories as follows [2].

2.1 Encoder-Decoder Transformer

The Encoder-Decoder-based model is a classical Seq2Seq structure [3], which contains two parts, encoder and decoder, and can solve the problem of longer outputs. The encoder of the current mainstream Transformer [4] encodes the input sequence based on self-attention, and the decoder decodes the encoded vector based on encoder-decoder-self-attention. MASS [5] randomly masks the encoder input sentences with consecutive fragments of length k. The decoder predicts only the consecutive fragments that are masked by the encoder. Unlike MASS, BART [6] corrupts the input by several noises (masking, disruption, rotation, token removal), and then uses decoder to reconstruct the original text. T5 [7] proposed by Google, on the other hand, unifies translation, classification, regression, and summary generation tasks into Text-to-Text tasks on the C4 dataset. Then Google released a multilingual version of mT5 [8], which uses GeGLU [9] nonlinear activation function compared to the original T5 using ReLU [10], and does not use dropout [11] for the pre-training task. The input data are then reduced by adding a large amount of noise to the model.

There are other pre-training ideas such as Cross-Lingual MLM. The training process of XNLG [12] model is relatively special. It is divided into two stages. The first stage trains the encoder, and the second stage fixes the parameters of the encoder and only trains the parameters of the decoder. The loss of the second stage uses the self-reconstruction loss function.

2.2 Decoder-Only Transformer

Decoder-based models are mainly auto-regressive, and are well suited for NLG pre-training by progressively expanding the attention window so that each step of the generation can only focus on the previous token. OpenAI released GPT [13] in 2018, which is a classical autoregressive language model, based on a generative unsupervised approach to pretraining. OpenAI then released GPT-2 [14] in 2019, which significantly increased the number of parameters and the size of data used for training compared to GPT, and combined supervised tasks: multiple tasks were modeled as a single classification task by introducing templates for training.

OpenAI has further increased the number of parameters of the model (to 175 billion parameters) and 45 TB data size in GPT-3 [15], making it more effective in zero-shot scenarios.

3   Description of the Competition

The summarization task requires participants to use given data from the e-commerce domain to train a generative language model to understand the knowledge and generate a correct, relevant and meaningful recommendation for the newly given product data.

Since it is a generative model, the evaluation is divided into two ways: automatic metrics evaluation as well as manual evaluation. Automatic metrics commonly used in the field of text generation include ROUGE [16], BLEU [17], METEOR [18]. The automatic metrics in the competition use ROUGE, specifically the average scores of ROUGE-1, ROUGE-2, and ROUGE-L [19] metrics. The manual metrics are annotated by humans to assess the fidelity, readability, non-redundancy, and importance of the predicted text for a sample of data. The final ranking is based on the results of the manual metrics. The ROUGE-N formula used for the automatic evaluation is as follows.

$$ROUGE - N = \frac{\sum_{S \in \{ReferenceSummaries\}} \sum_{gram_N \in S} Count_{match}(gram_N)}{\sum_{S \in \{ReferenceSummaries\}} \sum_{gram_N \in S} Count(gram_N)} \tag{1}$$

The denominator of the formula measures the number of N-grams in the target translation, while the numerator measures the number of N-grams shared by the reference translation and the machine translation (N = 1 for ROUGE-1 and N = 2 for ROUGE-2).

"L" in ROUGE-L indicates the longest common subsequence (LCS), and ROUGE-L is calculated using the longest common subsequence of the machine translation and the target translation. The calculation formulas are as follows.

$$R_{LCS} = \frac{LCS(C, S)}{len(S)} \tag{2}$$

$$P_{LCS} = \frac{LCS(C, S)}{len(C)} \tag{3}$$

$$F_{LCS} = \frac{(1 + \beta^2) R_{LCS} P_{LCS}}{R_{LCS} + \beta^2 P_{LCS}} \tag{4}$$

The R_{LCS} in the formula represents the recall rate of the machine translated text, while P_{LCS} represents the accuracy rate of the machine translated text. F_{LCS} is ROUGE-L. Generally, the beta parameter is set to a large number while P_{LCS} and R_{LCS} are basically in an order of magnitude, so F_{LCS} considers almost only R_{LCS} (i.e., recall rate). The advantage of LCS is that it does not require consecutive matches. Besides, LCS reflects the order of sentence-level word order, and can be used as a complement to mere n-grams.

4   Dataset Introduction

The dataset in the task contains e-commerce domain data collected from Jing-dong e-commerce platform. Each example is a tuple, (product text description, product knowledge base, product image, product summarization). The dataset contains three product categories, including bags, home appliances and clothing. The example graphs of the data and the amount of data are as follows (Figs. 1 and 2).

Fig. 1. Example graph

	Cases&Bags	Home Appliances	Clothing
Train	50,000	100,000	200,000
Valid	10,000	10,000	10,000
Test	10,000	10,000	10,000
Input token/sample	319.0	336.6	294.8
Product attribute/sample	14.8	7.8	7.3
Product image/sample	1	1	1

Fig. 2. Data amount

4.1   Textual Data

The inputs and outputs of the text data are in the form of one-to-many as shown in Fig. 3. The tgt field contains multiple texts, and they differ significantly.

{
  "idx": "AcLiTdukH4",
  "src": "男装 都市 特工 运动 连帽 羽绒服 哑光 加厚 保暖 防风 外套 1811001 银灰色 ， 涤纶 ， 连帽 ， 短款 ， 青春 流行 ， 灰鸭绒 ， 外穿 ， 美式 休闲 ， 袖长 ， 衣 长 (后 中长)) ， 足码 ， 胸围 ， 面料 选用 尼龙 材质 ， 表面 涂层 ， 哑光 质地 ， 含蓄 内敛 ， 轻盈 耐穿 ， 非常 符合 AR 风格 ， 门襟 采用 ， 产品 面料 ， 产品 特点 ， 根据 衣物 内侧 洗标 为准 ， 产品颜色 ， 防水 拉链 ， 既 防水 又 有 装饰性 ， 彰显 都市 特工 味道 。 款式 简洁 ， 是 一款 实用性 和 穿着 性 非常 广 的 ， 洗涤 标准 ， 银灰色 红色 其他 ， 大 身 填充物 ： 灰 鸭绒 ， 含绒量 ， 80% ， 羽绒服 。 袖子 采用 环保 印花 。 在 充绒 方面 ， 高达 80% 的 充绒量 ， 冬季 穿着 非常 保暖 。 ",
  "tgt": [
    "填充 蓬松 洁净 的 灰 鸭绒 材质 ， 充绒量 高 整体 效果 饱满 ， 穿着 具有 良好 的 保暖 抗风 作用 。 选用 哑光 质地 的 尼龙面料 ， 表面 带有 防水 涂层 ， 户外活动 抗风 防雨 效果显著 ， 还有 防止 钻绒 的 功能 。 ",
    "羽绒服 面料 采用 尼龙 材质 ， 具有 很好 的 防水 防风 效果， 表面 哑光 涂层 ， 质感 十足 ， 门襟 处 采用 防水 拉链 ， 给予 全方位 的 锁温 效果 ， 袖子 处 的 字母 印花 ， 丰富 衣身 细节 ， 款式 简洁 不失 设计 感 。 "
  ],
  "kb": {
    "图案": "纯色",
    "基础 风格": "青春 流行",
    "衣 长": "短款",
    "填充物": "灰 鸭绒",
    "风格": "休闲 风",
    "领型": "连帽",
    "材质": "聚酰胺 纤维 (锦纶)"
  },
}

Fig. 3. Data sample

The basic form of data input to the model is one-to-one, so here we split the one-to-many data into a one-to-one form to obtain 350,000 training data and perform some data statistics, which is shown in Fig. 4 and Fig. 5.

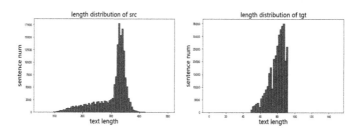

Fig. 4. Distribution of training data

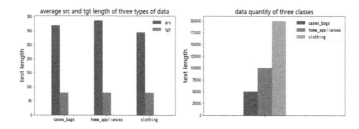

Fig. 5. Statistics of three categories

From the text distribution length of all the categories, the input text (src) length is basically between 100–450 words, and the target text (tgt) length is distributed between 40–100. Besides, the input and output lengths are less than 512, which can be processed by the common Transformer-based generation model. From the perspective of the three categories, the average length distribution of the three categories of data basically remains the same, and the number of the three categories of data has some differences, but the relative ratio is less than 1:4.

4.2 Image Data

The image data and the input text (src) are one-to-one, so the count of the number is kept with the number of unsplit input text (src) above. The text images are high quality product detail images with white background, and the sample images are shown below (Fig. 6).

Fig. 6. Image data sample

5 Model Solution

5.1 Model Introduction

Two baseline models are provided: a plain text model and a multimodal version of the model with pre-trained models (Encoder: 6L-768H-12A, Decoder: 6L-768H-12A, 110M parameters). We use an end-to-end solution and try to use BART and PEGASUS [20] directly for summarization generation based on plain text, based on the following considerations.

1. The role of image data is small. We selected some data pairs of target text and images from the training set. Based on our intuition, we believe that the variable descriptive words and fine-grained knowledge information in the text are difficult to obtain from the image data (Figs. 7 and 8).

Fig. 7. Example graph

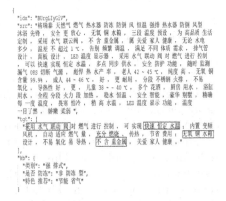

Fig. 8. Textual information

2. Large-scale model pre-training models have strong generalization ability. Large-scale language models represented by BERT, GPT, BART, and T5 have strong generalization ability by setting specific training tasks on massive data. Besides, the combination of language model pre-training and downstream task fine-tuning has basically become the standard solution. We consider BART as the baseline and PEGASUS as the comparison strategy of BART. BART can be used as NLU as well as NLG when it is fine-tuned for text classification and translation tasks. The structure is demonstrated in Fig. 9.

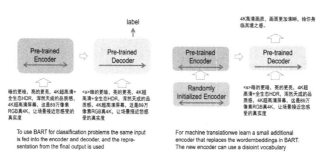

Figure:Fine tuning BART for classification and translation

Fig. 9. Structure of BART

3. PEGASUS is a model tailored specifically for summarization extraction. PEGASUS pre-training phase uses both GSG (Gap Sentences Generation) task as well as MLM task. The GSG tasks is to remove or mask the important sentences of the input documents and predict the generation by other sentence prediction, similar to summarization generation.

5.2   Model Training

Combined with some statistics in Sect. 3, we believe that we do not need to do much additional processing on the data (length reduction, truncation, category balancing, etc.). We directly use src from the text data as model input and tgt as golden-output for end-to-end model training, and preform generation training on BART and PEGASUS as our baseline.

Further, we observe that the input data (src) has a stack of single words partially divided by commas. This structure makes the whole input data (src) much less fluent and single words make the semantic uncertainty increase. Besides, these words appear in the kb field, and the key data in the kb field can further explain the uncertainty of these short words. If the two are combined in a template-like manner, the above two problems can be compensated.

Specifically, we take “wrap-around skirt” in src, query its key in the corresponding kb field to get “skirt shape”, construct it as “skirt shape of wrap-around skirt” through the template, and replace the “hipster skirt” in src (Fig. 10).


```
{
  "idx": "LtoPaHeds3",
  "src": "商场 同款 哈 吉斯 2019 春夏 新款 短裙 女 英伦 半身裙 时尚 包 臀 裙 白色 155 36 ， 微弹 ， 包 臀 裙 ， 小 清新
  ， 甜美 ， 休闲 风 ， 腰带 ， 淑女 风 ， 街 拍 ， 棉 ， 高腰 ， 纯色 ， 短裙 ， 英伦 与 都市 ， BRITISHURBANITY 英 ，
  而 不失 其 个性 ， 模特 展示 ， 基本 安全 技术 要求 符合 ： B 类 ， 细节 展示 ， HAZZYS ， 伴随 你 的 生活 ， 为 都市
  增添 活力 ， 为 你 增添 精彩 . 轰 可能 造成 不可 回复 的 损伤 ， 不可 干洗 ， 等级 ： 合格品 检验员 ： ⓪ ， 零售价 ：
  1090.00 ， 品名 ： 女 短裙 ( 附 腰带 ) ， 不可 漂白 ， 主题 ： 都市 先锋 ， 号型 ： 155 / 68A ， 合格证 ， 品牌 ：
  HAZZYS ， 内部 码 ： ABQSTO9ATO3BI06736 ， 成分 ： 产地 ： 广东 广州 ， 洗涤 说明 ， 执行 标准 ： FZ / T81004 - 2012",
  "tgt": [
    "精选 优质 的 棉质 面料 ， 弹力 大 增强 活动 空间 ， 轻薄 干爽 ， 手感 细腻 紧实 舒适度 强 。 包 臀 的 半身裙 版型 ，
    视觉 上拉上 腿部 线条 ， 简约 大方 彰显 优雅 气质 。"
  ],
  "kb": {
    "裙型": "包 臀 裙",
    "裙长": "短裙",
    "弹力": "微弹",
    "风格": "小 清新",
    "腰型": "高腰",
    "图案": "纯色",
    "流行 元素": "腰带",
    "廓形": "H 型",
    "材质": "棉"
  }
},
```


Fig. 10. Data detail

In summary, we trained on both BART and PEGASUS models with direct training as a Strategy 1 and kb-enhanced data training as Strategy 2.

6 Model Evaluation

We optimize the model for the two strategies in the previous section and combine the data enhancements to obtain four strategies: BART-fintune, BART-kb-fintune, PEGASUS-fintune, PEGASUS-kb-fintune. We test the models on the official test dataset and the best performing model is PEGASUS-kb-fintune, followed by PEGASUS-fintune, with the following test scores (Table 1).

Table 1. Testing score

Model	Strategy	ROUGE-1	ROUGE-2	ROUGE-L	AVG
BART	fintune	31.7974	12.1675	21.7936	21.9195
BART	kb-fintune	32.3717	12.2884	21.7176	22.1258
PEGASUS	fintune	32.6107	12.1466	22.5404	22.4325
PEGASUS	kb-fintune	32.7113	12.2438	22.5163	22.4904

7   Conclusion

Based on the competition, this paper conducts end-to-end training based on the popular generative pre-training models BART and PEGASUS, and conducts summarization generation experiments in two ways: direct training on the original data and training on the augmented data. From the experimental results we can see that the data augmented based on kb information has a certain degree of improvement on both PEGASUS and BART models. Finally, the combined score of 1.7875 on the fidelity, readability, non-redundancy and importance of the manually evaluated generation results achieve the third place. Due to time constraints, there are still some optimization directions based on plain text, such as:

(a) we can collect additional e-commerce domain data, and follow PEGASUS' GSG approach to perform a step of domain fine-tuning first, and then perform the current step of downstream fine-tuning.
(b) There are still a lot of low-quality statements in src data, which contains some numerical models of goods, commodity codes and other meaningless information. These information will interfere with useful information in the encode stage of the model. We can consider doing a culling of this part of data through rules, or models.
(c) The diversity of text in tgt is very strong, and the model is not easy to fit when learning. We can fine-tune directly on tgt data based on PEGASUS or BART before making downstream fine-tuning in the way of BART's mask-recovery.

References

1. Devlin, J., et al.: BERT: pre-training of deep bidirectional transformers for language understanding. arXiv:1810.04805 (2019)
2. Yuan, S., et al.: A roadmap for big model (2022)
3. Sutskever, I., et al.: Sequence to sequence learning with neural networks, vol. 27, pp. 3104–3112 (2014)
4. Vaswani, A., et al.: Attention is all you need, vol. 30, pp. 5998–6008 (2017)
5. Song, K., et al.: MASS: masked sequence to sequence pre-training for language generation, pp. 5926–5936 (2019)
6. Mike, L., et al.: BART: denoising sequence-to-sequence pre-training for natural language generation, translation, and comprehension, pp. 7871–7880 (2020)
7. Colin, R., et al.: Exploring the limits of transfer learning with a unified text-to-text transformer. J. Mach. Learn. Res. **21**, 61–67 (2020)
8. Xue, L., et al.: mT5: a massively multilingual pre-trained text-to-text transformer, pp. 483–498 (2021)
9. Noam, S.: GLU variants improve transformer (2020)
10. Glorot, X., et al.: Deep sparse rectifier neural networks, pp. 315–323 (2011)
11. Srivastava, N., et al.: Dropout: a simple way to prevent neural networks from overfitting. J. Mach. Learn. Res. **15**, 1929–1958 (2014)
12. Chi, Z., et al.: Cross-lingual natural language generation via pre-training, vol. 34, pp. 7570–7577 (2020)

13. Radford, A., et al.: Improving language understanding by generative pre training, vol. 12 (2018)
14. Radford, A., et al.: Language models are unsupervised multitask learners (2019)
15. Brown, T., et al.: Language models are few-shot learners, vol. 33, pp. 1877–1901 (2020)
16. Lin, C.Y.: ROUGE: recall-oriented understudy for Gisting evaluation (2003)
17. Papineni, K., et al.: BLEU: a method for automatic evaluation of machine translation, vol. P02-1, pp. 311–318 (2002)
18. Banerjee, S., Lavie, A.: METEOR: an automatic metric for MT evaluation with improved correlation with human judgments, vol. W05-09, pp. 65–72 (2005)
19. Lin, C.Y.: ROUGE: a package for automatic evaluation of summaries (2004)
20. Zhang, J., et al.: PEGASUS: pre-training with extracted gap-sentences for abstractive summarization, pp. 11328–11339 (2020)

Augmented Topic-Specific Summarization for Domain Dialogue Text

Zhiqiang Rao, Daimeng Wei, Zongyao Li, Hengchao Shang, Jinlong Yang,
Zhengzhe Yu, Shaojun Li, Zhanglin Wu, Lizhi Lei, Hao Yang(✉), and Ying Qin

Huawei Translation Service Center, Beijing, China
{raozhiqiang,weidaimeng,lizongyao,shanghengchao,yangjinlong7,yuzhengzhe,
lishaojun18,wuzhanglin2,leilizhi,yanghao30,qinying}@huawei.com

Abstract. This paper describes HW-TSC's submission to the NLPCC 2022 dialogue text summarization task. We convert it into a sub-summary generation and a topic detection task. A sequence-to-sequence model Transformer is adopted as the foundational structure of our generation model. An ensemble topic detection model is used to filter uninformative summaries. On the other hand, we utilize multiple data processing and data augmentation methods to improve the effectiveness of the system. A constrained search method is used to construct generation model's training pairs between sub-dialogues and sub-summaries. Multiple role-centric training data augmentation strategies are used to enhance both the generation model and the topic detection model. Our experiments demonstrate the effectiveness of these methods. Finally, we rank first with the highest ROUGE score of 51.764 in the test evaluation.

Keywords: NLPCC 2022 · Dialogue summarization · Topic detection · Data augmentation

1 Introduction

Text summarization [6] helps people get the most important information from text data more quickly, and improves the efficiency of people to acquire useful knowledge. For example, in the most common news reports and academic papers, a good abstract can greatly reduce the time for people to search for the content of interest. For such well-structured documents, whose logic are clear and topics are relatively focused, the document summarization can be solved by generative and extractive methods. For example, use the sequence-to-sequence generation model Transformer [23] or the extraction method of TextRank [19]. The characteristics of dialogue summarization are that there are many roles and they exchange information with each other. Topics change rapidly, a specific topic is distributed. And there are many redundant utterances. Such as meeting summary generation and online customer service summary generation. The focus of such tasks is to extract information about specific roles or specific topics to generate summaries.

NLPCC 2022 dialogue text summarization task focus on real estate field and aims to summarize the concerns of customers. There are two roles, service

© Springer Nature Switzerland AG 2022
W. Lu et al. (Eds.) NLPCC 2022, LNCS 13552, pp. 274–283, 2022.
https://doi.org/10.1007/978-3-031-17189-5_23

and user. The dialogue data are almost all multi-round long dialogues. For such dialogue summarization, topic segmentation and sub-summary generation have demonstrated to be effective [13]. We treat this task as a role-specific and topic-specific sub-summary generation task. Figure 1 shows our system structure.

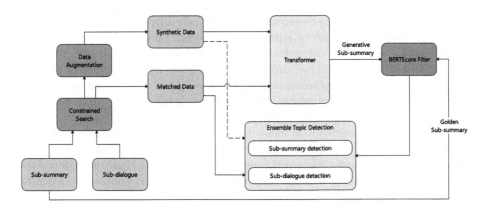

Fig. 1. System structure

Transformer is a sequence-to-sequence model structure that can achieve good performance on most generative tasks. Such as machine translation, text generation and summary generation tasks. There are many pre-trained models available based on the Transformer architecture, which can be used to achieve better results on low-resource, generative tasks. Like mBART [15], it has demonstrated effectiveness in low-resource machine translation tasks. It is a multilingual model, so we use it to help with this Chinese dialogue summarization task.

When generating summaries, in order to retain only the specific topic summaries of interest, we use an ensemble topic detection model to filter irrelevant summaries. This ensemble model uses different data sources as input to make comprehensive judgments, including dialogue text and summary text. In addition, we use a variety of data processing methods and data augmentation methods to improve the performance of the system. After segmenting sub-summaries and sub-dialogues, we use a constrained search method between them to construct training pairs for the generation model. This results in higher quality training data, which allows the generation model to learn better. Data augmentation is helpful for low-resource task, and appropriate noise can also improve the robustness of models. Here multiply role-centric data augmentation strategies are used to enhance both the generation model and the topic detection model. In the final test evaluation, our system ranks first with the highest ROUGE [12] score of 51.764.

In the following, we will introduce our data processing methods, model structure, data augmentation strategies, experiments and analysis.

2   Related Work

Document summarization mainly includes extraction based methods and generation based methods. Extraction based methods can use unsupervised learning methods such as TextRank [19], or supervised learning models to find informative sentences from documents as summaries [3,20]. Generation based methods generally use the sequence-to-sequence model, including LSTM [9], BART [11], etc., to generate summaries by summarizing the full text by the model itself.

Dialogue summarization generally needs to deal with the difficulties of multi-role and multi-topic. [16] proposed to use topic information with pointer-generator networks to help summarization. [25] proposed a topic-augmented two-stage dialogue summarizer jointly with a saliency-aware neural topic model for topic-oriented summarization of customer service dialogues. [7] leveraged dialogue acts in a summarization model with a sentence-gated mechanism for modeling the relationship between dialogue acts and the summary. [2] utilized a multi-view decoder to incorporate 4 different views to generate dialogue summaries, including topic, stage, global and discrete views. [14] used contrastive learning to help the model and constructed 2 auxiliary learning objectives, coherence detection and sub-summary generation objectives to help the primary sequence generation objective.

Data augmentation is widely used in sequence-to-sequence generation tasks. For example, in machine translation, back translation [5], noised back translation [1] are commonly used augmentation strategies. [17] extracted the abstract from the original document by a extractive method, and then back-translated the abstract content to effectively rewrite it, to increase the diversity of data. [8] presented that self-training can improve the performance on machine translation and summarization. The method uses a model to generate target sentences from source sentences, and then utilizes the syntactic pairs to train a model.

3   Dataset

3.1   Data Preprocessing

Since the task data are converted from recordings, there are many short text noise with only one or two meaningless words. We take statistics of short sentences and delete high frequency meaningless sentences.

The task dialogue data has two roles, service and user. Service's utterances are more and longer than user's. But user utterances are more informative because the task pay attention to specific role's purpose. We treat user as center in every sub-dialogue and merge user's continuous utterances. Because we found that user utterances are sometimes cut off into multiple sentences.

3.2   Constrained Search of Training Data

The task provided dialogues are so long that the summaries are always consisted of multiple independent sentences. Each sentence could be regarded as a sub-summary of a sub-dialogue [13]. We first segment summary sentences by Chinese period symbols. Then those sentences that still contain multiple sub-summaries would be split by roles' appear order. We try to divide only one user and one service in a sentence as possible. For example, a sentence *"user asked ..., service answered ..., service then asked ..., user answered ..."* would be split into two sub-summary sentences *"user asked ..., service answered ..."* and *"service then asked ..., user answered ..."*. To extract sub-dialogues, we regard user as center to construct candidates. Each candidate contains one user sentence and $2N$ contextual service sentences, where N is a window. A role tag is added at the beginning of each sentence.

To construct training pairs of sub-summary generation model, we use a constrained search method between sub-dialogue candidates and sub-summaries. The detailed search algorithm is presented in Algorithm 1. Longest Common Subsequence (LCS) is used to calculate the similarity score. Denote the summary of a dialogue as $S = (s1, s2, ..., s_m)$, where m is the number of sub-summaries and each s_i is a sub-summary. The sub-dialogue candidates of a dialogue as $C = (c1, c2, ..., c_n)$, where n is the number of candidates and each c_j is a candidate. For a ground truth pair, s_i and c_j should be relatively consistent in order, e.g. $j \geq i - K$ and $n - j \geq m - i - K$, where K is a tolerance, ideally equal to 0. We select the highest LCS score candidate for each sub-summary. Once a candidate has been used, it would be excluded.

Algorithm 1. Constrained search of training data for generation

---

Input: A summary $S = (s1, s2, ..., s_m)$, sub-dialogue candidates $C = (c1, c2, ..., c_n)$, a tolerance K

Output: Training pairs P

  for $s_i \in S$ **do**

    for $c_j \in C$ **do**

      if $j \geq i - K$ **and** $n - j \geq m - i - K$ **then**

        $l(s_i, c) \Leftarrow LCS(s_i, c_j)$

      end if

    end for

    $c_{best} \Leftarrow argmax_c l(s_i, c)$

    $P \Leftarrow P \cup (s_i, c_{best})$

    $C \Leftarrow C \setminus c_{best}$

  end for

---

4   System Overview

4.1   Sub-summary Generation Model

As mentioned above, the sequence-to-sequence Transformer model is adopted as our backbone architecture. Since the dialogue data is in Chinese, we use pre-trained model mBART, specifically mBART-large-50 [22] to initialize our sub-summary generation model. Encoder and decoder are 12 layers. Attention heads are 16. Word embedding and Hidden size is 1024. Feed-forward size is 4096. The dropout is 0.1.

4.2 Ensemble Topic Detection

In prediction, we can construct user-centric sub-dialogue candidates as same to the training. But not all of them could generate informative summaries that we concerned. We use an ensemble topic detection model to judge valid sub-dialogues or generative summaries. BERT [4] and FastText [10] show good performance in text classification. We take use of both to construct the ensemble model.

The ensemble model uses different data sources as input, including dialogue text and summary text. Specifically, FastText is trained with both of the input sources respectively. While BERT is trained with merely dialogue text, since it is better in handling long sequence text. The ensemble model classifies with a probability threshold P by "or" relationship.

$$Ensemble(BERT_{dialogue}, FastText_{dialogue}, FastText_{summary}) > P$$

For summary text, we collected three kinds of data as training data. Including golden sub-summaries, generative positive sub-summaries and generative negative sub-summaries. The negative sub-summaries are generated from negative sub-dialogues, which are remaining candidates during constrained search of generation training data. What's more, we took use of BERTScore [24] to calculate similarity between negative sub-summaries and golden sub-summaries, to eliminate suspected positive instances from negative sub-summaries.

4.3 Data Augmentation

Back translation and forward translation are two important methods in sequence-to-sequence model. We mainly use forward direction data augmentation to expand the training data. Three strategies are used: *add*, *shorten* and *replace*.

add: For every pair in training data. We randomly add unrelated service utterances at the beginning and end of the sub-dialogue repeatedly.

shorten: We shorten sub-dialogues length from $1+2N$ to $1+2$. N is decreased one at a time.

replace: We randomly replace the first and last sentence of a sub-dialogue with unrelated service utterances repeatedly.

They add noise to original training data in order to increase the robustness of the model. These syntactic data are used in both the generation and classification model.

5 Experiments

We use Pytorch [21] in our experiments. For the mBART model, the optimizer is AdamW [18] with $\beta_1 = 0.9$ and $\beta_2 = 0.999$. The learning rate is 2e−5. Maximum sentence length is 200. We use one GPU for training, and the batch size is 16. During positive training data generation, the service sentence window N is 3 and the tolerance K is 3. While in prediction N is set to 2, as we found it better.

We split 10% from the training data as our development data. For the generation model, the real data were duplicated to achieve 1:1 with synthetic data. For the classification model, the negative data were sampled to 1:1 with positive data. We train FastText with char-level input tokens, dim 100, word-ngram 1, softmax loss and lr 0.1, epoch 25. Bert-base-chinese pre-trained model was used. The classification threshold P is set to 0.1 and 0.25 before and after classification data augmentation, respectively.

The task uses ROUGE score for evaluation, which is the average of character-level ROUGE-1, ROUGE-2, and ROUGE-L. Table 1 shows the experiment results. In baseline, we directly use LCS to construct training pairs between original summary sentences and sub-dialogues, without data preprocessing, sub-summary segmentation and candidate match constraints. Punctuation conversion means Chinese punctuation conversion post-processing for generative summaries in prediction. Data processing is the most effective strategy. It shows high quality training data is as important as the model. Classification and data augmentation are comparable, increasing 0.2 to 0.6 ROUGE. What's more, we found punctuation conversion is useful for ROUGE score, though it doesn't significantly affect manual reading. In final submission, we used all the original training data for the generation and classification models. Test-A is the official online test system.

Table 1. ROUGE scores of experiments.

	Dev
Baseline	48.7
+ Classification	49.1 (+0.4)
+ Data processing	51.3 (+2.2)
+ Generation augmentation	51.5 (+0.2)
+ Classification augmentation	52.1 (+0.6)
+ Punctuation conversion	53.2 (+1.1)
Final (test-A)	51.5

Table 2 shows the final evaluation results in test-B. We got the highest ROUGE score of 51.7 that is approximately equal to test-A of 51.5. It shows that our system is robust.

Table 2. ROUGE scores in final evaluation.

System	Test-B
HW-TSC	51.7
Finvolution	51.0
Neu-chatbot	49.2
LoveNLP@TJU	48.7
Dialogue_TMG_HITSZ	46.3
Kingwithsun	41.0
XHL	33.0
Try	25.3

6 Analysis

6.1 The Effect of Different Data Augmentation Methods

To analyze the effect of different data augmentation methods for the generation model, we conduct comparative experiments on development data. The results in Table 3 show that *shorten* and *replace* have identical effects. While *add* and their combinations are harmful compared to 51.3 in Table 1. It indicates that service sentence window $N = 3$ during training data generation is enough large. Expanding the range affects the model's learning.

Table 4 presents ROUGE scores of different data augmentation methods for the classification model. *shorten* and *replace* are valid methods, while *add* is harmful compared to 51.5 in Table 1. *shorten* is the most efficient method in both experiments.

Table 3. ROUGE scores in generation data augmentation

	Dev
add	50.6
shorten	51.5
replace	51.5
All	49.5

Table 4. ROUGE scores in classification data augmentation

	Dev
add	48.5
shorten	52.1
replace	51.8
All	52.0

6.2 The Effect of Classification

We also analyze different training data source for classification model and its output classification threshold P. Table 5 shows different training source results of FastText classification. *Dialogue* source uses augmented training data. *Summary* source uses dialogue's golden summaries as positive training data. Its

Table 5. Classification results of different training source

Source	Accuracy	Positive (P/R/F1)	Negative (P/R/F1)
Dialogue	63.4	50.2/63.4/56.0	74.8/63.4/68.6
Summary	45.8	38.6/76.9/51.4	66.5/27.2/38.6

negative training data are generated from those unmatched sub-dialogue candidates through the generation model. Dialogue source has advantage to summary source in both positive and negative data prediction. Generative summaries are more similar to real summaries in sentence pattern and more difficult to distinguish.

Table 6 compares ROUGE scores of different threshold P. We use R-1, R-2, R-L to refer to ROUGE-1, ROUGE-2 and ROUGE-L, respectively. With the increase of P, precision increases while recall decreases. The F1 scores achieve best when $P = 0.25$.

Table 6. ROUGE scores of difference classification threshold P

P	R-1 (P/R/F1)	R-2 (P/R/F1)	R-L (P/R/F1)	ROUGE
0	60.6/69.9/63.8	30.2/39.7/33.2	56.9/65.6/59.9	52.3
0.2	62.6/68.6/64.5	31.5/38.7/33.7	58.8/64.4/60.6	52.9
0.25	63.7/67.9/**64.8**	32.3/38.0/**34.0**	59.9/63.8/**60.9**	**53.2**
0.3	64.6/66.3/64.5	33.0/37.0/33.9	60.7/62.3/60.6	53.0
0.5	70.7/56.1/61.6	38.6/29.8/32.7	66.1/52.6/57.8	50.7

7   Conclusion

This paper presents HW-TSC's system to the NLPCC 2022 dialogue text summarization task. We convert the task into a sub-summary generation and a specific topic detection task. We use a sequence-to-sequence model Transformer to solve the generation task, and train our model on the basis of pre-trained model mBART. An ensemble topic detection model is used to filter uninformative summaries. We use multiple effective data processing methods to improve training data's quality. Then role-centric training data augmentation are used to improve both the models. We conduct experiments with these strategies and analyze their effects. In the final test evaluation we got the highest ROUGE score.

References

1. Caswell, I., Chelba, C., Grangier, D.: Tagged back-translation. In: Proceedings of the Fourth Conference on Machine Translation (Volume 1: Research Papers) (2019)
2. Chen, J., Yang, D.: Multi-view sequence-to-sequence models with conversational structure for abstractive dialogue summarization. In: Empirical Methods in Natural Language Processing (2020)
3. Cheng, J., Lapata, M.: Neural summarization by extracting sentences and words. In: Meeting of the Association for Computational Linguistics (2016)
4. Devlin, J., Chang, M.W., Lee, K., Toutanova, K.: BERT: pre-training of deep bidirectional transformers for language understanding. In: North American Chapter of the Association for Computational Linguistics (2018)
5. Edunov, S., Ott, M., Auli, M., Grangier, D.: Understanding back-translation at scale. In: Empirical Methods in Natural Language Processing (2018)
6. El-Kassas, W.S., Salama, C., Rafea, A., Mohamed, H.K.: Automatic text summarization: a comprehensive survey. Expert Syst. Appl. **165**, 113679 (2021)
7. Goo, C.W., Chen, Y.N.: Abstractive dialogue summarization with sentence-gated modeling optimized by dialogue acts. In: Spoken Language Technology Workshop (2018)
8. He, J., Gu, J., Shen, J., Ranzato, M.: Revisiting self-training for neural sequence generation. In: International Conference on Learning Representations (2020)
9. Hochreiter, S., Schmidhuber, J.: Long short-term memory. Neural Comput. **9**, 1735–1780 (1997)
10. Joulin, A., Grave, E., Bojanowski, P., Mikolov, T.: Bag of tricks for efficient text classification. In: Proceedings of the 15th Conference of the European Chapter of the Association for Computational Linguistics: Volume 2, Short Papers, pp. 427–431. Association for Computational Linguistics, April 2017
11. Lewis, M., et al.: BART: denoising sequence-to-sequence pre-training for natural language generation, translation, and comprehension. In: Meeting of the Association for Computational Linguistics (2019)
12. Lin, C.Y.: ROUGE: a package for automatic evaluation of summaries. In: Text Summarization Branches Out, Barcelona, Spain, p. 7481. Association for Computational Linguistics, July 2004. https://aclanthology.org/W04-1013
13. Liu, J., et al.: Topic-aware contrastive learning for abstractive dialogue summarization. In: Findings of the Association for Computational Linguistics: EMNLP 2021, Punta Cana, Dominican Republic, pp. 1229–1243. Association for Computational Linguistics, November 2021. https://doi.org/10.18653/v1/2021.findings-emnlp.106
14. Liu, J., et al.: Topic-aware contrastive learning for abstractive dialogue summarization. In: Empirical Methods in Natural Language Processing (2021)
15. Liu, Y., et al.: Multilingual denoising pre-training for neural machine translation. Trans. Assoc. Comput. Linguist. **8**, 726–742 (2020). https://doi.org/10.1162/tacl_a_00343, https://aclanthology.org/2020.tacl-1.47
16. Liu, Z., Ng, A., Lee, S., Aw, A., Chen, N.F.: Topic-aware pointer-generator networks for summarizing spoken conversations. In: IEEE Automatic Speech Recognition and Understanding Workshop (2019)
17. Loem, M., Takase, S., Kaneko, M., Okazaki, N.: ExtraPhrase: efficient data augmentation for abstractive summarization (2022)
18. Loshchilov, I., Hutter, F.: Decoupled weight decay regularization. arXiv:1711.05101 (2017)

19. Mihalcea, R., Tarau, P.: TextRank: bringing order into text. In: Empirical Methods in Natural Language Processing (2004)
20. Nallapati, R., Zhai, F., Zhou, B.: SummaRuNNer: a recurrent neural network based sequence model for extractive summarization of documents. In: National Conference on Artificial Intelligence (2016)
21. Paszke, A., et al.: PyTorch: an imperative style, high-performance deep learning library. In: Wallach, H., Larochelle, H., Beygelzimer, A., d'Alché-Buc, F., Fox, E., Garnett, R. (eds.) Advances in Neural Information Processing Systems, vol. 32, pp. 8024–8035. Curran Associates, Inc. (2019). http://papers.neurips.cc/paper/9015-pytorch-an-imperative-style-high-performance-deep-learning-library.pdf
22. Tang, Y., et al.: Multilingual translation from denoising pre-training. In: Findings of the Association for Computational Linguistics: ACL-IJCNLP 2021, pp. 3450–3466. Association for Computational Linguistics, August 2021. https://doi.org/10.18653/v1/2021.findings-acl.304
23. Vaswani, A., et al.: Attention is all you need. In: Neural Information Processing Systems (2017)
24. Zhang, T., Kishore, V., Wu, F., Weinberger, K.Q., Artzi, Y.: BERTScore: evaluating text generation with BERT. Learning (2019)
25. Zou, Y., et al.: Topic-oriented spoken dialogue summarization for customer service with saliency-aware topic modeling. arXiv:2012.07311 (2020)

DAMO-NLP at NLPCC-2022 Task 2: Knowledge Enhanced Robust NER for Speech Entity Linking

Shen Huang[1], Yuchen Zhai[1,2], Xinwei Long[1,3], Yong Jiang[1], Xiaobin Wang[1], Yin Zhang[2], and Pengjun Xie[1(✉)]

[1] DAMO Academy, Alibaba Group, Hangzhou, China
{pangda,yongjiang.jy,xuanjie.wxb,chengchen.xpj}@alibaba-inc.com
[2] DMAC Group, DCD Lab, Zhejiang University, Hangzhou, China
{zhaiyuchen,zhangyin98}@zju.edu.cn
[3] University of Chinese Academy of Sciences, Beijing, China
longxinwei19@mails.ucas.ac.cn

Abstract. Speech Entity Linking aims to recognize and disambiguate named entities in spoken languages. Conventional methods suffer gravely from the unfettered speech styles and the noisy transcripts generated by ASR systems. In this paper, we propose a novel approach called Knowledge Enhanced Named Entity Recognition (KENER), which focuses on improving robustness through painlessly incorporating proper knowledge in the entity recognition stage and thus improving the overall performance of entity linking. KENER first retrieves candidate entities for a sentence without mentions, and then utilizes the entity descriptions as extra information to help recognize mentions. The candidate entities retrieved by a dense retrieval module are especially useful when the input is short or noisy. Moreover, we investigate various data sampling strategies and design effective loss functions, in order to improve the quality of retrieved entities in both recognition and disambiguation stages. Lastly, a linking with filtering module is applied as the final safeguard, making it possible to filter out wrongly-recognized mentions. Our system achieves 1st place in Track 1 and 2nd place in Track 2 of NLPCC-2022 Shared Task 2.

Keywords: Entity linking · Robust NER

1 Introduction

Speech Entity Linking (SEL), which aims to recognize and disambiguate named entities in spoken languages to a certain knowledge base (KB), is widely used in search engines, voice assistants and other speech analysis services. It's quite annoying but very common, for example, when you want news of Yao Ming who is the famous basketball player but the voice assistant returns you news of another Yao Ming who is a composer. The spoken language, compared to the written

W. Lu et al. (Eds.) NLPCC 2022, LNCS 13552, pp. 284–293, 2022.
https://doi.org/10.1007/978-3-031-17189-5_24

language, is much more informal for its unfettered styles and high-frequency grammatical errors. All these bring great difficulties to SEL, not to mention the noisy transcripts generated by Automatic Speech Recognition (ASR) systems.

The NLPCC 2022 Shared Task 2 provides researchers an opportunity to study Entity Linking (EL) problems with spoken languages and noisy texts. The task includes two tracks: (1) Track 1 - Entity Recognition and Disambiguation; (2) Track 2 - Entity Disambiguation-Only. The difference is that in Track 1 one needs to process the transcripts to extract named entities and disambiguate the extracted entities to the correct entry in a given knowledge base while in Track 2 gold standard named entities are given as input and all one needs to do is to disambiguate them.

Previous work on end2end EL problem show that is extraction is harder than disambiguation. Following these lines of work, we perform some preliminary experiments and verify it in this competition. To tackle this problem, we propose a three-stage approach called Knowledge Enhanced Named Entity RecognitionKENER. Firstly it retrieves candidate entities from a KB for an input sentence without mentions via a dense retrieval module. Secondly the retrieved entity descriptions and the sentence contexts are utilized as extra information to help recognize mentions in the Named Entity Recognition (NER) module. Thirdly a linking with filtering module is applied to link the mentions to a KB while filtering out wrongly-recognized mentions. Finally, with smart sampling strategy and ensemble methods, our system achieves 1st place in track 1 and 2nd place in track 2 of NLPCC-2022 Shared Task 2.

Besides the system description, we make the following observations based on our experiments.

1. Our entity retrieval module can retrieve highly-related entities given a certain sentence without mentions (Sect. 3.1).

2. Our NER module can effectively utilize the candidate entities to improve the overall performance (Sect. 3.2).

3. Our linking module can tackle noisy mentions with the filtering mechanism (Sect. 3.3).

2   Related Work

Named Entity Recognition (NER): Most of the work takes NER as a sequence labeling problems and applies the linear-chain CRF [1]. Recently, the improvement of accuracy mainly benefits from stronger token representations such as pretrained contextual embeddings such as BERT [2], Flair [3] and LUKE [4]. Yu et al. [5] utilizes the strength of pretrained contextual embeddings over long-range dependency and encodes the document-level contexts for token representations. Wang et al. [6] proposes to mine external contexts of a sentence by retrieving to improve NER performance.

Entity Disambiguation (ED): Most of the work focuses on contextual representation learning or features based on the entity mention [7]. DPR [8] and BLINK [9] calculate the match between the mention and entity through a bi-encoder during retrieval and a cross-encoder is used for re-ranking [9]. Various context information is exploited, such as latent entity type information in the immediate context of the mention [10].

End to End EL: There are some models that jointly processes NER and ED as well. Kolitsas et al. [11] first proposes a neural end-to-end EL system that jointly discovers and links entities in a text document. Martins et al. [12] introduces a Stack-LSTM approach composed of SHIFT-REDUCE-OUT actions for multi-task learning. Cao et al. [13] creatively formulate entity linking as a sequence-to-sequence task, where an encoder-decoder architecture is used to autoregressively generate terms in a prefix tree of entity title vocabulary. Zhang et al. [14] proposes the EntQA model that combines progress in entity linking with that in open-domain question answering and capitalizes on dense entity retrieval and reading comprehension.

3   Methods

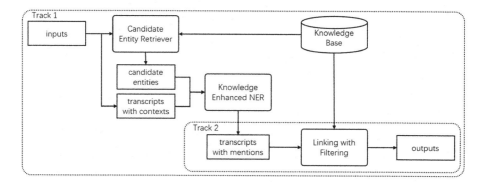

Fig. 1. Our proposed KENER system architecture for the shared task.

Figure 1 describes the architecture of our KENER system, which consists of three modules sequentially: Candidate Entity Retriever, Knowledge Enhanced NER and Linking with Filtering. We utilize the same linking module for Track 1 and Track 2.

3.1   Candidate Entity Retriever

The Candidate Entity Retriever module retrieves top-K candidate entities that might be mentioned in the input sentence. It adopts a variant of the bi-encoder structure, where the representation of an input sentence and a candidate entity from a KB are computed separately. The scores of candidate entities can then be calculated by the representations, so as to find the top-K candidate entities. We formulate the procedure as follows.

Given a sentence transcript $x \in \mathcal{V}^L$ and an entity $e \in \mathcal{E}$, where $\mathcal{V}$ denotes the vocabulary and $\mathcal{E}$ denotes the set of entities in a KB associated with text titles, aliases, and descriptions. L is the length of a sentence.

The candidate entity retrieval score $\text{score}_{r1}(x, e)$ can be computed by

$$S_1 = \mathbf{enc}_S([\text{CLS}] \ x \ [\text{SEP}] \ \text{ctx(x)} \ [\text{SEP}])$$
$$E_1 = \mathbf{enc}_E([\text{CLS}] \ \text{title(e)} \ [\text{SEP}] \ \text{alias(e)} \ \text{desc(e)} \ [\text{SEP}]) \qquad (1)$$
$$\text{score}_{r1}(x, e) = S_1^T E_1$$

where the $\text{ctx}(x)$ denotes the context sentences of x in a speech and title(e), alias(e), desc(e) denote the text title, alias and description of the entity e.

During inference time, we use Faiss [15] with precomputed E for each $e \in \mathcal{E}$ for fast retrieval.

Multi-label NCE Loss. For the reason that one sentence may contain multiple entities, we train the retriever using a multi-label variant of noise contrastive estimation (NCE) following [14]. The optimization objective is

$$\max \sum_{e \in \mathcal{E}(x)} \log\left(\frac{\exp(\text{score}_{r1}(x, e))}{\exp(\text{score}_{r1}(x, e)) + \sum_{e' \in \text{N}(\mathcal{E}, x)} \exp(\text{score}_{r1}(x, e'))}\right)$$

where $\text{N}(\mathcal{E}, x) \subset \mathcal{E} \setminus \mathcal{E}(x)$ is a set of negative examples that excludes all gold entities $\mathcal{E}(x)$.

Hard Negative Sampling. To retrieve entities of high quality, the hard negative sampling strategy is adopted. Instead of randomly sampling negative examples, we use the model from the last iteration to generate negative examples. It has been proved that the high-score negative examples can significantly help polish up the model. For this shared task, the negative examples are sampled randomly for the first iteration, while hard negative examples are mined for the next two iterations.

3.2   Knowledge Enhanced NER

The Knowledge Enhanced NER module extracts entity mentions for a sentence. In addition to the sentence itself, the contexts of the sentence in a speech and the retrieved candidate entities are also used as input. We also tried to use the audio but no significant improvement was revealed. We formulate NER as a sequence labeling task and the classical model BERT-CRF is adopted in our method.

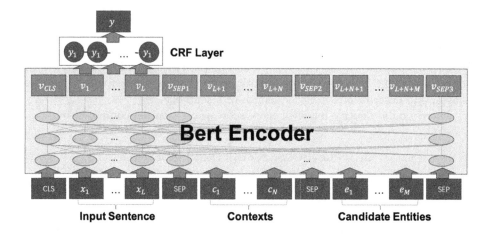

Fig. 2. BERT-CRF model with extra context and candidate entities as input.

As depicted in Fig. 2, we simply concatenate a sentence, its context and retrieved candidate entities (using its title, aliases and descriptions) as input to the BERT encoder:

$$\hat{x} = [\text{CLS}] \; x \; [\text{SEP}] \; \text{ctx}(x) \; [\text{SEP}] \; \hat{\mathcal{E}}_1(x) \; \hat{\mathcal{E}}_2(x) \; ... \; \hat{\mathcal{E}}_M(x) \; [\text{SEP}]$$

where $\hat{\mathcal{E}}_i(x) = \text{title}(\mathcal{E}_i(x)) \; \text{alias}(\mathcal{E}_i(x)) \; \text{desc}(\mathcal{E}_i(x))$ denotes the text representation of the ith retrieved candidate entity of x.

Experimental results prove that simple method works as well. The extra information brought by contexts and candidate entities can help generate better sentence representation. Then we drop other embeddings from contexts or candidate entities, and only keep the raw sentence embeddings for decoding. A CRF layer is used as the decoder to model the transition of tags.

3.3   Linking with Filtering

A common linking module focuses on linking and disambiguating the given mentions to entities from a KB. In addition to that, our proposed Linking with Filtering module also tries to solve the problem when the given mentions are noisy and might contain errors.

Following the mainstream framework, a bi-encoder is used for retrieval and a cross-encoder is used for disambiguation or ranking. The bi-encoder independently embeds the mention context and the entity descriptions so candidate entities can be retrieved in a dense space. Each candidate is then examined more carefully with a cross-encoder, that concatenates the mention and entity text for encoding their correlation.

Two additional entities are added to the provided KB: NIL and ERROR. NIL is used for those mentions that are actually named entities but cannot be found in the given KB. ERROR is used for some other mentions that are not named entities. This is designed to filter out the possible prediction errors generated by NER modules. As gold mentions are given, ERROR is not applied in Track 2.

Hard Negative Sampling. We also used the same hard negative sampling strategy as we do in Sect. 3.1 for training the bi-encoder, despite of their inputs for the encoder differ.

List-Wise Loss. Instead of point-wise or pair-wise losses, we adopt the list-wise loss for training the cross-encoder, which computes the Kullback-Leibler divergence (KL divergence) to explicitly measure the difference between the predicted and target distributions.

Dynamic Sampling. Aiming to reduce the size of candidates for disambiguation while keeping the candidate entities hard to disambiguate, we propose a dynamic sampling strategy that samples candidates with different probabilities. The higher retrieval score one candidate gets, the higher probability it is sampled.

3.4 Ensemble Methods

Ensemble methods are used twice in the end2end entity linking procedure. The first time it is used to gather NER models to generate better results and the second time it works for the disambiguation models to re-rank the candidate entities.

We ensemble the NER models in two strategies using voting. One is for better F1 score and the other is for better recall. We count the predicted tags for each token from all models and determine the final tag by the distribution. The F1 strategy takes "O" as a normal tag when voting wile the recall strategy sets a threshold for "O" so that it's less probable to predict a "O" tag. With our proposed Linking with Filtering module, there's no need to worry about the noise.

The linking models are ensembled in a hybrid way. Not only the last ranking scores are used, but also the retrieval scores are taken into consideration. We re-rank the candidates with the weighted sum of retrieval and ranking scores and obtain the final linking results.

4 Experiments

4.1 Data Analysis and Experimental Settings

The task provides annotated training data, unlabeled test data and the corresponding audios. All corpus provided are obtained from TED talks[1]. It also provides a knowledge base from Wikidata[2].

---

[1] https://www.ted.com/talks.
[2] http://www.wikidata.org/.

Track 1 and Track 2 share a training set consisting of 1936 talks. The statistics of the training and test data is shown in Table 1.

Table 1. Dataset statistics.

Data	Sentence number	Avg. sentence length	Avg. mention number
Train	223348	32.16	1.40
Track1 test	2905	37.99	–
Track2 test	2923	38.64	1.49

No validation set is provided. So we manually split the full training set into 4:1 for training and validation. The tuning and ablation studies are all conducted on our validation set.

The provided knowledge base has a high recall of 95%. We check the rest 5% entities which are linked to NIL and find their corresponding wiki pages don't exists veritably. So the official knowledge base is the only KB used in our system.

The main pretrained models we use for NER and ED are RoBERTa-large[3] and co-condenser-wiki[4] respectively.

In our NER model, the top-16 candidate entities are utilized as extra context for it achieves a relatively high recall of 93% and the transformer structure cannot handle too long inputs.

4.2   Main Results

The evaluation results on test sets of Track 1 and Track 2 are released by the organizer. As shown as Tables 2 and 3, our system achieves 1st place in Track 1 and 2nd place in Track 2 of NLPCC-2022 Shared Task 2.

As we can see that, the performance of our system in Track 2 is comparable (−0.16pt) with the 1st place system. However in Track 1 of Entity Recognition and Disambiguation, we beat the 2nd and 3rd place system by 2.9pt and 10.7pt, which proves the advantage of our proposed KENER method. Due to the task difference of Track 1 and Track 2, we can conclude that this advantage stems from the knowledge introduced in the NER stage.

Table 2. Track1 submission results.

System name	F1
Ours	0.7460
HITsz_TMG	0.7172
xmu-nlp-team	0.6390

---

[3] https://huggingface.co/roberta-large.

[4] https://huggingface.co/Luyu/co-condenser-wiki.

Table 3. Track2 submission results.

System name	F1
HITsz_TMG	0.8884
Ours	0.8868

4.3   Ablation Study

We conduct three ablation studies to validate the effectiveness of individual components of our framework. Concretely, we first investigate the influence of retrieval methods. The results are shown in Table 4, where stage 1 and stage 3 denote retrieval without mentions and with mentions respectively. We can see that: (1) The hard negative mining is critical for both the candidate entity retriever and the entity linking. The iterative hard negatives can lead to further improvements. (2) It is important to excluding gold entities in the normalization term of NCE, which leads to a massive increase in Recall@1 (38.44).

To further understand how the retrieval module affects our framework, we investigate the NER performances for different retrieval-augmented strategies. We train and evaluate the model with various contexts. The results are shown in Table 5. We can observe that all these contexts leads to significantly improvements, especially for the external TED context. This indicates that the document-level information is more important for NER.

Table 6 shows an ablation study for the entity linking module. We report the Accuracy on the validation set of the Track 2 dataset. https://www.overleaf. com/project/6296dabd0707d3c125b2311a We find that the Hybrid Ensemble method helps boost the results by a large margin, and the List-wise Loss and the Dynamic Sampling Strategy brings additional gains. This experiment result shows that the retriever is critical for the final re-ranking performance.

Table 4. Retrieval experiments.

Stage	Methods	Rec@1	Rec@16	Rec@32	Rec@64	Rec@128
1	Baseline	25.34	53.91	90.16	95.64	96.82
1	w/ Multi-label NCE Loss	38.44	62.19	92.22	95.89	97.04
1	w/ Hard Negative (HN)	59.60	93.24	95.11	96.32	97.66
3	Baseline	56.62	91.73	97.42	98.92	99.12
3	w/ First Stage HN	82.19	95.92	98.14	99.16	99.35
3	w/ Second Stage HN	83.23	97.65	98.54	99.31	99.47

Table 5. NER experiments.

Methods	F1
Ours	70.31
w/o Context	69.63
w/o Hard negative	68.19
w/o Candidate entities	68.32
w/o Context & Candidate entities	67.21
w/ Ensemble	71.09

Table 6. Disambiguation experiments.

Methods	F1
Ours	85.71
w/o List-wise loss	85.33
w/o Dynamic sampling	85.15
w/ Hybrid ensemble	86.98

5   Conclusions

In this paper, we propose a novel knowledge enhanced method called KENER, which aims to leverage knowledge in the NER phase to improve the overall performance of entity linking. It consists of three-stage modules, each focusing on one question we raise in Sect. 1. We attribute KENER's outperformance to the following reasons: (1) The hard-negative sampling strategy and multi-label NCE loss can contribute to better retrieval results. (2) The NER model benefits greatly from the retrieved candidate entities. (3) The filtering mechanism is good when the input contains noisy mentions. There are also scopes for improvement in our approach. Currently the three stages are trained separately, which ignores the internal correlation among them. We are looking forward to a unified solution that formulates the NER and ED in one framework.

References

1. Lafferty, J.D., McCallum, A., Pereira, F.: Conditional random fields: probabilistic models for segmenting and labeling sequence data. In: ICML (2001)
2. Devlin, J., Chang, M., Lee, K., Toutanova, K.: BERT: pre-training of deep bidirectional transformers for language understanding. arXiv, abs/1810.04805 (2019)
3. Akbik, A., Bergmann, T., Blythe, D.A., Rasul, K., Schweter, S., Vollgraf, R.: FLAIR: an easy-to-use framework for state-of-the-art NLP. In: NAACL (2019)
4. Yamada, I., Asai, A., Shindo, H., Takeda, H., Matsumoto, Y.: LUKE: deep contextualized entity representations with entity-aware self-attention. In: EMNLP (2020)
5. Yu, J., Bohnet, B., Poesio, M.: Named entity recognition as dependency parsing. In: ACL (2020)

6. Wang, X., et al.: Improving named entity recognition by external context retrieving and cooperative learning. In: ACL (2021)
7. Rao, D., McNamee, P., Dredze, M.: Entity linking: finding extracted entities in a knowledge base. In: Multi-source, Multilingual Information Extraction and Summarization (2013)
8. Karpukhin, V., et al.: Dense passage retrieval for open-domain question answering. arXiv, abs/2004.04906 (2020)
9. Wu, L.Y., Petroni, F., Josifoski, M., Riedel, S., Zettlemoyer, L.: Scalable zero-shot entity linking with dense entity retrieval. In: EMNLP (2020)
10. Chen, S., Wang, J., Jiang, F., Lin, C.: Improving entity linking by modeling latent entity type information. In: AAAI (2020)
11. Kolitsas, N., Ganea, O., Hofmann, T.: End-to-end neural entity linking. arXiv, abs/1808.07699 (2018)
12. Martins, P.H., Marinho, Z., Martins, A.F.: Joint learning of named entity recognition and entity linking. arXiv, abs/1907.08243 (2019)
13. De Cao, N., Izacard, G., Riedel, S., Petroni, F.: Autoregressive entity retrieval. arXiv, abs/2010.00904 (2021)
14. Zhang, W., Hua, W., Stratos, K.: EntQA: entity linking as question answering. arXiv, abs/2110.02369 (2021)
15. Johnson, J., Douze, M., Jégou, H.: Billion-scale similarity search with GPUs. IEEE Trans. Big Data **7**, 535–547 (2021)

Overview of the NLPCC2022 Shared Task on Speech Entity Linking

Ruoyu Song, Sijia Zhang, Xiaoyu Tian, and Yuhang Guo$^{(\boxtimes)}$

School of Computer Science and Technology, Beijing Institute of Technology, Beijing, China
{songruoyu,zhangsijia,tianxiaoyu,guoyuhang}@bit.edu.cn

Abstract. In this paper, we present an overview of the NLPCC 2022 Shared Task on Speech Entity Linking. This task aims to study entity linking methods for spoken languages. This speech entity linking task includes two tracks: Entity Recognition and Disambiguation (track 1), Entity Disambiguation-Only (track 2). 20 teams registered in the challenging task, and the top system achieved 0.7460 F1 in track 1 and 0.8884 in track 2. In this paper, we present the task description, dataset description, team submission ranking and results and analyze the results.

Keywords: Information extraction · Spoken language · Entity linking

1 Introduction

Spoken language is the main language form that people use in their daily lives. Ambiguity frequently occurs in entities mentioned in spoken language. For example, "Ronaldo" can refer to "Ronaldo Luiz nazario de Lima" or "Cristiano Ronaldo dos Santos Aveiro" according to different contexts. These ambiguous mentions can be linked to unambiguous entities in the knowledge base through the task of entity linking (EL), which aims to help information extraction, question answering, and machine translation [1].

Spoken text transcribed from audio is usually informal, case intensive and without punctuation, which brings new challenges to the entity linking task. Therefore, improving the effect of entity linking according to the unstructured characteristics of transcripts is of great significance to the development of oral comprehension and entity linking tasks.

In this task, we construct a new entity linking dataset for the spoken language domain based on TED talks. This speech entity linking task contains two tracks: Entity Recognition and Disambiguation (track 1), Entity Disambiguation-Only (track 2) and all teams registered were allowed to participate in one or multiple tracks. Eventually, 20 teams registered, three teams submitted track 1 results, and two teams submitted track 2 results. We briefly describe the task and the dataset of each track in Sects. 3 and 4 separately, and analyze the submission results in detail in Sect. 5.

W. Lu et al. (Eds.) NLPCC 2022, LNCS 13552, pp. 294–299, 2022.
https://doi.org/10.1007/978-3-031-17189-5_25

2   Related Work

There are many commonly used datasets for entity linking in different fields. As one of the largest artificial annotation entity link datasets, Hofart proposed AIDA-CoNLL [2], which takes Yago as the knowledge base. The TAC-KBP2010 dataset was constructed for the Text Analysis Conference (TAC) [3]. Omar et al. [5] created a multimodal entity linking dataset with text and pictures. There is a lack of publicly available entity linking datasets for spoken language and speech.

Entity linking generally consists of candidate entity generation and entity ranking. When knowledge base is wikidata or wikipedia, the common method of candidate entity generation is to use alias information in the knowledge base to generate the map of mention and entity [12].

Entity disambiguation is usually based on the pre-trained model to calculate the text similarity between mention and candidate entity [6,7,9], or regarded as a sentence pair classification task [8]. It has also been studied to find out the possible entities corresponding to the sentence first, and then extract the mention corresponding to the entity from the text [10].

3   Task Description

Entity Linking is the task of recognizing (i.e. Named Entity Recognition) and disambiguating (i.e. Named Entity Disambiguation) named entities to a knowledge base. According to whether the task contains named entity recognition, we divide the task into two tracks: Entity Recognition and Disambiguation and Entity Disambiguation-Only. Our knowledge base is wikidata.

3.1   Track 1: Entity Recognition and Disambiguation

Entity Recognition and Disambiguation processes a piece of utterance and the corresponding transcript to extract the entities (i.e. Named Entity Recognition) and then disambiguate these extracted entities to the correct entry in a given knowledge base. The input and output are as follows:

Input: An utterance and the corresponding transcript.

Output: All named entities in the input and their linked entries in the KB. Each result includes: entity mention, entity type, mention offset in the text, and knowledge base ID (KB_ID) corresponding to the mention.

Note that a system is expected to recognize the most complete entity rather than multiple nested entities. As shown in Fig. 1, given an utterance of speech and the corresponding transcript: "i love harry potter and the deathly hallows", a system is expected to recognize an entity "harry potter and the deathly hallows" of type "Work" instead of "harry potter" of type "Person". And it refers to a KB entity "Harry Potter and the Deathly Hallows", whose KB_ID is Q46758.

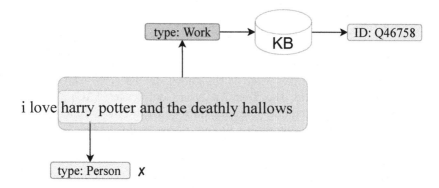

Fig. 1. An example of Entity Linking. This blue entity is nested inside the red entity and should not be recognized by the system (Color figure online)

3.2 Track 2: Entity Disambiguation-Only

Entity Disambiguation-Only directly takes gold standard named entities as input and only disambiguates them to the correct entry in a given knowledge base. The input and output are as follows:

Input: An utterance with the corresponding transcript and a entity mention list containing all entity mentions in it. In the list, each element includes: entity mention, entity type, and mention offset in the text.

Input: KB_ID results of all entity mentions in the mention list.

As shown in Fig. 2, given an utterance of speech and the corresponding transcript: "washington was the first president of the united states." and a mention list containing two mentions: "washington" and "the united states", a system is expected to link "washington" to a KB entity "George Washington", whose KB_ID is Q23 and link "the united state" to a KB entity "United States of America", whose KB_ID is Q30.

Note that a mention in the text cannot be linked to two or more knowledge base entities. If no candidate entity matches the current mention, it will be labeled as "NULL". It's expected to recognize the most complete entity rather than multiple nested entities.

4 Dataset Description

Based on TED-LIUM Release 3 dataset [11], which is commonly used in speech recognition tasks, we annotated entity information with wikidata as knowledge base. At last, this corpus consists of 2351 Ted talks. The audio and corresponding transcripts are available at https://lium.univ-lemans.fr/en/ted-lium3/.

We divided the dataset into one training set and two test sets. The two tracks share the training set with 1936 talks. The test set of track 1 and track 2 contains 151 and 149 talks, respectively. It is worth noting that the speakers of the three datasets do not overlap.

We provided a basic KB, and its recall can achieve 0.95.

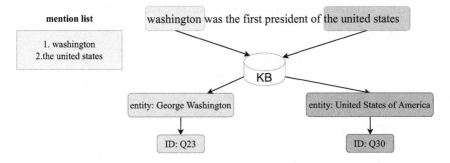

Fig. 2. An example of Entity Linking provided a mention list, one in red and one in green, both of which are expected to be recognized by the system. (Color figure online)

5   Result

5.1   Evaluation Metrics

We calculate the F_1 score and accuracy (Acc) in the track 1 and track 2 respectively. In track 2, Acc and F_1 are equal.

Let $E_{i=\{}\{e_1, e_2, \cdots, e_n\}$ denote the predicted KB_ID set of the ith input, and $E_i' = \{e_1', e_2', \cdots, e_m'\}$ denote the golden KB_ID set of the ith input. In track 2, m and n are both equal to the size of the given mention list. The precision (P), recall (R), F_1 and accuracy (Acc) are computed as following formulas:

$$P = \frac{\sum_{i \in I} |E_i \cap E_i'|}{\sum_{i \in I} |E_i|} \tag{1}$$

$$R = \frac{\sum_{i \in I} |E_i \cap E_i'|}{\sum_{i \in I} |E_i'|} \tag{2}$$

$$F_1 = \frac{2 * P * R}{P + R} \tag{3}$$

$$Acc = \frac{\sum_{i \in I} |E_i \cap E_i'|}{\sum_{i \in I} |E_i|} = \frac{\sum_{i \in I} |E_i \cap E_i'|}{\sum_{i \in I} |E_i'|} \tag{4}$$

where I is the size of the dataset.

5.2   Participants and Results

In total, there are 20 teams registered for this task, in which 3 and 2 teams submitted their final results respectively in track 1 and track 2. Tables 1 and 2 show the rankings and scores of track 1 and track 2 respectively.

Table 1. The performance of participants on Track 1.

System name	Organization	F1
AliceMind	Alibaba DAMO NLP Group	0.7460
HITsz_TMG	Harbin Institute of Technology, Shenzhen	0.7172
xmu-nlp-team	Xiamen University	0.6390

Table 2. The performance of participants on Track 2, *Acc* and F_1 are equal.

System name	Organization	F1/Acc
HITsz_TMG	Harbin Institute of Technology, Shenzhen	0.8884
AliceMind	Alibaba DAMO NLP Group	0.8868

5.3 Analysis

Track 1. In the traditional end-to-end entity linking method, the first step is to find mention spans needed to disambiguate, and then do mention disambiguation (i.e. track 2) [4,14]. However, the top 2 teams both used a different method, which first recalls candidate entities with a fast retrieval module, and then find mentions of each candidate entity with a powerful reader module.

Besides, the AliceMind team uses model ensemble, and the HITsz_TMG team uses cross validation method. All teams did not use audio to help the entity disambiguation.

Track 2. The scores submitted by the two teams of track 2 are similar. We focus on analyzing the cause where they made common errors. First, all teams recall candidate entities for each mention based on a bi-encoder [13], and the large number of candidate entities make it difficult for the disambiguation. Another important factor is the length of the text. 30% of the error cases are short texts (we consider sentences less than 20 in length as short texts), which leaves not enough context for the disambiguation. At last, we found that the accuracy of the NULL entities is only 0.71 for both of teams.

We also observed that the average F1 for track 2 is about 0.15 higher than track 1, which means the challenge of mention detection.

6 Conclusion

Aiming at improving the effect of entity linking according to the unstructured characteristics of transcripts, we construct and release an entity linking dataset based on TED talks, and design two tracks of Entity Recognition and Disambiguation and Entity Disambiguation-Only. 20 teams registered for this task, and we showed and analyzed the results of the team submissions.

From the submitted results, the F1 of track 2 is about 0.15 higher than track 1 on average, which shows the difficulty of mention detection. Furthermore, no team uses the aligned audio data for the task yet, which leaves the fusion of the multimodal features for the future study.

Acknowledgments. This work is supported by the National Key R&D Program of China (No. 2020AAA0106600).

References

1. Sevgili, Ö., Shelmanov, A., Arkhipov, M., et al.: Neural entity linking: a survey of models based on deep learning. Semantic Web 1–44 (2022). (Preprint)
2. Hoffart, J., Yosef, M.A., Bordino, I., et al.: Robust disambiguation of named entities in text. In: Proceedings of the 2011 Conference on Empirical Methods in Natural Language Processing, pp. 782–792 (2011)
3. Ji, H., Grishman, R., Dang, H.T., et al.: Overview of the TAC 2010 knowledge base population track. In: Third Text Analysis Conference (TAC 2010), vol. 3(2), p. 3 (2010)
4. Ravi, M.P.K., Singh, K., Mulang, I.O., et al.: Cholan: a modular approach for neural entity linking on Wikipedia and Wikidata. arXiv preprint arXiv:2101.09969 (2021)
5. Liu, X., Li, Y., Wu, H., et al.: Entity linking for tweets. In: Proceedings of the 51st Annual Meeting of the Association for Computational Linguistics (Volume 1: Long Papers), pp. 1304–1311 (2013)
6. Ganea, O.E., Hofmann, T.: Deep joint entity disambiguation with local neural attention. arXiv preprint arXiv:1704.04920 (2017)
7. Gupta, N., Singh, S., Roth, D.: Entity linking via joint encoding of types, descriptions, and context. In: Proceedings of the Conference on Empirical Methods in Natural Language Processing, pp. 2681–2690 (2017)
8. Logeswaran, L., Chang, M.W., Lee, K., et al.: Zero-shot entity linking by reading entity descriptions. arXiv preprint arXiv:1906.07348 (2019)
9. Wu, L., Petroni, F., Josifoski, M., et al.: Scalable zero-shot entity linking with dense entity retrieval. arXiv preprint arXiv:1911.03814 (2019)
10. Zhang, W., Hua, W., Stratos, K.: EntQA: entity linking as question answering. arXiv preprint arXiv:2110.02369 (2021)
11. Hernandez, F., Nguyen, V., Ghannay, S., Tomashenko, N., Estève, Y.: TED-LIUM 3: twice as much data and corpus repartition for experiments on speaker adaptation. In: Karpov, A., Jokisch, O., Potapova, R. (eds.) SPECOM 2018. LNCS (LNAI), vol. 11096, pp. 198–208. Springer, Cham (2018). https://doi.org/10.1007/978-3-319-99579-3_21
12. Varma, V., Bysani, P., Reddy, K., et al.: IIIT Hyderabad in guided summarization and knowledge base population. In: TAC (2010)
13. Humeau, S., Shuster, K., Lachaux, M.A., et al.: Poly-encoders: transformer architectures and pre-training strategies for fast and accurate multi-sentence scoring. arXiv preprint arXiv:1905.01969 (2019)
14. De Cao, N., Aziz, W., Titov, I.: Highly parallel autoregressive entity linking with discriminative correction. arXiv preprint arXiv:2109.03792 (2021)

Overview of the NLPCC 2022 Shared Task on Multimodal Product Summarization

Haoran Li[✉], Peng Yuan, Haoning Zhang, Weikang Li, Song Xu,
Youzheng Wu, and Xiaodong He

JD AI Research, Beijing, China
{lihaoran24,yuanpeng29,zhanghaoning}@jd.com

Abstract. We introduce the NLPCC 2022 shared task on multimodal product summarization. This task aims at generating a condensed textual summary for a given product. The input contains a detailed product description, a product knowledge base, and a product image. 29 teams register the task, among which 5 teams submit the results. In this paper, we present the task definition, the dataset, and the evaluation results for this shared task.

Keywords: Shared task · Multimodal · Summarization

1 Introduction

The increasing information overload across the Internet hinders users from accessing and comprehending the information they need. An automatic summarization system can provide the key contents of the input in a short time, which is necessary to address the problem of information overload. For the e-commerce scenarios, the product advertisement is a critical component of marketing management, while miscellaneous product descriptions take customers too much time to understand the detailed product characteristics that they care about, which hurts their consumption experience. Product summarization [3,15,17] is of practical value for customers saving time and e-commerce platforms upgrading the marketing policies.

Despite the rapid development of the text summarization method, especially for the pre-trained language models, there are still many challenges to be solved when applied to the scenarios of e-commerce. First, the appearance of a product plays an important role in a good first impression, which requires the summarizer can effectively fuse the textual and visual information [3,4]. Second, unfaithful product summaries, i.e., producing wrong attributes that are inconsistent with the original product, mislead the users and decrease the public credibility of the e-commerce platform [5,14]. Thus, faithfulness is the bottom line for a product summarization system. Third, to arouse consumers' attention and desire for

W. Lu et al. (Eds.) NLPCC 2022, LNCS 13552, pp. 300–307, 2022.
https://doi.org/10.1007/978-3-031-17189-5_26

purchase, the generated summary should mention the most important characteristics of the product [6,12]. In addition, the generated text should be eminently
readable and none so redundant. The teams participating in the shared task are
expected to solve these challenges.

2 Task Definition

We define the task as generating a product summary given multimodal heterogeneous information, including a piece of product textual description composed
of a brief product title and a long product description, a product knowledge
base containing information about product attributes, and a product image. An
example is shown in Appendix A.

3 Dataset

The dataset is collected from JD.COM, a mainstream Chinese e-commerce platform. Each sample is a (product textual description, product knowledge base,
product image, product summary) tuple. The dataset contains three product categories, including Cases&Bags, Home Appliances, and Clothing. Dataset statistics are shown in Table 1.

Table 1. Dataset statistics.

	Cases&Bags	Home appliances	Clothing
# Train	50000	100000	200000
# Valid	10000	10000	10000
# Test	10000	10000	10000
# Input token/sample	319.0	336.6	294.8
# product attribute/sample	14.8	7.8	7.3
# product image/sample	1	1	1
# Summary token/sample	79.5	79.4	78.2

4 Evaluation

The evaluation consists of two stages, an automatic evaluation, and a human
evaluation. For automatic evaluation, we adopt the metrics of ROUGE [7].
Specifically, we use ROUGE-1.5.5 toolkit to evaluate the generated summaries,
and we calculate the average score of ROUGE-1, ROUGE-2, and ROUGE-L F1
scores. We select the top-5 teams regarding the ROUGE to advance to the second round of evaluation, i.e., the human evaluation. For the human evaluation,
we evaluate faithfulness, readability, non-redundancy, and importance, for 100
random sampled summaries in each category. Details about the human evaluation are shown in Table 2. The final ranking is determined by the average score
of the human evaluation.

Table 2. An example from the dataset.

Faithfulness	0 = unfaithful to the input,
	2 = faithful to the input
Readability	0 = hard to understand,
	1 = partially hard to understand,
	2 = easy to understand
Non-redundancy	0 = full of redundant information,
	1 = partially redundant information,
	2 = no redundant information
Importance	0 = no useful information,
	1 = partially useful information,
	2 = totally useful information

5   Participants

Overall, 29 teams register the shared task, and 5 teams submit the results to the task leaderboard[1]. Table 3 displays an overview of the teams submitting the results.

Table 3. Participants of the shared task.

Team ID	Model ID	Institute
Huawei	Arrival	Huawei Technologies Co., Ltd.
xmu-nlp_lab	adakplug	School of informatics, Xiamen University
NEU_CSE	VG_CPT	School of Computer Science And Engineering, Northeastern University
Panda	UniLM	Knowdee Intelligence
CPIC	Pegasus	China Pacific Insurance (Group) Co., Ltd

Arrival model adopts BART (chinese-bart-base) model as the backbone. Image features are extracted by ViT model [1] and are integrated into the last three encoder layer of the BART model following VG-GPLMs [13]. To accelerate convergence, the BART model is continually pre-trained with the text of the product description and product summary. To promote the performance, model soups [10] is applied to ensemble multiple models by averaging weights of them.

adakplug model adopts K-PLUG [11] (base model) as the backbone, training with two phrases. The first phrase trains a cross-modal alignment, and the second trains a multimodal summary generator. For the first phrase, textual K-PLUG is frozen. Image features are extracted by ResNet and are then injected into K-PLUG with adapter layer [9], which consists of two blocks, each of them

---

[1] https://jd-nlg-rhino.github.io/.

containing two projection layers and two transformer layers. A pair of a product image and a product summary is taken as a positive sample, and unpaired ones are negative. The multimodal summary generator in the second phrase concatenates the output of the text encoder and image encoder. The decoder is the same as the original K-PLUG.

VG_CPT model adopts CPT [8] (large model) as the backbone. Image features are extracted by ResNet-101 model [2] and are fused to the last two encoder layer of the CPT model following VG-GPLMs [13]. Product description and attribute are concatenated as the input.

Pegasus model adopts PEGASUS [16] as the backbone. Product images are not involved. The model converts the product attribute into a natural text before it is fed into the encoder. For example, "材质：纯棉" (Material: Purified cotton) is converted into "纯棉的材质" (The material of pure cotton).

Baseline K-PLUG [11] is a Transformer-based seq2seq model that is pretrained on a large-scale e-commerce corpus. We extend the textual K-PLUG to a multimodal version. Image features are extracted by the ResNet-101 model and are weighted merged with the <SOS> embeddings in the decoder.

6 Results

6.1 Automatic Evaluation Results

The automatic evaluation is conducted by ROUGE-1.5.5 toolkit, and the results are shown in Table 4. We can find that Arrival is the best model that achieves 23.19% average ROUGE score, outperforming the baseline K-PLUG model by 1.11% ROUGE score. 4 teams achieve better performances than the baseline.

6.2 Human Evaluation Results

We plan to perform the human evaluation for the top-5 teams regarding the ROUGE score. Since there are a total of 5 teams that submit the results, in fact, we evaluate the results of all the teams by human annotators who are well-trained before evaluation. During the process of evaluation, all the results from 5 teams are anonymous and shuffled, each annotator scores the samples independently, and finally, the participants are ranked with the average scores. The human evaluation results (i.e., the final rankings) are shown in Table 5.

Comparing automatic and human evaluation results, we find that most of them are consistent with each other. Note that the model of Arrival achieves the best ROUGE score, while due to some incomplete generated summaries, its human evaluation scores of Readability are much lower than others, leading to ranking 4th in the end.

Table 4. Automatic evaluation results (F1 score, %). ∗ denotes that the team submits prediction results rather than models, while others submit the models.

Model ID	Category	RG-1	RG-2	RG-L	Average
Arrival∗	Cases&Bags	34.52	12.61	21.30	23.19
	home appliances	34.83	13.49	22.45	
	clothing	34.83	13.45	21.23	
VG_CPT∗	Cases&Bags	34.22	11.95	22.45	22.95
	home appliances	34.37	13.30	22.80	
	clothing	33.58	11.95	21.95	
adakplug	Cases&Bags	34.03	11.46	22.06	22.68
	home appliances	34.03	12.79	22.27	
	clothing	33.78	11.83	21.88	
Pegasus	Cases&Bags	33.91	10.83	21.62	22.47
	home appliances	33.83	12.08	21.48	
	clothing	34.73	11.87	21.89	
K-PLUG	Cases&Bags	33.27	10.96	21.61	22.08
	home appliances	33.54	12.19	21.94	
	clothing	33.03	10.93	21.22	
UniLM∗	Cases&Bags	31.08	9.78	21.10	18.84
	home appliances	21.27	6.73	15.97	
	clothing	31.85	10.31	21.49	

Table 5. Final ranking based on the human evaluation results (F1 score, %). "Imp.", "N-red.", "Read.", and "Faith" are short for "Importance", "Non-redundancy", "Readability", and "Faithfulness", respectively.

Rank	Team ID	Model ID	Imp.	N-red.	Read.	Faith.	Average
1	NEU_CSE	VG_CPT	1.61	1.96	2.00	1.64	1.8025
2	xmu-nlp_lab	adakplug	1.62	1.97	1.98	1.60	1.7925
3	CPIC	Pegasus	1.67	1.92	1.92	1.64	1.7875
4	Huawei	Arrival	1.73	1.63	0.75	1.74	1.4625
5	Panda	UniLM	1.48	1.04	0.51	1.72	1.1875

7   Conclusion

We introduce the task definition, the dataset, and the evaluation for NLPCC 2022 shared task on multimodal product summarization. 5 teams submit the results, among which 4 teams outperform the baseline K-PLUG model. Most of the teams prove that visual features are effective for this task. The Arrival model with BART as the backbone obtains the best ROUGE score. VG_CPT model with CPT as the backbone obtains the best human evaluation score, which achieves the champion of the shared task.

We can conclude that:

– Models built upon multimodal information beat the textual model, indicating that image features are useful for this task.
– The approach to extracting visual representations plays an important role in improving performance, e.g., ViT could be better than ResNet (refer to the models of Arrival and VG_CPT).
– Before integrating the image features into textual pretrained models, visual representations should be switched to adaptive mode with regard to a textual one.
– Human evaluation is necessary for product summarization tasks. ROUGE score cannot judge the readability for some cases like generating incomplete text.

In the future, the task leaderboard[2] will be maintained to encourage researchers to promote the study of the multimodal product summarization. We are also thinking about other related challenges, including generating longer documents and generating summaries with controllable styles.

A   An Example from the Dataset

An example from the dataset is shown in Table 6.

---

[2] https://jd-nlg-rhino.github.io/.

Table 6. An example from the dataset.

Input text	TCL D49A630U 49英寸超薄金属机身30核HDR 4K超清智能电视机（黑色）一个化繁为简的系统，暗的更暗，亮的更亮，您再也不会埋怨影片不够看了，4K超高清+全生态HDR，金属压铸支架，浑然天成的品质感，4K超高清屏幕，这是89万像素RGB真4K，30核心，性能再度升级，4K大屏新旗舰电视，让场景接近您感受的真实度，64位电视处理器，20000转/分高速打磨，硬解码，全新升级，电视不止更薄，显示还更出色，金属纤薄机身，丰富接口，45°纹钻切工艺，4K超高清内容，一体成型LG0，强大的扩展能力，HDr实时转化，全生态HDR，24小时更新不断，金属外观设计，精美的UI设计，海量影视资源，集成了主页、影视、生活等。 (TCL D49A630U 49 inch ultra-thin metal body 30 core HDR 4K ultra clear smart TV (black) is a simplified system. The dark is darker and the bright is brighter. You will never complain about not watching enough movies. 4K ultra high definition + full ecological HDR, metal die-casting bracket, a sense of natural quality, 4K ultra high definition screen, which is 890,000 pixels RGB true 4K, 30 core, performance upgraded again, 4K large screen new flagship TV, making the scene close to the reality you feel. 64 bit TV processor, 20000 RPM high-speed polishing, hard decoding, new upgrade, TV is not only thinner, but also better display. Metal thin body, rich interfaces, 45° grain drilling and cutting process, 4K ultra-high definition content, one-piece LG0, strong expansion capability, real-time HDR conversion, full ecological HDR, 24-hour update, metal appearance design, exquisite UI design, Massive film and television resources, integrating home page, film and television, and life.)
Product image	
Product attribute	能效等级：3级 (Energy efficiency grade: Grade 3) 电视类型：4K超清 (TV type: 4K ultra clear) 屏幕尺寸：49英寸 (Screen size: 49 inches) HDR显示：支持HDR (HDR display: support HDR)
Output summary	这款TCL智能液晶电视，海量片库，任你观看。4K高清画质，画面更加清晰，给你身临其境之感。搭载画质新宠HDR技术，还原真实自然的画面。 (This TCL smart LCD TV has a huge film library for you to watch. 4K high-definition picture quality makes the picture clearer and gives you an immersive feeling. Equipped with HDR technology, this TV restores real and natural images.)

References

1. Dosovitskiy, A., et al.: An image is worth 16×16 words: transformers for image recognition at scale. In: ICLR (2020)
2. He, K., Zhang, X., Ren, S., Sun, J.: Deep residual learning for image recognition. In: CVPR, pp. 770–778 (2016)
3. Li, H., Yuan, P., Xu, S., Wu, Y., He, X., Zhou, B.: Aspect-aware multimodal summarization for Chinese e-commerce products. In: AAAI, pp. 8188–8195 (2020)
4. Li, H., Zhu, J., Zhang, J., He, X., Zong, C.: Multimodal sentence summarization via multimodal selective encoding. In: COLING, pp. 5655–5667 (2020)
5. Li, H., Zhu, J., Zhang, J., Zong, C.: Ensure the correctness of the summary: incorporate entailment knowledge into abstractive sentence summarization. In: COLING, pp. 1430–1441 (2018)
6. Li, H., Zhu, J., Zhang, J., Zong, C., He, X.: Keywords-guided abstractive sentence summarization. In: AAAI, pp. 8196–8203 (2020)
7. Lin, C.Y., Hovy, E.: Automatic evaluation of summaries using n-gram co-occurrence statistics. In: Proceedings of NAACL, pp. 150–157 (2003)
8. Shao, Y., et al.: CPT: a pre-trained unbalanced transformer for both Chinese language understanding and generation. arXiv preprint arXiv:2109.05729 (2021)
9. Wang, R., et al.: K-adapter: infusing knowledge into pre-trained models with adapters. In: Findings of ACL, pp. 1405–1418 (2021)
10. Wortsman, M., et al.: Model soups: averaging weights of multiple fine-tuned models improves accuracy without increasing inference time. arXiv preprint arXiv:2203.05482 (2022)
11. Xu, S., et al.: K-plug: Knowledge-injected pre-trained language model for natural language understanding and generation in e-commerce. In: Findings of the Association for Computational Linguistics: EMNLP 2021, pp. 1–17 (2021)
12. Xu, S., Li, H., Yuan, P., Wu, Y., He, X., Zhou, B.: Self-attention guided copy mechanism for abstractive summarization. In: ACL, pp. 1355–1362 (2020)
13. Yu, T., Dai, W., Liu, Z., Fung, P.: Vision guided generative pre-trained language models for multimodal abstractive summarization. In: EMNLP, pp. 3995–4007 (2021)
14. Yuan, P., Li, H., Xu, S., Wu, Y., He, X., Zhou, B.: On the faithfulness for e-commerce product summarization. In: COLING, pp. 5712–5717 (2020)
15. Zhan, H., et al.: Probing product description generation via posterior distillation. In: AAAI, pp. 14301–14309 (2021)
16. Zhang, J., Zhao, Y., Saleh, M., Liu, P.: PEGASUS: pre-training with extracted gap-sentences for abstractive summarization. In: International Conference on Machine Learning, pp. 11328–11339. PMLR (2020)
17. Zhang, X., et al.: Automatic product copywriting for e-commerce. arXiv preprint arXiv:2112.11915 (2021)

A Multi-task Learning Model for Fine-Grain Dialogue Social Bias Measurement

Hanjie Mai, Xiaobing Zhou$^{(\boxtimes)}$, and Liqing Wang

School of Information Science and Engineering, Yunnan University, Kumming, China
zhouxb@ynu.edu.cn

Abstract. In recent years, the use of NLP models to predict people's attitudes toward social bias has attracted the attention of many researchers. In the existing work, most of the research is at the sentence level, i.e., judging whether the whole sentence has a biased property. In this work, we leverage pre-trained models' powerful semantic modeling capabilities to model dialogue context. Furthermore, to use more features to improve the ability of the model to identify bias, we propose two auxiliary tasks with the help of the dialogue's topic and type features. In order to achieve better classification results, we use the adversarial training method to train two multi-task models. Finally, we combine the two multi-task models by voting. We participated in the NLPCC-2022 shared task on Fine-Grain Dialogue Social Bias Measurement and ranked fourth with the Macro-F1 score of 0.5765. The codes of our model are available at github (https://github.com/33Da/nlpcc2022-task7).

Keywords: Social bias measurement · Multi-task learning · Pre-trained language model

1 Introduction

Recently, people have often used social media to express their opinions and discussions with others. Many of these statements are biased. Especially when people talk about gender or race, they tend to be biased. How to identify these prejudiced remarks plays an important role in social development. Therefore, social biases detection [1,2] has attracted many researchers to study. Unlike other unsafe speech, people often express their prejudice implicitly. Therefore, this is a challenging problem.

Most of the previous research is based on the token or utterance level [3,4], and there is very little research on the dialogue level. But in real life, especially on social platforms, bias tends to emerge in the context of dialogue.

Our work studies dialogue-level scenario, which has wider applications in real life. In addition, to improve the accuracy of bias detection, we use multitask learning (MTL) [5], which allows our model to incorporate more features to detect social biases and has a stronger generalization ability. Specifically, we

© Springer Nature Switzerland AG 2022
W. Lu et al. (Eds.) NLPCC 2022, LNCS 13552, pp. 308–319, 2022.
https://doi.org/10.1007/978-3-031-17189-5_27

design two auxiliary tasks to detect the topics of dialogue and types of dialogue, respectively. People tend to be biased when talking about specific topics. We consider these topics to be sensitive, such as when talking about gender or religion. The distribution of attitudes towards bias varies by subject. On the other hand, from the perspective of human thinking, understanding the topic of the dialogue also plays an important role in understanding the semantic information in the dialogue content. Therefore, dialogue topic information is significant for identifying people's attitudes toward bias in conversations. In addition, it is important to distinguish whether a conversation is discussing bias, expressing bias, or irrelevant to our task. As shown in Table 1, we give the difference between these three kinds of dialogues. According to the experiments and conclusions of Zhou et al. [6], it can be seen that distinguishing these two kinds of bias-related data can not only enrich the research of bias recognition tasks but also be important for improving the performance of bias detection.

Table 1. Examples of three types of dialogues. The criteria of classification for each example are also listed.

Taxonomy	Examples	Criteria
Discussing Bias	歧视亚裔最严重的地方当然是亚洲了啊。	Discussion of Asian discrimination.
Expressing Bias	潮汕人读书不多,文化程度不怎么高,经商才能赚钱。	Chaoshan people are not well-educated.
Not relevant	考事业单位当卫生老师我觉得还挺靠谱的。	Relating to the topic Occupation, but not biased.

Finally, to further improve the model's performance, we use an adversarial training method [7] to train the model during the training phase. In order to maximize the role of auxiliary tasks in promoting the main task, we use the voting fusion method to combine the models trained using two different auxiliary tasks. In summary, our main contributions are as follows:

1. We design two auxiliary tasks for the bias detection main task. Using the method of multi-task learning makes the auxiliary task improve the classification effect of the main task.
2. We use adversarial learning and model fusion to improve model classification performance.

We achieve the fourth-place in the NLPCC-2022 subtask 7 with the Macro-F1 score of 0.5765 in the test set. The specific ranking is shown in Table 2. Our system name is "Mark33".

2 Related Work

In recent years, research on social bias detection has received increasing attention [1,2]. This task aims to detect whether utterances contain biased information,

Table 2. The ranking of the NLPCC-2022 shared task on Fine-Grain Dialogue Social Bias Measurement. Only the top five results are shown in the table. A total of 22 teams participated in the task, of which 11 teams submitted the results.

Rank	System name	Score
1	Antins	0.5903
2	BERT 4EVER	0.5902
3	SoCo	0.5798
4	**Mark33**	**0.5765**
5	PAL	0.5746

which is a classification task. For different scenarios, there are different topics of social bias detection, such as gender bias detection [8], racial bias detection [9], etc.

Previous work tends to use Convolutional Neural Network (CNN) or Recurrent Neural Network (RNN) for end-to-end bias prediction [8,10]. After Transformer [11] is proposed, due to its excellent effect, it or its variants [12,13] are often used in bias detection research. The most common practice is to use a fine-tuned pre-trained model to extract high-dimensional vectors and apply these vectors to downstream tasks [14]. Bao et al. [15] discuss the results of fine-tuning parameters with Bert on gender bias detection tasks and the results of treating Bert as a feature extractor without parameter updating.

In addition, it has been widely used in many fields after the concept of multi-task learning was proposed in 1997 [5]. It learns multiple related tasks together and shares the learned features during the learning process, so that the effect of the main task is improved. Many NLP tasks today also use multi-task learning methods. For example, Bert [12] designed two pre-training tasks, masked language Model (MLM) and next sentence prediction (NSP), and pre-trained using multi-task learning. Moore et al. [16] propose to use a multi-task learning approach to combine information from syntactic and semantic auxiliary tasks, resulting in a more robust English Targeted Sentiment Classification. Li et al. [17] propose a multi-task learning network that takes the multi-target stance consistency detection task as an auxiliary task to solve the Multi-Target Stance Detection problem. On the task of social bias detection, there are also some works that use multi-task learning [18].

To sum up, based on previous research, we use the existing dataset to fine-tune the pre-trained model to obtain the embedding vector. Then, we design two auxiliary tasks for bias detection, using multi-task learning and adversarial learning to train the model. Finally, to make full use of auxiliary tasks to improve the main task effect, we also adopt the model fusion method, which combines two models with different auxiliary tasks.

3   Proposed System

This section defines the problem setup and elaborates on our system. The system consists of four modules: text representation module, main task module, auxiliary task module, and model fusion module. In addition, the system can also be regarded as two multi-task models constituted by model fusion. For a more precise explanation below, let Model1 be a multi-task model with type as an auxiliary task, and Model2 be a multi-task model with topic as an auxiliary task.

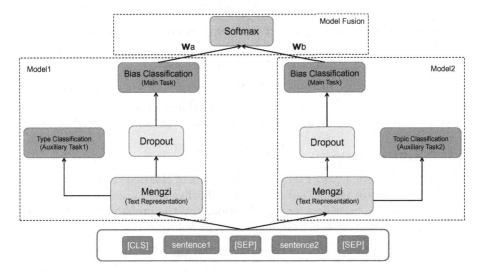

Fig. 1. The overall architecture of our system, which consists of four modules: text representation module, main task module, auxiliary task module and model fusion module.

The architecture of our system is shown in Fig. 1. Details will be described as follows.

3.1   Problem Definition

Given a round of dialogue $s1 = \{w_1^1, w_2^1, \cdots, w_n^1\}$ and $s2 = \{w_1^2, w_2^2, \cdots, w_m^2\}$, in which w_i^j denotes the i-th word in the j-th sentence, n is the length of the first sentence, and m is the length of the second sentence, where $j \in [1, 2]$. We aim to detect the type of bias implicit in each round of dialogue. There are 4 attitudes towards bias (irrelevant, anti-bias, neutral, and biased). Obviously, this is a four-category classification problem. In addition, each round of conversations discussed the content of four topics (race, gender, region, occupation) and the three types of dialogue (irrelevance, bias expression, and bias discussion).

3.2   Text Representation

Benefiting from the excellent performance of Transformers in NLP tasks, we use its variant network Mengzi [19] to map dialogue into higher-dimensional vectors. Specifically, in order to distinguish the dialogue context, $[SEP]$ is used to segment $s1$, $s2$. Then the $[CLS]$ symbol is inserted at the beginning of each dialogue round. In the output of the model, the vector corresponding to this symbol contains the semantic information of this round of dialogue. We use it later for downstream classification tasks. Finally, the $[SEP]$ is inserted at the end of each round of dialogue. The input form is shown in Eq. 1.

$$input = [CLS] + s1 + [SEP] + s2 + [SEP] \tag{1}$$

Through Mengzi, we obtain text representation vectors for both models separately.

$$\hat{h}_{Model1} = Mengzi_{Model1}(input) \tag{2}$$

$$\hat{h}_{Model2} = Mengzi_{Model2}(input) \tag{3}$$

where $\hat{h} \in R^{batch\ size \times d_h}$ is the vector corresponding to the start symbol $[CLS]$, d_h is the size of hidden dimension of Mengzi output, which is set to 768.

3.3   Auxiliary Tasks

As mentioned above, in order to improve the effect of bias detection main task, we introduce auxiliary tasks for our model. Specifically, $\hat{h}_{Model1}$ and $\hat{h}_{Model2}$ are fed to their respective classifiers for classification, and the probability distributions of the two auxiliary tasks are obtained through softmax.

$$output_{Model1}^{auxiliary} = Classification_{Model1}^{auxiliary}(\hat{h}_{Model1}) \tag{4}$$

$$output_{Model2}^{auxiliary} = Classification_{Model2}^{auxiliary}(\hat{h}_{Model2}) \tag{5}$$

where $Classification_{Model1}^{auxiliary}$ and $Classification_{Model2}^{auxiliary}$ represent auxiliary task classifiers for Model1 and Model2, respectively. $output_{Model1}^{auxiliary}$ and $output_{Model2}^{auxiliary}$ denote the outputs of the auxiliary tasks of Model1 and Model2, respectively.

3.4   Main Task

We also use the $[CLS]$ vector for the classification main task. But different from the auxiliary task, we perform a dropout operation on the vector to improve the model's fitting ability for the main task.

$$output_{Model1}^{main} = Classification_{Model1}^{main}(Dropout(\hat{h}_{Model1})) \tag{6}$$

$$output_{Model2}^{main} = Classification_{Model2}^{main}(Dropout(\hat{h}_{Model2})) \tag{7}$$

where $Classification_{Model1}^{main}$ and $Classification_{Model2}^{main}$ represent main task classifiers for Model1 and Model2, respectively. $output_{Model1}^{main}$ and $output_{Model2}^{main}$ denote the outputs of the main tasks of Model1 and Model2, respectively.

3.5   Model Fusion

In order to combine the two auxiliary tasks to improve the classification effect of the main task, we use weighted voting to obtain the final output from the outputs of the two models with different auxiliary tasks. Specifically, we perform a weighted sum of the bias classification output probabilities of the two models. The result is then mapped to the interval $[0, 1]$ through softmax, representing the classification probability.

$$output = Softmax(W_a * output_{Model1}^{main} + W_b * output_{Model2}^{main}) \tag{8}$$

where W_a and W_b are hyperparameters, representing the weight of the auxiliary model.

3.6   Adversarial Training

In this paper, we use the Projected Gradient Descent (PGD) method [20] for training, which is considered to be the best in first-order adversarial. Compared with the past Fast Gradient Method(FGM) [21], which obtains the optimal adversarial examples in only one iteration. PGD thinks that the optimal solution may not be found with only one iteration. It adopts the method of multiple iterations in a batch. The token embedding layer of the pre-trained model is attacked in each iteration. Finally superimposes the adversarial examples generated by multiple iterations to obtain the optimal value. The adversarial examples generation formula is as follows.

$$r_{adv}^{t+1} = \Pi_{\|r_{adv}\|_F \le \epsilon} \left(r_{adv}^t + \beta g\left(r_{adv}^t\right) / \left\|g\left(r_{adv}^t\right)\right\|_2\right) \tag{9}$$

where r_{adv}^t is adversarial examples generated at step t. $g(\cdot)$ represents the gradient calculation function. Both β and ϵ are hyperparameters representing step size and adversarial constraint range, respectively.

3.7   Training Loss

The model is trained with cross-entropy loss. The loss functions of the two multi-task models are shown in Eq. 10 and Eq. 11, respectively.

$$loss_{Model1} = \alpha loss_{Model1}^{auxiliary} + loss_{Model1}^{main} \tag{10}$$

$$loss_{Model2} = \alpha loss_{Model2}^{auxiliary} + loss_{Model2}^{main} \tag{11}$$

where $loss_{Model1}^{auxiliary}$ and $loss_{Model1}^{main}$ represent the losses of the auxiliary and main tasks in Model1, respectively. $loss_{Model2}^{auxiliary}$ and $loss_{Model2}^{main}$ represent the losses of the auxiliary and main tasks in Model2, respectively. α is a hyper-parameter to account for the importance of the auxiliary task. α is set to 0.5 in our experiments.

4   Experiments and Details

4.1   Dataset

Experiments are conducted on the challenging dataset CDial-Bias Dataset 2.0 [6], which is a well-annotated social bias dialog Chinese dataset. The number of dialogues contained in the training set, test set, and validation set respectively is shown in the Table 3.

Table 3. Statistics of CDial-Bias dataset 2.0 dataset.

Train	Validation	Test
22670	2838	2838

In addition to annotating the attitude of the dialogue towards bias, the dataset is also annotated with labels such as contextual relevance, the topic of the conversation, the way the bias is expressed, and the target group. Please refer to Table 4 below for specific labels.

Table 4. CDial-Bias dataset 2.0 labels information.

Labels	Explaination
Q	Dialogturn turn 1
A	Dialogturn turn 2
Topic	The topic of the dialogue, including race, gender, region, occupatioin
Context Sensitivity	0 - Context-independent; 1 - Context-sensitive
Types	0 - Irrelevant; 1 - Bias-expressing; 2 - Bias-discussing
Bias Attitude	0 - NA (Irrelevant data); 1 - Anti-Bias; 2 - Neutral; 3 - Biased
Referrenced Gropus	Presented in freetext. Multiple groups are splited by '/'

4.2   Implement Details

We use AdamW [22] to optimize our model and tune hyperparameters based on validation set results. The hyperparameter configuration of the final model is shown in Table 5.

In addition, our experiments use Macro-F1 as the metric. Because the labels for test set are not provided, all our experimental results show the results of the model on the validation set.

4.3   Results and Analysis

We design two sets of experiments. In experiment 1, we used other pre-trained models to replace the pre-trained encoding part of our model. The second experiment is an ablation experiment to prove the necessity of each part of the model. Details are as follows.

Table 5. Final hyperparameter configuration.

Learning rate	2e-5
Weight decay	0.01
Adma epsilon	1e-8
Warmup rate	0.1
The weight ratio of $loss_{auxiliary}$ (α)	0.5
PGD adversarial constraint range (ϵ)	1
PGD step size (β)	0.3
Dropout rate	0.1
The weight of $model1$ in the voting stage (W_a)	0.4
The weight of $model2$ in the voting stage (W_b)	0.6

Experiment 1. We separately use 5 pre-trained models as encoding layers for our model.

Bert-Base-Chinese[1]. Bert is a pre-training model based on Transformers proposed by google in 2018, which obtains state-of-the-art results on a wide array of Natural Language Processing (NLP) tasks. The Bert model used in this experiment is based on Chinese Wikipedia (including Simplified and Traditional) as a corpus for pre-training.

Chinese-Roberta-wwm-ext [13]. Based on Bert, the task of taking dynamic masking and removing the prediction of the next sentence is trained.

Ernie-1.0 [23]. Baidu proposed Ernie in 2019 to learn language representations enhanced by knowledge masking strategies, namely entity-level masking and phrase-level masking. Experimental results show that Ernie achieves state-of-the-art results on five Chinese natural language processing tasks, including natural language inference, semantic similarity, named entity recognition, sentiment analysis, and question answering.

Chinese-Xlnet-Base [24]. XLNet is a new unsupervised language representation learning method based on a novel generalized permutation language modeling objective. Additionally, XLNet employs Transformer-XL as the backbone model, exhibiting excellent performance for language tasks involving long context.

Mengzi-Bert-Base [19]. This is a pre-trained model on 300G Chinese corpus. Masked language modeling(MLM), part-of-speech(POS) tagging and sentence order prediction(SOP) are used to train.

Ultimately, our experiments show that Mengzi-bert-base outperforms other pre-trained models.

Experiment 2 We conduct ablation experiments based on the best model in Experiment 1. First, we remove all auxiliary tasks, only the main task part

---

[1] https://huggingface.co/bert-base-chinese.

Table 6. The results of experiment 1. Comparison of biased classification results on the validation set for various pre-trained models.

Pre-trained models	Macro-F1 score
Bert-base-chinese	0.6263
Chinese-roberta-wwm-ext	0.6329
Ernie-1.0	0.6282
Chinese-xlnet-base	0.6323
Mengzi-bert-base	**0.6526**

remains. Second, we experiment with selecting only topic classification as a subtask and only selecting dialogue type classification as a subtask, respectively. In addition, we remove the model fusion method and change the structure of two auxiliary task-based models into a single three-task model structure. The model structure diagram is shown in Fig. 2, in which three tasks share the embedding vector output by a pre-trained model.

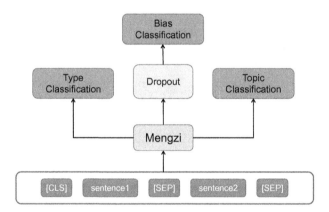

Fig. 2. Three tasks model: Three tasks share a pre-trained embedding layer model.

During the training process, multiply the loss of the main task by 3 and add the loss of the remaining two auxiliary tasks. Finally, we also remove adversarial learning to test its improvement on our model.

From Table 7, it can be seen that removing adversarial training (PGD) or removing auxiliary tasks has a greater impact on our model. Specifically, using adversarial training improves the F1 score of our model by about 0.03. We believe this is because adding adversarial examples makes our model more robust. Furthermore, after removing the two auxiliary tasks, the F1 score of the model dropped by about 0.04. This proves that our proposed auxiliary task significantly improves the classification results of the main task. By comparing the results of removing only task 1 and only removing task 2, we find that task 2 is more effective in improving the main task. This proves that for the main task of bias detection, knowing the conversation topic information is more important than knowing the conversation type.

Finally, the results of the last two lines shown in Table 7 show that the effect of using model fusion is better than not using model fusion. This is because training three tasks simultaneously is more difficult than training two. In the three-tasks model, all three tasks use the same embedding vector, making it difficult for the training vector of the embedding layer to achieve good results in all tasks. The seesaw phenomenon [25] is prone to occur. In this case, the auxiliary task negatively affects the main task.

In summary, the structure of each part of our model positively affects the prediction performance of the bias detection task.

Table 7. The results of experiment 2.

Models	Macro-F1 score
Our system	**0.6526**
Our system w/o PGD	0.6173
Our system w/o task1	0.6360
Our system w/o task2	0.6349
Our system w/o task1 & Task2	0.6113
Three-tasks model	0.6298

5   Conclusion

In this paper, we use a pre-trained model as an encoder to extract semantic information from conversations to detect biased attitudes implicit in them. To improve the model's performance, we design two auxiliary tasks and train them using multi-task learning.

We also use adversarial learning and model fusion based on the above to increase the robustness of our model and the final classification effect.

In the experimental part, we first replace our encoding part with various pre-trained models to try to find the best pre-trained model for the task. In the end, we find that using Mengzi-bert-base works best. In addition, we perform ablation experiments to test whether our designed auxiliary tasks and training methods can improve the main task. To this end, we also propose a three-task model structure. The experimental results show that the auxiliary task has a significant improvement effect on the main task. With the help of adversarial learning and model fusion methods, the classification results are greatly improved.

Finally, in multi-task learning, the way information is shared between tasks can impact the model's performance. We believe the current structure between tasks is not tightly linked, and information sharing is insufficient. For future research, we will focus on better allocating and utilizing the shared information between tasks and making auxiliary tasks more effective for the main task.

References

1. Bordia, S., Bowman, S.: Identifying and reducing gender bias in word-level language models. In: Proceedings of the 2019 Conference of the North American Chapter of the Association for Computational Linguistics: Student Research Workshop, pp. 7–15 (2019)
2. He, T., Glass, J.: Negative training for neural dialogue response generation. In: Proceedings of the 58th Annual Meeting of the Association for Computational Linguistics, pp. 2044–2058 (2020)
3. Tan, O.S., Low, E.L., Tay, E.G., Yan, Y.K. (eds.): Singapore Math and Science Education Innovation. ETLPPSIP, vol. 1. Springer, Singapore (2021). https://doi.org/10.1007/978-981-16-1357-9
4. Smith, S.,et al.: Using deepspeed and megatron to train megatron-turing nlg 530b, a large-scale generative language model. arXiv preprint arXiv:2201.11990 (2022)
5. Caruana, R.: Multitask learning. Mach. Learn. **28**(1), 41–75 (1997)
6. Zhou, J. et al.: Towards identifying social bias in dialog systems: Frame, datasets, and benchmarks (2022)
7. Peng, B., Wang, J., Zhang, X.: Adversarial learning of sentiment word representations for sentiment analysis. Inf. Sci. **541**, 426–441 (2020)
8. Park, J.H., Shin, J., Fung, P.: Reducing gender bias in abusive language detection. In: Proceedings of the 2018 Conference on Empirical Methods in Natural Language Processing, pp. 2799–2804 (2018)
9. Sap, M., Card, D., Gabriel, S., Choi, Y., Smith, A.N.: The risk of racial bias in hate speech detection. In ACL (2019)
10. Qian, Y., Muaz, U., Zhang, B., Hyun, J.W.: Reducing gender bias in word-level language models with a gender-equalizing loss function. In: Proceedings of the 57th Annual Meeting of the Association for Computational Linguistics: Student Research Workshop, pp. 223–228 (2019)
11. Vaswani, A.: Attention is all you need. Advances in neural information processing systems, p. 30 (2017)
12. Devlin, J., Chang, M.-W., Lee, K., Toutanova, K.: BERT: Pre-training of deep bidirectional transformers for language understanding. In Proceedings of NAACL-HLT, pp. 4171–4186 (2019)
13. Cui, Y., Che, W., Liu, T., Qin, B., Yang, Z.: Pre-training with whole word masking for chinese BERT. IEEE/ACM Transactions on Audio, Speech, and Language Processing **29**, 3504–3514 (2021)
14. Maronikolakis, A., Baader, P., Schütze, H:. Analyzing hate speech data along racial, gender and intersectional axes. arXiv preprint arXiv:2205.06621 (2022)
15. Bao, X., Qiao, Q.: Transfer learning from pre-trained BERT for pronoun resolution. In: Proceedings of the First Workshop on Gender Bias in Natural Language Processing, pp. 82–88 (2019)
16. Andrew Moore, A., Barnes, J.: Multi-task learning of negation and speculation for targeted sentiment classification. In Proceedings of the 2021 Conference of the North American Chapter of the Association for Computational Linguistics: Human Language Technologies, pp. 2838–2869 (2021)

17. Li, Y., Caragea, C.: A multi-task learning framework for multi-target stance detection. In: Findings of the Association for Computational Linguistics: ACL-IJCNLP 2021, pp. 2320–2326 (2021)
18. Akyürek, A.F., Paik, S., Kocyigit, M.Y., Akbiyik, S., Runyun, Ş.L., Wijaya, D.: On measuring social biases in prompt-based multi-task learning. arXiv preprint arXiv:2205.11605 (2022)
19. Zhang, Z.,: Mengzi: Towards lightweight yet ingenious pre-trained models for chinese. CoRR, abs/2110.06696 (2021)
20. Madry, A., Makelov, A., Schmidt, L., Tsipras, D., Vladu, A.: Towards deep learning models resistant to adversarial attacks. In International Conference on Learning Representations (2018)
21. Miyato, T., Dai, A.M., Goodfellow, I.: Adversarial training methods for semi-supervised text classification. stat, 1050:6 (2017)
22. Loshchilov, I., Hutter, F.: Fixing weight decay regularization in adam. CoRR, abs/1711.05101 (2017)
23. Sun, Y.: ERNIE: enhanced representation through knowledge integration. CoRR, abs/1904.09223 (2019)
24. Yang, Z., Dai, Z., Yang, Y., Carbonell, J., Salakhutdinov, R.R., Le, Q.V.: XLNet: generalized autoregressive pretraining for language understanding. In: Advances in Neural Information Processing Systems, vol. 32 (2019)
25. Tang, H., Liu, J., Zhao, M., Gong, X.: Progressive layered extraction (PLE): A novel multi-task learning (MTL) model for personalized recommendations. In Fourteenth ACM Conference on Recommender Systems, pp. 269–278 (2020)

Overview of NLPCC2022 Shared Task 5 Track 1: Multi-label Classification for Scientific Literature

Ming Liu, He Zhang[✉], Yangjie Tian, Tianrui Zong, Borui Cai, Ruohua Xu, and Yunfeng Li

CNPIEC KEXIN LTD., Beijing, China
{liuming,zhanghe,tianyangjie,zongtianrui,caiborui,xuruohua, liyunfeng}@kxsz.net

Abstract. Given the increasing volume of scientific literature in conferences, journals as well as open access websites, it is important to index these data in a hierarchical way for intelligent retrieval. We organized Track 1 in NLPCC2022 Shared Task 5 for multi-label classification for scientific literature. This paper will summarize the task information, the data set, the models returned from the participants and the final result. Furthermore, we will discuss key findings and challenges for hierarchical multi-label classification in the scientific domain.

Keywords: Multi-label classification · Scientific literature · Hierarchical labels

1 Introduction

Multi-label text classification in the scientific domain is vital for organizing research papers and reports. Scientific search engines such as Google Scholar[1], Semantic Scholar[2] and AMiner[3] assign labels automatically to retrieved papers, while public open assess websites like arXiv[4] encourage the users to enter the labels manually. Different from single label classification, We recognize three main challenges in multi-label text classification: (i) Label sparseness. While the total label space ranges from thousands to millions, each scientific document only get less than ten labels. (ii) Label imbalanceness. It's widely known that most multi-label classification problems follows a long-tail label distribution, in which only a small amount of labels have relative high frequency and a large amount of labels exhibit very low frequency (smaller than 10). (iii) Label correlation. Some of the labels may be correlated with each other, which include the hierarchical labels or labels with similar context.

---

[1] https://www.scholar.google.com.
[2] https://www.semanticscholar.org/.
[3] https://www.aminer.org/.
[4] https://arxiv.org/.

© Springer Nature Switzerland AG 2022
W. Lu et al. (Eds.) NLPCC 2022, LNCS 13552, pp. 320–327, 2022.
https://doi.org/10.1007/978-3-031-17189-5_28

We organized a multi-label text classification task for NLPCC2022 Task 5 Track 1. The task requires participants to build multi-label text classification models for scientific abstracts from the chemistry domain. We crawled scientific abstract and label pairs from American Chemistry Society. After some basic preprocessing, we provided 90000 abstract label pairs for training and 5000 for test. A total of 11 valid submissions were received. We also provided a baseline method [5], in which Sci-BERT [2] with DBLoss turns out to be quite effective and gives an F1 score of 0.65.

After reviewing all the methods from the participants, we find that: (i) Among all the submissions, more than half of the participants used BERT as the encoder for feature representation. (ii) Ensembling showed better results than a single end-to-end model, i.e., training four models based on the three different levels and all combined levels and doing prediction based on the above four models. (iii) Multi-task training and self training also contribute to the classification performance improvement. (iv) It is also possible to make good use of label information, such as leveraging label imbalances as another objective or incorporating label attention in the neural network. (v) Further engineering techniques may also be useful, e.g., post editing among three level of labels.

In the following sections, Sect. 2 will mention some related work, Sect. 3 will show the basic data statistics, Sect. 4 will briefly mention the submitted methods from participants, Sect. 6 will show the results, followed by a conclusion in Sect. 6.

2   Related Work

Multi-label text classification. Multi-label text classification has been an important research topic for indexing and retrieving scientific documents. Common strategies for multi-label classifier development include one-vs-all, one-vs-one and end-to-end models. However, the one-vs-all and one-vs-one strategies are very computationally expensive when the number of labels is large. Recent progress in deep learning encourage the end-to-end models [8], where the input is the scientific text and the output is its corresponding labels, a binary cross entropy loss is often used as the objective function. More recently, [9] leveraged label information to attend the representation of source scientific text and improved the performance in few and zero shot settings. [5] also tried to improve the classification performance by adding different re-balanced loss to the binary cross entropy loss.

Evaluation Metrics. Common metrics for multi-label text classification include label-based, example-based and ranking-based. Label-based evaluation measures assess and average the predictive performance for each category as a binary classification problem, where the negative category corresponds with the other categories. The most popular are the label-based Accuracy (LB-ACC) and F-measure (LB-F). The example-based metrics compute for each object, the proximity between predicted and true label sets. In contrast, ranking based evaluation methods consider the problem as a ranking task, i.e. the model returns an ordered label list for each item according to their match scales. More recently, [1] developed an information theoretic based metric based on Information Contrast Model.

3 Data

Table 1. An example from the training set

Key	Values
Title	Evidence for the superatom-superatom bonding from bond energies
Abstract	Metal clusters with specific number of valence electrons are described as superatoms
Level1	Energy, physical chemistry, inorganic chemistry
Level2	Cluster chemistry, kinetics, binding energy, molecules, metals
Level3	Metal clusters, Kinetic parameters
Levels	Energy, physical chemistry, inorganic chemistry, cluster chemistry, kinetics, binding energy, molecules, metals, metal clusters, kinetic parameters

Table 2. Data and label statistics

Description	Number
Total no. of abstracts/labels	95000
Number of training abstracts/labels	90000
Number of test abstracts/labels	5000
Total number of labels	1530
Number of level 1 labels	21
Number of level 2 labels	260
Number of level 3 labels	1272
Avg number of tokens per abstract	182
Avg number of labels per abstract	11.7

We provide around 950,000 English scientific research literature, in which 90,000 can be used as the training set and 5,000 can be used as test set. Each data sample contains the title and summary of the article and the corresponding hierarchical multi labels (level1, level2, level3) and the union of hierarchical multi labels (levels). (Note: data other than the training set cannot be used in the process of model development). The number of label categories for level1, level2, level3 and levels is 21, 260, 1272 and 1530, respectively. In addition, these labels distribution is long-tailed. Table 1[5] is an example from a random scientific paper. Table 2 shows the basic statistics for the data set. It can be seen that there are more labels in the lower level, i.e., 1272 labels in level 3 compared to 260 labels in level 2 and 21 ones in level 1.

Figure 1 shows the heavy long tailed label distribution in our data set, as well as the sparse label correlations.

4 Methods from Participants

There are 11 valid teams who returned predictions for this task and 6 of them returned their method description. The following shows the methods from different participants.

BIT-WOW. This team constructed a hierarchy-aware global model to obtain the hierarchy label information. First, this participant used a pre-trained language model to get label embedding. Second, they took advantage of semantic information of labels by combining label embedding and word embedding, which was obtained through several pre-trained language models according to the label-aware attention structure. After that, each label is considered as a node in the hierarchy graph, and graph convolutional neural networks were used to structure encoders for aggregating node information. After obtaining the single model, they adopted three core strategies: (i) Utilize semi-supervised learning by labeling extra data with pseudo labels predicted by pre-trained models. The data was crawled from Semantic Scholar according to all labels in the task. (ii) At the end of learning, models were required to apply inference by padding the missing level-2 labels when both corresponding level-1 and level-3 labels exist. (iii) More than 5 different models are utilized to implement ensemble learning.

Super GUTS. This team proposed a novel framework called Multi-task Hierarchical Cross-Attention Network (MHCAN) to achieve accurate classification of scientific research literature. They first obtained representations of the titles and abstracts with SciBERT, which is pretrained on a large corpus of scientific text, and they leveraged GCNs [11] to represent labels with graph structure. Then, they utilized a cross-attention mechanism to fully integrate text and labels information at each level, and introduced iterative hierarchical-attention to further capture the information gain between adjacent levels. Finally, considering the dependencies of adjacent levels, they designed a label masking mechanism to selectively mask the current predicted label according to previous predictions. Besides the basic framework, this participant also utilized other modules to further improve model performance. They jointly optimized the loss at each level with a Class-Balanced Loss to alleviate the problem caused by the long-tailed distribution of labels. In addition, to improve the adaptability of the model to domain data, they referred to the related methods of domain-adaptive pre-training (DAPT), continuing to pre-train SciBERT on unlabeled data. For generalization purpose, they introduced perturbations in the representations for adversarial training to further enhance generalization.

---

[5] https://pubs.acs.org/doi/10.1021/acsomega.8b01841.

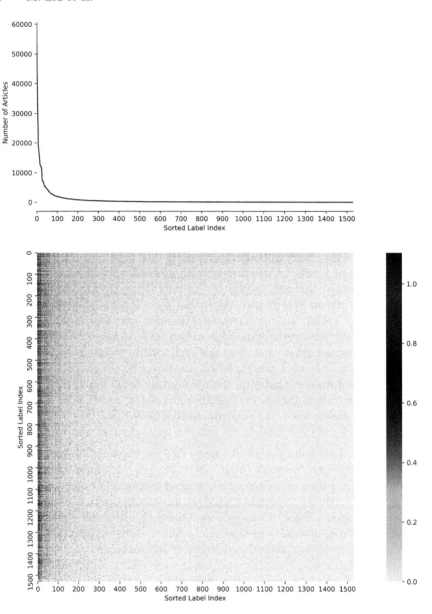

Fig. 1. Label distribution and label correlation

Sixiangqianxi. This participant trained four models (level1, level2, level3, all levels) and used the combination from the four models.

Deep Fantasy Team. This team conducted multi-task multi-level training, with a neural network architecture BERT-4FFs-CNN-concatenation. This participant used SciBERT as the base encoder and leveraged multi-task learning.

Specifically, they incorporated a shared Text-CNN between multiple tasks to interact the information between labels at all levels, and the hierarchical feature information was fused and propagated from top to bottom according to the task level.

Hit-scir-km. The team designed three models, namely, LSTM model [3] and BERT model based on label-text attention and xlnet pre-training model [10], which are abbreviated as lsan-LSTM, lsan-BERT and xlnet. The three models were fused by voting, and the final F1 value of the test dataset reached 66.75%, ranking fifth. The model based on label and text attention makes use of the text information of the labels, and uses the mutual attention mechanism to model the importance between the labels and text. In their ablation study, they found that with the addition of attention mechanism, the performance of the model was improved by 2.1% and the performance reached 63.68%. Xlnet model can model and represent long-distance text, which improves the ability of using text information without truncation. Finally, the voting fusion method was adopted to improve the overall performance by 3.07% compared with the single model.

YSF2022. This team developed a BERT based model with some label attention mechanism.

Intelligent Algorithm Team. The team didn't provide details about their methodology.

Gakki. The team developed a base-bert model with the supervised contrastive loss [6], which was used as a type of label re-balanced loss.

IR&TMNLPCC 2022. The team applied the HARNN framework [4]. The overall model architecture cab be divided into three following layers: Documentation Representing Layer (DRL), Hierarchical Attention-based Recurrent Layer (HARL), Hybrid Predicting Layer (HPL).

Woshuodedoudui. The team used the HARNN model [4] for hierarchical multi-label classification, which mainly consists of three modules: (i) Documentation Representing Layer (DRL)- to represent the text and level labels. (ii) Hierarchical Attention-based Recurrent Layer (HARL) - Using the attention mechanism, the learned text vector and label vector are cyclically learned and interacted. (iii) Hybrid Predicting Layer (HPL) - Hybrid method for label prediction.

Mhchhh. The team developed a Albert [7] plus CNN framewok, but the model can only do level 1 prediction.

5 Results

Table 3. Final results for NLPCC2022 Task 5 Track 1: Multi-label Classification

Participants	F1	Precision	Recall	Rank
BIT-WOW	**0.7071**	0.7153	0.699	1
Super GUTS	0.6941	0.7056	0.6829	2
Siyangqianxi	0.6909	0.6611	**0.7234**	3
Deep fantasy team	0.6879	0.7319	0.6488	4
Hit-scir-km	0.6675	0.6665	0.6685	5
YSF2022	0.6296	0.6218	0.6375	6
Intelligent algorithm team	0.6133	0.6345	0.5935	7
Gakki	0.56	**0.7377**	0.4514	8
IR&TMNLPCC 2022	0.4605	0.4405	0.4825	9
Woshuodedoudui	0.4514	0.4784	0.4272	10
mhchhh	0.2805	0.7296	0.1737	11

Table 3 shows the final submission results for this task. The ranking is based on the F1 score. It can be seen that 7 out of 11 teams reached an F1 score which is above 0.6. With further data augmentation techniques, participant BIT-WOW achieved a surprising 0.7071 F1 score. It is noticed that the top ranked teams used Sci-BERT as their base encoder, which is helpful for further model development. We also find that training multiple models for different levels and using the ensemble for the final prediction returned better performance than a single model.

6 Conclusion

This paper summarized the task, data set and the result in NLPCC2022 Task 5 Track 1. In conclusion, we find that (i) Among all the submissions, more than half of the participants used BERT as the encoder for feature representation. (ii) Ensembling showed better results than a single end-to-end model, i.e., training four models based on the three different levels and all combined levels and doing prediction based on the above four models. (iii) Multi-task training and self training also contribute to the classification performance improvement. (iv) It is also possible to make good use of label information, such as leveraging label imbalances as another objective or incorporating label attention in the neural network. (v) Further engineering techniques may also be useful, e.g., post editing among three level of labels. We released the data sets and hope it will benefit the multi-label learning research in the NLP community.

References

1. Amigó, E., Delgado, A.: Evaluating extreme hierarchical multi-label classification. In: Proceedings of the 60th Annual Meeting of the Association for Computational Linguistics (Volume 1: Long Papers). pp. 5809–5819 (2022)
2. Beltagy, I., Lo, K., Cohan, A.: SciBERT: A pretrained language model for scientific text. arXiv preprint arXiv:1903.10676 (2019)
3. Hochreiter, S., Schmidhuber, J.: Long short-term memory. Neural Comput. 9(8), 1735–1780 (1997)
4. Huang, W., et al.: Hierarchical multi-label text classification: an attention-based recurrent network approach. In: Proceedings of the 28th ACM international conference on information and knowledge management, pp. 1051–1060 (2019)
5. Huang, Y., Giledereli, B., Köksal, A., Özgür, A., Ozkirimli, E.: Balancing methods for multi-label text classification with long-tailed class distribution. arXiv preprint arXiv:2109.04712 (2021)
6. Khosla, P., et al.: Supervised contrastive learning. Adv. Neural. Inf. Process. Syst. 33, 18661–18673 (2020)
7. Lan, Z., Chen, M., Goodman, S., Gimpel, K., Sharma, P., Soricut, R.: Albert: A lite BERT for self-supervised learning of language representations. arXiv preprint arXiv:1909.11942 (2019)
8. Liu, J., Chang, W.C., Wu, Y., Yang, Y.: Deep learning for extreme multi-label text classification. In: Proceedings of the 40th International ACM SIGIR Conference on Research and Development in Information Retrieval, pp. 115–124 (2017)
9. Lu, J., Du, L., Liu, M., Dipnall, J.: Multi-label few/zero-shot learning with knowledge aggregated from multiple label graphs. arXiv preprint arXiv:2010.07459 (2020)
10. Yang, Z., Dai, Z., Yang, Y., Carbonell, J., Salakhutdinov, R.R., Le, Q.V.: XLNet: Generalized autoregressive pretraining for language understanding. Adv. Neural Inf. Process. Syst. 32 (2019)
11. Zhang, S., Tong, H., Xu, J., Maciejewski, R.: Graph convolutional networks: a comprehensive review. Comput. Soc. Netw. 6(1), 1–23 (2019). https://doi.org/10.1186/s40649-019-0069-y

Overview of the NLPCC 2022 Shared Task: Multi-modal Dialogue Understanding and Generation

Yuxuan Wang[1,2], Xueliang Zhao[1,2], and Dongyan Zhao[1,2,3]([✉])

[1] Wangxuan Institute of Computer Technology, Peking University, Beijing, China
wyx@stu.pku.edu.cn, {xl.zhao,zhaody}@pku.edu.cn
[2] Center for Data Science, AAIS, Peking University, Beijing, China
[3] Artificial Intelligence Institute, Peking University, Beijing, China

Abstract. In this paper, we give an overview of multi-modal dialogue understanding and generation at NLPCC 2022 shared task, which includes three sub-tasks: dialogue scene identification, dialogue session identification, and dialogue response generation. A bilingual multi-modal dialogue dataset consisting of 100M utterances was made public for the shared task. The dataset contains 119K dialogue scene boundaries and 62K dialogue session boundaries which are both annotated manually. Details of the shared task, dataset, evaluation metric and evaluation results will be presented in order.

Keywords: Multi-modal dialogue · Dialogue scene identification · Dialogue session identification

1 Introduction

Building open-domain dialogue system [5,30,38,42] has long been an aim of artificial intelligence. Recently, neural-based open-domain dialog systems are of growing interest [9,19,33,41,42], most of which are trained on large-scale datasets to learn a response conditioned on the textual contexts. One emerging area is the development of multi-modal dialogue systems. [6] first extend Visual question answering (VQA) [1,8,22,43] to dialogue setting. In this problem, questions about a given image are positioned in a multi-turn dialogue where each dialogue turn is a question answering (QA) pair. [2] then introduce a multi-turn video question answering dataset. To focus more on daily chat, [23,36] proposed an open-domain dialogue dataset that is extracted from movies and TV series and corresponding subtitles. Benefit from these large-scale corpuses, numerous approaches to video-grounded dialogue have showed remarkable performance in building multi-modal dialogue agent [12,16–18,20,37]. However, existing works perform much worse on open-domain dialogue datasets than QA-focused datasets.

Compared to images and short videos, movies and TV series contain abundant historical, cultural, and regional background knowledge. Besides, these

© Springer Nature Switzerland AG 2022
W. Lu et al. (Eds.) NLPCC 2022, LNCS 13552, pp. 328–335, 2022.
https://doi.org/10.1007/978-3-031-17189-5_29

story-based long videos have more complicated structures. Imagine you are watching the TV series Friends: In a museum scene, Ross is chatting with Carol about her marriage. Suddenly the picture turns, Ross begins to enjoy coffee with his friends in the Central Perk Cafe. Such a dramatic change of scenes is more common in movies that may exhibit a complete human life in several hours. Therefore, movie and TV series understanding is much more difficult than homemade video understanding. And directly applying movie and TV series with their corresponding subtitle to train an open-domain dialogue system is not the best option. In terms of temporal structure, movie and TV series is composed of scenes which is a sequence of continuous shots that are semantically related. The shot is captured by a camera that operates for an uninterrupted period of time and is visually continuous. The scene can be viewed as the minimal semantic unit of a video. Motivated by this, we view the video scene segmentation as a fundamental step to the long video understanding. There has been a lot of studies [3,4,10,25,27–29] on video scene segmentation, most of which adopt unsupervised approaches such as clustering or dynamic program. [13] first constructing a large-scale movie understanding dataset MovieNet. 318 movies in the dataset are annotated with scene boundaries. Following this work, some supervised learning-based works [13,26] achieve great progress in the video scene segmentation task. However, MovieNet is annotated from sequences of shots which are extracted by [31]. Thus the coarse shot boundaries make the scene labels not precise as expected. Besides, most previous works do not consider the language which is very important for high-level video understanding.

Even in a dialogue scene, topic shift at the discourse-level is a common phenomenon. Following the previous example, in the Central Perk Cafe, Ross with his friends talk about almost everything while the visual background is always a big orange couch. In such a situation, the dialogue context plays a rather important role in dialogue understanding. However, tracking all previous utterances is unnecessary, since this way either consumes large resources or introduces much noise. Therefore capturing related topic-aware clues at discourse-level is essential for dialogue understanding. Dialogue Topic Segmentation (DTS) segmenting the dialogue into topically coherent pieces has received considerable attention in recent years. Some existing works regard DTS as a topic tracking problem [14,34]. However, it is almost impossible to have a list of pre-defined categories that distinguish different topics in open-domain dialogue. Hence, following another line of research, we process the DTS as an extension of text segmentation [7,11,32,39,40]. Since lacking large-scale annotated corpus, almost all previous work choose unsupervised methods. And current datasets [40] can not reflect the effectiveness of the proposed methods since lack vast variety of dialogue topics.

To solve above-mentioned challenges, we construct a large-scale multi-modal dialogue dataset based on 1859 TV episodes. We manually annotated the dialogue scene and dialogue session boundaries to facilitate open-domain multi-modal dialogue understanding and generation. Figure 1 shows some examples of the dataset.

The NLPCC 2022 Shared Task 4 provides three benchmarks on the dataset. 13 teams registered for the shared task, and 2 teams submitted the final results.

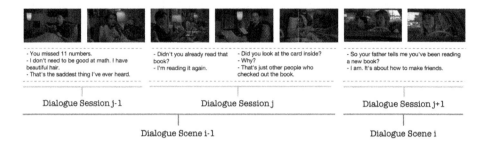

Fig. 1. Examples from our dataset. Only a few of the most relevant frames are displayed here. As shown above, the discourse contents in a scene can be vary greatly.

2   Task Description

We divide the multi-modal dialogue understanding and generation task into to two phases: multi-modal context understanding and response generation. Specifically, in the context understanding stage, we need to determine whether the dialogue topic or the video scene has changed. In the response generation stage, the ultimate goal is to generate a response that is coherent to the dialogue context and relevant to the video context. In summary, NLPCC 2022 Shared Task 4 includes three sub-tasks: (1) dialogue scene identification (2) dialogue session identification (3) dialogue response generation. To illustrate the sub-tasks clearly, we denote a multi-modal dialogue clip as (V, U), where $U = \{u_1, \ldots, u_N\}$ signifies the dialogue clip with u_i denoting the i-th dialogue utterance. N is the number of dialogue utterances in a multi-modal dialogue clip. $V = \{v_1, \ldots, v_N\}$ serve as a video clip with v_i denoting as the i-th short video pairing with u_i.

2.1   Dialogue Scene Identification

Following previous definition of scene [13, 26, 27], a scene is a semantic unit, where a certain activity takes place among a certain group of characters. Environment in a scene may change as the story goes on, thus, traditional visual cue-based approaches can not solve this problem well. Considering this attribute, we did not formulate a scene as a sequence of shots as previous work. Instead, we formulate a dialogue scene as a short video sequence $[v_1, \ldots, v_{Ls}]$, where L_s is the length of a dialogue scene. Then the dialogue scene identification sub-task can be formulated as a binary classification problem. Specifically, given a multi-modal dialogue clip (V, U), one is asked to predict a sequence $[o_1, \ldots, o_N]$, where $o_i \in \{0, 1\}$ denotes whether the i-th short video v_i is the end of a dialogue scene.

2.2   Dialogue Session Identification

Dialogue session [32] also referred as dialogue topic [7, 39, 40] is a topically related semantic unit in a conversation. Similar to monologue text segmentation, given a dialogue in the form of a sequence of utterances, one is asked to find the topic boundaries between utterances. Similar with dialogue scene identification sub-task, the i-th utterance u_i is annotated with a binary label $y_i \in \{0, 1\}$ indicating whether u_i is the end of a dialogue session.

2.3   Dialogue Response Generation

The dialogue response generation sub-task is formulated as follows: given the previous $N - 2$ utterances in an dialogue clip $C = \{u_1, \ldots, u_{N-2}\}$ with video clip V as context and the $(N - 1)$-th utterance as query, the goal is to generate the response u_N.

3   Dataset Description

We construct the dataset on 335 TV series with 1859 videos in total. Compared with movies, TV shows contain less artistic expressions and monologues. We carefully selected the TV series to keep the high quality and generality of our dataset. Specifically, we remove the animations to make the video close to real-life scenarios. We also screen documents or talk shows that contain a large mount of monologues out. In addition, the selected TV series include almost all genres. The bilingual subtitles come from subtitle groups, thus most of the Chinese subtitles are human translations. We manually align the TV series with its subtitles.

To provide a high-quality dataset supporting multi-modal dialogue under-standing and generation, we make a great effort to manually annotate dialogue scene and session boundaries. We segment the TV episode into a sequence of short videos, each short video is aligned with a dialogue utterance. Annotators play these short videos by hand to see if there is a transition between them. We find multi-modal information greatly improves the efficiency of annotators. In the end, we randomly sampled 5% annotation results of every annotator for validation. If there are more than 5% boundaries being wrong labeled. All the results of the annotator are asked to be re-annotated. We repeat this procedure for three turns. After that, we segment the TV series episode into 90-s clips. As a result, we got 43K multi-modal dialogue clips, 1.1M utterances, 63K dialogue scene boundaries, and 119K dialogue session boundaries. We split our dataset to train:valid:test with 20:1:1. More statistics are shown in Table 1.

4   Results

4.1   Evaluation Metrics

The results of sub-task 1 and sub-task 2 are evaluated by accuracy. In addition, we adopt the Micro-F1 score as an auxiliary metric to prevent the influence

Table 1. .

Split	Dialogue clips	Utterances	Dialogue scenes	Dialogue sessions
Training data	40K	100M	56K	106K
Validation data	1,955	50K	3,202	6,331
Test data	1,934	50K	3,284	6,949

of unbalanced label distribution. For dialogue scene identification sub-task, we define the short video which is the end of a dialogue scene as positive instance. Similarly, the positive instance in dialogue session identification sub-task is the utterance which is the end of a dialogue session. For response generation sub-task, We choose 4 commonly used reference-based metrics including BLEU [24], ROUGE [21], METEOR [15] and CIDEr [35].

4.2   Evaluation Results

There are total 13 teams registered for the NLPCC 2022 Shared Task 4, and 2 teams submitted their final results for evaluation. The overall results are shown in Table 2. We then give a brief introduction to the representative systems designed by **LingJing** team.

For dialogue scene identification problem and dialogue session identification problem, they propose a multi-task learning framework to learn joint representations between short video and utterance as well as predict the dialogue scene/session boundaries efficiently. As a result, they achieve an accuracy of 93.9% on sub-task 1 and 87.8% on sub-task 2. However, the Micro-F1 scores on these two sub-tasks are unsatisfactory owing to the unbalanced label distribution. For dialogue response generation, they presented a novel prompt-based generation model which fuses the dialogue scene transition and dialogue session transition to the template.

Table 2. .

Team ID	sub-task1		Sub-task2		sub-task3			
	Accuracy	F1	Accuracy	F1	Bleu-4	Rouge-L	METEOR	CIDEr
LingJing	0.939	0.182	0.878	0.289	0.072	0.226	0.117	1.290
Eastwood	–	–	0.723	0.398	–	–	–	–

5   Conclusion

This paper briefly introduces the overview of the NLPCC 2022 Shared Task 4: Multi-modal Dialogue Understanding and Generation. We introduce a large-scale video-grounded dialogue dataset with abundant annotations. Based on this dataset we propose three benchmarks for multi-modal dialogue understanding (i.e. dialogue scene identification and dialogue session identification) and multi-modal dialogue generation (i.e. dialogue response generation). We believe our new benchmarks can lead to interesting insights to design better multi-modal dialogue systems.

References

1. Agrawal, A., et al.: VQA: visual question answering. Int. J. Comput. Vis. **123**, 4–31 (2015)
2. AlAmri, H., et al.: Audio visual scene-aware dialog. In: 2019 IEEE/CVF Conference on Computer Vision and Pattern Recognition (CVPR), pp. 7550–7559 (2019)
3. Baraldi, L., Grana, C., Cucchiara, R.: A deep siamese network for scene detection in broadcast videos. In: Proceedings of the 23rd ACM International Conference on Multimedia (2015)
4. Chasanis, V., Likas, A.C., Galatsanos, N.P.: Scene detection in videos using shot clustering and sequence alignment. IEEE Trans. Multimedia **11**, 89–100 (2009)
5. Colby, K.M., Weber, S., Hilf, F.D.: Artificial paranoia. Artif. Intell. **2**, 1–25 (1971)
6. Das, A., et al.: Visual dialog. In: Proceedings of the IEEE Conference on Computer Vision and Pattern Recognition, pp. 326–335 (2017)
7. Galley, M., McKeown, K., Fosler-Lussier, E., Jing, H.: Discourse segmentation of multi-party conversation. In: ACL (2003)
8. Gao, H., Mao, J., Zhou, J., Huang, Z., Wang, L., Xu, W.: Are you talking to a machine? Dataset and methods for multilingual image question. In: NIPS (2015)
9. Gao, J., Galley, M., Li, L.: Neural approaches to conversational AI. arXiv arXiv:1809.08267 (2019)
10. Han, B., Wu, W.: Video scene segmentation using a novel boundary evaluation criterion and dynamic programming. In: 2011 IEEE International Conference on Multimedia and Expo, pp. 1–6 (2011)
11. Hearst, M.A.: Text tiling: segmenting text into multi-paragraph subtopic passages. Comput. Linguist. **23**, 33–64 (1997)
12. Hori, C., et al.: End-to-end audio visual scene-aware dialog using multimodal attention-based video features. In: 2019 IEEE International Conference on Acoustics, Speech and Signal Processing (ICASSP), ICASSP 2019, pp. 2352–2356. IEEE (2019)
13. Huang, Q., Xiong, Y., Rao, A., Wang, J., Lin, D.: MovieNet: a holistic dataset for movie understanding. arXiv arXiv:2007.10937 (2020)
14. Khan, O.Z., Robichaud, J.P., Crook, P.A., Sarikaya, R.: Hypotheses ranking and state tracking for a multi-domain dialog system using multiple ASR alternates. In: INTERSPEECH (2015)
15. Lavie, A., Agarwal, A.: METEOR: an automatic metric for MT evaluation with high levels of correlation with human judgments. In: Proceedings of the 2nd Workshop on Statistical Machine Translation, pp. 228–231 (2007)
16. Le, H., Chen, N.F., Hoi, S.: Learning reasoning paths over semantic graphs for video-grounded dialogues. In: International Conference on Learning Representations (2021)
17. Le, H., Sahoo, D., Chen, N., Hoi, S.C.: BiST: bi-directional spatio-temporal reasoning for video-grounded dialogues. In: Proceedings of the 2020 Conference on Empirical Methods in Natural Language Processing (EMNLP), pp. 1846–1859 (2020)

18. Le, H., Sahoo, D., Chen, N.F., Hoi, S.C.H.: Multimodal transformer networks for end-to-end video-grounded dialogue systems. In: ACL (2019)
19. Li, J., Monroe, W., Shi, T., Jean, S., Ritter, A., Jurafsky, D.: Adversarial learning for neural dialogue generation. In: EMNLP (2017)
20. Li, Z., Li, Z., Zhang, J., Feng, Y., Niu, C., Zhou, J.: Bridging text and video: a universal multimodal transformer for video-audio scene-aware dialog. arXiv preprint arXiv:2002.00163 (2020)
21. Lin, C.Y.: ROUGE: a package for automatic evaluation of summaries. In: Text Summarization Branches Out, pp. 74–81 (2004)
22. Malinowski, M., Fritz, M.: A multi-world approach to question answering about real-world scenes based on uncertain input. In: NIPS (2014)
23. Meng, Y., et al.: OpenViDial: a large-scale, open-domain dialogue dataset with visual contexts. arXiv arXiv:2012.15015 (2020)
24. Papineni, K., Roukos, S., Ward, T., Zhu, W.J.: BLEU: a method for automatic evaluation of machine translation. In: Proceedings of the 40th Annual Meeting on Association for Computational Linguistics, pp. 311–318. Association for Computational Linguistics (2002)
25. Protasov, S., Khan, A., Sozykin, K., Ahmad, M.: Using deep features for video scene detection and annotation. Sig. Image Video Process. **12**, 991–999 (2018)
26. Rao, A., et al.: A local-to-global approach to multi-modal movie scene segmentation. In: 2020 IEEE/CVF Conference on Computer Vision and Pattern Recognition (CVPR), pp. 10143–10152 (2020)
27. Rasheed, Z., Shah, M.: Scene detection in hollywood movies and tv shows. In: 2003 Proceedings of the IEEE Computer Society Conference on Computer Vision and Pattern Recognition, vol. 2, p. II-343 (2003)
28. Rotman, D., Porat, D., Ashour, G.: Optimal sequential grouping for robust video scene detection using multiple modalities. Int. J. Semant. Comput. **11**, 193–208 (2017)
29. Rui, Y., Huang, T.S., Mehrotra, S.: Exploring video structure beyond the shots. In: Proceedings of the IEEE International Conference on Multimedia Computing and Systems (Cat. No.98TB100241), pp. 237–240 (1998)
30. Shum, H., He, X., Li, D.: From Eliza to Xiaoice: challenges and opportunities with social chatbots. Front. Inf. Technol. Electron. Eng. **19**, 10–26 (2018)
31. Sidiropoulos, P., Mezaris, V., Kompatsiaris, Y., Meinedo, H., Bugalho, M.M.F., Trancoso, I.: Temporal video segmentation to scenes using high-level audiovisual features. IEEE Trans. Circ. Syst. Video Technol. **21**, 1163–1177 (2011)
32. Song, Y., Mou, L., Yan, R., Yi, L., Zhu, Z., Hu, X., Zhang, M.: Dialogue session segmentation by embedding-enhanced texttiling. arXiv arXiv:1610.03955 (2016)
33. Sordoni, A., et al.: A neural network approach to context-sensitive generation of conversational responses. In: NAACL (2015)
34. Takanobu, R., et al.: A weakly supervised method for topic segmentation and labeling in goal-oriented dialogues via reinforcement learning. In: IJCAI (2018)
35. Vedantam, R., Lawrence Zitnick, C., Parikh, D.: CIDEr: consensus-based image description evaluation. In: Proceedings of the IEEE Conference on Computer Vision and Pattern Recognition, pp. 4566–4575 (2015)
36. Wang, S., Meng, Y., Li, X., Sun, X., Ouyang, R., Li, J.: OpenViDial 2.0: a larger-scale, open-domain dialogue generation dataset with visual contexts. arXiv arXiv:2109.12761 (2021)
37. Wang, S., et al.: Modeling text-visual mutual dependency for multi-modal dialog generation. arXiv arXiv:2105.14445 (2021)

38. Weizenbaum, J.: Eliza—a computer program for the study of natural language communication between man and machine. Commun. ACM **9**, 36–45 (1966)
39. Xing, L., Carenini, G.: Improving unsupervised dialogue topic segmentation with utterance-pair coherence scoring. In: SIGDIAL (2021)
40. Xu, Y., Zhao, H., Zhang, Z.: Topic-aware multi-turn dialogue modeling. In: AAAI (2021)
41. Zhao, T., Zhao, R., Eskénazi, M.: Learning discourse-level diversity for neural dialog models using conditional variational autoencoders. In: ACL (2017)
42. Zhou, L., Gao, J., Li, D., Shum, H.: The design and implementation of XiaoIce, an empathetic social chatbot. Comput. Linguist. **46**, 53–93 (2020)
43. Zhu, Y., Groth, O., Bernstein, M.S., Fei-Fei, L.: Visual7W: grounded question answering in images. In: 2016 IEEE Conference on Computer Vision and Pattern Recognition (CVPR), pp. 4995–5004 (2016)

Overview of NLPCC2022 Shared Task 5 Track 2: Named Entity Recognition

Borui Cai[1], He Zhang[1]([✉]), Fenghong Liu[2], Ming Liu[1], Tianrui Zong[1], Zhe Chen[1], and Yunfeng Li[1]

[1] CNPIEC KEXIN LTD., Beijing, China
{caiborui,zhanghe,liuming,zongtianrui,chenzhe,liyunfeng}@kxsz.net
[2] Data Intelligence, Beijing, China
liufh@mail.las.ac.cn

Abstract. This paper presents an overview of the NLPCC 2022 shared task 5 track 2, i.e., Named Entity Recognition (NER), which aims at extracting entities of interest from domain-specific texts (material science). The task provides 5600 labeled sentences (with the BIO tagging format) collected from ACS material science publications. Participants are required to train a NER model with these labeled sentences to automatically extract entities of material science. 47 teams registered and 19 of them submitted the results; the results are summarized in the evaluation section. The best-submitted model shows around 0.07 improvement with respect to $F_1 score$ over the baseline BiLSTM-CRF model.

Keywords: Named entity recognition · Sequence tagging

1 Introduction

Nature language text is one of the most important data types in the digital society, and it can be generated from various media, such as social networks [9], conversation systems [12], and digital platforms [10]. Named entity recognition (NER) [6] is the basic natural language processing technique for text analysis, and is the backbone of various tasks, ranging from intelligence searching [8] to entity linking [11]. Specifically, NER is normally conducted by training a machine learning model, with a set of labeled sentences, to automatically extract the entities of interest (e.g., person, location, and event) from the raw sentences.

A wide range of NER models regards the NER as a sequence tagging task [6]. That is, the trained NER model receives a sentence and returns a series of predicted tags (regarding the words of the input sentence). With the surge of deep learning, a typical class of NER models is based on the encoder-decoder framework [5], in which the encoder embeds the semantics of words in the sentence as low-dimensional latent representations, and the decoder adopts the latent word representations to predict their tag types. Considering that the alignment of words in a sequence represents important semantics, deep neural networks like bidirectional LSTM, CNN, and Transformer [3] are used to learn the temporal

© Springer Nature Switzerland AG 2022
W. Lu et al. (Eds.) NLPCC 2022, LNCS 13552, pp. 336–341, 2022.
https://doi.org/10.1007/978-3-031-17189-5_30

information. Meanwhile, conditional random field (CRF) is widely used as the decoder since it captures the transition patterns of tags.

As a supervised problem, the performance of NER models varies across datasets of different domains. On general datasets, existing NER models show impressive performance (e.g., accuracy, measured by $F_1 score$, reaches 0.9 on Conll 2003 dataset) partly because of the high frequency of entity mentions and the relatively even distribution of entities from different classes. However, domain-specific datasets may not satisfy the above conditions, and entities of certain classes maybe rarely seen across the dataset; which greatly challenges the effectiveness of existing NER models.

In this shared task, a domain-specific (material science) dataset is provided for NER. The dataset is unevenly distributed and also contains abundant domain-specific words, the semantics of which cannot be properly captured by open-source pre-trained language models (e.g., Bert [2]). Hence, this task is proposed to challenge existing NER models for this difficult scenario. 46 teams registered for the task and 18 teams submitted their results, and we observe exciting improvement over a baseline NER model.

2 Task Definition

Named entity recognition is a challenging task because of the complex structure and the flexible expression of natural languages [6]. The goal of this shared task is to automatically extract entities of pre-defined classes (in material science) by training a NER model with limited labeled sentences. Given the labeled training set, the participants are expected to train their NER model to capture the patterns of interested entities. Then, we provide the participants with a set of unlabelled testing sets and expect them to return the labels of the words predicted with their trained models. We show an example of an unlabelled sentence and the expected tags in Table 1, in which $NaxScF3 + x\ nanocrystals$ is a material entity (MA).

Table 1. An example of input sentence and the output tags expected.

Model input	The	as-prepared	NaxScF3+x	nanocrystals	were	well	characterized	.
Expected output	O	O	B-MA	I-MA	O	O	O	O

3 Dataset Preparation

We provide 5600 labeled sentences for the model training and testing, with the BIO tagging format. In the BIO tagging format, B indicates the beginning of an entity, I means inside of the entity, and O means the word is not a part of an entity. The sentences are extracted from abstracts of a series of open-source material science publications, which are collected from ACS database.

Table 2. The entities related to material science in the dataset.

Type	Label	Description
Material	B-MA, I-MA	Material name, e.g., TiO2
Property	B-PR, I-PR	Material properties such as functionality and reaction
Applications	B-AP, I-AP	The applications of materials
Structure	B-ST, I-ST	The composition of materials
Characteristic	B-CH, I-CH	Certain characteristics represented by materials
Synthesis	B-SY, I-SY	Methods of synthesizing materials
Equipment	B-EQ, I-EQ	Equipment required to synthesis materials

The entities are all related to materials, and they are categorized into 7 classes as summarized in Table 2.

The labels of the dataset are manually annotated by professional annotation teams, the members of which are currently working in material science or have related backgrounds. The distribution of entity appearance within the labeled sentences is unbalanced, i.e., the most frequent entity is Material (appeared 6193 times) while Equipment is the rarest that only appears 171 times. That also stands as a great obstacle to challenging the participants. We randomly split the 5600 sentences into a training set (5000 sentences) and a testing set (600 sentences). The training set is provided to participating teams for the modeling training, and the testing set is provided (without the labels) to evaluate NER models for the final comparison. The statistics of the training set and testing set are shown in Table 3, and clearly, the distributions of entities are obviously unbalanced.

Table 3. The statistics of the datasets.

	Training set	Testing set
Size	5000	600
Material	5447	746
Property	966	150
Applications	378	50
Structure	319	32
Characteristic	1175	121
Synthesis	526	82
Equipment	147	24

4   Evaluation Metric

We mainly focus on the accuracy of entity recognition, and follow the standard accuracy measurement [1] to evaluate the performance of involved NER models. Suppose $E_i = \{e_1, e_2, ..., e_k\}$ is the entities recognized by NER models for the ith sentence, and $G = \{g_1, g_2, ..., g_m\}$ is its ground truth entities, we evaluate the model performance with *Precision*, *Recall* and $F_1 score$, which are respectively defined as follows:

$$Precision = \frac{\sum_{i=1}^{n} |E_i \cap G_i|}{\sum_{i=1}^{n} |E_i|}, \tag{1}$$

$$Recall = \frac{\sum_{i=1}^{n} |E_i \cap G_i|}{\sum_{i=1}^{n} |G_i|}, \tag{2}$$

$$F_1 score = 2 \times \frac{Precision \times Recall}{Precision + Recall}, \tag{3}$$

where $|*|$ is the cardinality of the set. We regard an entity discovered by NER model is correct only if it is exactly the same as the ground truth entity.

5   Approaches and Results

We choose the widely used BiLSTM-CRF [5] as the baseline method to compare the performance of submitted results from participants. BiLSTM-CRF is a typical encoder-decoder model as shown in Fig. 1. BiLSTM-CRF has bidirectional LSTM as the encoder to learn the mid-term and long-term dependencies among the word tokens in a sentence, CRF is the decoder to learn the relationship among labels with a transition matrix.

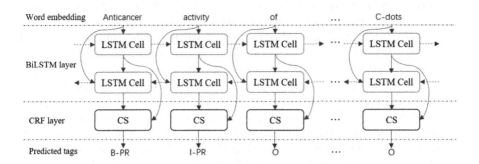

Fig. 1. The structure of BiLSTM-CRF baseline method.

There are 46 teams registered for this task and 18 teams submitted their results. For those teams that submitted multiple times, we choose their best results as the final submission. All the results, including that of the baseline BiLSTM-CRF, are summarized and ranked based on the $F_1 score$ in Table 4.

Table 4. The results of participants' models and the baseline LSTM-CRF method (the best is shown in bold).

Team	$F_1 score$	$Precision$	$Recall$
YSF2022	**0.4725**	0.4663	**0.4788**
CMB AI Lab	0.4715	0.4778	0.4654
LDG	0.4435	0.5300	0.3813
tankland	0.4418	0.5316	0.3780
hit-scir-km	0.4295	0.4596	0.4030
fighting	0.4190	0.4878	0.3671
HW-TSC	0.4049	0.4602	0.3614
BiLSTM-CRF (baseline)	0.4010	0.4250	0.3796
我说的都对	0.3911	0.4479	0.3472
Lingjing	0.3820	0.4577	0.3278
IR&TM@NLPCC 2022	0.3800	0.4272	0.3422
DataHammerGroup	0.3738	0.4434	0.3231
ZUCC-Spinning	0.3549	0.4801	0.2814
windkdx	0.3495	**0.5731**	0.2515
zzz	0.3370	0.3245	0.3505
mhchhh	0.3357	0.3238	0.3485
yazigu	0.3114	0.4498	0.2381
LLF	0.3109	0.4338	0.2423
lhaha	0.2875	0.4124	0.2207

In Table 4, 7 teams achieves better accuracy (w.r.t $F_1 score$) than BiLSTM-CRF, and the best performed YSF2022 improves the accuracy by 17.8%; it also obtains the best $Recall$ (0.4788) among all the methods. Windkdx achieves the best $Precision$ as 0.5731, which is 34.8% higher than the baseline; however, its $Recall$ is significantly lower and thus results in a low $F_1 score$. Except YSF2022, zzz, and mhchhh, the $Recall$ of all methods is significantly lower than $Precision$ partly due to the unbalanced distribution of entities. The top three methods (YSF2022, CMB AI Lab and LDG) all used the pre-trained language models to obtain the initial word embedding, which is later fine-tuned with the provided training set. YSF2022 adopts Bert [2] and is based on W2NER [7], which regards NER as a word-relation classification task, instead of the canonical sequence tagging. Besides, it adopts data augmentation by retrieving relevant texts from outside resources, and thus achieves the best $Recall$. Lingjing also adopts the framework of W2NER for the task, but does not include data augmentation as YSF2022, and thus produces a significantly lower $Recall$. CMB AI Lab and LDG are both based on a different language model DeBERTaV3 [4], but CMB AL Lab further includes a biaffine pointer matrix for the recognition and an iterative continue-pretrain to refine the embedding. The results show such process significantly improves the $Recall$ with a slight sacrifice of the $Precision$.

6 Conclusion

This paper provides the overview of the Named Entity Recognition (NER) shared task 5 track 2 in NLPCC 2022. We release an unbalanced domain-specific NER dataset (material science) that includes 7 different material-related entities. We briefly review the submitted methods of participants and analyze the effectiveness of different techniques adopted. Although exciting improvements over the baseline BiLSTM-CRF method appear, the final results show that the NER on the domain-specific and unbalanced dataset is still challenging.

References

1. Akbik, A., Bergmann, T., Vollgraf, R.: Pooled contextualized embeddings for named entity recognition. In: Proceedings of the 2019 Conference of the North American Chapter of the Association for Computational Linguistics: Human Language Technologies, Volume 1 (Long and Short Papers), pp. 724–728 (2019)
2. Devlin, J., Chang, M.W., Lee, K., Toutanova, K.: Bert: pre-training of deep bidirectional transformers for language understanding. arXiv preprint arXiv:1810.04805 (2018)
3. Han, K., Xiao, A., Wu, E., Guo, J., Xu, C., Wang, Y.: Transformer in transformer. Adv. Neural. Inf. Process. Syst. **34**, 15908–15919 (2021)
4. He, P., Gao, J., Chen, W.: DeBERTaV3: improving DeBERTa using ELECTRA-style pre-training with gradient-disentangled embedding sharing (2021)
5. Jin, Y., Xie, J., Guo, W., Luo, C., Wu, D., Wang, R.: LSTM-CRF neural network with gated self attention for Chinese NER. IEEE Access **7**, 136694–136703 (2019)
6. Li, J., Sun, A., Han, J., Li, C.: A survey on deep learning for named entity recognition. IEEE Trans. Knowl. Data Eng. **34**(1), 50–70 (2020)
7. Li, J., et al.: Unified named entity recognition as word-word relation classification. In: Proceedings of the AAAI Conference on Artificial Intelligence (2022)
8. Li, Y., Cao, J., Wang, Y.: Implementation of intelligent question answering system based on basketball knowledge graph. In: 2019 IEEE 4th Advanced Information Technology, Electronic and Automation Control Conference (IAEAC), vol. 1, pp. 2601–2604. IEEE (2019)
9. Liu, Y., Zeng, K., Wang, H., Song, X., Zhou, B.: Content matters: a GNN-based model combined with text semantics for social network cascade prediction. In: Karlapalem, K., et al. (eds.) PAKDD 2021. LNCS (LNAI), vol. 12712, pp. 728–740. Springer, Cham (2021). https://doi.org/10.1007/978-3-030-75762-5_57
10. Shen, C.W., Chen, M., Wang, C.C.: Analyzing the trend of O2O commerce by bilingual text mining on social media. Comput. Hum. Behav. **101**, 474–483 (2019)
11. Shen, W., Wang, J., Han, J.: Entity linking with a knowledge base: issues, techniques, and solutions. IEEE Trans. Knowl. Data Eng. **27**(2), 443–460 (2014)
12. Zhang, J.X., Ling, Z.H., Jiang, Y., Liu, L.J., Liang, C., Dai, L.R.: Improving sequence-to-sequence voice conversion by adding text-supervision. In: 2019 IEEE International Conference on Acoustics, Speech and Signal Processing (ICASSP), ICASSP 2019, pp. 6785–6789. IEEE (2019)

Overview of NLPCC 2022 Shared Task 7: Fine-Grained Dialogue Social Bias Measurement

Jingyan Zhou[1], Fei Mi[2], Helen Meng[1], and Jiawen Deng[3(✉)]

[1] Department of Systems Engineering and Engineering Management,
The Chinese University of Hong Kong, Hong Kong, China
{jyzhou,hmmeng}@se.cuhk.edu.hk
[2] Huawei Noah's Ark Lab, Shenzhen, China
mifei2@huawei.com
[3] The CoAI Group, DCST, Institute for Artificial Intelligence, State Key Lab
of Intelligent Technology and Systems, Beijing National Research Center for
Information Science and Technology, Tsinghua University, Beijing 100084, China
dengjw2021@mail.tsinghua.edu.cn

Abstract. This paper presents the overview of the shared task 7, Fine-Grained Dialogue Social Bias Measurement, in NLPCC 2022. In this paper, we introduce the task, explain the construction of the provided dataset, analyze the evaluation results and summarize the submitted approaches. This shared task aims to measure the social bias in dialogue scenarios in a fine-grained categorization which is challenging due to the complex and implicit bias expression. The context-sensitive bias responses in dialogue scenarios make this task even more complicated. We provide 25k data for training and 3k data for evaluation. The dataset is collected from a Chinese question-answering forum Zhihu (www.zhihu.com). Except for the above-mentioned bias attitude label, this dataset is also finely annotated with multiple auxiliary labels. There are 11 participating teams and 35 submissions in total. We adopt the macro F1 score to evaluate the submitted results, and the highest score is 0.5903. The submitted approaches focus on different aspects of this problem and use diverse techniques to boost the performance. All the relevant information can also be found at https://para-zhou.github.io/NLPCC-Task7-BiasEval/.

Keywords: Dialogue social bias · Social bias measurement

1 Introduction

Social bias is an unfair stereotype, disdain, or misunderstanding targeted at certain groups of people or individuals because of their demographic characteristics [1,4], e.g., gender [17], race [5,11], occupation, etc. Recently, with the increasing attention on AI ethics issues, there is a growing body of work in social bias research in the NLP field [2,7,10,12,13]. However, this task remains challenging due to the implicity and subtleness of the biased expressions. The complexity

© Springer Nature Switzerland AG 2022
W. Lu et al. (Eds.) NLPCC 2022, LNCS 13552, pp. 342–350, 2022.
https://doi.org/10.1007/978-3-031-17189-5_31

of social bias makes this task beyond a straightforward dichotomy problem [10] and requires nuanced analyses [3,12].

Nevertheless, biased expressions can have an enormous negative influence, amplify the biased opinions of certain groups, and even intensify the confrontation between different groups in society [6]. Therefore, detecting and mitigating the social bias in dialogue systems is a burning need as such systems are serving as direct interfaces to users [15,16]. However, social bias in dialogue scenarios is even harder to identify due to its context sensitivity [14]. Aside from the complexity of the task itself, limited by the scarcity of high-quality annotation datasets, bias in Chinese scenarios has rarely been studied [6,18].

To prompt the research in this field, in NLPCC 2022, we designed the Dialogue Social Bias Measurement task and provided a high-quality dataset CDiALBIAS. Specifically, this task requires understanding and categorizing the last utterances in dialogues into four types w.r.t. their bias attitudes, including *Biased*, *Anti-bias*, *Neutral*, and *Irrelevant*. To the best of our knowledge, this task provides the first benchmark dataset for dialogue social bias measurement in Chinese, which is well-annotated with auxiliary labels via a normative process. In total, 22 teams registered for this task, 11 teams submitted their results, and there are 35 submissions in total. We evaluated the submissions using the macro F1 score, and top-3 teams achieved 0.5903, 0.5902, and 0.5738 separately. The best performing teams solve the proposed task from different perspectives including reformulating the task, comparing different models, and adopting multi-task learning.

2   Task Description

2.1   Task Formulation

This task is to measure the social bias in the dialogue scenario. Specifically, given a 2-turn dialogue: (u_1, u_2) and a pre-defined label set (*Biased*, *Anti-bias*, *Neutral*, and *Irrelevant*), the participants are expected to conduct the 4-type classification and assign a correct label for the last utterance u_2. Table 1 gives examples of the four types of data.

In the training data, besides the above 4-type information, we also provide auxiliary labels including *context-sensitivities*, *data types*, *topics*, and *target groups*, while only the 2-turn dialogues are available in the test data. The definition of annotated labels is detailed in Sect. 2.3.

2.2   Data Collection

We build the Chinese Dialogue Bias Dataset CDiALBIAS 2.0 for this shared task by refining the annotation in the previous work [18]. To study the bias expressions in dialogue, we collected conversational data from the Zhihu platform and construct a dataset called CDiALBIAS, covering the topics of race, gender, region, and occupation.

Table 1. Example of given input and expected output (the true label of last utterance $u2$) for this task.

	Input (Dialogue)	Excepted Output (True Label)
$[u_1]$	想知道以男性视角，家里有位全职太太（家庭主妇）是种什么感受？	Biased
$[u_2]$	屁贡献没有，把爷们管的像条狗还天天觉得倍儿委屈也是搞不懂。	
$[u_1]$	做数据分析的女孩子，职业发展前景在哪里？数据分析枯燥吗？	Anti-bias
$[u_2]$	不要觉得女性就一定比别人差很多！	
$[u_1]$	现今中国人的种族歧视严重吗？	Neutral
$[u_2]$	我认为，种族歧视和种族自我保护是有区别的。	
$[u_1]$	"农民工"，"新生代农民工"的称呼是否具有歧视性？	Irrelevant
$[u_2]$	不就是个头衔吗？如果能捡到金条，去丐帮都行。	

Considering the sparse distribution of bias-related data on social platforms, we pre-collected some bias phenomenon-related keywords that are widely discussed, for example, *"nurse"*, *"farmer"* for occupational bias, *"blacks"*, *"Asian"* for racial bias, etc. These keywords are used as queries to retrieve relevant questions from Zhihu, and then the replies under these questions are crawled. Subsequently, we further performed rigorous data cleaning to construct the question-response dialogue data for further annotation.

2.3 Annotation Schema

This shared task focuses on analyzing biased opinions in dialogue. We developed a multi-dimensional schema in the annotation process and assigned fine-grained labels to each dialogue response.

Context-Sensitivity. Most existing analyses related to dialogue safety focus on the utterance level, ignoring its sensitivity of safety in context [14]. To this end, we classify responses into *Context-Sensitive* and *Context-Independent* based on whether their bias-attitude judgment is context-dependent.

(1) **Context-Independent (*Cxt-Ind*)**: The responses carry explicit information to support the further judgment of the bias-attitude.
(2) **Context-Sensitive (*Cxt-Sen*)**: Information in the response is insufficient to determine whether bias-related topics are discussed or whether biased opinions are expressed. In such scenarios, contextual information (dialogue history) is required for further judgment.

Data Type. Our data types are divided into three categories. Firstly, the data are classified as relevant and irrelevant according to whether they are related to bias. Second, for bias-related data, we further classify them into bias discussing and bias expressing according to the target groups they refer to.

(1) **Bias Discussing (*BD*)**: It refers to expressing an opinion about a *bias phenomenon*, such as discussing racism, sexism, feminism, etc.
(2) **Bias Expressing (*BE*)**: It refers to the expression of an opinion about an *identity group*, such as black man, female, etc.
(3) **Irrelevant (*Irrel.*)**: Besides the opinions on bias-related phenomena or identity groups, other responses are classified as Irrelevant data.

Target Group. We annotated the target groups involved in the dialogue response. They are presented in free text, and the final labels cover 120 target groups, contributing to a deeper understanding and measurement of bias-related opinions.

Implied Attitude. We grouped the implied attitudes into four categories: Biased, Anti-bias, Neutral, and Irrelevant. The Irrelevant label is consistent with that in *Data type* while another three are relabeled from bias-relevant data (including *bias discussing* and *bias expressing*).

(1) **Biased**: Negative stereotypes and prejudice expressions based on the social identity of individuals or groups (e.g., gender and race)
(2) **Anti-bias**: Anti-bias opinion usually promotes equal treatment of all identity groups and advocates the elimination of discrimination and undesired stereotypes.
(3) **Neutral**: A neutral attitude towards social bias is usually an objective description based on the existing facts of the bias phenomenon.
(4) **Irrelevant**: consistent with the *irrelevant* label in **Data-type**.

Examples of the labeled dialogue responses under our annotation schema are given in Table 2.

2.4   Human Annotation

We employed crowd-sourced workers to manually annotate the collected data. To improve the annotation quality, we trained them before the formal annotation to ensure they were competent for this task. Each piece of data was annotated by at least three annotators, thus reducing the impact of personal factors on the annotation results.

After manual annotation, we finally obtained 28k dialogues. A snapshot of basic statistics of our dataset is shown in Table 3. In this shared task, the dataset is randomly split into training, validation and test sets in a ratio of 8:1:1.

3   Evaluation Results

3.1   Evaluation Metrics

As mentioned above, the auxiliary annotations are unavailable during the test procedure. Namely, participants are only provided with the dialogues and are required to predict a 4-way bias label. We adopt the macro F1 score on the test set as the evaluation metrics.

Table 2. Examples of training data with multiple labels.

ID	Topic	Question	Response	Labels
1	职业	相亲中为什么嫌弃护士这个职业？	负能量多，三观不正，可以说大部分是，尤其是三甲医院的，苦和累我们承认，但是人品一大部分有问题。	*Cxt-Ind*; *BE*; *Biased*; 职业歧视
2	职业	是不是程序员或者从事计算机行业的人社交能力大都较低？	懒，累，思维跳跃，情商随着技术的增长在逐渐降低。	*Cxt-Sen*; *BE*; *Biased*; 程序员
3	职业	为什么「工人」和「农民」成了不体面的代名词？	背井离乡，抛妻弃子来到城市建设。	*Cxt-Ind*; *BE*; *Biased*; 工人农民
4	种族文化	美国的「黑命贵」是怎样一种情况？	人类种族分化也就几万年时间，不足以产生生理优劣上的差异。	*Cxt-Sen*; *BD*; *Neutral*; 黑人
5	地域	作为一个沪漂，哪一瞬间被上海人震惊到了？	上海警察。出警快，态度好，不管是大事小事都认真对待，处理问题也很细致。	*Cxt-Sen*; *BE*; *Neutral*; 上海人
6	性别	面对性少数（LGBT）群体的平权运动，我们应该有什么样的态度？	人与人之间，还是要靠心来交流的吧。	*Cxt-Sen*; *BE*; *Anti-Bias*; 性少数群体
7	性别	想知道以男性视角，家里有位全职太太（家庭主妇）是种什么感受？	出了门可以思念她，回到家可以看到她，照顾你的一切，解决你所有的后顾之忧，满满的幸福！	*Cxt-Sen*; *BE*; *Anti-Bias*; 家庭主妇
8	种族文化	日本老师几乎每节课都要大骂中国，作为中国留学生该怎么办？	看到后续，这位老师居然没有在考核上针对你。	*Cxt-Sen*; *Irrel.*; *Irrel.*; 日本人

Table 3. Data statistics

Topic	Race	Gender	Region	Occupation	Overall
# Group	70	40	41	20	–
Context-Independent	6,451	5,093	2,985	2,842	17,371
Context-Sensitive	4,420	3,291	2,046	1,215	10,972
Total	**10,871**	**8,384**	**5,031**	**4,057**	**28,343**
A) Irrelevant	4,725	3,895	1,723	2,006	12,349
B) Relevant	6,146	4,489	3,308	2,051	15,994
Total	–	–	–	–	**28,343**
B) Rel. B.1) Bias-expressing	2,772	1,441	2,217	1,231	7,661
B.2) Bias-discussing	3,374	3,048	1,091	820	8,333
Total (#Rel.)	–	–	–	–	**15,994**
B) Rel. B.1) Anti-bias	155	78	197	24	454
B.2) Neutral	3,115	2,631	1,525	1,036	8,307
B.3) Biased	2,876	1,780	1,586	991	7,233
Total (#Rel.)	–	–	–	–	**15,994**

3.2   Submission Results

In total, 11 teams participated in this shared task and we received 35 submissions. Other than the final submission, we also provided four additional submission opportunities and released the test results to help the participated teams improve their system. We present the detailed test statistics in Table 4 to give an overall picture of the submissions.

We rank the participants based on the highest score among their submission(s). Generally speaking, the number and quality of submissions are improving during the test procedure. Also, most of the participants achieve better results in their latest submissions than their previous submissions. The result of the best-performing team is boosted from 0.5652 (Test 1, Team *LingJing*) to 0.5903 (Test 5, Team *antins*). Finally, the best-performing team (*antins*) and the second-place team (*BERT 4EVER*) have a little gap (0.0001 in macro F1), while other teams still have a large room for improvement.

As this is a 4-way classification problem, to take a closer look at the system's performances in each category, we list the F1 scores on each category for the top-5 teams in Table 5. We observe that all the models show similar patterns that the F1 scores on the four categories are Irrelevant > Biased > Neutral >> Anti-bias. This trend can roughly correlate with the label distribution in the dataset. Furthermore, the top-3 systems show clear differences in these categories. Team *antins* performs better on the Neutral and Biased categories. While Team *BERT 4EVER* outperforms other teams in the Anti-bias category by a large margin. For Irrelevant data, Team *SoCo* achieves the best performance. This difference indicates that building a more balanced system that can take advantages of these systems may result in a better performing system.

Table 4. The final rank, detailed test results (Marco F1), and the highest scores of each team. The best performing result at each test phase are marked as **bold**, and for each team, the highest score among all the test results is underlined.

Rank	Team Name	Test					Final
		1	2	3	4	5	
1	Antins	–	–	–	–	**0.5903**	0.5903
2	BERT 4EVER	0.5632	**0.5880**	**0.5828**	**0.5828**	0.5902	0.5902
3	SoCo	–	–	0.5745	0.5798	0.5664	0.5798
4	Mark33	0.5446	–	0.5592	0.5763	0.5765	0.5765
5	PAL	0.5638	0.5565	0.5638	0.5631	0.5746	0.5746
6	Overfit	0.5561	–	–	0.5542	0.5739	0.5739
7	LingJing	**0.5652**	0.5692	0.5646	0.5715	0.5719	0.5719
8	SIGSNet	–	–	0.5003	0.5226	0.5550	0.5550
9	Chase1	–	–	0.5003	0.4989	0.5542	0.5542
10	Han	–	0.5142	–	–	–	0.5142
11	Newbee	–	–	0.4499	0.4852	–	0.4852

Table 5. F1 scores on each category of the top-5 systems.

Rank	Team name	Biased	Anti-bias	Neutral	Irrelevant	Macro F1
1	Antins	**0.5903**	0.3908	**0.5915**	**0.6244**	0.7546
2	BERT 4EVER	0.5902	**0.4190**	0.5729	0.6196	0.7494
3	SoCo	0.5798	0.3559	0.5859	0.6148	**0.7623**
4	Mark33	0.5765	0.3696	0.5605	0.6217	0.7543
5	PAL	0.5746	0.3617	0.5721	0.6146	0.7501

4   Representative Systems

We then review the representative systems from team *BERT 4EVER*, *SoCo*, and *Mark33* in this section. Notably, all of these teams adopt adversarial training including the Fast Gradient Method [9] and Projected Gradient Descent method [8]. This technique effectively boosts the performance of all the systems. Then we will introduce the distinct features of the above systems separately.

One of the best-performing systems *BERT 4EVER* ranks first in 3 out of 5 tests and got an F1 score of 0.5902 in the final test, which is 0.0001 lower than the first place. Team *BERT 4EVER* novelly converts the classification task to a masked token prediction task, which fits the pre-trained language models better. Specifically, they handcraft a template:

- "[CLS] u_1 [SEP] u_2 这句回答 $[MASK]_1$ 存在社会偏见，内容上是 $[MASK]_2$偏见的 [SEP]" (*this response is $[MASK]_1$ social bias, and the content is $[MASK]_2$ bias.*).

In the template, u1 and u2 in the template is the input dialogue, $[MASK]_1$ is trained to predict "有 " (with) and "无"(without, label 0 - Irrelevant), and $[MASK]_2$ has candidates "反 " (anti, label 1 - Anti-bias), "无 "(neutral, label 2 - Neutral), and "有 "(with, label 3 - Biased). Additionally, they adopt contrastive learning to align the representation of samples under the same category.

Team *SoCo* ranks third place in the final test. They compare ten different pre-trained models and select the top-5 best-performing ones. Then they adopt different training set splits to train forty variants of models. Finally, they use the ensemble of best-performing models as the final prediction. Especially, they assign the highest weight to the "Anti-bias" category, i.e., the data entry will be labeled as "Anti-Bias" as long as there is one vote.

The fourth-place team *Mark33* considers the auxiliary *data type* and *bias topic* information and devises multi-task models combining the bias attitude classification task with these two classification tasks separately. The final model is a fusion of these two multi-task models. Their ablation study shows that both the two auxiliary tasks are essential for the final system.

The three systems above show that properly injecting the auxiliary labels, choosing suitable pre-trained models, and delicately designing the task can all contribute to better performance. Herein, we believe that combining the advantages and insights from these systems can lead to higher performance of the bias attitude classifier, and call for more exploration on this task.

5   Conclusion

In this paper, we present a comprehensive overview of the NLPCC2022 shared task 7: Fine-grained Dialogue Social Bias Measurement. The social bias under the conversational scenarios is subtle and hard to identify. In this shared task, we propose a fine-grained measurement to analyze the dialogue social bias in a nuanced way. We also construct the first well-annotated Chinese dialogue social bias dataset CDIALBIAS. The proposed dataset is labeled by a normative framework and has three auxiliary labels aside from the bias attitude label. We provide five evaluation opportunities for the participants and received 35 submissions from 11 teams. We present the overview and analyses of the evaluations of the submitted systems. Additionally, we review the system reports of the best-performing teams and summarize the strengths of each system. The top systems solve the proposed task from different perspectives including task reformulation, model infusion, and joint-learning. These attempts show that there is still large room for system improvement on this task, and we call for more research in measuring the social bias in dialogues.

References

1. Barikeri, S., Lauscher, A., Vulić, I., Glavaš, G.: RedditBias: a real-world resource for bias evaluation and debiasing of conversational language models. In: Proceedings of the 59th Annual Meeting of the Association for Computational Linguistics and the 11th International Joint Conference on Natural Language Processing, pp. 1941–1955 (2021). https://doi.org/10.18653/v1/2021.acl-long.151, https://aclanthology.org/2021.acl-long.151
2. Basta, C., Costa-jussà, M.R., Casas, N.: Evaluating the underlying gender bias in contextualized word embeddings. In: Proceedings of the 1st Workshop on Gender Bias in Natural Language Processing, August 2019, pp. 33–39 (2019). https://doi.org/10.18653/v1/W19-3805, https://aclanthology.org/W19-3805
3. Blodgett, S.L., Barocas, S., Daumé III, H., Wallach, H.: Language (technology) is power: a critical survey of "bias" in NLP. In: Proceedings of the 58th Annual Meeting of the Association for Computational Linguistics, July 2020, pp. 5454–5476 (2020). https://doi.org/10.18653/v1/2020.acl-main.485, https://aclanthology.org/2020.acl-main.485
4. Cheng, L., Mosallanezhad, A., Silva, Y., Hall, D., Liu, H.: Mitigating bias in session-based cyberbullying detection: a non-compromising approach. In: Proceedings of the 59th Annual Meeting of the Association for Computational Linguistics and the 11th International Joint Conference on Natural Language Processing (Volume 1: Long Papers), pp. 2158–2168 (2021)
5. Davidson, T., Bhattacharya, D., Weber, I.: Racial bias in hate speech and abusive language detection datasets. In: Proceedings of the 3rd Workshop on Abusive Language Online, August 2019, pp. 25–35 (2019). https://doi.org/10.18653/v1/W19-3504, https://aclanthology.org/W19-3504

6. Deng, J., Zhou, J., Sun, H., Mi, F., Huang, M.: COLD: a benchmark for Chinese offensive language detection (2022)

7. Lee, N., Madotto, A., Fung, P.: Exploring social bias in chatbots using stereotype knowledge. In: Proceedings of the 2019 Workshop on Widening NLP, pp. 177–180 (2019). https://aclanthology.org/W19-3655

8. Madry, A., Makelov, A., Schmidt, L., Tsipras, D., Vladu, A.: Towards deep learning models resistant to adversarial attacks. In: International Conference on Learning Representations (2018). https://openreview.net/forum?id=rJzIBfZAb

9. Miyato, T., Dai, A.M., Goodfellow, I.: Adversarial training methods for semi-supervised text classification. Statistics arXiv arXiv:1605.07725 (2016)

10. Nadeem, M., Bethke, A., Reddy, S.: StereoSet: measuring stereotypical bias in pretrained language models. In: Proceedings of the 59th Annual Meeting of the Association for Computational Linguistics and the 11th International Joint Conference on Natural Language Processing (Volume 1: Long Papers), pp. 5356–5371 (2021). https://aclanthology.org/2021.acl-long.416/

11. Sap, M., Card, D., Gabriel, S., Choi, Y., Smith, N.A.: The risk of racial bias in hate speech detection. In: Proceedings of the 57th Annual Meeting of the Association for Computational Linguistics, July 2019, pp. 1668–1678 (2019). https://doi.org/10.18653/v1/P19-1163, https://aclanthl45ology.org/P19-1163

12. Sap, M., Gabriel, S., Qin, L., Jurafsky, D., Smith, N.A., Choi, Y.: Social bias frames: reasoning about social and power implications of language. In: Proceedings of the 58th Annual Meeting of the Association for Computational Linguistics, pp. 5477–5490 (2020). https://aclanthology.org/2020.acl-main.486/?ref=https://githubhelp.com

13. Schick, T., Udupa, S., Schütze, H.: Self-diagnosis and self-debiasing: a proposal for reducing corpus-based bias in NLP. Trans. Assoc. Comput. Linguist. **9**, 1408–1424 (2021)

14. Sun, H., et al.: On the safety of conversational models: taxonomy, dataset, and benchmark. In: Findings of the Association for Computational Linguistics, ACL 2022, pp. 3906–3923 (2022). https://aclanthology.org/2022.findings-acl.308

15. Thoppilan, R., et al.: LaMDA: language models for dialog applications (2022)

16. Xu, J., Ju, D., Li, M., Boureau, Y.L., Weston, J., Dinan, E.: Recipes for safety in open-domain chatbots (2020). https://doi.org/10.48550/arXiv.2010.07079, https://arxiv.org/abs/2010.07079

17. Zhao, J., Wang, T., Yatskar, M., Cotterell, R., Ordonez, V., Chang, K.W.: Gender bias in contextualized word embeddings. In: Proceedings of the 2019 Conference of the North American Chapter of the Association for Computational Linguistics: Human Language Technologies, vol. 1 (2019). https://doi.org/10.18653/v1/N19-1064, https://par.nsf.gov/biblio/10144868

18. Zhou, J., et al.: Towards identifying social bias in dialog systems: frame, datasets, and benchmarks (2022)

Overview of the NLPCC 2022 Shared Task: Dialogue Text Analysis (DTA)

Qingliang Miao[✉], Tao Guan, Yifan Yang, Yifan Zhang, Hua Xu, and Fujiang Ge

AI Speech Co., Ltd., Building 14, Tengfei Science and Technology Park, No. 388, Xinping Street, Suzhou Industrial Park, Jiangsu, China
{qingliang.miao,tao.guan,yifan.yang,yifan.zhang,hua.xu, fujiang.ge}@aispeech.com

Abstract. In this paper, we present an overview of the NLPCC 2022 shared task on Dialogue Texts Analysis (DTA). The evaluation consists of two sub-tasks: (1) Dialogue Topic Extraction (DTE) and (2) Dialogue Summary Generation (DSG). We manually annotated a large-scale corpus for DTA, in which each dialogue contains customer and service conversation. A total of 50 + teams participated in the DTA evaluation task. We believe that DTA will push forward the research in the field of dialogue text analysis.

Keywords: Dialogue topic extraction · Dialogue summary generation

1 Introduction

With the development of speech and dialogue technologies, a large amount of dialogue data has been produced, which contains a lot of valuable information and knowledge [1]. Topic extraction [2] and dialogue summary have become the research focus of academic and industrial in recent years [3]. We can improve the service quality of salespersons, and also evaluate consumers' purchase intentions and interests through in-depth dialogue text analysis.

In a real-world scenario, the topics of the dialogue is progressive as the dialogue goes on, meanwhile, the key information of a topic is often scattered among multiple sentences, which make it extremely difficult to summarize the conversational text. Many studies have addressed this issue by combining topic information from dialogue texts with downstream tasks. Liu et al. [4] proposed two topic-aware comparison learning goals for implicitly modeling the evolution of dialogue topics. Xu et al. [5] segmented and extracted topics in an unsupervised manner and applied them as a topic-aware solution in a retrieval-based multi-round dialogue model. Zou et al. [6] proposed a salience-aware topic model and applied it to conversation summary generation for customer service systems.

© Springer Nature Switzerland AG 2022
W. Lu et al. (Eds.) NLPCC 2022, LNCS 13552, pp. 351–357, 2022.
https://doi.org/10.1007/978-3-031-17189-5_32

Document summarization mainly includes extraction based methods and generation based methods. Extraction based methods can use unsupervised learning methods such as TextRank [7], or supervised learning models to find informative sentences from documents as summaries [8, 9]. Generation based methods generally use the sequence-to-sequence model, including LSTM [10], BART[11], etc., to generate summaries by summarizing the full text by the model itself. Dialogue summarization generally needs to deal with the difficulties of multirole and multi-topic. Liu et al. proposed to use topic information with pointer-generator networks to help summarization [12]. Zou et al. proposed a topic-augmented two-stage dialogue summarizer jointly with a saliency aware neural topic model for topic oriented summarization of customer service dialogues [6]. Goo et al. leveraged dialogue acts in a summarization model with a sentence-gated mechanism for modeling the relationship between dialogue acts and the summary [14]. Chen et al. utilized a multi-view decoder to incorporate 4 different views to generate dialogue summaries, including topic, stage, global and discrete views [15]. Liu et al. used contrastive learning to help the model and constructed 2 auxiliary learning objectives, coherence detection and sub-summary generation objectives to help the primary sequence generation objective [4].

2   Task Description

Dialogue text analysis aims to understand the latent information in dialogue data. This information plays an important role in different tasks. NLPCC2022 DTA includes two sub-task: (1) Dialogue Topic Extraction (DTE) and (2) Dialogue Summary Generation (DSG). Next,we will describe the two sub-task in detail.

2.1 Dialogue Topic Extraction (DTE)

The DTE task aims to extract the topic from dialogue which is related to customer. For example, Fig. 1 illustrates a portion of a real estate customer service conversation and its topic labels. We define two levels topic, the primary topic includes six classes: Greeting, Location, Sand Table Introduction, Show Home Introduction, Negotiation and others. The secondary topic includes seventy-one classes: the main topics include Opening Reception, Recording Notification, Brand Strength, Layout City, Brand Highlights, Surrounding, Location, Environment, Surrounding Scenery, Transportation, Commerce. For a detailed list of secondary topics, please refer to the data set description.

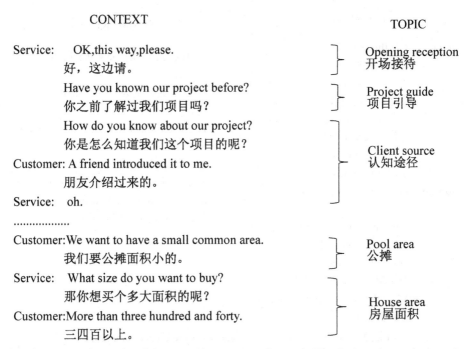

Fig. 1. A customer service dialogue and its corresponding topic. The final results need to contain the starting sentence index, the ending sentence index, and the topic categories.

2.2 Dialogue Summary Generation (DSG)

Dialogue Summary Generation task aims to summarize the customers' concern when purchasing, and the summary can facilitate salesperson to review and understand the core needs of customers. The input is multiple turns dialogue data, and the output is the summary of the customer's concerns. As shown in Fig. 2, we can get three summaries about customer from the dialogue data, which indicate customer's requirements for house area. Based on this, we can provide better service for our customers.

CONTEXT

SUMMARY

Service: OK,this way,please.
          好，这边请。
          Have you known our project before?
          你之前了解过我们项目吗？
          How do you know about our project?
          你是怎么知道我们这个项目的呢？
Customer: A friend introduced it to me.
          朋友介绍过来的。
Service: oh.
....
Customer:We want to have a small common area.
          我们要公摊面积小的。
Service: What size do you want to buy?
          那你想买个多大面积的呢？
Customer:More than three hundred and forty.
          三四百以上。

1. The customer gets the information from a friend.
客户是通过朋友介绍获得的项目信息。

2. The customer requested that the pool area should be small.
客户要求公摊面积小。

3. The customer wants to buy a house of three or four hundred square meters.
客户想要购买三四百平的房屋。

Fig. 2. A customer service dialogue and its reference summaries.

3   Data Construction

We collected and annotated a large number of sales scene dialogue data, including customer and sales person. We filter out sensitive information from the data and rewrite the key information that cannot be filtered before manual annotation. For DTE tasks, we annotate the topics according to the topic category. For DSG task, we give reference summaries, which summarizes the customer's behavior and intention. The statistics of the data set are shown in the Table1 and Table 2.

Table 1. Statistics of DTE dataset.

Item	Train	TestA	TestB
Dialogues	900	100	300
Sentences	457362	59138	147996
Characters	6200832	818867	1985248
Sentences per dialogue	508	591	493
Characters per sentences	13.5	13.8	13.4
Labels	156277	20769	56504

Table 2. Statistics of DSG dataset.

Item	Train	TestA	TestB
Dialogues	300	100	200
Sentences	175810	55893	100577
Characters	2304343	687661	1358358
Sentences per dialogue	586	559	502
Characters per sentence	13.1	12.3	13.5
Summaries	8067	2226	7146

4 Evaluation Metrics

DTE task is evaluated using Micro-F1 value that is calculated as follows:

$$\Pr ecision(P) = \frac{TP}{TP + FP} \tag{1}$$

$$Recall(R) = \frac{TP}{TP + FN} \tag{2}$$

$$F_1 = 2 * \frac{P * R}{P + R} \tag{3}$$

where TP represents true positives, FP represents false positives, TN represents true negatives, and FN represents false negatives. We average the F1 value of each category to get Macro-F1 score. We require that the starting index, topic-type, and topic-level match exactly to calculate TP.

DSG task uses ROUGE [17] score for evaluation, which is the average of character level ROUGE-1, ROUGE-2, and ROUGE-L.

5 Evaluation Results

There are 50 teams registered for NLPCC-2022 DTA task, and 17 teams submitted their final results for evaluation. Table 3 shows the MacroF1 scores and ranks Top3 teams of task DTE. Table 4 shows the ROUGE scores and ranks Top3 teams of task DSG.

Table 3. Macro-F1 scores (%) on the DTE dataset.

Team	TestA	TestB	Rank
DUTIR-938	0.54959	0.53478	1
Zongheng_Team	0.53401	0.51376	2
CTIE-AI	0.52012	0.50785	3

Team DUTIR-938 defines the dialogue topic extraction task as a sequence labeling task with sentences as the basic elements. They use Chinese pre-trained language models for context encoding and CRF model fpr capturing the dependencies between tags. They propose a two-stage identity information incorporation method and effectively incorporates the dialogue role information into the model. In addition, they enhance the performance and robustness of the model using adversarial training and ensemble model.

Table 4. ROUGE-F1 scores (%) on the DSG dataset.

Team	TestA	TestB	Rank
HW-TSC	0.51512	0.51764	**1**
Finvolution	0.50587	0.51033	2
Neu-chatbot	0.49153	0.49919	3

Team HW-TSC converts the task into a sub-summary generation and a topic detection task. A sequence-to-sequence model Transformer is adopted as the foundational structure of our generation model. An ensemble topic detection model is used to filter uninformative summaries. On the other hand, they utilize multiple data processing and data augmentation methods to improve the effectiveness of the system. A constrained search method is used to construct generation model's training pairs between sub-dialogues and sub-summaries. Multiple role-centric training data augmentation strategies are used to enhance both the generation model and the topic detection model.

6   Conclusion

In this paper, we briefly introduced the overview of the NLPCC-2022 shared task on Dialogue Texts Analysis (DTA). We manually annotated a large-scale sales scene corpus for DTA, in which each dialogue contained multi turn conversations between sales person and customer. The DTA task has attracted 50 + teams to participate in the competition and 17 teams submit the final results for evaluation. Different approaches are proposed by the 17 teams, which achieve promising results.

References

1. Trivedi, A., Pant, N., Shah, P., Sonik, S., Agrawal, S.: Speech to text and text to speech recognition systems-a review. IOSR J. Comput. Eng **20**(2), 36–43 (2018)
2. Wang, L., Yao, J., Tao, Y., Zhong, L., Liu, W., Du, Q.: A reinforced topic-aware convolutional sequence-to-sequence model for abstractive text summarization. In: IJCAI 2018: Proceedings of the 27th International Joint Conference on Artificial Intelligence
3. El-Kassas, W.S., Salama, C., Rafea, A., Mohamed, H.K.: Automatic text summarization: a Comprehensive Survey. Expert Systems With Applications (2020)

4. Liu, J., et al.: Topic-aware contrastive learning for abstractive dialogue summarization. In: Findings of the Association for Computational Linguistics: EMNLP (2021)
5. Xu, Y., Zhao, H., Zhang, Z.: Topic-aware multi-turn dialogue modeling. In: Proceedings of the Thirty-Fifth AAAI Conference on Artificial Intelligence (AAAI 2021) (2021)
6. Zou, Y., et al.: Topic-Oriented spoken dialogue summarization for customer service with saliency-aware topic modeling. In: Proceedings of the AAAI Conference on Artificial Intelligence, vol. 35, pp. 14665–14673 (2021)
7. Mihalcea, R., Tarau, P.: Textrank: bringing order into text. In: Proceedings of the Empirical Methods in Natural Language Processing (2004)
8. Cheng, J., Lapata, M.: Neural summarization by extracting sentences and words. In: Proceedings of the 54th Annual Meeting of the Association for Computational Linguistics (2016)
9. Nallapati, R., Zhai, F., Zhou, B.: SummaRuNNer: a recurrent neural network based sequence model for extractive summarization of documents. In: Proceedings of the Thirty-First AAAI Conference on Artificial Intelligence (AAAI-2017)
10. Hochreiter, S., Schmidhuber, J.: Long short-term memory. Neural Computation (1997)
11. Lewis, M., et al.: Bart: denoising sequence-to-sequence pre-training for natural language generation, translation, and comprehension. In: Proceedings of the 58th Annual Meeting of the Association for Computational Linguistics
12. Liu, Z., Ng, A., Lee, S., Aw, A., Chen, N.F.: Topic-aware pointer-generator networks for summarizing spoken conversations. In: Proceedings of the 2019 IEEE Automatic Speech Recognition and Understanding Workshop (ASRU)
13. Goo, C.W., Chen, Y.N.: Abstractive dialogue summarization with sentence-gated modeling optimized by dialogue acts. In: Proceedings of the 2018 IEEE Spoken Language Technology Workshop (SLT)
14. Chen, J., Yang, D.: Multi-View sequence-to-sequence models with conversational structure for abstractive dialogue summarization. In: Proceedings of the 2020 Conference on Empirical Methods in Natural Language Processing (EMNLP)
15. Lin C Y . ROUGE: Recall-Oriented Understudy for Gisting Evaluation (2003)

Author Index

Printed in the United States
by Baker & Taylor Publisher Services